THE BOND BOOK

Everything Investors Need to
Know About Treasuries,
Municipals, GNMAs, Corporates,
Zeros, Bond Funds, Money
Market Funds, and More

THE BOND BOOK

Everything Investors Need to
Know About Treasuries,
Municipals, GNMAs, Corporates,
Zeros, Bond Funds, Money
Market Funds, and More

SECOND EDITION

ANNETTE THAU

McGRAW-HILL
New York San Francisco Washington, D.C. Auckland Bogotá
Caracas Lisbon London Madrid Mexico City Milan
Montreal New Delhi San Juan Singapore
Sydney Tokyo Toronto

Library of Congress Cataloging-in-Publication Data

Thau, Annette.
    The bond book / by Annette Thau.—[Rev. ed.]
        p. cm.
    ISBN 0-07-135862-5
    1. Bonds.   2. Portfolio management.   3. Investments.   I. Title.

    HG4651.T447 2000
    332.63'23—dc21

                                                                00-041587

McGraw-Hill

A Division of The McGraw·Hill Companies

    3 4 5 6 7 8 9 0   AGM/AGM   0 9 8 7 6 5 4 3 2 1

ISBN 0-07-135862-5

This book was set in Palatino by Pro-Image Corporation.

Printed and bound by Quebecor World/Martinsburg.

McGraw-Hill books are available at special quantity discounts to use as premiums and sales promotions, or for use in corporate training programs. For more information, please write to the Director of Special Sales, Professional Publishing, McGraw-Hill, Two Penn Plaza, New York, NY 10121-2298. Or contact your local bookstore.

This publication is designed to provide accurate and authoritative information in regard to the subject matter covered. It is sold with the understanding that neither the author nor the publisher is engaged in rendering legal, accounting, futures/securities trading, or other professional service. If legal advice or other expert assistance is required, the services of a competent professional person should be sought.

—From a Declaration of Principles jointly adopted by a Committee of the American Bar Association and a Committee of Publishers.

DEDICATION

TO FRED

CONTENTS

Chapter 8

Mortgage-Backed Securities   165

Chapter 9

Corporate Bonds   199

Chapter 10

International Bonds   219

PART THREE INVESTING THROUGH FUNDS 235

PART FOUR PORTFOLIO MANAGEMENT 351

PREFACE

This is a revised edition of a book that was initially published in December of 1991. While working as a bond analyst, I started exploring the literature on investing in bonds. I found two types of books. The first, intended for institutional investors, was heavily quantitative, and not understandable by anyone not trained in finance. The second, meant for individual investors, dealt primarily with credit risk, that is, the risk that bond investors might not get their money back.

As I started investing in bonds personally, it became clear to me that interest rate risk (that is, rates going up and down), and not credit risk, had become the major risk to any bondbuyer. In addition, so many new instruments had come on the market that any book written earlier was clearly obsolete.

I looked in vain for a book that would explain in clear English some of the basic concepts used by professionals in managing bond portfolios; and that would contain information on the major types of securities available to any individual investor, so that the merits and disadvantages of each could be compared. Since I was unable to find such a book, after working for several years as a bond analyst, I decided to write the book that I would have liked to read.

The first edition of this book was written between 1990 and 1991. Since then, enormous changes have occurred in the bond market. First of all, there have been significant changes in the interest rate environment. At the time I wrote this book, interest rates on the Treasury's 30-year bond were about 9%; and that rate, high as it may seem today, represented a significant decline from the highs of 15% and 16% which had been reached in 1982 and 1983. Money market rates hovered around 7%. Interest rates continued to be extremely volatile, and this volatility caused a lot of concern. Returns from investments in bonds, however, were extremely high by historical standards, and investments in bonds were in high favor. In fact, strange as it may appear today, more money was actually going into bond funds than into stock funds.

Today, by comparison, the unprecedented bull market in stocks has created an enormous change in investor psychology. Some "experts" now recommend that individuals invest 100% of their portfolios in equities (or perhaps keep a small percentage— say 10%—in cash), and nothing at all in bonds. Indeed, many investors in bonds may feel like losers, or like fools, given the huge disparity between the returns of stocks and those of bonds, particularly between 1996 and 1999. Therefore, the case for investing in bonds (or in bond funds) needed to be re-examined.

In spite of this change in investor psychology, there has been a veritable explosion in the number and variety of mutual funds that invest in bonds. Many bond funds have proved as volatile and unpredictable as stock funds. Many investors have experienced significant losses in bond funds; and indeed, some of those occurred in bond funds that had been initially marketed as very low risk investments. On the other hand, returns of some bond funds have been high.

A number of new instruments have emerged within the last few years: for example, inflation-indexed bonds. Other securities, such as GNMAs, still considered exotic and new at the time the first edition was published, have become staples. Some sectors of the bond market have also undergone significant changes and expansion: the CMO market, for example; as well as the market for emerging markets debt (chiefly Brady bonds) and the market for junk bonds.

Another significant change has been the advent of the Internet. While buying and selling bonds on the Internet is not yet as easy as it is for stocks, the Internet still represents an important resource for investors in bonds and in bond funds, and this resource is bound to improve with time.

All of these changes pointed to a need to update the book. It is difficult to summarize the changes that I have made: there is no chapter of the book that has not undergone some changes. But here is a summary of the most significant changes.

First, large sections of several chapters have been rewritten.

- Chapters 1–5 have been updated to incorporate current conditions in the bond market; and to include relevant discussions of the Internet. Some sections have been expanded (for example, the section on duration).

- Chapter 6 (Treasuries) includes new sections on inflation-indexed bonds; and on I, EE, and HH Savings Bonds.
- Chapter 8 (Mortgage-Backed Securities) includes expanded sections on CMOs and other asset-backed securities.
- Chapter 9 (Corporate Bonds): the section concerning junk bonds has been rewritten.
- Chapter 10 is a new chapter on international bonds.
- Chapters 11 and 12 (on bond funds) have been entirely rewritten, to reflect the investment experience of the decade of the 90s.
- Chapters 14 and 15 (on portfolio management) include a lot of changes, again, to reflect the investment experience of the 90s.

Throughout the book, I have incorporated information on how to use the Internet to research and to buy bonds. This has been frustrating because I am chasing a moving target. Also, listing every website that has any information on bonds would require a book in itself. What I have done, first of all, is to focus on primary trends. Only currently vital website names have been included. Second, I have described recent developments on the web; the type of information currently available and where to find it; and how to buy and sell bonds online to the extent that is currently possible.

While a good deal of material in the book is new, my initial orientation remains the same. This book is meant to be practical. It assumes little or no knowledge of any bond investment, but it explains all of the critical information required to buy any security, be it a Treasury bond, a municipal bond, or a bond fund.

Several basic themes run through the book. First, I explain in detail the risks that underlie the purchase of any security. The main reason for this is that it is patently silly to lose money because you are buying a security thought to be riskless only because the risk factors are unknown. After you read this book, this will no longer happen.

Second, this book will define areas of opportunity. Just as you can lose money because you don't realize that an investment is risky, you can also earn less because you are restricting yourself unnecessarily. There may be areas of opportunity that you just don't know are out there.

Third, at minimum, any investor needs to understand enough technical information to be able to discriminate between sound analysis and hot air. You will learn a lot of technical terms and concepts so that, in the future, no one can intimidate you. If you sound like an informed investor, the next time you talk to a bond salesman, he will be much more likely to be honest with you and less likely to try to sell you a bill of goods.

This will, in turn, enable you to locate knowledgeable salespeople. You will learn to find such salespeople by asking questions. This book will suggest a lot of questions. The answers you get by talking to salespersons will tell you whether they have the technical expertise that you are looking for.

Fourth, another theme is how to obtain information. Many chapters contain sample tables and graphs along with explanations on how to interpret them. Similar tables appear in the three bibles of the financial press, that is, *The Wall Street Journal*, *The New York Times*, and *Barron's*; in the financial pages of many major daily newspapers, as well as on the Internet. Also, references for additional research (books, trade journals, and now the Internet) are listed at the end of many chapters. If you wish to pursue any topic in greater depth, you will know where to look.

I kept in mind that investors differ both in the amount of time they have to devote to investing and the amount of personal interest. Throughout the book, I have pointed out techniques that minimize risk for safety-minded investors who have limited time to devote to investing.

Ultimately, this book should enable you to select the instruments that match your tolerance for risk and your overall investment goals and strategies. If you wish to purchase only the safest securities, you will learn what those are. If you love risk, well then, you will learn what instruments in the bond market are the most speculative.

A word about the organization of the book. It is divided into four parts. The first, consisting of five chapters, is introductory, and it is basic to understanding everything that follows. It explains the fundamentals of bond investing, namely, what a bond is and how it originates; how the bond market works; what you must know before buying or selling bonds; the specifics of interest rate risk and credit risk; key concepts used to measure bond returns; and the key data you will want to consult in the financial pages of your newspaper (or on your favorite website).

The second part of the book discusses the major individual securities purchased by individual investors: Treasuries, municipals, GNMAs, corporate bonds, and international bonds. One chapter is devoted to each security. The third part of the book analyzes the major types of bond funds. Most of that is devoted to mutual funds, but closed-end bond funds and unit investment trusts are discussed as well. The fourth part of the book, portfolio management, deals in a more general way with management of bond investments and illustrates how the information contained in various sections of this book may be put together and used.

Some vocabulary notes are in order. First, a word about the term "bond": the term designates any debt instrument or fixed-income security available on the market. Unfortunately, no nifty term exists to cover this type of instrument. For the sake of variety, the terms bond, fixed-income security, or debt instrument are used interchangeably throughout the book. Second, it was necessary to decide how to deal with gender to refer to men and women as investors, or as salespeople. I considered using "he/she" but rejected it as too clumsy. Instead, I decided to use either "he" or "she" in random fashion. This should introduce some variety in the text. It is not meant to offend anyone.

Finally, I have no axe to grind. This is not a book for bonds or against bonds. Bond investments are more complex and less predictable than is generally realized. This book will explain how and why. You may, after reading it, decide to allocate more of your portfolio, or less, to bonds, or to change the mix. What I hope is that whatever you decide, the information contained in this book will enable you to invest in a more informed manner and in turn, increase your returns.

So, many happy returns!

Annette Thau
Teaneck, N.J.

ACKNOWLEDGMENTS

Many individuals provided invaluable help when I wrote the first edition of this book. This book would not have existed without them.

First of all, I would like to thank those persons who not only spent hours answering questions but who also subsequently read portions of the manuscript. This book benefitted enormously from their many insights and suggestions. These individuals include: Bill Reynolds, director of the Municipal Funds Division of T. Rowe Price Mutual Funds; John Charlesworth, chief debt strategist for retail at Merrill Lynch; Richard Wilson, director of Research Products and Services at Fitch Investors; Thomas Herzfeld, president, Thomas Herzfeld Associates; Greg Hickok, formerly head of the municipal division of the Chase Manhattan Bank (now president of Hydra-Clean); John Campbell and Jim Musson, vice presidents at Dean Witter Reynolds; Michael Lipper, president, Lipper Analytical Services.

I would also like to thank the many individuals who answered questions without end while I researched this book. They were incredibly generous with their time. They include Fred Stoever, president, Stoever Glass Securities; the late Steven Hueglin, principal, Gabriele, Hueglin and Cashman; Richard Potter, senior vice president (and director of fixed-income portfolios) at the Fiduciary Trust Bank; Theresa Havell, president, Fixed-Income Funds, Neuberger and Berman; Gary Pollack, vice president, Bankers Trust; Jeffrey Baker, vice president at The Chase Manhattan Bank; Michele Worthy of the Investment Company Institute; and Judy Otterman, vice president at Salomon Brothers.

Most special thanks go to Tom Murphy, who not only acted most capably as my literary agent but who also read several versions of the manuscript; and to my husband, for cheering me on through all the stages of writing this book.

In writing the second edition of this book, I consulted many people within the industry, whose help was again invaluable. Most special thanks go to individuals who read portions of the manuscript, and made many useful suggestions: David Askin, now of the Globecon group; Michael Shamosh, chief strategist at Gabriele, Hueglin and Cashman; Don Cassidy, senior analyst with the Denver Office of Lipper; and Martin Mauro, senior economist at Merrill Lynch. Many other individuals answered innumerable questions and supplied materials: Martin Fridson, senior economist at Merrill Lynch; Janet Dugo, at Gabriele, Hueglin and Cashman; Gary Rudow, now at Gruntal; Dick Wilson, now retired; Len Abazzia and Camilla Altamura, from Lipper; and Shushma Singh, from Merrill Lynch.

Special thanks go to the Lipper organization for generously supplying me with data concerning bond funds. Special thanks also go to Catherine Schwent, my editor at McGraw-Hill, for her support and assistance.

To one and all who made this book possible: thank you!

The opinions expressed in this book are my own. Any omissions or errors are, of course, entirely my own responsibility.

PART ONE

The Basic Basics

This part of the book is introductory and basic to understanding all that follows. Its purpose is to explain the fundamentals of bond investing.

- Chapter 1 defines bonds and explains how they are originated and sold.
- Chapter 2 explains the workings of the bond market and what you must know before buying or selling bonds. This chapter also contains an overview of how to use the Internet to research and buy bonds.
- Chapter 3 is at the heart of the book: it explains why bond prices go up and down through a detailed discussion of interest rate risk and credit risk.
- Chapter 4 is an introduction to basic bond mathematics. It defines the key concepts used to measure return from bond investments as well as bond cash flows.
- Chapter 5 explains how to read and understand tables or data presented in newspapers and on the Internet about bonds and bond prices. It also introduces you to some of the key information you will want to consult when you are researching bond prices or interest rates.

CHAPTER 1

The Life of a Bond

This chapter

- Defines a bond
- Explains how bonds are issued and trade
- Defines some key terms used in buying and selling bonds

FIRST, WHAT IS A BOND?

Basically, a bond is a loan or an IOU. When you buy a bond, you lend your money to a large borrower such as a corporation or a governmental body. These borrowers routinely raise needed capital by selling (or, using Wall Street vocabulary, by "issuing") bonds for periods as brief as a few days to as long as 30 or 40 years. The distinguishing characteristic of a bond is that the borrower (the issuer) enters into a legal agreement to compensate the lender (you, the bondholder) through periodic interest payments in the form of coupons; and to repay the original sum (the principal) in full on a stipulated date, which is known as the bond's "maturity date."

HOW BONDS ARE ISSUED AND TRADE

The process of issuing bonds is complex. Because the sums involved are so large, issuers do not sell bonds directly to the public. Instead, bonds are brought to market by an investment bank (the underwriter). The investment bank acts as an intermediary between the issuer and the investing public. Lawyers are hired by both parties (that is, the issuer and the underwriter) to draw up the formal terms of the sale and to see to it that the sale conforms to the regulations of the Securities and Exchange Commission (the SEC).

To illustrate the process, let us say that the State of New Jersey needs to borrow $500 million in order to finance a major project. New Jersey announces its intention through trade journals and asks for bids. Underwriters (major broker-dealer firms such as Merrill Lynch, Goldman Sachs, Morgan Stanley, Shearson Lehman, etc.) or smaller, less well-known firms (there are dozens of them) compete with each other by submitting bids to New Jersey. A firm may bid for the business by itself in its own name. More often, firms form a group called a syndicate, which submits a joint bid. The State awards the sale to the firm or syndicate which submits the bid which results in the lowest cost to the state. The underwriters then get busy selling the bonds.

The underwriter (or the syndicate) handles all aspects of the bond sale, in effect buying the bonds from the issuer (New Jersey) and selling them to the investing public. The investing public is made up of large institutions such as banks, pension funds, and insurance companies as well as individual investors and bond funds. The large institutional investors are by far the biggest players in the bond market. Once the bonds have been sold, the underwriter retains no connection to the bonds. Payment of interest and redemption (repayment) of principal are—and will remain— the responsibility of the issuer (New Jersey). After the sale, the actual physical payment of interest, record-keeping chores, and so forth are handled for the issuer by still another party, a fiduciary agent, which is generally a bank that acts as the trustee for the bonds.

KEY TERMS FOR BONDS

The exact terms of the loan agreement between the issuer (the State of New Jersey) and anyone who buys the bonds (you or an institution) are described fully in a legal document known as the *indenture,* which is legally binding on the issuer for the entire period that the bond remains outstanding.

First, the indenture stipulates the dates when coupons are paid, as well as the date for repayment of the principal in full: that is, the bond's maturity date.

The indenture then discusses a great many other matters of importance to the bondholder. It describes how the issuer intends to cover debt payments; that is, where the money to pay debt service will come from. In our example concerning the State of New Jersey, the indenture would specify that the State intends to raise the monies through taxes; and in order to further document its ability to service the loan, there would be a description of the State's economy. The indenture also describes a set of conditions that would enable either the issuer or the bondholder to redeem bonds at full value before their stipulated maturity date. These topics are discussed in greater detail in the sections dealing with "call" features and credit quality.

All of the major terms of the indenture, including the payment dates for coupons, the bond's maturity date, call provisions, sources of revenue backing the bonds, and so on, are summarized in a document called a *prospectus.* It is a good idea to read the prospectus if you can. For bonds bought at issue, that is, during the initial few days that the bonds are sold to the public, a prospectus is easily obtained. But for older issues, the prospectus may be hard to find. (As we will see in the next chapter, the prospectus of some older issues can now be found on the Internet.) When the prospectus is printed before the sale, it is known as a "preliminary prospectus," or a "red herring" because certain legal terms are printed on the cover of the prospectus in red ink. After the sale, it is sometimes called an *official statement,* or OS.

The most elementary distinction between bonds is based on who issued the bonds. Bonds issued directly by the U.S. government are classified as Treasury bonds; those issued by corporations are known as corporate bonds; and those issued by local and state governmental units, which are generally exempt from federal taxes, are called "municipals," or "munis" for short. The actual process of selling the bonds differs somewhat from sale to sale but generally conforms to this process.

Many bonds are issued in very large amounts, typically between $100 million and $500 million for corporates and munis and

billions for Treasuries. To sell the bonds to the public, the investment bank divides them into smaller batches. By custom, the
smallest bond unit is one bond, which can be redeemed at maturity for $1,000. The terms *par* and *principal value* both refer to the
$1,000 value of the bond at maturity. In practice, however, bonds
are traded in larger batches, usually in minimum amounts of
$5,000 (par value).

Anyone interested in the New Jersey bonds may buy them
during the few days when the underwriter initially sells the bonds
to the investing public (this is known as buying "at issue") or
subsequently from someone who has decided to sell them. Bonds
purchased at the time of issue are said to have been purchased in
the "primary market." Bonds may be held to maturity, or resold
anytime between the original issue date and the maturity date.
Typically, a bondholder who wishes to sell his bonds will use the
services of a broker, who pockets a fee for the service. There is a
market in older issues, called the "secondary market." Some
bonds (for example, 30-year Treasuries) enjoy a very active market. For many bonds, however, the market becomes moribund and
inactive once the bonds have "gone away" (that is an expression
used by traders) to investors. It is almost always possible to sell
an older bond; but if the bond is not actively traded, then commission costs for selling may be very high. Pricing, buying, and
selling bonds, as well as bond returns, are discussed in greater
detail in Chapters 2 and 4.

During the time that they trade in the secondary market,
bond prices go up and down continually. Bonds seldom, if ever,
trade at par. In fact, bonds are likely to be priced at par only twice
during their life: first, when they are brought to market (at issue),
and second, when they are redeemed. But, and this is an important but, regardless of the purchase price for the bonds, they are
always redeemed at par.

But, you may well ask, if the issue price of a bond is almost
always $1,000, and the maturity value is always $1,000, why and
how do bond prices change? That is where the story gets interesting, so read on.

CHAPTER 2

Buying and Selling Bonds

This chapter discusses

- The bond market: an overview
- Bond pricing and commissions
- Terms used in buying, selling, and discussing bonds
- The Internet and the bond market

THE BOND MARKET: AN OVERVIEW

While people speak of the bond market as if it were one market, in reality there is not one central place or exchange where bonds are bought and sold. In fact, there are not even several exchanges where bonds are traded and prices for each trade are posted. Rather, the bond market is a gigantic over-the-counter market, consisting of networks of independent dealers, organized by type of security, with some overlaps. Most U.S. Treasury securities, for example, are sold through a network of "primary dealers" who sell directly to large institutions and to large broker-dealer firms. The broker-dealer firms, in turn, resell the bonds to the investing public and to smaller institutional investors. Municipals are sold by dealers, by banks, and by brokerage firms. A small number of corporate bonds are sold on each of the stock exchanges and through bond dealers. Whereas stocks sell ultimately in one of three independent exchanges (the New York Stock Exchange, the American Stock Exchange, or the Nasdaq), most bonds are sold dealer to dealer.

This market is so vast that its size is difficult to imagine. Although the financial press reports mainly on the stock market, the bond market is several times larger. Overwhelmingly, this is an institutional market. It raises debt capital for the largest issuers of debt, such as the U.S. government, state and local governments, and the largest corporations. The buyers of that debt are primarily large institutional investors such as pension funds, insurance companies, banks, corporations, and, increasingly, mutual funds. These buyers and sellers routinely trade sums that appear almost unreal to a nonfinance professional. U.S. government bonds trade in blocks of $1 million, and $100 million trades are routine. The smallest blocks are traded in the municipal market, where a round lot is $100,000. Another way of characterizing this market is to call it a wholesale market.

Enter the individual investor. In the bond markets, individual investors, even those with considerable wealth, are all little guys, who are trying to navigate a market dominated by far larger traders. Indeed, many of the new fixed-income securities created over the last ten years were specifically tailored to the needs of pension funds or insurance companies and may not be appropriate for individual investors. The individual investor faces many disadvantages when compared to institutions. Commission costs are much higher. Institutions have developed a vast amount of information concerning bonds, as well as mathematical models and sophisticated trading strategies for buying and selling bonds, which are simply not available to individual investors.

BOND PRICING AND COMMISSIONS

Individuals may purchase bonds from a number of sources, such as full service brokerage firms, banks, or firms that specialize in debt instruments; and discount brokers. (U.S. Treasuries, as we shall see, may also be bought directly from the Federal Reserve Bank.) In this connection, a comparison with stocks may be helpful. If you want to buy a stock listed on the New York Stock Exchange—say International Business Machines (IBM)—any broker can sell you shares of IBM, and any broker knows and can tell you the price of the last trade. Whether you deal with a large brokerage firm or a small brokerage firm, you can buy IBM at the market price (although commissions may differ). If you want to find out the high, low, and closing price of IBM on the previous day, you can look them up in the financial pages of any of the major daily newspapers in the country. In fact, if you have access to the Internet, you can now follow the price of IBM in real time on any computer screen.

However, the situation is very different for bonds. First, the availability of bonds varies from dealer to dealer. If you want to buy a specific type of bond (say, an intermediate muni with a rating of A or better), you cannot just assume that you can buy that bond from any dealer. Instead, you may have to approach several dealers before you find one who has what you want. Discount brokers generally do not maintain inventories. If you want to buy a certain type of bond, their traders have to buy it from another dealer; if you want to sell the bond, their traders ask for bids from other dealers. The best sources for individual bonds tend to be larger broker-dealer firms, or firms that specialize in selling bonds to indiviudal investors. These firms typically maintain inventories of bonds. They may also be able to obtain desirable new issues, whereas smaller firms may not.

Pricing also varies from dealer to dealer. Dealers mark up their bonds independently. The markup depends on their own cost, the size of the order, and how much profit they want to earn. Commission costs, moreover, are hidden, so that the buyer does not know either the cost to the dealer or the size of the markup. Basically, buying a bond is analogous to buying a stock without knowing either the size of the commission or the price on which the commission is based. When you shop for that A-rated intermediate muni, you are likely to be offered a variety of bonds with different yields and prices by different dealers.

Pricing information has been difficult to obtain and that continues to be true. The large bond dealers consider pricing information to be proprietary, and they have resisted efforts to make pricing information more widely available. The financial press publishes some pricing information. But it is limited. The tables that appear in the financial newspapers—including most of those listed in this book—list a few representative widely traded issues. Most of the prices apply to institutional size trades of $1 million or more. If you want to either buy or to sell smaller-size lots (that is, fewer bonds), the price per bond will be higher if you buy, lower if you sell.

Two additional factors further muddy bond pricing. With the exception of Treasuries, many bonds trade infrequently. If a bond has not traded for months, there is obviously no current valid pricing on it. Furthermore, the bond market includes literally well over millions of issues of all types, sizes, maturity dates, and credit quality. The same bond may be sold by different dealers for widely different prices, based on the price at which they bought the bond, the size of their markup, the size of the lot, and the direction of interest rates, and these are only a few of the relevant factors.

To sum up, buying bonds continues to be very different from buying stocks. To return to our original example, if you want to buy a bond, at the current time it is still not possible to type a ticker symbol on your favorite financial website, as you would for IBM, and look up the last price at which this bond traded. You have to call up a number of brokers and see if they own or can get this bond for you, and if so, at what price. If you own a bond and want to sell it, once again you really ought to call a number of different brokers and see how much they will offer you for that bond. (As noted earlier, Treasuries are an exception.)

In addition, many stockbrokers who also sell bonds don't really understand the bond market very well. It is not clear why this is so. But the bull market in equities of the last two decades has done nothing to improve this situation. Many of the brokers who specialized in bonds, and really understood the bonds they were selling, have moved to the equity side because that is where the action has been. Finding a good source for bonds requires effort. Try to locate either a firm that specializes in bonds, or within a bank or brokerage firm, an individual who specializes in selling particular types of bonds to individual investors. Take the trouble to interview brokers and discuss your needs with them. This book will suggest a lot of questions that you can ask. Unfortunately, it may be difficult to find salespeople who can answer these questions. In order to protect your own interests, if you want to buy individual bonds, you need to become an informed investor; and you need to stick to bonds whose characteristics and risks you understand.

Finally, be aware that there is nothing wrong with bargaining; for example, asking the broker if she can do a little better. To a broker, a smaller commission is better than no sale. Commissions in the bond market are often negotiable. Even if you have always done business with a particular firm (or a particular broker), it pays to shop around and be as well informed about market conditions as possible. You are more likely to negotiate a better price if your broker realizes that you are shopping around.

The chapters dealing with specific sectors of the bond market will address the issues involved in buying or selling those bonds in greater detail.

You can judge the quality of a firm partly by what that firm tries to sell you. If you tell a broker that stability of principal is important to you, and you are consistently offered only high-yielding—and therefore risky—securities, go elsewhere. Certain firms, referred to unceremoniously as "bucket shops," are known for their high-pressure tactics. Such firms rely on cold-calling, that is, telephoning strangers in order to spot buyers who will buy without investigating carefully. Typically, the cold caller will tell you that he is offering you a unique opportunity to buy a terrific bond, but that if you do not purchase this bond immediately, the opportunity will disappear. Never buy anything over the phone from a person or a firm that you do not know well or without comparing prices with several dealers.

TERMS USED IN BUYING, SELLING, AND DISCUSSING BONDS

Par, Premium, and Discount Bonds

The "par" value of a bond is its value at maturity; that is, $1,000. When a bond begins to trade, it normally ceases to sell at par. If it sells at less than par (less than $1,000), it is said to be selling at a "discount." If it sells at more than par (above $1,000), it is called a "premium" bond.

CUSIP Numbers

The CUSIP numbering system was established in 1967 in order to provide a uniform method for identifying bonds. (CUSIP stands for Committee on Uniform Security Identification Procedures.)

This is a nine-digit number which identifies individual bonds. It is equivalent to a ticker symbol for a stock, and it identifies each bond issue precisely. Suppose, for example, you own a State of New Jersey bond. That bond is only one of perhaps hundreds of State of New Jersey bonds that are outstanding at any given time. Each one of these bonds has very precise and individual provisions: coupon, issue date, maturity, and call provisions. These bonds are not interchangeable. If you want to buy or sell a bond, the CUSIP number identifies the precise issue you are dealing with.

CUSIP numbers are assigned to municipal, corporate, and pass-through securities. International issues are identified by a CINS number.

"Bid," "Ask," and "Spread"

Commission costs for buying or selling bonds are hidden. The price is quoted net. Indeed, if you ask a broker about the commission, you may be told that there is no commission. But that is not the case.

Prices of all fixed-income instruments—including mutual funds—are always quoted in pairs: the "bid" and the "ask," also known as the offer. The difference between the bid and the ask is known as the "spread." It represents the commission. Technically, the bid is what you sell for; the ask, the price at which you buy. But it is not difficult to remember which is the bid and which is the ask. Just remember this: if you want to buy, you always pay the *higher* price. If you want to sell, you receive the *lower*.

For example, a bond may be quoted at "98 bid/100 ask." If you are buying the bond, you will pay 100; if you are selling, you will receive 98 (see below for the answer to 98 and 100 what).

Technically, the bid/ask spread is a market spread, which means that it is the cost of buying or selling for the broker. A broker starts with the market spread, and figures out how much additional commission she needs to charge in order sell a bond to you at a profit. Suppose, for example, that the market spread is "98 bid/100 ask." If you are selling an inactively traded bond (and that description applies to most bonds), then the broker makes sure that she buys it from you cheaply enough so that she will not lose money when she resells. She might then quote a spread to you of "97 bid/101 ask." For that reason, commission costs to an individual investor are often wider than the market bid/ask spread.

For an individual investor, commission costs typically range from 1/2 of 1% (or even less) for actively traded Treasury issues to as much as 4% on inactively traded bonds. Commissions vary for many reasons:

+ The dealer's cost and his markup
+ The type of bond being sold (Treasury, muni, mortgage-backed, or corporate)
+ The amount of the bond being traded (that is, the size of the lot)
+ The bond's maturity
+ Its credit quality
+ The overall direction of interest rates
+ Demand for a specific bond
+ Demand for a particular bond sector

As a rule, bonds that have very low risk have narrower (that is, lower) commission (spreads); bonds that are riskier or less in demand sell at wider (that is, higher) spreads. Any characteristic that makes a bond less desirable makes it more expensive to sell. For example, lower-quality bonds are more expensive to resell than bonds with higher credit quality. Bonds with longer maturities have higher markups than short-term bonds. Selling a small number of bonds is more expensive than selling a large quantity (or a round lot). Market conditions are also important. For instance, if interest rates are rising, spreads normally widen; if interest rates are dropping, spreads usually narrow.

Let's illustrate with some concrete examples. Treasury bonds sell at the narrowest spreads (less than 1/2% or even less), no matter how many bonds, or the direction of interest rates. High-quality intermediate munis (AA or AAA, maturing between three and seven years) sell at commissions of between 3/4% to perhaps 2%. Thirty-year munis sell at spreads of between 3% and 4%. The more strikes against a bond, the more difficult it is to sell. Trying to sell a long maturity, low credit quality bond in a weak market is a worst-case scenario because you may have to shop extensively just to get a bid.

The size of the spread (or commission) reflects what is known as a bond's *liquidity*; that is, the ease and cost of trading a particular bond. A narrow spread indicates high demand and low risk: the dealer is sure she can resell quickly. Conversely, a wide spread indicates an unwillingness on the part of the dealer to own a bond without a substantial price cushion. An unusually wide commission (4% or more) constitutes a red flag. It warns you that at best, a particular bond may be expensive to resell and, at worst, headed for difficult times. The dealer community, which earns its living buying and selling bonds, has a very active information and rumor network that is sometimes quicker to spot potential trouble than the credit rating agencies.

Note also that when you buy a bond at issue, even though the commission is built into the deal, commission costs are usually closer to the actual market price for that bond, at that point in time, than when bonds trade in the secondary market. Hence, the individual investor may receive a fairer shake by buying at issue than by buying in the secondary market.

As already noted, it is difficult to obtain information on spreads and pricing. Dealers are reluctant to reveal markups. And pricing is variable. It bears repeating that the only way to protect yourself is to comparison shop and to do some arithmetic. A difference of 2% in the spread may not seem like a lot; but on a $10,000 investment, that's $200. On a $100,000 investment, it's $2,000. Such differences in markups are common.

Always try to find out the bid/ask spread when you are buying a bond. If the broker does not directly quote the spread, ask what you could resell the bond for if you had to resell it that afternoon (or the next day).

Discussing Bonds

When the broker "shows" you a bond (that is the term generally used), she will say something like "I want to show you this great bond we just got in. It is the State of Bliss 7 1/4 of 05, and it is priced at 96 bid and 97 ask." Well, what did she say?

Actually, that statement is easily decoded. Bonds are always identified by several pieces of information; namely, the issuer (State of Bliss); the coupon (7 1/4); the maturity date, of "05"; and the price, quoted as 97.

Let us examine each of these details more closely. First, the coupon. Coupons are always quoted in percentages. That percentage is set at issue and is therefore a percentage of par. The percentage value, however, is immediately translated into a fixed dollar amount, and that amount remains the same throughout the life of the bond no matter what happens to the price of the bond. In the previous example, the 7 1/4 coupon represents 7 1/4% of $1,000, that is, $72.50. Unless stipulated otherwise, coupons are paid semiannually. You will receive half of that amount, that is, $36.25, twice a year, for as long as the bond remains outstanding. (Floating-rate bonds vary from this pattern. For floating-rate bonds, coupon rates are reset at predetermined intervals.)

The maturity date is designated by the last two digits, in this instance, 05. This has to be 2005. Note that with few exceptions, bonds are not issued with maturities above 30 years.

Finally, the price was quoted as 97. Bond prices are quoted in percentages, and again, percentages of par. So the quote of 97 should be interpreted as 97% (or 0.97) times $1,000, which equals $970. To compute price, add a zero to the percentage quote.

You can now translate what the bond broker is telling you. She would like to sell you a State of Bliss bond, maturing in 2005, with a coupon of $72.50, at a price of $970.

Accrued Interest

Let us suppose you decide to buy the State of Bliss bonds. When you receive your confirmation notice, it is probable that the price will turn out to be somewhat higher than the $970 that you were quoted. No, the broker is not ripping you off. The difference between the price that you pay and the $970 that you were quoted is "accrued interest." Let's explain.

You will remember that interest payments are made twice a year. But actually, bonds earn (the Wall Street word is "accrue") interest every single day. The owner of a bond earns or accrues interest for the exact number of days that he owns the bond.

Now suppose you are buying the State of Bliss bonds three months after the last coupon payment was made (and therefore, three months before the next interest payment occurs). In three months, you will receive an interest payment for the past six months; but you will have earned that interest for only three months. The gentlemanly thing to do is to turn over three months' worth of interest to the previous owner.

In fact, that is what you do when you buy the bond—only you do not have any choice in the matter. The three months of interest due to the previous owner are automatically added on to the purchase price. The buyer pays the seller the accrued interest. When you (the buyer) receive the next coupon payment, the interest you receive will cover the three months' worth of interest you earned and the three months of interest that you paid the previous owner.

Accrued interest is easily computed. For bond pricing purposes, for many bonds (but not for notes), the year has 360 days. To compute accrued interest, divide the annual coupon by 360 days and multiply the result by the number of days accrued interest is owed. Add accrued interest to the purchase price. The day count varies somewhat, depending on the type of bond.

Accrued interest is paid on par, premium, and discount bonds. The amount of accrued interest depends entirely on the coupons, divided by the number of days interest is owed. It has nothing to do with the price.

Call Risk

"Call risk" is the risk that bonds will be redeemed ("called") by the issuer before they mature. Municipal and corporate bonds are subject to call; Treasuries generally are not. Some older 30-year Treasuries may be callable five years before they mature, but the Treasury no longer issues any callable bonds.

The ability to call bonds protects issuers by enabling them to retire bonds with high coupons and refinance at lower interest rates. Calls are usually bad news for bondholders. A call reduces total return because bonds are called when interest rates are lower than the coupon interest of the bond that is being called. A high interest rate, thought to be "locked in," disappears, and the bondholder is forced to reinvest at lower rates.

If a bond was purchased at par, there is no loss of principal. But if it was purchased at a premium (say for $1,200), an unexpected early call can result in a substantial loss of principal since bonds are typically redeemed at or close to par. If the $1,200 bond is redeemed at par, then that translates into a $200 loss per bond.

The prospectus spells out call provisions by stipulating both specific call dates and call prices, which are typically somewhat above par. Call provisions differ, depending on the type of bond you are buying. Call provisions for corporates can be obscure. Mortgage-backed securities do not have stipulated call dates, but prepayments constitute a type of call risk. Call features of municipal, corporate, and mortgage-backed securities will be discussed in greater detail in the chapters dealing with these securities. But I mention call features at this point because you should be aware that call provisions are one of the complicating factors when you buy bonds. Never buy a bond without specifically inquiring about the call provisions for that particular bond.

When a bond is offered, the broker should quote not only the yield-to-maturity (see Chapter 4), but also the yield to the earliest call date (appropriately known as the *yield-to-call*). Brokers usually quote the yield-to-call for munis, but seldom for corporates. If the coupon rate is a lot higher than the current interest rate on similar bonds, it is prudent to assume that the bond will be called and to evaluate the bond based on the yield-to-call. If, for example, a broker offers you a bond with an 8% coupon, maturing in ten years, callable in one year, and interest rates are now at 6% for similar maturities, you should assume the bond will be called.

Let us note in passing another term that has come into use as an alternate to yield-to-call: *yield-to-worst*. That is the lowest yield that a bond would earn, under some provision in the indenture, whether that is a call, or a sinking fund provision or even the yield-to-maturity. If you are buying a bond, always inquire about the yield-to-worst.

How can you protect yourself against calls?

+ First, check call provisions carefully whenever you are buying munis or corporate bonds.
+ Be particularly careful in checking call provisions if you are purchasing premium bonds; that is, bonds whose price is well above par.
+ Buy deeply discounted bonds; that is, bonds with very low coupons selling well below par. They are much less likely to be called than high coupon bonds. Remember that the coupon represents the cost of money to the

issuer. The issuer is therefore most likely to call the bonds with the highest coupons rather than those with lower coupons.

The Form of a Bond: Certificate, Registered, and Book-Entry

If you bought a muni bond before 1980, you received as proof of ownership an ornate document with coupons attached at the side. This document was known as a "certificate." The certificate did not have your name on it. To collect interest, it was necessary to physically clip the coupons and to send them to the trustee, who would then mail you the interest payment. (That is the origin of the term "coupon.") The certificate functioned like a dollar bill. It was presumed to be owned by the bearer. Those bonds were also known as "bearer bonds."

In the early 1980s, certificates began to be issued with the name of the owner imprinted on the certificate. Those are called "registered" bonds. Interest payments are sent automatically to the owner of record.

With the spread of computerization, the process has become even more automated. Many bonds are now issued in "book-entry" form. No certificates are issued. Instead, when you buy a bond, you receive a confirmation statement with a number on it. That number is stored in a computer data bank and is the only proof of ownership. Coupon payments are wired automatically to the checking or bank account that the owner designates. Notification of calls is automatic.

Most bonds are now issued in book-entry form. Older bonds are still available in bearer form, but the supply is diminishing as these bonds mature.

You may hold certificates in your own possession or leave them in your account with a broker. Brokers always prefer holding the certificates. There are two good reasons for letting them do so. First, if the firm is covered by the Securities Insurance Protection Corporation (SIPC), and most are, the bond is protected against loss—that is, against physical loss of the certificate—not against a decline in price due to market conditions. Second, the firm is more likely than you to be immediately aware of calls. If a bond is called, the firm should immediately redeem the bonds. That should protect you against loss of interest.

Leaving a bond in a brokerage account does not prevent you from selling the bond through a different broker. To transfer a book-entry bond, you need only to notify your broker to transfer it by wire to any other firm.

If your bond is in certificate form, however, the matter becomes more complicated because you need to deliver the certificate within three days after the sale. (A recommendation has been made that trades should settle one day after the sale, but that is not yet the rule except for Treasuries.) And six weeks or more may be needed to obtain the document because it is usually not stored in the branch office. Selling through the firm holding your bond eliminates actually having to get your hands on the document, and it permits you to sell at any time. If you want to sell through a different broker, then you must allow enough time to obtain the certificate.

Basis Points

Interest rates rise from 6% to 7%. How much have they gone up?

No, they have not gone up 1%. On a percentage basis, that increase represents a percentage difference of 16.67%. This may seem like nitpicking. But suppose, for example, that interest rates rise from 6% to 6.12%? How would you label that increase, using percentages?

The answer to that question would be either imprecise or confusing. Since institutional investors make or lose thousands of dollars on seemingly minute percentage changes, they have divided each percentage point into 100 points, each of which is called a "basis point" (bp). The difference between an interest rate of 6% and one of 7% is 100 basis points; between 5% and 6%, it is still 100 basis points. An increase in interest rate yield from 6% to 6.12% represents an increase in yield of 12 basis points (which would be recorded as 12 bp).

The term "basis point" is used to compare both price and yield. If, for example, you are comparing two different bonds, you might note that the three-year bond yields 6.58%, whereas the two-year bond yields 6.50%. In this instance, the three-year bond yields 8 basis points more than the two-year bond. Changes in interest rates from one day to the next, or from one year to the next, are denoted in basis points.

Under normal circumstances, yields of most bonds vary from day to day by no more than a few basis points. But occasional moves are higher. A rise or a decline in yield from one day to the next of more than 10 basis points constitutes a major price move and therefore a major change in the direction of interest rates. Remember that changes in yield translate into changes in price and vice-versa. Experienced investors and salespeople think in basis points. It is far easier and more precise than using percentages. Using the term will immediately mark you as a knowledgeable investor. It will be used through the rest of the book.

BONDS AND THE INTERNET

Writing this section of the book made my grey hair turn just a little whiter. The reason is that writing about bonds and the Internet is writing about a constantly changing work-in-progress. There is no question in my mind that a year from now, some of this section will be obsolete, because changes are occurring at such a rapid pace.

The issue, therefore, was what to focus on that would remain useful.

I decided, first of all, to include only vital website names. Firms are being formed, bought, merging, and going out of existence on a daily basis. For that reason, this overview will focus on trends.

Second, I will describe recent developments on the web: the type of information currently available on the web; the securities that are available for sale; and how to buy and sell bonds online.

Finally, I will describe some potential developments.

Fixed-Income Securities and the Web: An Overview

Over the past few months, a number of articles have appeared in various financial publications proclaiming that the revolution has arrived, and that we can now buy bonds online. The authors of these articles took the position, moreover, that this was a giant step forward, and the wave of the future.

It may be the wave of the future; but the future has not yet arrived.

As stated earlier, the fixed-income markets remain dominated by institutions: the large institutions that buy the bulk of fixed-income securities; and the very large dealers that service those institutions. Firms that sell bonds include very large dealers, who also underwrite and distribute bonds. These firms are known as broker-dealers. The largest of these firms sell to smaller brokerage firms. Some broker-dealer firms have separate departments that service both individual investors and institutions. Up to now, the biggest push for electronic or online business has occurred within the institutional community, to service the large broker-dealer firms. A number of the electronic platforms that have been recently announced in the financial press have been established to service only broker-dealers and brokers. They do not deal with individual investors.

The push to use the web has not been limited to sales and distribution of fixed-income securities. A number of recent initiatives are intended to make the process of underwriting and bringing bonds to market more efficient. For example, in the municipal sector, several issuers have solicited bids from underwriters directly online. These have been mainly smaller issuers, who hoped to obtain more favorable bids. These issuers, however, were dealing with underwriters, not selling directly to the public. Another initiative would allow underwriters to submit official documents (such as the prospectus or official statement) online. This may not seem like a big deal, unless you realize that official statements are usually over 100 pages long, and have to be printed, mailed, and stored. Documents filed electronically would cost a lot less to produce, and would remain much more accessible to everyone including the public. Further initiatives are bound to occur, which will change the way bonds are brought to market and distributed to interested buyers, including individual investors.

No doubt, what interests you the most at this point is how you can currently use the Internet to research bonds; and to buy or sell bonds. You can now buy Treasuries and savings bonds directly online, from the U.S. Treasury, in the privacy of your home, without paying fees or commissions of any kind, and if you are on the web, that is clearly the way to go. But for other sectors of the bond market (municipals, corporates, or mortgage-backed securities), even though you can now find listings for different types of bonds on the websites of dealers, as well as on several free websites, progress has been limited. Here is why.

How Bonds Are Listed Online: Markups

Before proceeding further, let's explain how bonds come to be listed. If you see a bond listed by a broker on the website of that broker, the logical conclusion is that this is a bond that broker owns and is listing for sale. But that is usually not the case.

The entity behind most bond websites is a database currently called *Bond Express*. Prior to its current incarnation, Bond Express existed as an inter-dealer broker. Before 1987, that firm would call hundreds of firms daily to find out what bonds they owned and wanted to sell. The advent of the fax machine revolutionized the business. Dealers were now able to fax, on a daily basis, the list of bonds they wanted to sell. Those faxes were then used to compile a master list, which was circulated among dealers. In effect, it became a central database for dealers.

In 1999, the business was sold to a purveyor of financial market data, named Barra and renamed Bond Express. Barra has announced its intention to turn Bond Express into a genuine bond trading exchange at some future date. This exchange would allow individual investors to execute trades directly by matching buy and sell orders. But at the current time, Bond Express remains mainly an electronic bulletin board. Bond Express makes the entire list, as well as its software, available to discount brokers, full service brokers, and also, to some free websites. When you are searching for bonds on the website of an online broker, what you are looking at is the list supplied by Bond Express. (Currently, there are two free websites which also make the list available for informational purposes: *Bondsonline* and *CNNfn*. Neither is a broker. If a bond interests you, you have to contact a broker to place an order.)

At this point, further explanations are in order. First of all, you should realize that the price you see includes at least one, and perhaps two markups. This is how that happens.

When a broker-dealer reports its inventory to Bond Express, that dealer lists the bid side of the market. But when Bond Express lists the bond, Bond Express immediately marks up the price to reflect the ask (or offer) side of the market. This is done in either of two ways. If the list is shown by an online broker, Bond Express marks up the price according to the instructions of that broker. If the inventory is shown on a free website, average markups are applied. Because of this, depending on which website you log on to, you may see the same bond listed with different prices. Note also that at the current time, with very few exceptions, few online dealers display the bid and the ask. The markup remains hidden.

Now let us assume that you are logging on to the website of your favorite online broker and you see a list of municipal bonds for sale. Most online brokers claim two advantages: that commissions will be lower; and execution will be fast and convenient. At the current time, however, neither is certain.

Let's first look at the price. Bear in mind that in all likelihood, the dealer does not own the bonds that are listed on its website. The site is displaying the list supplied by Bond Express, after the markup has been tacked on. If you order a bond from an online broker, the dealer will first have to buy the bond from the listing dealer and then turn around and sell it to you. So the price you pay will then actually include two different markups. The first one is the markup required by the dealer selling the bond to your dealer. And the second markup is the one your dealer is charging you. On top of that, most dealers charge a small fee per bond, which they sometimes call a "transaction" fee, and sometimes, a commission. (Several recent articles on the topic listed that fee as if that was the total amount of the markup, but that is not correct.)

There are other shortcomings. Bear in mind that Bond Express updates its list once a day. Therefore, when you see the list, many bonds may no longer be available. If they are available, they may not be available at the price at which you see them listed. Some websites contain disclaimers stating that: "Prices, yields, and availability are subject to change with the market." If the site lists 500 bonds for sale, and you want to buy a smaller lot, say 15 bonds, the price per bond will probably be higher than the listed price. But that may not be clearly stated. Finally, some of the listed bonds may not really be available for sale: they may simply be requests for bids.

One final word about markups. Are the markups online higher than they are with more traditional brokers? Clearly, that question does not have one answer. But you should first of all be aware that seeing a listing on the web does not mean you are automatically getting a better price. There may be some good deals online. But you have to be familiar enough with the market to be able to spot a bargain, or at least, to know whether or not you are getting a fair deal.

One recently published book on the bond market makes the claim that online buying of bonds is the best deal the individual investor has gotten. That claim is trumpeted in ads by a number of online brokers. If online trading expands, and if online brokers begin to compete on price, that may become a fact. But for the moment, the claim is, at the very least, premature.

Buying and Selling Bonds Online

First, what bonds can you currently buy online?

In this section, I will briefly summarize general sources. More detailed information will be provided in the chapters dealing with individual securities.

Let's first mention *publicdebt.treas.com*. This is not a commercial broker-dealer. It is a website maintained by the Treasury, which enables you to buy any security issued by the government, whether it's a savings bond or a Treasury obligation, online, without any additional fees or commissions. This website is in a class by itself, and if you are considering buying any obligation of the U.S. government, this is the way to go. (This website is described in detail in Chapter 6.)

All brokers (online or offline) also sell Treasuries, but for a fee. So why would you want to buy from them?

Surprisingly, only a few brokers currently sell other fixed-income securities online. A few sell listed corporate bonds and a limited number of municipal bonds. (Bear in mind that few of these are likely to be owned by the broker. Most brokers post the list provided by Bond Express.) Surveys indicate that at the current time, the brokers with the largest selection, and most diversified offerings are *E*Trade* and *Discover*.[1] E*Trade sells Treasuries,

1. See, for example, Elizabeth Roy, "TSC's Guide to Bonds Online," *The Street.com*, July 24, 2000.

municipals, and corporates; and has a wider selection of bonds available for immediate execution than most. Discover sells Treasuries and corporates, but not municipals.

Finally, opening an account and buying bonds from an online broker involves a number of different steps. In all cases, you can download an application to open an account from the web. But that has to be mailed in, with your signature, and the account has to be funded before you can buy any bonds. Once your account is open, you can search the website of the broker for a bond, but in order to actually complete the transaction, and buy the bond, you may need to phone a broker. Selling bonds is also more complicated than buying bonds. Few online brokers are currently set up to allow you to sell bonds conveniently.

Now consider execution. Execution is unlikely to be as quick as you might expect. To get a better idea of how placing an order would work, you can scroll through the website of *E*Trade*, currently (as mentioned earlier) considered to have the largest selection of bonds for sale online, as well as some of the best software. To order a bond, you select from among several criteria (maturity, credit rating, price, and so on) those that are most important to you. You then have a choice. You can specify the price at which you are willing to buy a bond; but that does not guarantee execution. Or, you can buy at the market price; but then the price may change. You will not know the exact price you are paying until you receive a confirmation. Finally, if you are ordering a bond after normal trading hours, your order goes into a queue for the following day. Then your order may or may not be executed. In comparison, when you buy a bond from a broker on the phone, you know immediately if you have bought the bond, and at what price.

What Is Likely to Change?

I have described in some detail the process of listing bonds, and markups, because that is the most entrenched aspect of the market, and probably, the least likely to change over the near term.

You may very well wonder why there is so much secrecy in this market. One answer is that this is the way the market has always functioned, and there is always resistance to change. But another reason is that many large bond dealers consider pricing information to be one of their main competitive advantages, and they are reluctant to part with this advantage. They are resisting change ferociously.

What is more likely to change, and more rapidly, is the availability of bonds online. A number of firms, Schwab and Fidelity among them, have announced plans to expand their bond offerings sometime later this year. But firms you are unlikely to be familiar with may very well become major players. For example, today's issue of *The Bond Buyer*[2] carries a story stating that two firms, one formed several months ago to specialize in municipals and another also launched within the last year to sell a variety of fixed-income securities primarily to dealers and financial advisers, were merging. The combined company, named *Bonddesk.com*, intends to market all types of fixed-income products to both dealers and individual investors. Backers of this firm include some of the largest investment banks on Wall Street, including Goldman Sachs, Paine Webber, and Donaldson, Lufkin and Jenrette. But in the last month, few days have gone by without another story about another entrant into this market.

What would need to happen for pricing to become much more competitive? Software would have to be developed which would allow individual investors to place their orders directly with the dealer listing a bond for sale. Similarly, that software should allow an individual investor who wants to sell bonds to solicit bids directly from dealers. Dealers would then have to compete anonymously on price.

This, however, is not just a technical software issue. It involves important regulatory issues which exist to protect individual investors. At the current time, the Municipal Securities Rulemaking Board (MSRB), which is the regulatory agency for municipal bonds, has announced the creation of a task force which will look into some of the important regulatory issues that need to be addressed as electronic sales of municipal bonds expand. Specific rules that are being investigated include:

+ Rule G-13, dealing with the fact that quotes for bond prices are not firm;
+ Rule G-30 on fair pricing requiring dealers acting as principals to set "fair and reasonable prices and commissions";

2. August 10, 2000, p. 1

- Rule G-17, which requires dealers to provide "all material" information about a security before its sale;
- Rule G-19 on suitability, which requires dealers to ensure they recommend securities suitable for a particular investor. One issue raised by consideration of this rule is whether posting a bond for sale on a website constitutes a *de facto* recommendation of that security.[3]

The Bond Market Association (the association representing dealers of fixed-income securities) will also publish a paper later this year addressing some of the same issues. These issues are complex and unlikely to be resolved instantly. But they point to the need for caution when individual investors buy bonds online. Until pricing information becomes much more transparent, you will still need to shop around and consult a variety of sources to protect yourself on price.

Finally, look for online brokers to develop and add sophisticated software to their websites which will make available to individual investors some of the tools used by professionals to manage risk or tax efficiency.

Information Available on the Web

There is a lot of useful information about bonds available on the web.

First, the Bond Market Association provides actual price (that is, trade) information on its website: *investinginbonds.com* for two sectors of the bond market. The most detailed information is provided for municipal bonds. Less detailed information is provided for corporate bonds. This information is intended to supply representative, not exact pricing, for bonds. Also, that website makes it very clear that the listings are for information only. To actually buy or sell a bond, you need to contact a broker. Still, the listings give you some idea where the market is for the securities listed. These listings will be described in detail in Chapters 7 and 8.

Also, a good deal of information is available on the web concerning different sectors of the bond market; and a lot of that information may not be available in the printed press. Websites providing this type of information will be listed along with

---

3. "MSRB Plans Guidance on Online Sales," *The Bond Buyer,* Aug. 2, 2000, p. 1.

sources available in the printed media, at the end of each chapter dealing with individual issues and with bond funds. Websites providing general information on bonds are listed at the end of Chapter 5 along with additional general references on the bond market.

Finally, the websites of online dealers can be viewed, at the very least as a source of information about prices in various sectors of the bond market, and sometimes, as a resource for buying some bonds. If, for example, you are used to dealing with a broker, and you see a bond you like, by all means, call your broker. She may actually be able to buy that bond for less than you could buy it yourself. And you will get a second opinion on the bond.

CHAPTER 3

Volatility: Why Bond Prices Go Up and Down

This chapter discusses

- Interest rate risk
- Credit ratings
- A short history of interest rates

Bond prices go up and down in response to two factors: changes in interest rates and changes in credit quality. Individual investors who purchase bonds tend to worry a lot about the safety of their money. Generally, however, they tie safety to credit considerations. Many individual investors do not fully understand how changes in interest rates affect price. Since the late 1970s, changes in the interest rate environment have become the greatest single determinant of bond returns. Managing interest rate risk has become the most critical variable in the management of bond portfolios. In this chapter we'll see why.

INTEREST RATE RISK, OR A TALE OF PRINCIPAL RISK

"Interest rate risk," also known as "market risk," refers to the propensity bonds have of fluctuating in price as a result of changes in interest rates.

All bonds are subject to interest rate risk.
All bonds are subject to interest rate risk.
All bonds are subject to interest rate risk.

Why am I repeating this statement so many times?

Because if nothing else makes an impression, but you learn that all bonds are subject to interest rate risk, regardless of the issuer or the credit rating or whether the bond is "insured" or "guaranteed," then this book will have served a useful purpose.

The principle behind this fact is easy to explain.

Let us suppose you bought a 30-year bond when 30-year Treasuries were yielding 4%. Further suppose that you now wish to sell your bond and that interest rates for the same maturity are currently 10%. How can you convince someone to purchase your bond, with a coupon of 4%, when he can buy new issues with a 10% coupon?

Well, there is only one thing you can do: you mark down your bond. In fact, the price at which a buyer would buy your bond as readily as a new issue is that price at which your bond would now yield 10%. That would be approximately 30 cents on the dollar, or about $300 per bond.

But, you will object, if I sell my $1,000 bond for $300, I have lost $700 per bond! That is precisely the point.

Significant changes in the interest rate environment are not hypothetical. During the past decade, swings of 1% (100 basis points) have occurred on several occasions over periods of a few weeks or a few months. During the late 1970s and 1980s, rates moved up and down, in sharp spikes or drops, as much as 5% (500 basis points) within a few years. Between September of 1998 and January of 2000, interest rates on the Treasury's long bond moved from a low of 4.78% to a high of 6.75%, almost 200 basis points. If you held bonds during that period, you will remember it as a period when returns from all types of bonds were dismal.

The basic principle is that interest rates and prices move in an inverse relationship. When interest rates went from 4.78% to 6.75%, that represented an increase in yield of over 40%. The price of the bond declined by a corresponding amount. On the other hand, when interest rates decline, then the price of the bond goes up. The section on bond math (Chapter 4) will expand on this relationship.

The following questions and answers discuss management of interest rate risk.

Is There Anything You Can Do to Protect Your Money Against Interest Rate Fluctuations?

Yes. You can buy bonds with maturities that are either short (under one year) or short-intermediate (between two and seven years).

Again, the reason for that is easy to explain. While all bonds are subject to interest rate risk, *that risk is correlated to maturity length*. As maturity length increases, so do potential price fluctuations. Conversely, the shorter the maturity of the bond you buy, the lower the risk of price fluctuations as a result of changes in interest rate levels. For the moment, let us leave aside the question of exactly how much the price of a bond will go up and down in response to changes in interest rates. The main point to remember is that price fluctuations for bonds are correlated directly to maturity length. If interest rates rise, the value of bonds with very short maturities (under a year) changes only a little. That is why such bonds are considered cash equivalents. Each additional year in maturity length adds some degree of volatility. A very rough rule of thumb is that a 100-basis-point rise in yield (say, from 7% to 8%) will result in a loss of value of about 10% of principal (a loss of $100 per $1,000 par value bond) for bonds with 30-year maturities. Steeper rises in interest levels devastate the price of long-term bonds.

To illustrate, let's look at Table 3–1. This table shows what would happen to the price of a bond selling at par ($1,000), with a 7% coupon, for several different maturities, under three different scenarios: if interest rates were to go up modestly by 50 basis points, to 7.5%; or by 100 basis points, to 8%; or, more steeply, by 200 basis points, to 9%.

Table 3–1 shows that if interest rates rise very modestly, by 50 basis points, the price of the two-year bond changes very little. But even that modest rise results in a decline of 3.5% ($35) for the ten-year bond and 5.9% ($59) for the 30-year bond. For the 30-year bond, the decline of 5.9% wipes out almost the total amount of interest income for the entire year. If a much sharper rise in interest rates occurs, from 7% to 9%, declines become correspondingly larger: from 3.6% ($36) for the two-year bond, through 13%

T A B L E   3–1

What Would Happen to the Price of a $1,000 Par Value
Bond with a 7% Coupon if Interest Rates Rise by 50
Basis Points, to 7.5%? By 100 Basis Points, to 8%? And
by 200 Basis Points, to 9%?

Maturity	to 7.5%	to 8%	to 9%
2 yrs	−0.9%	−1.1%	−3.6%
5 yrs	−2.1%	−3.5%	−4.7%
10 yrs	−3.5%	−6.8%	−13.0%
30 yrs	−5.9%	−11.3%	−20.6%

Source: Merrill Lynch. Material supplied to the author.

($130) for the ten-year, and 20.6% ($206) for the 30-year bond. (All
numbers are rounded.) Clearly, if interest rates go up, the holder
of bonds with shorter maturities would be less unhappy than the
holder of bonds with long maturities.

This phenomenon, happily, operates in reverse. As interest
rates decline, bond prices rise. This is illustrated in Table 3–2.

Table 3–2 illustrates changes in price for various maturities
under three different scenarios: first, if interest rates decline by a
small amount, 50 basis points, to 6.5%; or by 100 basis points, to
6%; or more steeply, by 200 basis points, to 5%. Once again, the

T A B L E   3–2

What Would Happen to the Price of a $1,000 Par Value
Bond with a 7% Coupon if Interest Rates Decline by 50
Basis Points, to 6.5%? By 100 Basis Points, to 6%? And
by 200 Basis Points, to 5%?

Maturity	to 6.5%	to 6%	to 5%
2 yrs	+0.9%	+1.9%	+3.8%
5 yrs	+2.1%	+4.3%	+8.7%
10 yrs	+3.6%	+7.4%	+15.6%
30 yrs	+6.6%	+13.8%	+30.9%

Source: Merrill Lynch. Material supplied to the author.

change in price is much smaller for the two-year maturity. But it rises gradually through the maturity spectrum. If interest rates decline by 50 basis points, the price of the two-year increases by a minor amount, 0.9% ($9). But the value of the 30-year rises by 6.6% ($66). A decline in rates of 200 basis points would result in more significant price increases for all maturities, ranging from 3.8% ($38) for the two-year to 30.9% ($31) for the 30-year. (Again, all numbers are rounded.) In this instance, the holder of a bond would benefit from holding the longest maturities because the longer the maturity, the higher the gain. That is the reason that investors anticipating a decline in interest rates position themselves at the long end, in order to realize the largest capital gains.

Several qualifications need to be made concerning both of the preceding tables. First, the exact price changes illustrated are assumed to have occurred as a result of instantaneous changes in yield. In practice, such changes may take weeks, months, or even years. Changes occurring over longer time periods would result in somewhat different numbers because, as noted earlier, the price of a bond moves towards par as it gets closer to maturity, and those price changes occur regardless of what happens to interest rates.

Secondly, the exact price changes illustrated apply only to bonds selling at par, with a 7% coupon. The numbers would be different for bonds with coupons that are either higher or lower. Price changes would be somewhat *larger,* in both directions, if the coupons are *lower* than 7%, and the price changes would be *lower* if the coupons are somewhat *higher* than 7%.

Thirdly, if you look at the price changes that occur in both directions, you will note that these changes are not linear. If interest rates rise, the price of a bond declines as maturity length increases, but those increases occur at a declining rate. That decline in the rate of increase begins to be noticeable approximately after the ten-year mark. Similarly, if interest rates decline, the price of bonds increases as maturity length increases, but again, at a declining rate that begins to be noticeable at the approximate ten-year mark. Nonetheless, it remains the case that price changes are greatest at the highest maturity length.

Finally, note that the price changes that occur if interest rates move up or down are somewhat larger if interest rates decline than if they go up. For example, for the 30-year bond, if interest rates go up by 100 basis points, the price of the bond declines by 11.3%. But if interest rates decline by 100 basis points, the price of the same bond goes up by 13.8%. Similarly, if interest rates go up by 200 basis points, the price of the 30-year bond declines by 20.6%. But if interest rates decline, the price of the same bond goes up by 30.9%. That distinction is obviously a desirable characteristic: your bond appreciates more in value if interest rates decline than it loses if interest rates rise. This characteristic has a somewhat formidable name: it is known as *convexity*.

In summary, while the numbers vary somewhat for different bonds, both Table 3–1 and Table 3–2 illustrate two basic principles. First, the price of bonds and interest rates move in opposite directions. If interest rates decline, the price of a bond goes up, and if interest rates rise, the price of a bond declines. Second, bonds with longer maturities incur significantly higher interest rate risk than those with shorter maturities. That is a disadvantage if interest rates rise, but an advantage if interest rates decline.

So now we have the two faces of interest rate fluctuations: risk and opportunity. It may sound paradoxical, but a rising or strong bond market is one in which interest rates are declining because that causes bond prices to rise. You can sell a bond for more than you paid for it and make a profit. A weak bond market is one in which interest rates are rising and, as a result, prices are falling. If you have to sell your bonds, you have to do so at a loss. In either case, the changes in price are correlated to maturity length.

For more on the relationship between interest rate and bond prices, see the section on duration later in this chapter.

If Long-term Bonds Are so Risky, Why Would Anyone Purchase Them?

Mainly because many investors believe that long-term bonds provide the highest yields (or maximum income). That, however, is not necessarily true. If all other factors are equal, long-term bonds have higher coupons than shorter-term bonds of the same credit quality. But, intermediate bonds in the A to AA range often yield as much as AAA bonds with far longer maturities, and they are much less volatile. (Note that this relationship is considered normal. But there are times when interest rates on short maturities are higher than interest rates on longer maturities. This will be discussed in the section on yield curves in Chapter 5.)

You might, of course, want to purchase long-term bonds for other reasons. One would be to "lock in" an attractive interest rate for as long as possible, if you think you are not going to sell the bonds before they mature. Also, if you think interest rates are about to decline, buying bonds at the long end positions you for maximum capital gains. That would imply that you consider potential capital gains as important (or more so) than interest yield, and in all likelihood that you intend to resell the bonds before they mature.

How Do Interest Rate Fluctuations Affect the Price of a Bond if I Hold It to Maturity?

If you hold bonds to maturity, you recover your principal in full (assuming there has not been a default). No matter what kind of roller coaster ride interest rates take during the life of a bond, its value will always be par when the bond is redeemed. Bonds purchased either above par (premium bonds) or below par (discount bonds) are also redeemed at par. The price of discounts gradually rises to par; the price of premiums falls to par. These changes occur very gradually, in minute annual increments and are reflected in the current price of any bond.

I Own Bonds Issued Years Ago, When Coupon Rates Were 4%. Rates Are Now Much Higher. Can't I Sell My Old Bonds and Buy New Ones with Higher Coupons in Order to Earn More Income?

The swap by itself will not result in higher yields: if you buy a bond that is comparable in maturity length and credit quality, the transaction will be a wash. This is because you would sell at that price at which the buyer of your old bonds would be "indifferent" (using a word from economics) to buying your bond, or one carrying a higher coupon, meaning at the exact price which would result in the prevailing yield. Therefore, your income from the bonds would not change.

For example, let us assume you own bonds with a par value of $10,000 and a coupon rate of 4%. That means that annually you receive interest (coupon) income of $400. Assume further that over a period of several years, interest rates have risen to 8%. You sell your bonds for approximately $500 per bond, for a total of $5,000, which you now reinvest. You now own $5,000 (par value) bonds, and you will now receive annual interest of 8%; that is, $400. Therefore, even though you are now earning a coupon rate of 8%, you will be earning the same dollar amount as before the swap. Moreover, you would be out the transaction costs (commissions) incurred in selling the old bonds and buying the new bonds.

This does not mean that you should never consider swaps. There are other valid reasons for swapping. On the preceding transaction, you would generate a capital loss of approximately $5,000 and that might be used for tax purposes to offset capital gains on other transactions. Or you might swap to upgrade credit quality. You might increase yield by buying lower-quality bonds, or by buying different bonds.

Please note two caveats. In the preceding example, you would have taken an enormous hit to principal. Also, costing out a swap accurately is complex. For more on swaps, see Chapter 15.

CREDIT RATINGS: HOW CREDIT QUALITY AFFECTS THE VALUE OF YOUR BONDS

There is widespread misunderstanding about what credit ratings really mean, and how they affect the returns that you earn and the overall riskiness of your portfolio. This section explains what credit ratings mean. It then discusses two related topics: how credit ratings are assigned, and the relationship among credit ratings, credit risk, and overall returns. Finally, this section answers some of the most frequently asked questions concerning credit ratings.

Credit Risk and Credit Ratings: What Ratings Tell You

Investors generally rely on bond ratings to evaluate the credit quality of specific bonds. Credit ratings indicate on a scale of high to low the probability of default; that is, the probability that debt will not be repaid on time in full. Failure to redeem principal at maturity would constitute a default. Failure to make interest payments on time (that is, to pay coupons to bondholders) would also constitute a default. In plain English, ratings answer two questions: how likely am I to get my money back at maturity, and how likely am I to get my interest payments on time?

All bonds are not subject to default risk. Any security issued *directly* by the U.S. government is considered free of default risk. Although these bonds are not rated, they are considered the safest and highest-quality securities that you can buy because a default by the U.S. government is deemed impossible. This includes all Treasury securities, as well as savings bonds.

Bonds issued by entities other than the U.S. government, such as corporate bonds and municipal bonds, are rated by a number of agencies that specialize in evaluating credit quality. The best-known rating agencies are Moody's, Standard & Poor's (S&P), and Fitch (now Fitch IBCA). Bonds are rated when issuers initially come to market, and subsequently, as issuers bring additional issues to market. Issuers pay the agencies for the rating.

On a scale from the best credit quality to the lowest, Exhibit 3–3 lists the symbols used by each of the major credit rating agencies. These symbols are on the lefthand side. The righthand side of Exhibit 3–3 is a translation into plain English of what the ratings mean. Standard & Poor's adds plus (+) and minus (−) signs to its ratings. A plus signifies higher quality; a minus signifies somewhat lower quality. For instance, a rating of B+ is slightly higher than a rating of B. A rating of B− is slightly lower than a B rating. Moody's adds a 1 to indicate slightly higher credit quality; for instance, a rating of A1 is a higher quality credit rating than an A rating.

In order to protect their investments, many individual investors limit their purchases to bonds that are at minimum rated "investment grade," which corresponds to BBB (Standard & Poor's) and Baa (Moody's). The term "investment grade" stems from the fact that fiduciary institutions, such as banks, are permitted by law to invest only in securities rated at the minimum "investment grade." That rating denotes a fair margin of safety. Note that some ads for bond funds use the term "investment grade" to imply extraordinarily high quality, which is misleading.

How Ratings Are Assigned

Ratings are assigned on the basis of extensive economic analysis by the rating agencies. While the general principles are the same,

E X H I B I T   3-3

Credit Quality Ratings and What They Mean

Moody's	Standard & Poor's	Fitch	
Aaa	AAA	AAA	Gilt edged. If everything that can go wrong, goes wrong, they can still service debt.
Aa	AA	AA	Very high quality by all standards.
A	A	A	Investment grade; good quality.
Baa	BBB	BBB	Lowest investment grade rating; satisfactory; but needs to be monitored.
Ba	BB	BB	Somewhat speculative; low grade.
B	B	B	Very speculative.
Caa	CCC	CCC	Even more speculative. Substantial risk.
Ca	CC	CC	Wildly speculative. May be in default.
C	C	C	In default. Junk.

the exact approach differs for munis and for corporates. This section describes how munis are rated.

Ratings are assigned through a three-part process. First, the agencies identify the specific revenues that will be available for payment of debt service: taxes, fees, and so on. They then estimate those revenues over the life of the bond. Finally, revenues are compared to costs of debt service. Remember that costs are known. They are the interest payments on the bonds, and these were fixed when the bonds were issued. Revenues, on the other hand, must be forecast based on models of future economic activity.

The more money that is predicted to be available for debt service, compared to costs of debt service, the higher the rating. An issuer whose revenues are estimated to equal ten times costs of debt service would be assigned a very high rating. But if revenues are forecast to be less than the costs of debt service, and therefore insufficient to cover debt service, the rating would be likely to be somewhere below investment grade.

· . . . and Why They Are Subject to Change

When forecasting economic conditions for the next six months or for perhaps one year, experts stand on reasonably secure ground. But the further they predict into the future, the more imprecise and unreliable their forecasts become. Any prediction of economic conditions that goes out more than five years becomes guesswork. Bear in mind, however, that bonds are rated for their entire life, even if that is 30 years.

As a result, some forecasts turn out to be incorrect. When ratings are reviewed, they may change. As the economic fortunes of the issuer vary, so will the ratings. Over time, changes in ratings can be major. For example, State of Louisiana bonds were rated AAA in the middle 1980s. In early 1990, they were rated barely investment grade. Occasionally, changes in rating are more sudden. For instance, State of Massachusetts ratings went from AA to barely investment grade within the space of one year. More dramatic rating changes sometimes occur in the corporate bond sector: for example, if a company buys another with debt, the amount of debt may increase sharply virtually overnight. And that increase would cause the rating to deteriorate virtually overnight as well.

Credit Ratings and Bond Returns: How Credit Ratings Affect Interest Income

Above all, credit ratings affect the cost of borrowing; that is, the interest rate that will have to be paid by the issuer to attract buyers. The interest cost to the issuer, you will remember, is the coupon you will earn.

The principle for this is easy to explain. Think of a bond as a loan (which, you will recall, is what it is) and imagine that you are a bank that is lending to a borrower. You would ask a lot of questions relating to the probability of repayment. To whom would you rather lend money: to a struggling businessman with no collateral who wants to start a business, or to IBM? To someone who has one million dollars in the bank and wants to borrow money for a yacht, or to John Doe, who has barely enough earnings to cover his mortgage payments and who wants to borrow money for home improvements? The answer is obvious. Now suppose you are the struggling businessman or John Doe. Chances are that if your banker turns you down, you will find a different banker, who will charge you higher interest costs. You may even go to your neighborhood loan shark (or equivalent), who will lend you the money, but charge you a much higher interest rate than the bank.

This is also true for bonds. The most creditworthy issuers—say, large states with diverse economies, blue chip corporations with very little debt, or the U.S. government—borrow at a lower cost. Less creditworthy clients have to pay higher interest. Consequently, bonds with the highest quality credit ratings always carry the lowest yields; bonds with lower credit ratings yield more. Note that the yield, in a sense, provides a scale of creditworthiness: higher yields generally indicate higher risk—the higher the yield, the higher the risk.

How Changes in Ratings Affect
the Price of Bonds

If bonds are downgraded (that is, if the credit rating is lowered), the price declines. If the rating is upgraded, the price goes up. In fact, bond prices sometimes change if there is even a strong possibility of an upgrade or a downgrade. This is because anxious investors sell bonds whose credit quality is declining and buy bonds whose credit quality is improving.

Unless there is a genuine risk of default, however, price changes in response to upgrades or downgrades are far less major than those occurring due to changes in interest rate levels. With rare exceptions, ratings go up one notch or down one notch in the rating scale, and prices go up or down by perhaps 1% or 2% per bond in response to rating changes. The change in price corresponds to the amount necessary to bring the yield of a bond (and therefore its price) in line with other bonds rated at the same level. For bonds rated AA, for example, a downgrade to A+ may not make a noticeable difference in the price.

This point needs to be emphasized because many individual investors are needlessly worried about relatively minor downgrades and this fear is sometimes exacerbated by the financial press. For bonds that have very high credit quality (AA or AAA), a deterioration in the rating is not a major cause for concern. It would not result in a serious deterioration in the price of the bond. The financial press sometimes overstates how much a downgrade would affect the price of bonds. A more serious concern would be a series of downgrades, particularly if downgrades drop the credit rating to below investment grade.

There is one notable exception to the preceding statements. During the takeover craze of the 1980s, corporate bond prices were exceptionally volatile because of the possibility of downgrades due to takeovers. This unique situation is discussed in detail in Chapter 9.

The following questions and answers deal with some common concerns concerning ratings.

Doesn't a Downgrade Mean My Bonds Are No Longer Safe?

That is usually not the case. The rating scales used by the agencies are very conservative. Distinctions between rating levels are often based on nuances. Any bond rated investment grade or better continues to have good margins of safety, even after a downgrade.

However, certain downgrades are more significant than others and should be viewed as red flags. Those would include any downgrade that drops a bond rating to below investment grade; a downgrade of more than one notch (say from AA to A−); or a string of downgrades in close succession. If any of these occurs, you might want to review whether you wish to continue owning that security.

My Bonds Are Insured, or AAA, or Government Guaranteed. Won't that Guarantee that Principal Remains Safe?

No. What is guaranteed is that interest payments will be made on time and that principal will be redeemed in full at the bond's maturity. There is no connection between that guarantee and what happens to the price (or value) of bonds due to fluctuations in interest rates. If interest rates rise, the value of your bonds will decline. If interest rates decline, the value of your bonds will rise. Period. No exceptions.

I am repeating this point because this is one of the most widely misunderstood aspects of investing in bonds. Many investors assume that if bonds are insured, or obligations of the U.S. government, then somehow the bonds are not risky, and will not fluctuate in price. That is a major and costly mistake. Changes in interest rates affect *all* bonds, whether they are those of Fly-by-Night airlines or obligations of the U.S. government. The major variant in the size of the decline (or appreciation) will be the maturity length of the bonds.

How Frequently Do Defaults Occur?

That depends, of course, on the type of bond under discussion. But overall, if you consider primarily bonds that are at least investment grade in credit quality, default rates are relatively low. Since the Second World War, and despite a few well-publicized defaults in the corporate sector no bonds have ever defaulted while currently rated AA. Only two defaults have occurred to bonds rated A. Similar statistics prevail for municipal bonds. (While some bonds that were initially highly rated eventually defaulted, these had been downgraded prior to the actual default. Hence, it is prudent to monitor the ratings of bonds in your portfolio.) Default rates for junk bonds, which by definition are bonds rated below investment grade, are higher.

Note, however, that even when defaults occur, bond investors seldom lose 100% of the principal value of the bond. Defaulted bonds usually have some salvage value. There is a good deal of speculation in the bonds of defaulted or bankrupt issuers. That is because such bonds may be purchased very cheaply, perhaps as little as 10 to 30 cents on the dollar. Many defaults have taken the form of a suspension of coupon payments. Such bonds are said to be trading flat. If coupon payments are resumed, the price of the bonds can soar. Bondholders may also benefit from the sale of assets of issuers under bankruptcy proceedings. Finally, some bankrupt companies emerge successfully from bankruptcy proceedings, leading to a bonanza for anyone who purchased the bonds while the company was in default.

There is a gradation in risk of default. Any bond that is a direct obligation of the U.S. government is deemed to have zero possibility of default. Bonds issued by federal agencies, or most types of mortgage-backed securities, are deemed to have almost equally high credit quality. Municipal bonds come in a wide variety of ratings, but in the aggregate they have low default rates. Corporates (particularly so-called junk bonds) are far less predictable. And debt of so-called emerging markets is highly speculative.

I Want Maximum Income and Maximum Safety. My Broker Advises Me to Buy 30-year Bonds with AAA Ratings and Just Hold Them to Maturity. Isn't that the Safest Thing to Do?

Not necessarily. That can be a costly and high-risk strategy. It is costly because AAA rated bonds yield less than bonds with lower ratings but with similar maturites. You are therefore sacrificing income. And it is high-risk for two reasons: one is that, as we have just seen, interest rate risk is far higher for bonds with longer maturities. If you need to resell your bonds before they mature, you might have to take a very costly hit to principal. But in addition, and for reasons we shall discuss in the next chapter, it is very difficult to predict how much you will really earn on bonds with the longest maturities.

This entire issue will be revisited in chapters concerning specific types of bonds. But as a general rule, if you are concerned about safety of principal and predictable income, it tends to be safer to buy bonds with maturities of five to ten years, rated at least investment grade or somewhat higher (depending on your preferences and tolerance for risk). Interest income from such bonds is likely to be close to (and occasionally higher) than that of AAA-rated bonds with long maturities, so you will not be sacrificing income. But risk to principal is dramatically lower.

Does All of This Mean that I Should Ignore Credit Ratings?

No. But I have tried to put credit ratings in perspective. Remember that ratings are opinions. The rating agencies do not have any connection to actual debt service payments, which are made by

the issuer. Nor do the ratings constitute any kind of recommendation either to buy or sell a particular security. A low rating does
not mean that default will occur; and a high rating guarantees
nothing, not even that a downgrade won't occur.

Here is a summary of what you will want to remember concerning ratings:

- When you purchase bonds, you should check credit
  ratings by the major agencies. Most of the time, ratings
  issued by the different rating agencies are close. If they
  are not, then to be safe, assume the lowest rating is
  accurate.
- Buy bonds rated investment grade (or higher),
  depending on your risk tolerance. A rating of A or better
  represents a sound rating, particularly for bonds with
  maturities under five years.
- Be sure that you understand the main reasons for the
  rating. What sources of revenue will pay debt? What is
  the credit history of the issuer? Has it been upgraded or
  downgraded? Why?
- When you own a bond, monitor its rating. Ask your
  broker to let you know if any rating changes occur (and
  check periodically). If a significant downgrade occurs,
  and you feel uncomfortable holding, you may want to
  consider selling that security. Note that occasionally the
  price of some bonds drops in advance of a rating change.
  The market is sometimes ahead of the rating agencies in
  sniffing out that a particular security may face potential
  problems.
- Diversify. Don't put all your assets in one bond. If you
  have a total of $50,000 to invest, it is more prudent to
  buy five $10,000 lots than one $50,000 lot. Buy bonds of
  different issuers to diversify credit risk. And buy bonds
  with different maturities to diversify interest rate risk.

A SHORT HISTORY OF INTEREST RATES

We read all kinds of discussions concerning interest rate levels.
Pundits expound on whether they are high or low, and above all,

where they are headed. Without some knowledge of historical interest rate levels, discussions concerning interest rate risk appear somewhat unfounded. Exhibit 3–4 presents a simplified history of interest rates between 1930 and 1999.

The interest rates shown are for the longest maturities issued by the U.S. government from 1930 to 1999. The government started issuing 30-year bonds regularly only in the early 1970s. But since that period, the 30-year bond has been the most widely traded bond, not only in the United States but worldwide. Because it has been such a key security, the most recently issued 30-year Treasury bond has been known as the "bellwether long bond," or the "long bond," for short. When people in the financial world refer to interest rates, they mean the long bond.

Exhibit 3–4 shows that between 1930 and 1940, during the Depression, the yield on bonds with the longest maturities declined gradually, from a little under 4% to around 2%. Between 1940 and 1950, interest rates barely budged. But in 1950, rates began a long and almost uninterrupted rise. They rose first slowly, then more steeply, from 2% in 1950 to 4% in 1960. (Some of you

E X H I B I T   3–4

A History of Interest Rates between 1930 and 1999

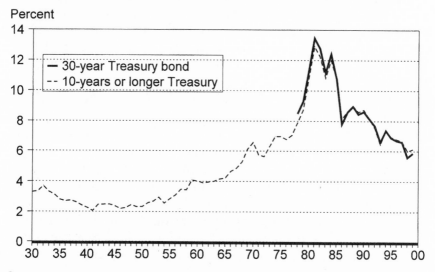

Percent

Source: Material supplied to the author by Merrill Lynch. Data source: the Federal Reserve Board.

may remember that in those days bank passbook accounts paid 2% to 2 1/2% interest.) By the late 1960s, yields began to rise, reaching 6% in 1970 and then after 1979, climbing sharply and steeply upwards. In 1981, the long bond briefly yielded above 15%. The actual peak was 15.2% in October 1981. (That peak level is not shown in Exhibit 3–4 because the graph shows *average* annual interest rates for each year.) Since all interest rates key off the bellwether bond, during the early 1980s, yields on tax-exempt bonds with 30-year maturities reached numbers that seem almost unbelievable at the current time: 12% to 14%, depending on credit quality.

The period between 1950 and 1982 represents a bear market in bonds that lasted well over 30 years. During many of those years, bonds were said not to "have earned their coupon," meaning that the principal value of bonds declined by more than the interest income received. During the disastrous 1970s, the worst of those three decades, satirists described long-term bonds as "fixed rate instrument(s) designed to fall in price" and "certificates of confiscation." Bondholders suffered staggering losses as bonds purchased in the 1960s and 1970s with coupons of 4% to 6% declined by 50% or more ($500 per $1,000 bond) as interest rates approached 15% on the long bond.

Note further that these bondholders suffered a double whammy. Not only was the value of their bonds sharply down, but to add insult to injury, they were earning meager returns of 4% to 6% while interest rates went into the double digits even on short-term and tax-exempt securities. The final blow was that during that period double-digit inflation was eroding the purchasing power of every dollar.

In 1982, however, bond yields began a very sharp decline. Bond prices soared! For most of the 1990s, the yield on the long bond has fluctuated somewhere between 8% at the high end and 5% at the low end (the exact low was 4.78%, in 1998).

The returns earned on long-term bonds between 1982 and 1990 have no precedent in the history of the United States: first, because yields reached historically high levels, and second, because anyone who purchased bonds during the late 1970s or early 1980s, at coupon rates between 11% and 15% for Treasuries (and correspondingly high rates in other sectors of the bond market), either is continuing to earn unprecedented rates of interest if those bonds are still in their possession or, if the bonds were sold, reaped exceptional capital gains. During the late 1980s, U.S. Treasury bonds with coupons of 14% to 15% sold for as much as $1,700 per bond, for a capital gain of 70%. Total returns for the decade of the 1990s were lower than during the 1980s, but still high by historical standards. The two decades, back to back, constitute a major bull market in bonds of the United States. In fact, hard as it may be to believe, in spite of the enormous bull market in stocks that has been ongoing since 1982 in the United States, anyone who was either clever enough or lucky enough to have purchased 30-year Treasury bonds in 1982 or 1983 still had returns on those bonds that exceeded those on stocks through 1997.

Since interest rates in all sectors of the bond market key off Treasuries, interest rate levels in other sectors of the bond market (corporates, munis, mortgage-backed, etc.) followed the general patterns seen in the Treasury market. Keep this history of interest in mind as you read the book. We will refer to it again and again. It is absolutely basic to understanding bond returns.

"Real" and "Nominal" Rates of Return

The terms "real" rate and "nominal" rate are sometimes used to refer to rates of return on bonds. These terms represent a method of adjusting bond yields for the rate of inflation. The nominal rate measures the actual dollars earned, based on interest rate yields. To obtain the real rate, subtract the inflation rate from the nominal rate. For example, the coupon rate on the long bond is currently close to 6%. That is the nominal rate. Subtracting the current rate of inflation, which is around 2.5%, results in a real rate of return of about 3.5%.

The relationship between the real rate of return and the nominal rate has varied during the century. So has the level of interest rates. Interest rate levels are governed, first, by what is happening to prices (that is, inflation or deflation) and secondly, by expectations of what will happen to prices. Until 1950, even though interest rates were low, bonds earned a real rate of return because inflation was low. As inflation began to rise, the real rate of return began to decline, despite a rise in nominal rates. The real rate of return throughout the 1960s and 1970s was negative even though rates were high and rising. Moreover, inflation eroded the purchasing power of older issues. That was the main reason interest rates rose to such high levels: few investors were willing to purchase long-term bonds because the nominal rate did not appear high enough to compensate for anticipated increases in yield as a result of continuing high inflation.

Historically, the real rate of return on long bonds has averaged about 3% above the inflation rate. Since that is an average, it has sometimes been higher and sometimes lower. During the 1990s inflation averaged under 3% a year, and that rate is considered benign. Inflation, moreover has been relatively benign worldwide. But note that benign as it may seem, the recent low inflation rate does not mean inflation is dead. Over a 30-year period, if inflation were to remain as low as a constant 2% a year, an item costing $100 at year one would cost $181 at year 30. If inflation rates were to rise to 3% over that same 30-year period, an item costing $100 at year one would cost $243 at year 30. Beginning in 1999, the inflation rate rose slightly, and since then, concerns about inflation have increased somewhat.

Unless there is an extended period of actual deflation, nominal rates will probably continue to remain 2% to 3% above the inflation rate. But none of this is predictable. No one knows whether the next 30 years will see deflation or whether higher inflation rates will return. Some experts worry that the current economic boom will inevitably lead to inflation worldwide. Others feel that central banks will be able to keep inflation at bay. Still others point out that the recent belief that central banks can successfully control inflation, and hence manage growth, is overly optimistic. The one point no one disputes is that crystal balls have been notoriously unreliable in predicting interest rates. More to the point, no one has ever consistently predicted interest rates correctly over a period of 30 years: that is, over the life of a long-term bond.

The strategies described in this book are predicated on the assumption that interest rates cannot be predicted but that you can manage your bond portfolio so that no matter what happens, your portfolio will not suffer severe erosion.

SUMMARY

Prior to the 1970s, individuals who purchased bonds tended to buy and hold and worry mainly about credit quality. Such an attitude made sense at a time when interest rates barely budged. The past few decades have witnessed both bull markets and bear markets in bonds. While swings in interest rates during the 1990s have not been as dramatic as those of the 1980s, interest rate volatility continues to be a significant risk factor for bond investors. Interest rate changes have wreaked far more devastating losses on bond portfolios, and far more often, than credit risk. Investors concerned about the safety of their principal should limit their purchases to bonds with maturities that are short to intermediate.

CHAPTER 4

Many Happy Returns, or Fundamentals of Bond Math

This chapter discusses basic bond math. This includes

- Simple interest
- Interest-on-interest, or the magic of compounding
- Yield (current yield and yield-to-maturity)
- Total return
- Duration

Discussions of bond returns begin and end with numbers. If your eyes glaze over when numbers and formulae appear, you may be tempted to skip this chapter. But that would be a mistake because it is impossible to evaluate bonds without an understanding of bond math. But fear not. I, too, am a charter member of the math anxiety crowd. The mathematics in this section is at the level of arithmetic, or at most, elementary algebra. More importantly, the emphasis is on concepts that help you to evaluate what you will actually earn, and not on mathematical formulae.

BOND CASH FLOWS

When you buy a bond, you earn money from three sources. The first source has already been mentioned. It is the simple interest derived from coupons, usually paid twice a year. The second source arises from the difference between the purchase price of a bond and its sale or redemption price. If you sell a bond for more than your purchase price, then you realize a capital gain. If you sell it for less than you paid, then you realize a capital loss. The third source is earned when coupons are reinvested: at that point, you earn interest on your interest income. This creates still another source of revenue, appropriately called "interest-on-interest." On Wall Street, each of these sources of income is called a "cash flow." Let's look at each in turn.

Simple Interest

Let's start with simple interest (that is, the coupon payments).

Let us say you invest $10,000 in 30-year bonds, paying 7% a year, semiannually. In return, you will receive two coupons (or interest) payments of $350 each at six-month intervals every year. If you hold the bonds until they mature, you will receive a total of 60 coupons, which add up to a total amount of $10,500. Those coupons represent coupon income, also called interest income.

Interest-on-Interest, or the Magic of Compounding

If you are investing primarily to receive income, and you spend the coupons, then the coupon interest is all you will earn. But if the coupons are reinvested, those produce additional interest; subsequently, if those earnings are reinvested, you earn interest on that interest, and so on. That entire income stream is called, logically enough, "interest-on-interest," or "compound interest."

Some illustrations will make clear how this works. After six months, you will have the following amounts:

Principal originally invested	$10,000.00
Interest income (1/2 of 7%)	350.00
Total amount	$10,350.00

You can choose to spend the coupon or to reinvest it. Let's assume you decide to reinvest the entire amount, and furthermore, that you reinvest it at the same 7% rate. At the end of the year, you would have not $10,700, but rather, $10,712.25. The $12.25 difference results from reinvesting your first interest payment. Compared to your original investment, this is how you get to the final number at the end of year one:

Principal originally invested	$10,000.00
First coupon payment	350.00
Second coupon payment	350.00
Interest on second coupon payment (1/2 of 7%, that is, 3.5% of $350)	12.25
Total at the end of year one	$12,712.25

You have earned a total of $700 in simple interest. The additional $12.25 represents interest on the first coupon payment of $350.00.

That may not sound like a major difference, and indeed, after one year and two coupon payments, interest-on-interest does not constitute a major amount of money. But that is only the beginning of the story. Table 4–1 shows how coupon payments and interest-on-interest would continue to grow if you held the bonds for 30 years and if you continue to reinvest the coupons at 7%.

T A B L E   4–1

Interest and Interest-on-Interest on 30-year, $10,000 Par Value Bond with a 7% Coupon. Coupons Reinvested at 7%, Semiannually.

Time	Number of Coupons	Coupon Interest A	Interest-on-Interest (Cumulative) B	Total Interest A + B	Total Value of Investment
Year 1	2	$ 700	$ 12.25	$ 712.25	
Year 5	10	3,500	605.99	41,005.99	
Year 10	20	7,000	2,897.89	12,897.89	
Year 20	40	14,000	15,592.60	29,592.60	
Year 30	60	21,000	47,780.91	68,780.91	$78,780.91*

*Year 30: redeem the bonds at par ($10,000)

A look at Table 4–1 shows that the income generated by coupon payments constitutes only a limited portion of the total income you receive from the bonds. Moreover, the longer you hold the bonds, the higher the portion of total income is generated by interest-on-interest. After five years, you would have received ten semiannual coupon payments, for a total of $3,500. Interest-on-interest would have increased to almost $606, approximately 15% of the total income generated by the bond. After 20 years, on the other hand, interest-on-interest actually exceeds the amount of income generated by the coupon payments: the 40 coupon payments total $14,000, but interest-on-interest amounts to almost $15,593. After 30 years, the amount of income generated by interest-on-interest ($47,781) is more than double the amount generated by the 60 coupon payments you would have received (which add up to a total of $21,000). At the 30-year mark, interest-on-interest constitutes approximately 69% of the total amount of earnings generated by the bond.

As Table 4–1 shows, the amount of interest-on-interest earned is directly related to the time allowed for compounding: the longer the time frame, the larger the percentage produced by interest-on-interest. For truly long-term holdings (30 years or more), interest-on-interest can comprise up to 80% of the total amount earned.

Increasing the frequency of compounding (compounding four times a year, for example, instead of twice; or, as some banks do, compounding daily) would translate into higher returns. So would increasing the rate, either of the original coupon or of the interest-on-interest. This would be true both on an absolute basis (more total dollars would be earned) and on a relative basis (the percentage that would consist of interest-on-interest would grow). Even apparently minute percentage differences, compounded over long periods of time, make a significant difference. For example, over a ten-year period, increasing the annual return to 7.5% from 7% would increase total earnings by almost 5%; after 20 years, by somewhat over 10%; and after 40 years (for the investor with a long-term perspective), by an astonishing 20%.

Compounded interest has been called the eighth wonder of the world. And yet it works for everyone. It requires no special aptitude and is totally automatic. In fact, only two ingredients are required: reinvesting and time.

The rate at which assets compound is critical to the total actually earned. Money reinvested (tax-free) at 4%, semiannually, will double every 17.5 years; at 6%, every 11.7 years; at 8%, every 8.8 years; and at 10%, every 7 years. Over very long periods, compounding achieves extraordinary results. Over a period of 50 years, $1,000, compounded semiannually at a rate of 8%, would grow to $50,504. For the investor with a truly long-term view, over a period of 100 years, $1,000 compounded semiannually would grow to $2,550,749.[1]

Compounding has been heavily advertised for zero coupon bonds, but it applies equally to all financial investments, whether stocks, bonds, or savings accounts. Wherever you consult information concerning an investment (a mutual fund, stocks, or bonds), the merits of that investment are usually illustrated with graphs showing that if you had invested in that particular vehicle, you would now be (or you will become) very rich. All those graphs basically illustrate the magic of compounding. The differences in the final result are not necessarily due to the particular product that is being advertised. Rather, those differences are the result of two variables, namely, the actual rates at which that instrument compounds (that is, the actual reinvestment rates) and the amount of time.

YIELD

When you buy a bond, you are quoted a "yield." That term appears in a number of phrases: "coupon yield," "current yield," and "yield-to-maturity." Each has a very precise meaning. Let's look at each in turn.

Coupon Yield

Coupon yield is set when a bond is issued. It is the interest rate paid by a bond, listed as a percentage (for example, 5 1/2% or 7 1/4%). That percentage is a percentage of par, and it designates

---

1. Sidney Homer and Martin Leibowitz, *Inside the Yield Book* (Englewood Cliffs, N.J.: Prentice Hall, 1973), p. 32.

a fixed-dollar amount which never changes through the life of the bond. If you buy a bond with a 7% coupon, you will receive $70 a year, usually paid out in two semiannual increments of $35. You will receive the same amount in dollars, no matter what happens to the price of the bond, until the bond is redeemed on its maturity date. The only exception to this is floating-rate bonds, whose interest rate is reset at predetermined intervals, based on a stipulated benchmark interest rate.

Current Yield

Almost as soon as a bond starts trading in the secondary market, it ceases to trade at par. Current yield is simply coupon divided by price.

Let us assume you purchase three bonds: the first at par ($1,000), the second at a premium ($1,200), and the third at a discount ($800), each bearing $100 in annual coupons. Dividing the coupon ($100) by the price results in a current yield of 10% for the par bond, 8.33% for the premium bond, and 12.5% for the discount bond. Current yield is equal to coupon yield for the par bond, higher than coupon yield for the premium bond, and lower than coupon yield for the discount.

Current yield is quoted for fixed-income securities of any maturity, whether short or long. In none of the preceding examples was the bond's maturity specified. That is because current yield is based only on coupon and price. Current yield, therefore, fails to measure two important cash flows earned from bonds: interest-on-interest and appreciation or depreciation in the price of the bond.

Yield-to-Maturity

Yield-to-maturity (YTM) is a far more comprehensive measure of return than current yield. It estimates the total amount that you will earn over the entire life of a bond, from all possible cash flows, namely: coupon income, interest-on-interest, and gains or losses due to the difference between the price you pay when you purchase the bond, and par (the redemption price).

Calculating YTM with paper and pencil involves a tedious trial-and-error algebraic procedure. In practice, no one actually uses the formula. Before the advent of calculators, the investor (or his broker) used bond yield tables to come up with an approximate YTM. Nowadays the process has been enormously simplified (and made more accurate) through the use of financial calculators.

For example, let's use a financial calculator to compute the YTM of a ten-year discount bond purchased for $800 and redeemed for $1,000, with one $50 coupon payment annually. Feed all of those numbers into the calculator as follows:

- Plug in the price of $800 as PV (present value), using the *PV* key, with a minus sign: −$800.
- Plug in the par price of $1,000 (the redemption value) as FV (future value), using the *FV* key.
- Enter the dollar amount of the coupon payment ($50), using the *PMT* (payment) key.
- Finally, enter the number of years to maturity, using the *n* key (10 years).
- Solve for YTM by hitting *i*, the interest key.

Result: the YTM is 7.98%. That is higher than the coupon rate, (5%) because you purchased this bond at a discount, for $800. When the bond is redeemed at par, you earn an additional $200, which represents the difference between the price you paid ($800) and the redemption price at par ($1,000).[2]

Note: the concepts of PV (present value) and FV (future value) will be explained in this chapter, in the section on duration.

The YTM is the measure of return most widely quoted by brokers, although it is not quoted for corporate bonds or for muni

---

2. The steps used in this calculation represent a quick way of calculating YTM. In this example, as well as the others in this chapter, I did not plug in the date of purchase and the date the bond matures. The better financial calculators enable you to compute YTM, prices, and total return with great precision, by plugging in the specific dates from date of purchase to date of maturity. They are inexpensive. Specifically request one that is set up for calculating bond yields. Programs for calculating bond yields are also available on the Internet, for example, a program called "Compound It" on *bondsonline.com*. Online brokers are also adding this capability to their website.

"dollar" bonds. The important point to remember about YTM is what it actually tells you. Many investors believe that YTM is a prediction of what they will actually earn. That is not the case. The actual return is likely to differ from the YTM, perhaps considerably, because the YTM will only be realized under certain conditions. Those conditions are:

♦ That you hold the bond to maturity
♦ That the coupons are reinvested (rather than spent)
♦ That coupons are reinvested at the YTM rate

Let's briefly look at each assumption.

That You Hold the Bond to Maturity

The YTM quote is based on the assumption that the bond will be redeemed at par at maturity. If you sell a bond before it matures at a price other than par, then you will realize either a capital gain or a capital loss. Either will change what you actually earn. If, for example, you purchase a bond at par and sell it at a premium, say, $1,200, the $200 difference represents a gain of approximately 20%. That boosts actual return by a very significant amount. But if you buy a bond at par and sell it at a loss, say, $800, you lose about 20%. Clearly, that will mean that you would earn far less than the YTM initially quoted.[3]

That You Reinvest Coupons and Also that You Reinvest Them at the YTM Rate

YTM calculations are based on the assumption that coupons are never spent; they are always reinvested.

Clearly, if you spend coupons, then the interest-on-interest goes out the window. You will then earn less than the anticipated YTM. How much less depends both on how many coupons you spend and on the maturity of the bonds.

---

3. For tax purposes, when you sell bonds, capital gains and losses are usually treated as ordinary capital gains and losses. If the purchase price is lower than the sale price, the sale results in a taxable capital gain. Note, however, that if you buy a premium bond, the YTM is quoted net. Even though the redemption price is lower than the purchase price, that difference is not treated as a capital gain for tax purposes.

In addition, the assumption is made that the coupons are reinvested at the quoted YTM rate. This may sound like double-talk. However, what this means is that if a broker quotes a YTM of 7% for a bond, then that yield will be earned *only if each and every coupon is reinvested at a rate of 7%*, that is, at the same rate as the quoted YTM. Clearly, that is highly unlikely to happen. Some coupons will be reinvested at more than 7%; others, at less than 7%. If you reinvest coupons at a higher rate, you will actually earn more than the bond's stated YTM. If you reinvest coupons at lower rates, you will earn less.

Reinvestment Rates and Actual Returns

Both of these factors alter what you actually earn, compared to the anticipated YTM. Table 4–2 shows what the actual yield would be for a 25-year par bond, with a 7.5% coupon, under a variety of reinvestment assumptions. The YTM quoted at the time of purchase is 7.5%.

As Table 4–2 shows, the anticipated 7.5% YTM is realized only if all coupons are reinvested at 7.5% (line 4). If no coupons

T A B L E   4–2

How the Reinvestment Rate Affects Actual Yield over the Life of a 25-year, 7.5% Par Bond

Assumed Reinvestment Rate (Semiannual Basis)	Coupon Income (A)	Interest-on- Interest (B)	Total Interest (A + B)	Interest-on- Interest as Percent of Total Interest	Actual Yield
0.0%	$1,875	$ 0	$1,875	0%	4.27%
5.0	1,875	1,781	3,656	49	6.25
6.0	1,875	2,355	4,230	56	6.73
7.5	1,875	3,426	5,301	65	7.50
8.0	1,875	3,850	5,725	67	7.77
10.0	1,875	5,976	7,851	76	8.91

Source: Frank Fabozzi et al., *The Handbook of Fixed-Income Securities*, 2nd ed., (Homewood, Ill.: Dow Jones Irwin), p. 596. Adapted with permission.

are reinvested (line 1), the anticipated 7.5% YTM is cut to 4.27%. On the other hand, if coupons are reinvested at a higher rate than 7.5%, the actual yield rises: to 7.77% if coupons are reinvested at 8%, but more significantly, to 8.91% if coupons are reinvested at 10%. The higher the reinvestment rate, the higher the actual return.

The amount of total earnings due to interest-on-interest varies both with the maturity of a bond and with the reinvestment rate. It is less significant for shorter than for longer bonds. This was actually illustrated by Table 4–1, in the section concerning compounding. As we saw, interest-on-interest constituted only a minor portion of the total amount of income generated by a bond at the two-year mark. For the same bond, however, interest-on-interest represented 15% of total income at the five-year mark, 53% at the 20-year mark, and almost 70% at the 30-year mark. Particularly if you are investing over the long term, for periods of over 20 or 30 years (as you would, for example, in a retirement plan), the importance of reinvestment rates cannot be stressed enough. Because interest-on-interest constitutes the major part of returns for long-term holdings, you need to be as aware of reinvestment rates as about initial YTM, or perhaps even more so.

When the YTM is quoted to you, reinvestment rates are assumed to be both constant and known: they are set at the YTM rate. In real life, of course, you cannot know at the time of purchase what the reinvestment rate is going to be, since you don't know where interest rates will be in the future. Consequently, you cannot know at the time of purchase exactly how much you will earn either in actual dollars or as a percentage value. That uncertainty is known as the *"reinvestment risk."*

Calling this uncertainty a "risk" is somewhat confusing in that there is no risk of an actual loss, either of principal or interest. But, as noted earlier, if you reinvest coupons at a lower rate than the YTM, actual return will then be lower than the YTM quoted to you when you bought the bond. Reinvestment risk may work in your favor if coupons are reinvested at a higher rate: you would then earn a higher amount than the YTM initially quoted to you.

Two other factors affect the reliability of the YTM quote. The first is the maturity of the bond: as maturities become longer, since the amount represented by the interest-on-interest becomes greater on a percentage basis, the YTM becomes increasingly less accurate and less reliable as a forecast of what you will actually earn. If you buy 30-year bonds, for example, and hold them for the entire period, the total return is likely to be very different from the YTM quoted at the time of purchase. Remember that for 30-year bonds, interest-on-interest may provide up to 80% of the total return. If you hold 30-year bonds until they mature, and you re-invest coupons at lower rates, then you will earn far less than the YTM you were initially quoted. But if interest rates go up and you are able to reinvest coupons at higher interest rates, then you will earn an amount higher than the YTM initially quoted.

The second factor that affects the reliability of the YTM quote is the size of the coupon. If interest rates are particularly high at the time you buy your bonds, or if you buy a bond that has a particularly high coupon (for example, a "junk" bond), again, it becomes more likely that you will earn less than the YTM quoted to you. The larger the size of the coupons, the more likely it is that you will be able to reinvest coupons only at rates lower than either the coupon interest or the YTM quote.

If YTM does not predict actual return, what does it tell you? The chief usefulness of YTM quotes is that they permit direct comparison between different securities, with dissimilar coupons and prices (par, premium, and discount). Suppose, for example, that you are considering three different securities for purchase, the first an A-rated bond, selling at a discount, and maturing in five years; the second a AAA bond selling at a premium and maturing in five years; and the third an A-rated bond selling at par and maturing in 30 years. The YTM enables you to evaluate, for instance, how much yield you might be giving up for higher credit quality; or how much yield you are picking up as you lengthen maturities.

In a sense, YTM and price are two sides of the same coin and they are interchangeable. Once you are familiar with the language of bonds, if someone tells you that the YTM of a bond went up, that tells you instantly that its price declined. Or vice-versa, if you know the YTM of a bond declined, that tells you its price went up. If you are comparing the price of different securities, say, one a discount, one a par bond, one a premium, the easiest way to compare price is to compare their YTM. Just be sure that the yield measure you are using is the YTM, and not, for example, the current yield.

Overall, there is too much emphasis on yield. YTM should not be the main criterion for selecting specific bonds. More appropriate criteria would depend on your objective when you purchase bonds. If, for example, you do not intend to reinvest coupons, then you might look for bonds with high current yield. If you are primarily interested in stability of principal, that would dictate selecting bonds with intermediate (two- to seven-year) maturities. Such criteria are discussed at greater length in other sections of the book.

One final note: as we will see in a later chapter, you can eliminate reinvestment risk by purchasing zero coupon bonds. That may be an attractive option under certain conditions.

TOTAL RETURN

Investors in fixed-income securities sometimes make the mistake of equating interest income or YTM with return without taking into consideration what is happening to principal. A more useful way of measuring return includes the changing value of principal. It is called "total return." Total return consists of whatever you earn in interest income, plus or minus changes in the value of principal. To be 100% accurate, you would also subtract taxes and commission expenses from return.

For example, let's assume that a year ago you invested $10,000 in a bond fund, purchasing 1,000 shares at $10.00 each. Assume also that the bond fund was advertising a yield of 10%, or $1.00 per share, which was maintained for the entire year. But suppose that in the meantime interest rates have risen so that now bond funds with similar maturity and credit quality yield 11%. As a result, your bond fund is now selling for $9.00 per share. What have you earned on that investment for the past year?

One answer is that you have earned simple interest income (based on the dividend distributions) of 10%, or $1,000. But that ignores the fact that your bond fund has now lost approximately $1 per share (10% of its principal value) and that your principal is now worth $9,000.

Add the dividend earnings of $1,000 to the current value of your fund ($9,000). Your investment is now worth $10,000. But it was worth that one year earlier. (For the sake of simplicity, I am ignoring interest-on-interest and commission costs.) Therefore, the net return is $0, or 0%. That is your total return, to date, even though you have received 10% dividend interest.

In the trade, among professionals, that kind of calculation is done daily and is known as "marking-to-market." It describes to each trader exactly what his holdings are worth at the end of the day if he had to or wanted to sell them. But you may say: "I am only interested in income. I am not interested in total return. I haven't sold my bond fund. Therefore, I have not lost anything. I'll just wait until the bond matures or until the bond fund goes back to what I paid for it."

Unfortunately, that is not true. Your fund is now worth $9.00 per share and you have lost 10% of your principal. It is gone. The future value of each share of the fund will depend on a variety of factors, such as the future course of interest rates and the specific management practices of the fund managers. At some future date, the fund may be worth more than $9.00 per share. But it also may not. The fund's price may or may not return to what you paid for it.

This scenario can become even more depressing. Let us assume, for example, that you were charged a 5% commission, which was paid when you bought the fund. Subtract the commission from the above calculation and you get: total return, minus 5% after one year, *even though the fund has paid out* 10% in dividend income, and is accurately quoting its current yield at 10%. If, disgusted with this turn of events, you decide to sell this bond fund, your total return, which in this instance would become your actual (or realized return), would then become minus 15%. (Some of this could be used to generate a tax loss, but for the moment I am leaving tax considerations aside.) So even though the dividend yield of 10% was paid out to you, after one year, your investment is worth 15% less than a year earlier.

To be totally precise, let's note again that if we were to substitute an individual bond for the bond fund, and if you hold the bond to maturity, the price will return to par. But, for a long-term bond, that may take 30 years! The price of bond funds, however, does not necessarily return to par. (This is discussed in the chapters on bond funds.)

The important point to remember is that when you are evaluating fixed-income securities, you must assess potential fluctuations in the value of the principal and not just look at dividend yield. Such fluctuations are not theoretical. They affect your assets in real dollars. This is why, when you buy a bond, you need to take into consideration when you may need to sell it. If you need to sell a bond, or a bond fund, before it matures, and if interest rates have moved against you, you may take a real hit to principal. Even if you decide not sell your bonds (or your bond fund) and do not realize the loss in principal value, you may experience another loss: you are unable to take advantage of the currently higher yields (that is called an "opportunity cost"), and you have lost liquidity because you may be unwilling to sell a bond if it has declined significantly in value.

If you look only at the dividend yield side, bond investments look very predictable. But if you include potential changes in a bond's principal value, and you look at bonds as total return vehicles, the picture changes vastly.

But, you may be thinking, "I just want to invest in bonds for income."

Unfortunately, whether you like it or not, like Molière's character who found out that he had been speaking in prose all his life without realizing it, if you are buying bonds with 30-year maturities, you are making a bet on interest rates, whether you know it or not.

Investors intent on boosting yield sometimes place their principal at risk for very little gain. When purchasing bonds, the first question to ask, always, is, "How much more am I really earning?" The second is, "What kinds of risk am I assuming in order to earn that extra amount?"

No one can quote total return to you ahead of time. Total return is actual return to you, based on your own investment experience. For any investment, you start out with a given sum. For a chosen period of time (say, one year), add all the income streams that have accrued (whether from dividends, interest-on-interest, or capital gains), subtract all transaction costs, and be sure to add or subtract any changes in principal value. You can also subtract taxes to obtain total return on a net-after-tax basis. For the year, calculate how much (as a percentage) your investment has grown or declined. That is your total return.

There is one further virtue to "total return": the concept is easy to understand. If you like precision, the exact formula for calculating total return is:

$$\frac{(\text{Ending Figure} + \text{Dividends} + \text{Distributions}) - \text{Beginning Figure}}{\text{Beginning Figure}}$$

The same formula can be used to calculate total return on any investment, whether it's stocks, gold bullion, baseball cards, or real estate. Calculating total return keeps you honest; it helps you to evaluate what your investments are really doing for you. It is, therefore, a very useful concept.

Actual Total Returns: A Prototypical Bond Transaction

A discussion of bond returns can appear dry as dust. So let's apply it to a prototypical bond transaction, in order to illustrate how a variety of factors affect your investment.

First, let's remember that when you buy a bond—or a bond fund—you cannot know at the time of purchase how interest rates are going to behave, and you may not know how long you will hold the security. Therefore, it follows that you cannot know at what rate(s) coupons will be reinvested and, if you need to resell before the bond matures, at what price. Let's briefly illustrate how to calculate what you have actually earned. In order to do that, let's buy and sell a bond, include some transaction costs, and figure out actual returns.

You decide to buy a bond. Your broker shows you the 6% State of Bliss bonds, of 10 (that is, maturing in 2010) quoted at 85 bid/87 ask. You buy the 10 bonds but do not hold them to maturity. Instead, you sell them two years later. At that date, the bonds are still being quoted at 85 bid/87 ask (interest rates are unusually stable). At the time of purchase, what was your current yield and your yield-to-maturity? And how much did you actually earn when you sold?

Well, first of all, since the coupon is 6% of par, you know that you will receive two interest payments every year, each $300, or $600 annually for 10 bonds. You will pay the "ask" (or offer) price, $870 per bond, for a total of $8,700 for the 10 bonds. The current yield will be $600 divided by $8,700, which equals 6.9%.

To calculate the YTM, take out your financial calculator. To proceed:

- Plug in the price you are paying for the bonds as PV
  (−$8,700).
- Plug in the par value of the bonds at maturity as FV
  ($8,500).
- Plug in the annual amount of the coupons as PMT
  ($600).
- Plug in the number of years to maturity, using the *n* key
  (10).
- Solve for YTM, using the *i* key.
- The answer is a YTM of 7.93%.

The YTM is significantly higher than the coupon yield because when the bond matures, it will be redeemed at par. (At par, the bonds will be worth $10,000, $1,300 more than you initially paid.) The YTM is also higher than the current yield, again because of the anticipated gain when the bond is redeemed at maturity.

But since you sell your bonds before they mature, you will not earn the YTM that was initially quoted. In this example, we specified that you sell your bonds after two years for $850 per bond ($8,500 for the 10 bonds). Since you paid $8,700 for the 10 bonds and you sell them for $8,500, you realize a loss of $200 on the principal. Because of that loss, it should be clear immediately that your actual return will be lower than either the anticipated YTM of 7.93%, or even, lower than the current yield of 6.9%. Since you sold the bond for less than you paid, you earned less than the coupon.

To calculate your actual total return, we can use the formula for total return stated earlier. To be accurate, let's assume you reinvested the coupons in a money market fund, and earned approximately $55 interest-on-interest. These are the cash flows on your bonds:

Sale price (ending figure)	$8,500
Interest income for 2 years (2 times $600)	1,200
Interest-on-interest	55
Beginning figure (purchase price)	8,700

Doing the arithmetic, you get

$$\frac{\left(\underset{\text{Ending Figure}}{\$8{,}500} + \underset{\text{Dividends}}{\$1{,}200} + \underset{\text{Distributions}}{\$55}\right) - \underset{\text{Beginning Figure}}{\$8{,}700}}{\underset{\$8{,}700}{\text{Beginning Figure}}}$$

$$= \frac{\$9{,}755 - \$8{,}700}{\$8{,}700}$$

$$= 0.121 \text{ or } 12.1\%$$

Your total return for two years has been approximately 12.1%, or slightly more than 6% per year. You can also calculate the total return, on a compounded basis. To solve for this number, you would use the procedure outlined earlier for calculating YTM. The answer turns out to be 5.89%. That is your average annual compounded return.

You can also consider that number as your actual YTM, as opposed to the projected YTM quoted when you bought the bond. It is a positive gain, but it is lower than the YTM initially quoted you. To reiterate, that is due to the fact that since you sold the bonds before they matured, you did not earn the $1,300 that the bonds would have gained simply by appreciating to par. In fact, you sold them at a small loss.

Let's assume a happier scenario: namely, that interest rates declined, enabling you to sell your bonds at a profit. Let's assume the price appreciated to $950 per bond. You would then sell your bonds for a total of $9,500, and you would realize a gain of $800 compared to the purchase price. The cash flows on your bonds would now look like this:

Sale price (ending figure)	$9,500
Interest income for 2 years (2 times $600)	1,200
Interest-on-interest	55
Beginning figure (purchase price)	8,700

Doing the arithmetic, you get

$$\frac{\left(\underset{\text{Ending Figure}}{\$9,500} + \underset{\text{Dividends}}{\$1,200} + \underset{\text{Distributions)}}{\$55}\right) - \underset{\text{Beginning Figure}}{\$8,700}}{\underset{\$8,700}{\text{Beginning Figure}}}$$

$$= \frac{\$10,755 - \$8,700}{\$8,700}$$

$$= 0.236 \text{ or } 23.6\%$$

Because you realized a profit of $800 on the sale of your bonds, your actual total return jumps to 23.6%. If you solve for the YTM, you will see that the average annual compounded rate of return on these bonds was approximately 11.2%. That is significantly higher than the anticipated YTM quoted when you bought the bonds, because the $800 profit is a significant short-term gain.

Commission costs are actually included in the above examples since for bonds, commission costs are the difference between the "bid" and the "ask" price. A wider spread would have translated into a lower total return since your purchase price would have been higher.

The preceding examples demonstrate the dramatic impact of changing bond prices on actual total returns. But note that I stacked the deck: both of these examples revolve around bonds with ten-year (intermediate) maturities that had to be sold well prior to maturity.

When you bought the bonds, if you thought there was a reasonable chance that the money from this investment would be needed in two years, you could have avoided having to sell your bonds at a loss by purchasing bonds with a two-year maturity. Your initial yield might have been a bit lower, but your total return would have been more predictable.

If you hold the bonds until their maturity date, then the total return would be closer to the YTM initially quoted because no matter what had happened to interest rates during your holding period, the bonds would be redeemed at par. The major variable then which would determine your actual total return would be whether you reinvested the coupons or spent them; and if you reinvested the coupons the rate at which you reinvested them.

What should have become clear by now is that when you buy bonds, YTM is only one of the factors that should be considered as a basis for selecting a particular bond. Many other factors should be considered, and they will be discussed throughout the book.

Finally, let us note that none of the preceding examples includes still another important transaction cost—taxes. In order to compare returns on fixed-income instruments accurately, any tax owed on dividends or capital gains should be subtracted from the estimated yield. The tax calculation would depend on current tax rates and your own tax bracket.

DURATION AND BOND PRICE VOLATILITY

The concept of "duration" originated in 1938. It has come into widespread use over the last 15 years or so. Duration does not measure return. It can be used as a gauge of the sensitivity of a bond to interest rate changes: that is, you can use duration to predict how much specific bonds will go up (or down) in price if interest rates change. Duration is used by professionals for the management of institutional portfolios. The term is also cropping up increasingly in newsletters or on websites that give financial advice concerning bonds. Even if you don't want to calculate duration for yourself, the concept is extremely useful in that it enables you to evaluate how much interest rate risk you are taking on whenever you buy a bond or a bond fund. And interpreting duration numbers is actually quite simple.

Duration is based on the same cash flows as YTM: that is, coupon payments, interest-on-interest, and the sale or redemption value of a bond. But duration adds in as important elements the timing (when you receive the cash flows) and the size of all the cash flows. It takes into account not only how many dollars will be received as coupons and repayment of principal, but also when those cash flows occur. That is because the timing and the size of the cash flows affect interest-on-interest. If, for example, you buy premium bonds, which have high coupons, that gives you more money to reinvest each time you receive a coupon payment. If you buy discount bonds, which typically will have lower coupons, you will then have less money to reinvest. Therefore, two bonds with the same YTM, but one a discount bond and the other a premium bond, will have different durations.

The Time Value of Money

To understand duration, first of all you have to become familiar with a concept known as "the time value of money." The time value of money can be calculated using either of two related concepts: future value and present value. Future value tells you how much a dollar today will be worth at some future date, based on assumed annual percentage increases. Present value tells you how much a dollar received at some future date is worth today, again based on an assumed annual percentage rate of return.

Both concepts can be illustrated with a financial calculator. Suppose you want to know how much $50,000 invested today will be worth in 20 years if you earn 7% per year: that would be the future value of the $50,000. Take out your financial calculator and plug in the following numbers:

- Plug in $50,000 as PV, using the *PV* (present value) key (you need to use a minus sign in front of the $50,000 number).
- Plug in 7, using the *i* (interest) key.
- Plug in 20, using the *n* key (for the number of years).
- Solve for FV (future value), using the *FV* key.
- The answer is $193,484.22.

If you want to test how much more you would earn if you earned 10% a year, simply plug in 10 using the *i* (interest) key. The answer is $336,375.00. (Incidentally, this provides another illustration of the magic of compounding.)

Present value is the reverse. Suppose you know that you will need $100,000 in 20 years. How much money would you need to put away today (assuming you are putting away a lump sum)? The answer to that question would be the present value of the $100,000. Well, once again, you have to assume a rate at which the money would compound; let's say 7%. Again, take out your financial calculator. You would plug in the following numbers:

♦ Plug in $100,000 as FV, using the *FV* key.
♦ Plug in 20, using the *n* key (for the number of years).
♦ Plug in 7, using the *i* (interest) key.
♦ Solve for present value (PV), using the *PV* key.
♦ The answer is $25,842. That number is the present value of $100,000 compounding at an annual rate of 7% for 20 years.

When you work from future value back to present value, the annual percentage rate at which money is assumed to compound is known as the *"discount"* rate. Both present value and future value are based on compounded numbers, that is, they assume interest-on-interest if you are calculating dollar amounts.

Now that we have defined the time value of money, let's apply it to the concept of duration. The definition of duration is "a weighted average term-to-maturity of a security's cash flows."[4] Solving for duration is a tedious process, involving several different steps. You first need to calculate the present value of all of a bond's known cash flows: coupon payments, redeemed principal, and capital gains (or losses), if you did not purchase the bond at par. (You calculate the present value of these known cash flows by discounting them—for interest-on-interest—at the assumed reinvestment rate.) The present values of all the bond's cash flows are then adjusted, by weight, for the exact time when they are received.

The resulting number is the bond's duration, in years. In effect, the number you have obtained readjusts the maturity date to account for the size of the coupons, as well as potential interest-on-interest. Duration is correlated to maturity length. But it is readjusted for the size and timing of the bond's cash flows. The reason for this, again, is interest-on-interest. If you own a premium bond with high coupons, you receive larger sums earlier, which can be reinvested to earn interest-on-interest. On the other hand, if you own a discount bond, with low coupons, you have less money to reinvest to earn interest-on-interest. Also, one of the

---

4. Frank Fabozzi, ed., *The Handbook of Fixed Income Securities,* 5th ed. (New York: McGraw-Hill, 1997), p. 85.

bond's cash flows—the capital gain you receive when you redeem a discount bond at par—is received when the bond matures. Therefore, throughout its life, the discount bond throws off lower cash flows than the premium bond.

As a result, bonds with lower coupons have longer durations than bonds with higher coupons. With the exception of zero coupon bonds, the duration of a bond is always shorter than its term-to-maturity. Because all of a zero coupon bond's cash flows are received on a single date, its maturity date, zero coupon bonds have the longest durations. In fact, the duration of zero coupon bonds equals their term-to-maturity.

How You Can Use the Concept of Duration

When you buy a bond or a bond fund, you should find out its duration. If all other factors are equal, a bond (or a bond fund) with a longer duration is always more volatile than one with a shorter duration. In fact, duration can be used to calculate approximately how much the price of a bond will go up or down if interest rates move up or down; that is, how much interest rate risk you are taking on. The general guideline is that for every 100 basis points (1%) that interest rates go up or down, the price of a bond will go up or down by the duration number. For example, suppose you own two different bonds with a 6% coupon: the first has a maturity of five years and an approximate duration of 4.4 years, and the second has a 20-year maturity and a duration of almost 12 years. If interest rates were to go up to 7%, the price of the five-year bond would decline by approximately 4 1/2% (or close to its duration of 4.4 years). That of the bond with the 20-year maturity would decline by approximately 12% (close to its duration of almost 12 years).

Bonds with the same maturity, but with larger coupons than the two preceding examples would have somewhat lower durations, and therefore, somewhat lower volatility. Suppose, for example, you own two other bonds with 9% coupons: one with a five-year maturity and one with a 20-year maturity. The respective durations of these two bonds would be approximately 4.2 years and 11 years. If interest rates were to go up by 100 basis points (1%), these two bonds would decline by approximately 4.2% and

11% respectively, somewhat less than the two bonds in the previous example.

Let's summarize a number of features of duration:

- With the exception of zero coupon bonds, the duration of a bond is always shorter than its term-to-maturity.
- The longer the duration of a bond, the higher its volatility.
- Bonds with lower coupons have longer durations than bonds with larger coupons. That is the reason that bonds with higher coupons are less volatile than bonds with lower coupons.
- For zero coupon bonds, duration and maturity are the same. That is why zero coupon bonds are the most volatile of all bonds.

Duration can be calculated both for individual bonds and for bond funds. For bond funds, the duration of the fund is the weighted average duration of all the bonds in the portfolio. The same guidelines for calculating price changes hold both for declines in price if interest rates go up and for increases in price if interest rates are declining.

If you are considering purchase of three bonds with the same YTM quotes, one a discount, one a premium, or one a zero, then the premium bond would be the least volatile, the discount would be more volatile, and the zero the most volatile. The same principle would apply to bond funds quoting the same yield but with different durations.

The concept of duration has some limits. For calculating how much the price of a bond will go up or down if interest rates change, duration works more accurately for smaller changes in interest rates than for larger changes. Also, as the term-to-maturity becomes longer, duration becomes somewhat less precise. Finally, the guidelines suggested above are somewhat approximate. But they are precise enough for the purposes of most individual investors. (There are actually two different definitions of duration and different formulas for calculating duration. But these would be of concern primarily to institutional investors for whom a difference to the fourth decimal point can translate into several thousand dollars.)

We shall use the concept of duration in several chapters of the book: when bond funds are discussed, and also in the discussion of portfolio management.

Finally, let's turn briefly back to the concepts of present value and future value. An entire industry seems to have grown up to tell you how much money you need to save periodically in order to have a certain amount of money in your retirement years. Brokerage firms and mutual fund groups are eager to supply this type of information, usually based on a questionnaire. This is actually a simple illustration of the concept of future value. These firms are using software programs which calculate the future value of whatever sums they start with, based on two assumptions: an assumed rate of inflation and an assumed rate of return. Both of those assumptions, of course, are absolutely critical. Particularly over long time periods, a difference of even 1/2% in the assumptions makes a significant difference in their conclusions. If you know how to use a financial calculator (or a spreadsheet), you can easily do the arithmetic yourself. But in any case, it is critical to be aware of the assumptions. Different firms come up with different numbers simply because they are using different assumptions for both inflation and annual percentage returns.

SUMMARY

This chapter discussed a number of ways of evaluating bond returns. It first showed how bond cash flows interact to compound over time and pointed out the importance of compounding (the eighth wonder of the world) in building assets. The different concepts of yield were then defined. Current yield is based on coupon and price only. It ignores all other cash flows. Yield-to-maturity (YTM) takes into account all of the bond's known cash flows. It is only a projection, however. Your actual realized return is likely to differ significantly from the YTM because neither the price at which you sell (if you sell before the bond matures) nor the rates at which you reinvest coupons can be predicted at the time you buy the bond. The YTM should be used primarily to compare different bonds to each other before you purchase a bond.

The only way to measure what you have earned in a bond accurately is to measure its total return. Total return includes changes in the value of your bond, commission costs, interest income, and interest-on-interest. A brief section illustrated the various steps involved in pricing and calculating total return for a bond purchase. This example illustrates how commission costs and changes in the price of bonds due to interest rate fluctuations affect returns from fixed-income securities. It is important to consider them when you buy bonds, and not just buy on the basis of the quoted YTM.

Finally, the concept of duration was also introduced. Duration can be used to predict potential changes in the value of a bond (or of a bond fund) if interest rates go up or if they go down. If you know the duration of a bond, you can anticipate how much interest rate risk you are taking on before purchasing the bond.

CHAPTER 5

A Guide for the Perplexed: How to Read the Financial Pages of Your Newspaper

This chapter discusses

- The Table of Treasury Bills, Bonds, and Notes
- The yield curve and what it can tell you

INTERPRETING THE TABLE OF TREASURY BILLS, BONDS, AND NOTES

You are on the train in the morning and reading the daily newspaper. If you are currently investing in bonds, what do you want to look at? Well, before you turn to sports, or gourmet cooking, or whatever else really turns you on, your newspaper probably contains its own version of a nifty table that looks like Table 5–1. Its title will be *Table of Treasury Bills, Bonds, and Notes,* and it will tell you very quickly almost everything you might want to know about what is happening in the credit markets.

Table 5–1 shows some of the format and a partial listing of the prices that would have been published in the financial pages of major dailies on March 28, 2000.

This table summarizes the major price changes that occurred the preceding day to securities issued by the U.S. government and trading in the secondary market. It lists specific issues, starting with the shortest maturities, and goes through the entire maturity

TABLE 5–1

Table of Treasury Bills, Bonds, and Notes

TREASURY BILLS

Date	Bid	Ask	Chg	Yield
Mar 30 00	5.60	5.58	+0.05	5.68
Apr 06 00	5.40	5.38	+0.05	5.48
Apr 13 00	5.50	5.48	+0,05	5.59
Apr 20 00	5.85	5.83	+0.30	5.95
Apr 27 00	5.83	5.81	...	5.94
May 04 00	5.72	5.70	+0.02	5.83
May 11 00	5.69	5.67	+0.03	5.80
May 18 00	5.60	5.58	...	5.72
May 25 00	5.61	5.59	−0.03	5.74
Jun 01 00	5.68	5.66	...	5.81
Jun 08 00	5.71	5.69	...	5.85
Jun 15 00	5.70	5.68	−0.01	5.85
Jun 21 00	5.69	5.67	−0.04	5.84
Jun 29 00	5.71	5.69	−0.01	5.87
Jul 06 00	5.73	5.71	...	5.90
Jul 13 00	5.68	5.66	−0.01	5.85
Jul 20 00	5.72	5.70	−0.01	5.90
Jul 27 00	5.72	5.70	...	5.91
Aug 03 00	5.78	5.76	+0.01	5.98
Aug 10 00	5.79	5.77	+0.01	6.00
Aug 17 00	5.83	5.81	+0.01	6.05
Aug 24 00	5.87	5.85	+0.01	6.09
Aug 31 00	5.89	5.87	+0.01	6.11
Sep 07 00	5.91	5.89	...	6.14
Sep 14 00	5.90	5.88	...	6.15
Sep 21 00	5.92	5.90	+0.01	6.16
Sep 28 00	5.90	5.88	...	6.14
Oct 12 00	5.93	5.91	...	6.20
Nov 09 00	5.97	5.95	...	6.25
Dec 07 00	5.99	5.97	+0.01	6.28
Jan 04 01	5.98	5.96	+0.01	6.29
Feb 01 01	6.00	5.98	+0.01	6.33
Mar 01 01	5.95	5.93	+0.02	6.28

BONDS AND NOTES

Month	Rate	Bid	Ask	Chg	Yld
Mar 00 p	5½	100.00	100.02	...	...
Mar 00 p	6⅞	100.00	100.02	...	...
Apr 00 p	5½	99.31	100.01	...	4.71
Apr 00 p	5⅝	99.30	100.00	...	5.50
Apr 00 p	6¾	100.01	100.03	...	5.35
May 00 p	6⅜	100.01	100.03	...	5.51
May 00 p	8⅞	100.12	100.14	...	5.17
May 00 p	5½	99.29	99.31	...	5.58
May 00 p	6¼	100.01	100.03	...	5.59
Jun 00 p	5⅜	99.27	99.29	+0.01	5.67
Jun 00 p	5⅞	99.31	100.01	+0.01	5.67
Jul 00 p	5⅜	99.24	99.26	+0.01	5.89
Jul 00 p	6⅛	100.00	100.02	+0.01	5.88
Aug 00 p	6	99.29	99.31	...	6.00
Aug 00 p	8¾	100.30	101.00	−0.01	5.97
Aug 00 p	5⅛	99.16	99.18	...	6.13
Aug 00 p	6¼	99.31	100.01	...	6.11
Sep 00 p	4½	99.02	99.04	...	6.25
Sep 00 p	6⅛	99.29	99.31	...	6.16
Oct 00 p	4	98.20	98.22	...	6.27
Oct 00 p	5¾	99.20	99.22	...	6.26
Nov 00 p	5¾	99.19	99.21	...	6.28
Nov 00 p	8½	101.09	101.11	−0.01	6.24
Nov 00 p	4⅝	98.27	98.29	...	6.28
Nov 00 p	5⅝	99.16	99.18	...	6.28
Dec 00 p	4⅝	98.22	98.24	...	6.33
Dec 00 p	5½	99.10	99.12	...	6.34
Jan 01 p	4½	98.14	98.16	...	6.35
Jan 01 p	5¼	99.01	99.03	−0.01	6.34
Feb 01 p	5⅜	99.03	99.05	...	6.36
Feb 01 p	7¾	101.03	101.05	−0.01	6.35
Feb 01	11¾	104.17	104.19	−0.01	6.29
Feb 01 p	5	98.23	98.24	...	6.39
Feb 01 p	5⅝	99.09	99.11	...	6.36
Mar 01 p	4⅞	98.15	98.16	...	6.44
Mar 01 p	6⅜	99.29	99.31	−0.01	6.39
Apr 01 p	5	98.15	98.17	...	6.41
Apr 01 p	6¼	99.24	99.26	−0.01	6.41
May 01 p	5⅝	99.01	99.03	−0.01	6.45
May 01 p	8	101.19	101.21	...	6.44
May 01	13⅛	107.03	107.05	−0.01	6.42
May 01 p	5¼	98.18	98.19	...	6.51
May 01 p	6½	99.30	100.00	−0.01	6.47
Jun 01 p	5¾	99.00	99.02	...	6.53
Jun 01 p	6⅝	100.01	100.03	−0.01	6.52
Jul 01 p	5½	98.19	98.21	...	6.54
Jul 01 p	6⅝	100.01	100.03	...	6.54
Aug 01 p	7⅞	101.20	101.22	−0.01	6.57
Aug 01	13⅜	108.24	108.26	−0.02	6.57
Aug 01 p	5½	98.15	98.17	−0.01	6.58
Aug 01 p	6½	99.26	99.28	−0.01	6.58
Sep 01 p	5⅝	98.18	98.20	−0.01	6.60
Sep 01 p	6⅜	99.20	99.22	−0.01	6.60
Oct 01 p	5⅞	98.27	98.29	−0.01	6.61
Oct 01 p	6¼	99.13	99.15	−0.01	6.59
Nov 01 p	7½	101.09	101.11	−0.01	6.61
Nov 01	15¾	113.26	113.28	−0.01	6.61
Nov 01 p	5⅞	98.25	98.27	−0.01	6.60
Dec 01 p	6⅛	99.05	99.07	−0.01	6.60
Jan 02 p	6¼	99.10	99.12	−0.01	6.61
Jan 02 p	6⅜	99.17	99.19	−0.01	6.60
Feb 02	14¼	113.07	113.09	−0.01	6.62
Feb 02 p	6¼	99.09	99.11	−0.01	6.61
Feb 02 p	6½	99.24	99.26	−0.01	6.60
Mar 02 p	6⅝	99.31	100.01	−0.01	6.61
Apr 02 p	6⅝	99.31	100.01	...	6.61
May 02 p	7½	101.21	101.23	−0.01	6.61
May 02 p	6½	99.23	99.25	−0.01	6.60
Jun 02 p	6¼	99.06	99.08	−0.01	6.60
Jul 02 f	3⅝	99.17	99.19	...	3.81
Jul 02 p	6	98.21	98.23	−0.01	6.59
Aug 02 p	6⅜	99.14	99.16	−0.01	6.60
Aug 02 p	6¼	99.05	99.07	−0.01	6.60
Sep 02 p	5⅞	98.08	98.10	−0.01	6.61
Oct 02 p	5¾	97.30	98.00	−0.01	6.60
Nov 02	11⅝	111.22	111.24	−0.02	6.66
Nov 02	5¾	97.26	97.28	−0.02	6.62
Dec 02 p	5⅝	97.15	97.17	−0.02	6.61
Jan 03 p	5½	97.04	97.06	−0.01	6.60
Feb 03 p	6¼	99.01	99.03	−0.01	6.60
Feb 03	10¾	110.14	110.16	−0.02	6.67
Feb 03 p	5½	97.02	97.04	−0.01	6.59
Mar 03 p	5½	97.00	97.02	−0.01	6.59
Apr 03 p	5¾	97.20	97.22	−0.01	6.59
May 03	10¾	111.08	111.10	−0.02	6.68
May 03 p	5½	96.27	96.29	−0.02	6.59
Jun 03 p	5⅜	96.15	96.17	−0.01	6.57
Aug 03 p	5¼	96.00	96.02	−0.01	6.57
Aug 03 p	5¾	97.15	97.17	−0.01	6.57
Aug 03	11⅛	113.06	113.08	−0.02	6.67
Nov 03 p	4¼	92.22	92.24	−0.01	6.52
Nov 03	11⅞	116.15	116.17	−0.02	6.66
Feb 04 p	4¾	93.30	94.00	−0.02	6.52
Feb 04 p	5⅞	97.23	97.25	−0.02	6.53
May 04	12⅜	120.07	120.09	−0.03	6.67
May 04 p	5¼	95.12	95.14	−0.02	6.52
May 04 p	7¼	102.12	102.14	−0.02	6.56
Aug 04 p	6	97.31	98.01	−0.02	6.52

k = Non U.S. citizen exempt from withholding taxes.
n = Treasury note.
p = Treasury note and non U.S. citizen exempt from withholding taxes.

spectrum. The table first lists *bills* (any security with a maturity of one year or less), *notes* (maturities between two and ten years), and *bonds* (maturities between ten and 30 years). (Note that the longest maturities do not appear in Table 5–1. They would be listed in still another column.) Any newspaper that covers finance will publish some version of this table. The most complete appears daily in *The Wall Street Journal* and on weekends in *Barron's*.

Spending one minute a day skimming this table is the most useful thing that you can do to be a well-informed bond investor. You will want to focus on the interest rate levels and on the price changes.

Let's go through a couple of sample listings in order to explain how to read this table. Exhibit 5–2 illustrates both the column headings, and a typical listing under *Bonds and Notes*.

Reading from left to right:

- The date is the maturity date of the note. This note matures in March of 01 (i.e., 2001). That is the current yield on Treasury notes with an approximate one-year maturity.
- The rate, 6 3/8, is the coupon rate.
- Both the "bid" and "ask" prices are listed. Translated into dollars, the bid price would be approximately $993. The ask price is slightly higher. (For more on pricing of Treasury bonds, see below.)
- The column headed "Chg" lists the change in price compared to the previous day (calculated from the bid). The previous day, the price of this note went down by one basis point (indicated by −.01).
- The last column lists the yield-to-maturity for the note, 6.39%.

E X H I B I T   5–2

Note Listing

Month	Rate	Bid	Ask	Chg	Yld
Mar 01	6 3/8	99.29	99.31	−0.01	6.39

Exhibit 5–3 illustrates longer-dated paper, which would be at the bottom of the Table.

Again, reading from left to right:

♦ The maturity date for this bond is February of 27 (i.e., 2027). This is a bond maturing in approximately 27 years.
♦ The rate, 6 5/8, is the coupon rate.
♦ Both the "bid" and "ask" prices are listed. (For more on pricing of Treasury bonds, see below.)
♦ Yesterday, the price of this note went up by one basis point (indicated by +.01).
♦ Yield is the YTM: 6.21%.

These listings may be used for a variety of purposes. First, the table tells you in very precise detail the interest rates available on the previous day for a broad spectrum of Treasury bonds, from the shortest to the longest maturities. Those are the yields-to-maturity of the individual bonds in the table. Exhibit 5–2 indicates that on March 27, 2000, one-year Treasury paper was yielding 6.39%. Exhibit 5–3 shows that on the same date, 27-year paper had a yield-to-maturity of 6.21%. Yes, that number is correct. Even though under normal circumstances, bonds with long maturities yield more than bonds with short maturities, in March of 2000 that was not the case. This reflected an unusual situation, known as an inversion of the yield curve. For more on this topic, see the next section of this chapter, concerning yield curves.

Suppose you want to invest some money and would like to know what one-year Treasuries are yielding. You would look for an issue maturing one year from the date that you are reading your paper. That would be March 2001, corresponding to Exhibit

E X H I B I T   5–3

Long-Term Bond Listing

Date	Rate	Bid	Ask	Chg	Yield
Feb 27	6 5/8	105.11	105.13	+0.01	6.21

5–2, which shows a yield of 6.39%. Similarly, if you are interested in four-year paper, you would look for a security that matures four years from the date you are reading the paper. In this instance, the closest date (shown in Table 5–1) would be May of 2004. The yield for that note is 6.67%.

The *Table of Treasury Bills, Bonds, and Notes* also tells you exactly what happened to interest rates the previous day in the Treasury market, through the information conveyed by price changes, under the "Chg" (Change) heading. All you need to do is to look at plus (+) or minus (−) signs.

Remember that prices and yields (that is, interest rates) move in opposite directions. Plus (+) signs indicate that prices moved up and therefore interest rates (yields) went down. Minus (−) signs indicate the reverse. If prices of bonds went down, interest rates (and therefore yields) went up.

On most days, all signs in the *Table of Treasury Bills, Bonds, and Notes* are either (+) or (−), indicating that short rates and long rates moved in the same direction. But it is not uncommon for short rates and long rates to move in opposite directions. That was the case on March 28, 2000. This is immediately apparent when you look at Table 5–1. A glance at the table shows that there are both (+) and (−) signs. The (−) signs indicate that for those maturities, yields rose and prices declined. The (+) signs indicate that for those maturities, prices rose and yields went down.

If you get into the habit of looking at the *Table of Bills, Bonds, and Notes,* you will notice that it gives you very precise information much more quickly than any other source. It will enable you to compare the yields available on Treasury issues (the safest instruments) to those of any other fixed-income instrument you might be considering. It will also tell you exactly what is happening to both long and short interest rates. They may or they may not be moving in the same direction.

One peculiarity of Treasury bond pricing should be noted. Prices are quoted in 32nds of a point. "Minus .01" (−.01) does not mean minus one cent. It means minus one 32nd (−1/32) of a point. One point represents $10.00 per $1,000 par value bond. Therefore, 1/2 of one point would be half that amount, that is, $5.00; 1/32 of a point would be $10.00 divided by 32, that is, 31.25 cents. One 32nd (1/32) of one point is called a "tick." Traders or anyone reporting on Treasuries may say something like "the long bond moved up one tick" or "the long bond moved down two ticks."

As an example of bond pricing, let's go back to Exhibit 5–2. The bid price, 99.29, should be read as 99 and 29/32nds. Translated into dollars that would be $999.06. The ask price should be read as 99 and 31/32nds. In dollars that would be $999.69. Both of these prices are about $6 higher than if the price were just read as a percentage of par. That may not seem like a major difference, but on ten bonds that would be a $60 difference; on 100 bonds a $600 difference.

The size of the price changes also conveys useful information. On some days, prices may not change at all, or they may move up one tick or down three ticks. Moves of this magnitude represent relatively minor changes in interest rates. However, if prices move a full point (represented by 1.0, amounting to $10.00 per $1,000 bond), this is a substantial price move. If prices move as much as two points (indicated by 2.0, that is, $20.00 per $1,000 bond) or more, this is a violent move, and it indicates significant turbulence in the credit markets. Therefore, if you look regularly at the *Table of Treasury Bills, Bonds, and Notes,* you will learn to distinguish between periods of relatively stable interest rates, with relatively minor changes from day to day, and periods of greater volatility.

Finally, note also that since the *Table of Bills, Bonds, and Notes* lists both bid and ask prices for a broad spectrum of Treasury issues trading in the secondary market, it permits you to calculate the price of any older issue you might want to buy or to sell fairly accurately. Since spreads between the bid and the ask prices of Treasuries are very narrow (3/32 or 4/32 of one point, or about $1.25 per $1,000 bond), you should be able to buy or sell older securities at close to the price listed in the table.

But why focus on this particular table?

The market in U.S. debt securities is considered the key interest rate market not only for the United States, but also for other countries worldwide. The shortest maturity paper—the three-month bill—is considered the safest security that you can buy. It is so short that it has virtually no interest rate risk, and its credit quality is the highest available. In fact, it is used as a proxy for risk-free returns by professionals. Similarly, the most recently issued 30-year bond, referred to as the long bond, is the key bellwether security for long maturities.

Any other type of bond is deemed to be riskier than a Treasury, even if the risk is slight. Therefore, all other securities of the same maturity will have a slightly higher (or a much higher) yield than a Treasury of the same maturity, depending on their credit quality. The difference in yield between that security and a Treasury security is known as the spread. No professional buys a debt instrument of any kind, in any maturity, without first comparing it to a U.S. government security of the same maturity, and neither should you.

The "Credit Markets" Column and Other Columns

After looking at the *Table of Treasury Bills, Bonds, and Notes,* and usually on the same page, there are several other columns you should read. The first is the one entitled "credit markets." It summarizes the previous day's developments in different sectors of the bond market:

- Whether a Treasury auction took place
- What yields resulted
- Any outstanding development in any other sector of the bond market (munis, GNMAs, corporates)
- Interest rates available in those markets

In addition, the column provides a running commentary on where professionals think the market, or interest rates, are headed, and why. It is must reading, if only because it is the best method for finding out how bond professionals view the market.

In addition, several briefer articles may be devoted to recent bond sales that appear newsworthy for a variety of reasons. Such an article might, for example, describe a very large sale of municipal bonds by an issuer in a neighboring state. The article might supply a variety of details, such as who were the underwriters, the yields for various maturities, whether demand was strong or weak, and so forth. Again, articles such as these are useful in that they give you some clues about developments in various sectors of the bond market. They also let you know what kinds of yields are available. Unfortunately, coverage of the bond markets is skimpy at best: some major financial dailies provide little coverage. Among national newspapers, *The Wall Street Journal, The New York Times,* and *Barron's* tend to have the most complete coverage of the bond markets.

Finally, the Monday issues of *The Wall Street Journal* and *The New York Times* list specific upcoming bond sales in both the municipal and the corporate market, and the date of the sale. If you want to buy bonds at issue, this will alert you to upcoming sales that may interest you.

The financial pages contain other tables and graphs relating to specific sectors of the bond market (municipals, corporates, and mortgage-backed), and these will be discussed in the appropriate chapters. Most financial websites such as *Bloomberg* and *CNBC* carry stories devoted to particular sectors of the bond market. Their advantage, compared to the printed media, is that they are closer to real time.

THE YIELD CURVE AND WHAT IT CAN TELL YOU

Located next to the "credit markets" column, the financial pages of the newspaper usually contain a small graph which looks like Exhibit 5–4.

This graph is called a "yield curve." The yield curve graphs some the key points along the *Table of Treasury Bonds, Bills, and Notes.* The exact points along the graph may vary, but the graph typically includes short, intermediate, and longer maturities—for example, interest rates for the three-month, six-month, one-year, two-year, five-year, ten-year, and 30-year Treasury maturities. The graph displayed in Exhibit 5–4, which appeared August 22, 2000, at 1:36 PM, is taken off the Bloomberg website. Note just below the graph that changes in yield along key points are also tracked.

For purposes of comparison, let's look at Exhibit 5–5, which shows three yield curves that differ significantly from each other. Pay particular attention both to the interest rate levels and to the shape of the curve.

E X H I B I T   5–4

Treasury Yield Curve

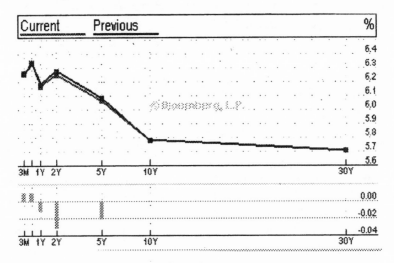

Source: *Bloomberg.com*. August 22, 2000, 1:36PM EDT. Reprinted with permission.

E X H I B I T   5–5

Three Different Treasury Yield Curves

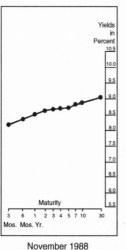

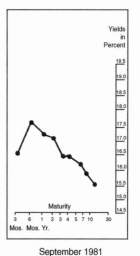

November 1988   December 1954   September 1981

The first graph, dated November 16, 1988, shows three-month bill rates at about 8 1/4% and 30-year rates at 9%. The difference in yield between the three-month rate and the 30-year rate (the spread) is about 80 basis points (less than 1%). That is considered very narrow. As a result, this would be considered a relatively flat yield curve.

The December 1954 graph shows bill rates at about 1.2% and 30-year bonds at about 2.7%. The spread between the shortest three-month paper and the 30-year maturity is about 150 basis points (1 1/2%). That is considered a normal, that is, an upward-sloping, yield curve, with long bonds yielding considerably more than short maturities. The 150-basis point spread is somewhat narrow for an upward sloping curve, due to the overall low interest rate level. At higher interest rate levels, the spread has been as high as 250 to 300 basis points.

Finally, look at the last graph, dated September 1981. Three-month rates are close to 16%; six-month rates are 17%; 30-year rates are actually below six-month rates, at 15%. That is called an inverted yield curve, with long rates actually lower than short rates. That suggests that the market is predicting lower rates at some future date, and therefore slower economic growth. For that reason, inverted yield curves are believed to predict recessions. Unfortunately for some would-be forecasters, it is also said that postwar, inverted yield curves have predicted nine out of five recessions. If you look back to Exhibit 5–4, you will note that the yield curve is also inverted, as it had been for a number of months prior to August 2000. For many experts, this was an indication that the economy would be slowing. It remains to be seen whether or not the forecasted recession will occur.

I have purposely used the December 1954 and September 1981 yield curves for shock value. The interest rate levels are so different from those of the past decade that they appear to be mistakes. These levels demonstrate "graphically" that current conditions may be no more normal, or permanent, than those that prevailed during earlier periods.

The Shape of the Yield Curve

The shape of the yield curve changes continually because interest rate expectations of the major users of credit (that is, large corporations and institutional investors) change constantly. If buyers expect an increase in inflation and a concurrent rise in interest rates, they seek the safety of short-term paper. As a result, short rates decline. If, on the other hand, they anticipate lower economic growth, recessionary times, and lower interest rates, they try to "lock in" high yields, which results in declines of long-term interest rates. These explanations are highly oversimplified. Anyone who follows interest rate movements soon learns that at any given time there are some "experts" who believe interest rates will go up and can make a good case for that, while other "experts" can make an equally strong case explaining why interest rates must go down.

Some professional economists argue that the shape of the yield curve contains an implicit consensus forecast of the future of interest rates and can, therefore, be used both to predict the direction of interest rates and future economic activity. But this entire subject is highly technical and controversial, with little agreement among professionals. Suppose, for example, that the yield curve is flat. The curve could return to a normal shape (upward sloping) in a number of ways. Short rates could fall, or long rates could go up, or both could occur. On the other hand, the curve could remain flat for another three years. Or, as happened in the early 1980s, all interest rates might rise for as long as two or three years. Not surprisingly, the experts are unlikely to agree about the likely outcome.

The Yield Curve and the Individual Investor

The yield curve, however, can be used by the individual investor in a number of ways:

- As a quick summary of current interest rate levels at all points of the maturity spectrum
- To pinpoint advantageous buy points as far as maturity length is concerned
- To provide, specifically, a very precise answer to the question, for the additional risk to principal incurred in going out further on the yield curve, how much more am I earning?

In the December 1988 yield curve, for example, there was a difference of about 50 basis points between one-year and 30-year paper. Now the question is, if you can buy one-year paper with no risk to principal, are you getting adequately compensated if you buy a 30-year bond with a great deal of risk to principal, for the additional yield of only 50 basis points? Similarly, at any one point along the curve, the investor should constantly ask how much more yield he is getting for the increasing risk to principal as maturities increase in length.

Often, two- to seven-year maturities yield perhaps only 30 to 50 basis points less than the 30-year bond, but the risk to principal is far lower. You have to ask yourself, if you can capture perhaps 90% of the yield of the 30-year bond with lower risk to principal, are you getting adequately compensated for the additional risk? This is a question that has no one correct answer, because everyone has a different reason for buying bonds. So the answer would vary with your reason for investing in the bonds. But the yield curve can let you know where relatively attractive buy-points are occurring at any given period in time.

Note that the highest yields are usually found somewhere between the ten and the 20-year, rather than the 30-year mark. While that seems illogical on the basis of risk, the explanation has to do with the fact that the 30-year bond is a more frequently traded issue among professionals than the 20-year maturity. Since the 30-year bond is in greater demand, it costs more to buy and yields less than the 20-year bond. That, of course, could change. Remember that the bond market is a dealer-to-dealer market. This explains pricing anomalies which can sometimes be exploited to advantage by an individual investor.

At the beginning of 2000, one reason being given for the very low yields of the 30-year bond was that the Treasury had announced that from this time forward, fewer 30-year bonds would be issued. Auctions of the 30-year bond would be held once a year instead of four times a year; and some older 30-year issues would be repurchased by the Treasury. Both of these announcements instantly conferred scarcity value on the 30-year bond. Higher demand for the bonds caused their price to rise and their yield to fall.

Investors intent on boosting yield sometimes place their principal at risk for very little extra gain. When purchasing bonds, always ask yourself, "How much more am I really earning?" and "What kinds of risk am I assuming in order to earn that extra amount?"

The 1981 yield curve deserves an additional comment. As indicated, on that date the yield curve was steeply inverted, with 30-year paper yielding 130 basis points less than short paper. Indeed, the very shortest rate, which is an overnight rate known as the "fed funds rate," was actually at 20%, making the inversion even more extreme. It would appear that at that point, the buyer of the 30-year bond was clearly not getting compensated for the risk of buying paper with a 30-year maturity. Or was he?

Well, with the wisdom of hindsight, you now know that in 1981 you should have squirreled away every possible dollar, hocked the house, and bought as many of those 15% Treasury bonds as possible, because that happened to be almost the peak of that interest rate cycle. At the time, however, many learned pundits were predicting that long rates would continue to climb and might possibly reach 20% at the long end. Mortgage rates did reach those levels. Is there some way you might have realized that these rates were highly advantageous, in spite of what the pundits were saying?

One indicator would have been some knowledge of the history of interest rates. The rates of the early 1980s were extraordinarily high; indeed, they were at the highest level that they had reached since the beginning of the century in the United States. To put this return into perspective, remember that historically the stock market has had an annual rate of return of about 11%. Therefore, a dividend yield of 15% on a government-guaranteed instrument, with call protection, represented an amazing opportunity. To some, another clue was the shape of the yield curve. The yield curve was inverted because many professionals (who dominate the bond markets) did not expect rates to continue climbing at the long end. They were buying the 30-year bonds, perhaps anticipating an end to the prevailing inflationary conditions. And they realized that with lower inflation rates, those very high interest rates would decline, as they did.

While I have discussed the yield curve for Treasuries only, a yield curve can be constructed for any other security as well; and that yield curve can be used to evaluate return versus risk for all maturities of that security. Yield curves in other sectors of the bond market are always related to some extent to the Treasury yield curve because, as noted previously, the yield of any security is always priced at a spread to Treasuries, based on the amount of risk that security is perceived to have, compared to Treasuries. But note that those perceptions vary as economic conditions change. For example, if Treasury yields at the long end are declining because the economy is slowing, then yields may rise in the market for "junk" bonds because the risk of default is considered to be rising for corporations with lower credit quality. That would translate into a widening spread between Treasuries and junk: the price of Treasuries might rise at the same time that the price of junk bonds might be falling.

Note also that yield curves in the municipal bond market tend to be more steeply upward sloping than those in the Treasury market, so that typically, to capture 90% of the yield of 30-year bonds, you may need to go out further along the yield curve than you would for Treasuries. Typically, for municipals, the best trade-offs between risk and yield are found between the seven-year and the 15-year maturities. But this is not a constant. Again, these issues will be revisited in the chapters on individual securities.

PRICING INFORMATION ON THE WEB

In reporting data, most financial websites follow the conventions of the print media. If you are familiar with data in print media, you can therefore easily interpret this information. But some formats may be more puzzling.

For example, the *Yahoo* finance website is cryptic. If you look up the web page summarizing quotes for the stock market, you will find one number for the bond market: it is the yield for the 30-year bond. That number is followed by either a (+) or a (−) sign. That indicates the change in yield compared to the previous day. For example, if you looked up the yield on Friday, April 7, 2000, this is what you would have seen:

30-year bond   5.724%   −0.069

The yield listed is the YTM of the most currently issued 30-year bond, priced to three decimal points. The change noted (−0.069) is the change in YTM compared to the previous day, in this instance, a decline of 6.9 basis points. As an informed investor, you know that a decline in the YTM indicates an inverse change in the price of the bond: on April 7 the price of the bond went up compared to the previous day. Moreover, a change of almost 7 basis points in yield is a pretty good-sized move. On the other hand, when the sign following the yield number is a (+), that tells you the price of the long bond declined.

Many websites (*Yahoo*, for example) which have limited information on the the bond market have links to other websites that have more information.

ADDITIONAL REFERENCES

The bond math in the preceding chapters is ample for the needs of most individual investors. If, however, you are more quantitatively oriented and want to understand bond mathematics more thoroughly, the bible of the fixed income markets is Frank Fabozzi, ed., *The Handbook of Fixed Income Securities*, 5th ed. (New York: McGraw-Hill, 1997).

The following websites contain general information on bonds:

- *investinginbonds.com*. This is the website maintained by the Bond Market Association. All the information on it is available for free. At the current time, it is the most complete website concerning bonds. It provides an overview of the U.S. bond market, a glossary of bond market terms, and links to a variety of other websites. The website also includes sections on municipal bonds, corporate bonds, mortgage-backed securities, and Treasuries. These sections are updated periodically to include major changes in each market. Finally, this website provides pricing information for both municipal and corporate bonds that is based on real trades that occurred the *previous* day. At the current time, that is unique, and it is probably the most useful feature of the website. This feature is illustrated in future chapters.
- *bondsonline.com*. This is a general website that lists different resources pretaining to bonds, such as books, and newsletters, which are available, mainly for a fee. Notes on the site indicate that it is undergoing changes

and that in the future, it will list pricing information, again probably for a fee.

- *Bloomberg.com, CBS.com,* and *CNBC.com* contain current pricing data and running commentary concerning current developments in various sectors of the bond market.

- The three major rating agencies all maintain extensive websites: *standardandpoors.com, moodys.com,* and *fitchibca.com.* The rating agencies all provide a variety of services, including monthly publications and rating information, which are fee-based. But a surprising amount of information, including extensive commentary on both domestic and foreign bond markets, is available for free on their respective websites. Inquiries concerning bond ratings may also be made by e-mail for free.

- *bondresources.com.* This is a brand new site, which lists itself as the "top source" for information on all types of bonds and bond funds, for the individual investor. It will have links to *Bond Express,* and will contain pricing information, as well as commentary on all types of bonds. It will also have links to brokers.

PART TWO

Individual Securities

If you have at least $50,000 to invest (less for Treasuries, since you can buy individual Treasury bonds with complete safety for as little as $1,000), you might consider purchasing individual securities.

I chose the sum of $50,000 because the first rule of investing, in bonds or anything else, is to diversify. If you do not have at least $50,000, you will be unable to buy a diversified portfolio. Also, your transaction costs, namely commission costs incurred in buying and selling, would be too high.

This section discusses five different types of fixed-income securities:

+ Treasury debt
+ Municipal bonds
+ Mortgage-backed securities
+ Corporate bonds
+ International bonds

They are discussed in order of their appeal for individual investors.

Treasuries are the benchmark against which all other debt instruments must be compared. They have the highest degree of safety. They are inexpensive to buy and sell. And they are easy to understand. Anyone looking for safety who does not have a great deal of time or interest in finance could very well limit himself to Treasuries alone, or for an investor in higher income brackets, to a combination of high-grade municipals and Treasuries.

Municipal bonds are perhaps the securities most widely held by individual investors. Their appeal is twofold. They are sound investments, and because of the exemptions from federal and some state and local taxes, they are among the highest-yielding fixed-income securities that an individual investor can own.

Mortgage-backed securities and corporates both yield more than Treasuries (on a current yield basis). Surprisingly, however, the total return for those securities may not be higher than for Treasuries. More importantly, mortgage-backed securities and corporates are more complex than either Treasuries or munis. Each requires owner involvement. They should not be purchased unless the investor has both the time and the interest to analyze specific securities in some depth before purchase and to monitor them after purchase.

A brief chapter on international bonds has been added. At the current time, it is still very difficult for individual investors to buy these as individual securities in the United States. But this is an area which is bound to grow in importance, given the enormous capital needs of the developing world and the increasing globalization of the more developed economies. This chapter gives some very basic information concerning the types of international bonds currently available in the U.S. market.

CHAPTER 6

Treasuries, Savings Bonds, and Federal Agency Paper

This chapter discusses

- Treasury Bills, Notes, and Bonds
- Inflation-indexed Treasuries
- Treasury Direct: How to buy Treasuries directly at auction, without paying commissions
- Zero coupon bonds
- Savings Bonds: EE, HH, and I bonds
- Federal agency debt

This chapter will discuss the main types of debt securities which are direct obligations of the U.S. government. There are four distinct types of instruments.

The first, perhaps the most familiar, are the securities issued by the Treasury, and sold at auction by the Federal Reserve Bank, popularly known as "Treasuries." They come in three different flavors, based on maturity length. The shortest instruments, called bills, mature in one year or less. Notes mature in two to ten years. Bonds mature in ten to 30 years. In 1997, the Federal Reserve Bank (the "Fed") brought out a new type of Treasury security: inflation-linked securities. These are also sold at auction, like other Treasuries. There is a very active secondary market in all Treasuries, which is the largest, most active, and most liquid debt market in the world.

The second type of Treasury is not sold by the Fed. It was actually created by investment bankers out of Treasury bonds and continues to be generated and sold by investment bankers. Those are zero coupon bonds ("zeros").

The third type of instrument are the familiar savings bonds, sold by the government directly to individuals through banks, and now, directly on the Internet. Savings bonds do not trade in the secondary market. As a result, the face value of savings bonds does not vary with changes in interest rates. That is a major difference between savings bonds and Treasuries. You may remember savings bonds mainly as those certificates given to you as presents by your least favorite aunt when you were a kid, to be cashed in at some far off future date. If so, you will be overlooking some extremely attractive opportunities. The savings bonds program has undergone dramatic changes. The government now sells three types of savings bonds: Series EE, HH, and I. Interest rates on older bonds are now more competitive, and new types of bonds have been introduced. I bonds are particularly attractive because their total return is linked to inflation and they offer an attractive vehicle for setting up a tax-deferred retirement plan.

Finally, we will turn to a fourth type of instrument. These are the debt instruments issued by the various Federal Agencies. They are not direct obligations of the Federal government. But they have implicit government backing. These are collectively called Federal Agencies.

Each of these instruments will be discussed in turn.

WHAT IS UNIQUE ABOUT TREASURIES

I want to buy a security that is completely safe, easy to buy, easy to sell, easy to understand, and high-yielding. Is there such an instrument?

Surprisingly, the answer is yes. Treasuries are that rare paradox: common and high quality. While they are not formally "insured," since Treasuries are a direct obligation of the U.S. government, itself the ultimate insurer, Treasuries are (if one can rate safety among issues backed by the U.S. government) safer than insured accounts. In addition, since 1985, long-dated Treasuries have not been callable before maturity—far more generous call protection than is afforded by any other debt instrument. Finally, Treasuries are the most liquid securities you can buy; they trade with lower markups than any other debt instrument.

Before buying any other fixed-income security, you should check out the yield of a Treasury with a comparable maturity. Professionals do. Every single debt instrument is priced by professionals off Treasuries. Never buy a security with a maturity comparable to a Treasury unless the additional yield (the spread to the Treasury yield) is large enough to compensate for the additional credit risk of the other security. The greater the risk, the wider the spread should be.

If you are risk-averse and/or don't have much time to devote to the management of your finances, then Treasuries are for you. Even if you have a lot of time, Treasuries may still be your best option.

The only real decision that has to be made when buying a Treasury is how much interest rate risk you want to assume; that is, where on the yield curve you will find the best trade-off between return and interest rate risk. If this were a perfect world, there would be no interest rate risk. But as we know, the price of long Treasury bonds is as volatile as the price of any other long-dated instrument. However, if you limit your purchases to maturities of five years or less and hold securities until maturity, you can put together a portfolio that has complete safety of principal and predictable returns.

What is surprising is that in spite of their high quality, on a total return basis, Treasuries often outperform other debt instruments. There are two main reasons for this. First, whenever any financial market becomes turbulent, investors sell these financial assets—stocks, for example—and put their money in Treasuries. This is referred to as a "flight to quality." And secondly, the significant call protection Treasuries enjoy, compared to other debt instruments, boosts the return of long-dated Treasuries whenever interest rates decline significantly.

Treasury bonds are issued periodically by the Treasury and sold through auctions run by the Federal Reserve Bank. Most Treasuries are sold to large dealers, called "primary dealers," who in turn sell to everyone else: to banks, to brokerage firms, to large and small institutions, to money market funds, or to individual investors. Individuals can purchase Treasuries from banks or from brokerage firms. But you can also purchase Treasuries directly at auction in amounts ranging from $1,000 to millions.

Treasuries are taxable at the federal level, but exempt from state and local taxes. As a rule, in states with high income taxes, this feature adds about 50 to 60 basis points (1/2 of 1% or slightly more) to the yield of a Treasury. As a result, net-after-tax yield of Treasuries (particularly those with maturities under five years) may sometimes be competitive with tax-exempt paper.

TREASURY BILLS, NOTES, AND BONDS

Treasury Bills

Treasury bills are short-dated instruments: they mature in a year or less. A Treasury bill (called a "T-bill" for short) is technically a non-interest-bearing instrument. When you purchase a T-bill, you do not receive interest in the form of a coupon. Instead, the T-bill is sold at a discount from par. When it matures, the Treasury redeems the T-bill at par. The difference between the discounted price paid and the face value of the Bill when it is redeemed is its yield.

The financial pages of major newspapers list T-bill yields daily, at the top of the Table of Bills, Bonds, and Notes. This table is very brief. Table 6–1 shows the format and some of the yields that appeared on August 14, 2000.

Reading from left to right, the listings show the same data as for longer-dated paper:

- The maturity date of the bill
- The days to maturity
- The bid and ask prices
- The change in price
- The yield

Note that the actual yield, rather than the price, is quoted, even under the bid and asked price columns. T-bills are always priced and sold on the basis of yield. The yield changes daily, but seldom by more than a few basis points.

You will see the yield on T-bills quoted in two ways: at the discount at which a T-bill sells from par; and on a so-called "bond

T A B L E   6–1

Treasury Bills Listing

Maturity	Days to Mat.	Bid	Ask	Chg.	Ask-Yld.
Aug 17 '00	3	6.05	5.97	+0.02	6.06
Aug 24 '00	10	6.13	6.05	+0.05	6.14
Aug 31 '00	17	6.08	6.00	+0.09	6.10
Sep 07 '00	24	6.13	6.05	+0.11	6.16
Sep 14 '00	31	6.14	6.10	+0.05	6.22
Sep 21 '00	38	6.35	6.31	+0.25	6.44
Sep 28 '00	45	6.17	6.13	+0.09	6.26
Oct 05 '00	52	6.10	6.06	+0.06	6.20
Oct 12 '00	59	6.11	6.07	+0.05	6.22
Oct 19 '00	66	6.07	6.05	+0.05	6.20
Oct 26 '00	73	6.07	6.05	+0.03	6.21
Nov 02 '00	80	6.07	6.05	+0.02	6.22
Nov 09 '00	87	6.10	6.09	+0.03	6.27

equivalent yield basis." The two are not identical. A simplified explanation is that the discount is quoted on the basis of the one-time premium earned when a T-bill is redeemed, which is equivalent to simple interest. But when a three-month or six-month bill is redeemed, the investor has the opportunity to reinvest that money and earn interest-on-interest. Therefore, the actual rate of return (annualized) is higher than the discounted rate. The bond-equivalent yield of T-bills is always slightly higher (by between ten and 20 basis points) than the discount rate. In effect, the bond equivalent yield of a T-bill, as its name implies, enables you to compare its yield to that of a coupon bearing security. The formula for converting discount rate to bond equivalent yield is complicated, but anyone selling a T-bill has tables quoting both rates.[1]

---

1. Several other factors go into the calculation of bond-equivalent yields. For one thing, the Treasury calculates the price of T-bills as if a year had 360 days. When the yield is annualized (to a 365-day year), the actual yield turns out to be slightly higher than the discount. Also, the bond-equivalent yield is computed on the assumption that the interest-on-interest will compound at the issue rate and for a 364-day year. (One-year bills are actually outstanding for 52 weeks, exactly 364 days.)

T-bills are currently issued in three-month, six-month, and one-year maturities. They are offered in minimum denominations of $10,000, with multiples of $5,000 thereafter. Individuals can purchase bills directly at the Fed's weekly auctions. They can also purchase T-bills trading in the secondary market for any desired maturity—from a few days to one year—from banks or from brokerage firms, for a small fee. T-bills may be resold any time; they are the most liquid of all instruments. T-bills are issued in book-entry form only.

Without a doubt, T-bills are the safest instruments that you can buy. They have zero credit risk. And they are so short that interest rate risk may be ignored. In fact, the yield on the shortest bills is used by investment professionals as a proxy for a risk-free rate of return, and institutions use them as cash equivalents.

Note, however, that while T-bills are perfect as a parking place for cash, they are not appropriate as long-term investments. Over long holding periods, total return is lower than for riskier investments; and reinvestment risk is very high.

Why Treasury Notes Should Be in Your Portfolio

Treasury notes mature in two to ten years. Currently, the Treasury is selling the following maturities:

- ◆ 2-year
- ◆ 5-year
- ◆ 10-year

The Treasury no longer sells three-year, four-year, and seven-year notes.

The price of notes fluctuates more than the price of T-bills in response to interest rate changes, as you would expect given their longer maturities. Consequently, if you need to resell a note before it matures, its price may be higher than you paid or lower than you paid. Price changes, you will remember, are directly tied to maturity length. The smallest price changes would occur for two-year notes and increase gradually as maturity lengthens. Interest rate risk becomes significant after the five-year mark.

Treasury notes are extremely attractive securities. They yield more than T-bills, typically by 50 to 150 basis points, depending on the shape of the yield curve. If you buy and hold to maturity, you are guaranteed to get back 100% of principal. In addition, on a net-after-tax basis, there are times when Treasury notes may actually yield more than tax-exempt paper. This can occur, for example, in states that have high state taxes because Treasury notes are exempt from state and local taxes. Also, whenever the yield curve is inverted (that is, when yields on shorter securities are higher than those on long-dated instruments), Treasury notes maturing in two to five years may yield more than municipal bonds, on an after-tax basis, by a significant amount. Yield curve inversions occurred in 1987 and 1988; as well as in 2000.

If you think you are giving up return by purchasing notes rather than longer-term instruments, think again. Studies have shown that over long periods of time, notes have actually outperformed long-dated Treasuries. One authoritative study, by Ibbotson Associates, showed that between 1926 and 1997, average annual total return for Treasury notes was 5.3%, compared to 5.2% for long-dated governments. (This study is updated annually.) Over long holding periods, the intermediate sector generally has shown the best average annual total returns. The same study shows that, as you would expect, over the same time period, average annual total return for T-bills was a lot lower, only 3.8%.[2]

The higher total return of two- to five-year Treasuries compared to longer-dated paper is due to the lower price volatility in response to interest rate changes and, compared to shorter dated paper, to the fact that two-year paper normally yields more than T-bills (assuming an upward-sloping yield curve).

Treasury Bonds

Treasury bonds are the longest-dated instruments issued by the Treasury, maturing in ten to 30 years. Currently, the Treasury sells a ten-year and a 30-year bond at auction. (It no longer sells either 15- or 20-year bonds.) But because the market in Treasuries is extremely active, any other maturity may be purchased in the secondary market.

---

2. *Stocks, Bonds, Bills and Inflation: 1998 Yearbook* (Chicago: Ibbotson Associates, 1998), 10–30.

You might expect that the 30-year bond would normally yield more than any shorter maturity, assuming that the yield curve is upwards sloping. Curiously, this is normally not the case. The highest yields are usually found somewhere between the ten-year and the 20-year mark. This is because these maturities are less actively traded by dealers and therefore less in demand than either shorter- or longer-dated bonds. They are therefore considered less liquid. The lower demand and lower liquidity result in a higher yield. For an individual investor who does not intend to trade, and therefore, for whom liquidity is not a major concern, that extra yield is a gift. If you want the highest yield possible when buying longer-term Treasuries, the ten-year to 20-year maturities are a good place to look.

Even slight differences in maturity may affect yield. You may see the term "off-the-run security." An off-the-run security is the most recently issued bond in any maturity. For example, the off-the-run 30-year bond is the 30-year bond sold at the most recently held auction. Considered the most liquid 30-year bond, this is the one usually listed as the "long" bond or the bellwether Treasury. Bonds issued just a few months earlier may yield as much as 20 basis points more because of the slightly lower liquidity. Again, if you do not intend to trade, it pays to look for issues with the higher yield.

If you want to "lock in" a return for the longest possible period, purchase an issue maturing close to the current off-the-run Treasury. Long-dated Treasuries enjoy generous call protection. They are not callable for 25 years.

INFLATION-INDEXED SECURITIES

Inflation-indexed securities (also called inflation-linked securities) are an entirely new type of Treasury bond, first introduced in January of 1997. These bonds have a unique feature: the value of the principal (that is, the par value of the bond) is adjusted daily based on the Consumer Price Index for all Urban Consumers, published by the Bureau of Labor Statistics (also known as the CPI-U). As a result, the value of the bond increases at the rate of inflation. In effect, you are guaranteed a real return over and above the inflation rate. Therefore, any money invested in these bonds should retain its purchasing power up until the time the bonds mature.

These bonds are like other Treasury bonds in many respects. They are backed by the full faith and credit of the United States and therefore have the highest credit quality. They are sold at Treasury auctions, on a quarterly basis. As with other Treasury securities, interest is paid twice a year.

But these bonds differ from other Treasuries in some significant ways. The interest rate on inflation-linked bonds is set at the time the bonds are sold at auction. That rate remains in force until the bond matures. But because the value of the principal is adjusted daily at the rate of inflation, interest income rises with inflation: the interest income is calculated based on a constantly higher base. Since the time these bonds were introduced, interest rates at auction have varied from a low of 3 3/8% to a high of 4 1/4%.

Suppose, for example, that you invest $10,000 in inflation-linked bonds and the interest rate is set at auction at 3%. The first interest payment will be 1/2 of 3% multiplied by $10,000, or $150.00. Now further suppose that the CPI rises by 1 1/2% in the first six months. The value of the principal will now rise by 1 1/2%. The bond will now be worth $10,150. The second interest payment will be based on the increased value of the bond. The second interest payment will therefore be 1/2 of 3% multiplied by the new value of the bond: $10,150 or $152.25.

You may be looking at these numbers and thinking something like: "Big deal. A 3% interest rate, and minute adjustments in the amount of the coupon don't amount to very much." But actually, if you estimate the numbers for a bond with a ten-year maturity, the numbers begin to look a lot more attractive. Assume, for example, that inflation averages out to 3% a year. Over that ten-year period, the value of the principal would rise to approximately $13,440. When the bond matures, therefore, instead of the $10,000 you invested, you would redeem the bond at its face value at that time, that is, $13,440. In addition, interest income would rise gradually until, during the 10th year, coupon payments would have increased to about $201.50 twice a year (or $403.00 annually). The nominal rate of return would be equivalent to somewhere between 6 1/2% and 7%.

In effect, what this accomplishes is that you are guaranteed a real rate of return. Historically, the real rate of return on Treasuries has averaged about 3% above the rate of inflation. The structure of inflation-linked bonds guarantees a return equivalent to the real rate of return. Moreover, the structure of these bonds guarantees that the purchasing power of the principal will not erode due to inflation. Finally, as an additional layer of protection, the Treasury guarantees that in the unlikely event deflation occurs, the final value of the bond will not be less than par, or the initial price paid for the bond.

There are, however, a couple of wrinkles to be aware of. In a number of respects, inflation-linked bonds resemble zero coupon bonds. While the value of principal is adjusted daily, any adjustment in the price is not paid out until the bond actually matures. The tax treatment of this adjustment is also similar to that of zero coupon bonds: while you do not receive any inflation adjustments to the value of principal until the bond matures, you will be taxed annually on that amount. (That is sometimes called a tax on "phantom income.") If you are in a high tax bracket, that feature might make these bonds suitable primarily for tax-deferred or tax-advantaged accounts. For investors in low income tax brackets, however, these bonds may be a very good deal. Note also that like other Treasury securities, interest income is not taxable at the state level.

Initially, bonds were sold in five-year and ten-year maturities. The five-year has not been sold recently; but a 30-year maturity has been added. In the future, other maturities may be added. Also, inflation-linked securities will be available for stripping; that is, as zero coupon bonds. Future interest rates may differ from those of the past two years: they will be reset at each auction.

An important point to bear in mind is that while the structure of these bonds is designed to protect the value of your principal, this does not eliminate market risk. An increase in interest rates may cause the price to decline. So can a lack of demand.

Since these bonds were introduced, they have met with very little investor enthusiasm. That may be due to the fact that since 1997 inflation has seemed benign. It may also be due to a lack of understanding of how these bonds actually work: an interest rate of 3% to 4% may have seemed paltry. Whatever the cause, the price of the bonds actually declined in the first year.

BUYING TREASURIES: TREASURY DIRECT

Treasuries can be purchased or sold through banks and brokerage firms. Fees are modest, typically $25 or $50 per transaction, regardless of the amount purchased. Nonetheless, if you buy Treasuries regularly over the course of a year, those small amounts can add up. Also, the smaller the face amount of the securities purchased, the higher those fees are as a percentage of the face amount. Fifty dollars represents 1/2 of 1% of a $10,000 purchase, but 5% of a $1,000 purchase.

Treasury Direct: Buying Treasuries at Auction

It is now possible for individuals to buy Treasury securities directly at auction by establishing an account with the Fed, through its Treasury Direct program. You can buy securities for as little as $1,000, with additional increments of $1,000. This is a very attractive option:

◆ It eliminates all transaction costs.

◆ Individuals receive the same yield as institutional investors.

◆ All of your Treasury securities can be consolidated in one account.

When you open an account through Treasury Direct, you are banking directly with the Fed. Since the program was begun, the Fed has continued to simplify the process of opening and maintaining a Treasury Direct account and of buying or selling Treasuries. Information and any necessary forms can all be downloaded directly from the Web (*publicdebt.treas.com*). If you do not have access to the Web, forms necessary to open an account can be obtained from any of the 12 Federal Reserve Banks or from any of their branches. (The phone numbers of these banks can be obtained from your local bank or from the reference desk of your local public library. Forms can also be obtained by telephoning the Treasury Direct Office in Washington: 1-202-874-4000.)

However you obtain the forms, establishing an account is simple. To open an account, you fill out a one-page form. In addition to your address and social security number, you need to provide the number of an account that you hold with either a commercial bank or a major brokerage firm (such as a cash management account). When you place an order for a bond, the Fed will automatically debit that account for any securities you purchase at auction on the day of the auction. The Fed will also wire interest payments and matured principal directly to that account. And the friendly Fed will notify you when securities mature and ask you whether you want to reinvest or redeem principal. Finally, the Fed will send written confirmations for any transactions that have occurred in your account. In short, the Fed will be your friendly banker. Moreover, the Fed will not charge you for any of this unless your account has over $100,000 in securities. If you have more than that amount, you will be charged an annual fee of $25.00.

Once you have opened an account, you can participate in any auction held by the Fed. To purchase a security, you submit a very brief form called a "noncompetitive tender" whereby you agree to purchase the maturity you select at the average yield of the auction—that is, the average of all the competitive tenders submitted by dealers purchasing billions of dollars worth of securities. Tenders may be submitted in several ways: directly on the Internet; by phone, through the toll-free *Buy Direct* telephone number (1-800-943-6864); or by mail. Bids submitted by phone or via the Internet must be received by the published cutoff time, generally 12:00 noon Eastern Standard Time of the day of the auction. Bids submitted by mail must be postmarked by the day prior to the auction. Finally, tenders may also be submitted in person at any of the 12 federal reserve banks until noon on the day of any auction. All securities are sold in book-entry form only.

Treasury Direct is a highly efficient operation. Interest payments are automatically wired to the account that you designate, as is matured principal. You can choose to automatically reinvest or to withdraw cash periodically. No matter how many different securities are in your account, in whatever combination of maturities you desire, all are held in one central account with one account number. You may access information about your account via the Web or through the Buy Direct toll-free telephone number.

The Treasury Direct program is primarily intended for individuals who intend to buy securities and hold them to maturity. But the Fed has now added a feature called *Sell Direct*, which enables you to sell securities before they mature. If you direct the Fed to sell securities, the Fed will obtain quotes from several brokers and sell at the highest quote obtained. Proceeds from the sale will be deposited automatically into the bank account you have designated. The Fed charges a modest fee for this service (currently $34.00).

A Treasury Direct account enables you to purchase any security, including inflation-linked bonds, in any maturity you desire, from three months to 30 years, and to put together a portfolio that is totally tailored to your needs. One possible strategy would be to stay with notes, in order to minimize interest rate risk. Another popular strategy is to constitute a so-called laddered portfolio, buying, for example, one-year, two-year, three-year, and five-year maturities, and automatically renewing with the same maturities as the securities are redeemed. The average yield of such a portfolio would be about 100 to 150 basis points above money market fund yields and exempt from state taxes. Interest rate risk is low because average maturity would be between two and three years. And the different maturities enable you to take advantage of higher yields as they occur. (Portfolio structure is discussed in greater detail in Chapter 15, dealing with portfolio management.)

Purchasing T-bills, notes, and bonds directly is actually safer than purchasing them through a mutual fund. This is because by buying individual securities and holding them to maturity, you can be certain that you will redeem your principal in entirety. As you will see in Chapters 11 and 12, on bond funds if you buy the same securities through a mutual fund, you may not.

Exact information about upcoming auctions is usually listed in the major financial dailies. In addition, the Fed publishes a tentative three-month calendar in February, May, August, and November which is listed on its website. Minimum amounts required for purchase are $1,000 for any security, with additional increments of $1,000, up to $1,000,000.

Would you like to know the probable yield before you purchase at auction? You can come fairly close by checking the *Table of Treasury Bills, Bonds, and Notes* a few days before the auction for the maturities that interest you. Also, dealers actually begin trading these securities a few days before the auction on a so-called "when issued" basis—that is, in anticipation of the interest rate they will bear when issued. The "when issued" yield is often mentioned in the "credit markets" column of either *The New York Times* or *The Wall Street Journal* on the days preceding the auction.

ZERO COUPON BONDS

Zero coupon bonds (zeros for short) are also colloquially known as "strips." This is not a humorous nickname. The word "strips" actually describes the process of creating zeros.

Behind every zero stands an ordinary so-called plain vanilla U.S. Treasury bond. In 1982, investment banks got the brilliant idea of separating the different revenue streams of government bonds (the coupons-only and the principal-only) and repackaging each separate stream as a distinct security. The zero was born.

Whether the zero is based on the interest-only or principal-only strip is unimportant to the buyer. In either case, the buyer of a zero (like that of a T-bill), does not receive any interest coupons. Instead, the zero is sold at a very deep discount from par, but it matures at par. The difference between the discounted price paid and par represents the interest earned. You will recall that when you invest in ordinary bonds, return on the bond includes interest-on-interest earned by reinvesting the coupons. For long-term maturities, the interest-on-interest is the major source of return. Since zeros have no coupons, you might think you lose that source of income. Quite the contrary. The final lump sum payment is calculated so that it includes the interest-on-interest that would have been received if the coupons had been reinvested periodically *at the yield-to-maturity rate*. That is why zeros seem to multiply like magic. Invest $197.00 in a zero with a coupon rate of 8.3%; in 20 years you will receive $1,000.

Advertising for zeros makes them look like a unique method of creating wealth. You invest a small sum. In a number of years—say, ten—you realize a huge profit, guaranteed. It looks magical. Actually, this is just another manifestation of the magic of compounding. The main difference between a zero and another Treasury of the same maturity is that the zero has no reinvestment risk. The actual return in dollars is known and guaranteed. Furthermore, reinvesting is automatic and efficient: it is built into the structure of the bond. If you buy a Treasury of comparable maturity, the actual return will vary depending on the rates at which you can reinvest coupons. Realized return may be higher or may be lower than for the zero, depending on reinvestment rates.

You should be aware that investing small sums in zeros can be expensive. Markups are high and vary a great deal from dealer to dealer. If the maturity of the zero is short (under five years), the conventional coupon Treasury may actually be the better buy. Locking in a YTM with a zero is an advantage only if the zero has a particularly attractive yield.

Before investing in zeros, you should carefully consider two unique aspects of these securities; namely, the tax treatment of zeros and their extreme volatility.

Even though the owner of a zero receives no interest payments prior to its maturity, the interest that is accrued (earned) is taxed annually as if it were actually paid out. (That interest is known as "imputed interest," or "phantom interest.") As a result of this feature, zeros are suitable mainly for two types of accounts: tax-sheltered accounts such as IRAs or Keoghs, and accounts taxed at low tax rates, such as accounts of children in a low tax bracket.

The volatility of zeros is unique. The basic explanation for the volatility of zeros is to be found in duration. As you will recall, bonds with long durations are more volatile than those with shorter durations. Because zeros have no coupons, their duration is the same as their maturity, far longer than that of ordinary coupon bonds with the same maturity. As a result, the volatility of zeros is much higher than that of ordinary coupon bonds with the same maturity.

To illustrate, let's look at Table 6–2, which shows the percentage price changes that would occur to both zero coupon bonds and ordinary coupon bonds, both yielding 7%, if interest rates rise by 50 basis points, to 7.5%; by 100 basis points, to 8%; and by 200 basis points, to 9%.

As Table 6–2 shows, zeros with two-year maturities are only slightly more volatile than ordinary coupon bonds. But as maturity lengthens, so does volatility. The volatility of the 30-year zero is more than two times that of the 30-year coupon security. If interest rates rise by 200 basis points, from 7% to 9%, the price of a zero with a 7% yield and a 30-year maturity would decline by

T A B L E 6-2

Price Changes for a Given Change in Yields: Coupon Security vs. Zero Coupon Bond, 7% Yield

Change in Yields (Basis Points)	2 yr		5 yr		10 yr		30 yr	
	Coupon Bond	Zero Coupon Bond	Coupon Bond	Zero Coupon Bond	Coupon Bond	Zero Coupon Bond	Coupon Book	Zero Coupon Bond
+50	−0.9%	−1.0%	−2.1%	−2.4%	−3.5%	−4.7%	−5.9%	−13.5%
+100	−1.8%	−1.9%	−4.1%	−4.7%	−6.8%	−9.2%	−11.3%	−25.1%
+200	−3.6%	−3.8%	−7.9%	−9.2%	−13.0%	−17.5%	−20.6%	−43.8%
−50	+0.9%	+1.0%	+2.1%	+2.4%	+3.6%	+5.0%	+6.6%	+15.6%
−100	+1.9%	+2.0%	+4.3%	+5.0%	+7.4%	+10.2%	+13.8%	+33.7%
−200	+3.8%	+4.0%	+8.7%	+10.2%	+15.6%	+21.4%	+30.9%	+79%

approximately 43.8% ($4,380 for a $10,000 investment) compared to 20.6% for the coupon security ($2,060 per $10,000 investment).

If interest rates decline, the price of a zero coupon bond also appreciates at a higher rate than that of a coupon security with the same maturity and yield. Once again, price changes are most dramatic for zero coupon bonds with long maturities. Table 6–2 also illustrates the percentage price changes that would occur to both zeros and ordinary coupon bonds, yielding 7%, if interest rates decline by 50 basis points, to 6.5%; by 100 basis points, to 6%; and by 200 basis points, to 7%.

Once again, price changes for the two-year bond are only modestly higher for the zero coupon bond compared to the regular coupon security. For bonds with intermediate or longer maturities, the sensitivity of a zero coupon bond to interest rate changes turns into a genuine bonanza at the longer end. For example, if interest rates decline by 100 basis points, the price of a zero coupon bond with a 30-year maturity rises by approximately 25% ($2,500 for a $10,000 investment). If interest rates decline by 200 basis points, the price of a zero coupon bond yielding 7%, with a 30-year maturity, goes up by an astonishing 79% ($7,900 for a $10,000 investment)!

Note that, as explained in the section on interest rate risk, the price changes that occur if interest rates fluctuate are greater if interest rates decline than if interest rates go up: you will remember that was called *convexity*. As is shown in Table 6–2, for example, if interest rates go up by 200 basis points, the price of the 30-year, 7% zero declines by 43.8%. But if interest rates decline by the same amount (200 basis points), the price of the 30-year, 7% coupon bond appreciates by 79%. You can readily understand why anyone who anticipates that interest rates will decline buys zeros.

The price changes illustrated assume an instantaneous change in yields. In real life, as noted in the section on interest rate risk, changes of this magnitude would in all likelihood take months, or perhaps years. The numbers in Table 6–2 would therefore have to be adjusted for time. For instance, if the interest rate change were to occur five years after the bonds were initially purchased, then five years would have to be subtracted from the age of the bond. Five years after the purchase date, the ten-year bond would have become a five-year bond, and so on.

Note also that the exact price swings illustrated in Table 6–2 are accurate only for bonds with a 7% yield. Price changes would be somewhat higher or lower for bonds with different yields.

Note once again that the interest rate changes illustrated are entirely plausible. Between September of 1998 and December of 1999, interest rates on the 30-year bond went from a low of 4.78% to a high of 6.75%. In the beginning of 2000, the interest rate on the long bond reversed steeply, declining to approximately 5.75% between January and the end of March.

In sum, while there is no risk to principal if you hold a zero to maturity, if you want to resell it before it matures, its value may have gone up a great deal or may have declined significantly.

Zeros for Investment Purposes

The peculiarities of zeros makes them ideal investments for several totally different purposes.

First zeros are ideal investments for tax-sheltered accounts such as IRAs or Keoghs, particularly if you would like to invest small sums periodically. Suppose, for instance, that you want to invest $2,000 annually in an IRA account. Because of the unique structure of zeros, $2,000 enables you to buy a much larger par amount of bonds, particularly if you are young and retirement is 20 or 30 years away. Furthermore, since the zeros are in a tax-deferred account, you can forget about paying taxes on phantom income. And finally, you can select maturities so that they coincide with any date you select. That can be the year you retire. Or you can build an annuity by buying bonds that will mature every year in succession starting with the year you retire and thereafter, for the next 15 or 20 years.

Second, zeros can be used to speculate on interest rate moves. As illustrated earlier, because of their extreme volatility, any change in interest rates has a dramatic impact on the price of zero coupon bonds, particularly those with long maturities. If you think interest rates are about to decline and you want to profit from such a move, you would buy zeros with long maturities. Then, if you are right, you will be able to resell your zeros with a significant capital gain. The legendary investor Warren Buffett was said to have made just such a purchase of zero coupon bonds with 30-year maturities in 1998, and for precisely this reason. Managers of many types of bond funds (or even of equity funds) routinely buy zeros to boost returns if they think interest rates are about to decline.

If you are wrong, on the other hand, and interest rates rise, then your downside risk is twofold. You may have to hold the zero to maturity (or longer than you expected). Also, and perhaps less important to you, there is the opportunity cost of not receiving the higher interest rate. There would be no risk of loss of principal, however, unless you actually decided to sell the zero. But, given the unreliability of interest rate forecasts, it is not advisable to buy zeros primarily in order to make interest rate bets unless you are prepared to hold them to maturity (or for a very long time) in the event that you are wrong.

Finally, zeros can be used to put aside money for a known future need such as a child's college tuition. The total return when the zero matures is known and guaranteed. The problem here would be the phantom interest generated by a Treasury zero, which generates annual taxes. You should be aware, however, that you can buy municipal zeros (they will be discussed in the next chapter), and municipal zeros might be more appropriate for this type of use if you are in a high income bracket.

U.S. SAVINGS BONDS

U.S. savings bonds were initially sold during World War II. The government now sells several types of savings bonds, and some of these have extremely attractive features. Savings bonds are described in excruciating detail in a continually updated website maintained by the Bureau of the Public Debt: *savingsbonds.gov,* as well as *publicdebt.treas.gov.* I will briefly describe some of the outstanding features of these bonds. Because the rules governing interest rates and actual bonds available have undergone so many changes, I will stick to the basics. If, after reading this section, you think savings bonds are for you, and you have access to the Internet, that is your best source of information. If you do not, then your local savings bank is your next best bet.

Several series of savings bonds are now available:

+ Series EE/E
+ Series HH/H
+ Series I

These bonds have important differences. *Series EE bonds* are accrual bonds; that is, as with zero coupon bonds or bills, you do not receive coupon interest while you hold the bonds. Instead, interest accrues until the bond matures or is redeemed for cash. The difference between the price you pay and the amount you receive when you redeem the bonds is based on interest rates prevailing during the life of the bond, as well as on accrued interest-on-interest.

Series HH bonds are purchased for current income. Interest income is paid twice a year.

Series I bonds are the newest of the savings bonds. They were first introduced in September 1998. To remember the main feature of I bonds, think "I" and inflation. I bonds resemble inflation-indexed bonds. They are an accrual bond, meaning that you do not receive coupon interest while you hold the bonds. Interest is added to the bond on a monthly basis and paid when the bond is cashed or redeemed. But, as for inflation-linked bonds, interest payments are adjusted for inflation based on the Consumer Price Index for All Urban Consumers (CPI-U). In effect, interest income grows at an inflation-indexed rate.

All series share a number of characteristics. Since all these bonds are direct obligations of the U.S. government, their credit quality is impeccable. Moreover, any of these series has attractive tax features. Interest income is exempt from state and local taxes. In addition, you may defer payment of taxes on *all* interest income until the bonds are redeemed, which makes these bonds very attractive for individuals who may not have other tax-deferred accounts. Finally, interest income of both I bonds and EE bonds, under certain circumstances, may be *entirely tax-free* if used to pay certain college expenses. You can purchase any of these series in very small amounts (as little as $25.00 for I bonds) to amounts as large as $1 million. But each of these bonds has some unique characteristics. I shall describe some of the key features.

Series EE Bonds

These are the first savings bonds that were issued. The government has changed the features of these bonds in order to make them more attractive. As a result, interest rates have varied widely since the inception of the program, depending on their issue date. Bonds issued in 1997 or thereafter earn the most generous rates: 90% of the average rate of five-year Treasury notes for the previous six months. Interest rates are reset every six months. Interest rates of EE bonds issued prior to 1997 were sometimes market based and other times set at time of issue.

As noted above, EE bonds are accrual securities. You receive accrued interest when the bonds are redeemed. EE bonds are sold at 50% of face value. For example, you would buy a $100 face value bond for $50. You cannot predict at the time you buy the bonds when they will reach face value, because that will depend on the interest rates prevailing while you hold the bonds.

EE bonds were originally sold with maturity dates ranging from eight to 17 years. But when the bonds reach maturity, most go into an automatic extension period, usually about ten years. At the current time, most EE bonds can earn interest for up to 30 years. You need not hold EE bonds until they mature, however. EE bonds can be redeemed anytime after six months. However, if you redeem prior to five years, there is a penalty, which is that you forfeit interest payments for the last three months.

EE bonds share the attractive tax features mentioned above. Taxes on these bonds are deferred until you actually cash in the bonds, as long as you hold the bonds for at least five years. EE bonds are also eligible for an education tax exclusion (see below).

EE bonds can now be purchased directly on line for face amounts of up to $1,000. They can also be purchased from your local bank. And employers can set up an automatic deduction plan called *EasySaver*. Minimum amounts that can be purchased are $25.00 ($50 face). The maximum amount is $5,000 ($10,000 face). There are no commissions of any type. The maximum that can be purchased during any one year is $15,000 purchase price ($30,000 face amount).

If you own EE bonds purchased prior to 1997 (or since that date, for that matter) and want to know what the bonds are currently worth or how much interest they are currently earning, you can, of course, check with your local bank. But there are also two sources of information on the Internet, both maintained by the government. One is called the *Savings Bond Wizard* (more about the Wizard below); and the other is called the *Savings Bonds Earnings Report*.

In February of 2000, EE bonds were being sold with an interest rate of 5.19%.

HH Bonds

Unlike EE bonds, HH bonds are purchased for income. These bonds do not change in value: interest income is paid every six months, at a rate set when you buy the bonds. The current rate, 4%, was set in 1993, when these bonds were first introduced. Interest rates will be reset on the 10th anniversary of the HH bonds issue date.

You cannot buy HH bonds for cash. You can get them only in exchange for EE bonds; and the securities you exchange must have a minimum value of $500. There is no maximum limit. These bonds are bought for face amounts ranging from $500 to $10,000. The price you pay is the face amount.

These are probably the least attractive of the savings bonds because the interest rate they pay is low and not market based. The most attractive feature of HH bonds is that you can continue to defer taxes on interest payments until you cash in the bonds or until they reach maturity. Also, because the rates are not market based, the bonds will not decline in value if interest rates rise.

I Bonds

These are the newest and most attractive of the savings bonds. They resemble EE bonds in a number of respects. Like EE bonds, they are accrual securities, which means that you do not receive interest payments (coupon income) until you redeem the bonds. Also, as with EE bonds, taxes on interest can be deferred until the bonds are redeemed or until maturity, that is, for up to 30 years. Finally, also like EE bonds, they are eligible for the education exclusion.

The major difference between I bonds and EE bonds, however, is to be found in the procedures followed to determine and to reset interest rates. I bonds are basically inflation-linked savings bonds. The earnings rate of I bonds is a combination of two separate rates: a fixed rate of return and a variable semiannual inflation rate. The fixed rate is set when the bonds are initially sold, and it remains the same throughout the life of the bond. But the semiannual inflation rate adjustment is reset every six months, based on the CPI-U. In the unlikely event that deflation occurs, the value of the bond remains at its pre-deflation level.

I bonds have several major advantages. Because interest rates of I bonds are indexed to inflation, and because interest rates are based on compounding of both principal and interest, the value of the bond rises with inflation, like that of inflation-linked bonds. But in addition, the interest rate set at the time of issue guarantees a minimum return. Finally, and this is an important difference, because I savings bonds do not trade in the secondary market, the value of the bonds can never go down. The value of inflation-linked bonds, on the other hand, fluctuates in the secondary market as interest rates change.

I bonds are sold for face amounts ranging from $50 to $10,000. They are purchased at face value: you pay $50 for a $50 bond. You can buy up to $30,000 worth of I bonds each calendar year. I Bonds can be bought directly through the Internet, at a local bank, or through an employer-sponsored plan such as *EasySaver*. I bonds have a maturity of 30 years, but they can be redeemed any time after six months. Because these bonds are structured primarily as long-term investments, there is a small penalty for redeeming I bonds within five years of purchase: you would forfeit three months of interest if you cashed out your bonds within five years.

In February of 2000, I bonds were being sold with a combined interest rate of 6.98%, which is a combination of a fixed rate of 3.4% and an inflation adjustment rate of about 3.5%. This combined rate was well above that of 30-year Treasuries and that of EE bonds at the same date. The combined rate is likely to decline if inflation continues to be low.

Using I Bonds to Set Up a Deferred-Tax Retirement Plan

Have I got a deal for you! I'm going to offer you a retirement plan with the following features:

+ You can invest any amount, from $50 to $10,000, and invest up to $30,000 per calendar year.
+ The amounts invested will accrue interest at a guaranteed minimum rate set at the time you buy; but

an additional interest component will be added, which
will be reset every six months, based on the inflation
rate. In the event deflation occurs, the minimum interest
rate will remain in effect. In the event interest rates rise,
the value of this bond (*unlike that of any other bond,
including Treasuries, that trade in the secondary market*) will
not decline.

+ Interest and interest-on-interest will compound, tax
  deferred, until you choose to cash in some bonds, for
  income or for any purpose you choose. You can cash out
  any sum you wish, any time you wish, after six months.
  But you can also leave the money to compound for up to
  30 years. Both purchases and withdrawals can be tailored
  to your needs.
+ Interest income is exempted from state and local taxes.
+ Interest rates are attractive: currently above those of the
  ten-year and 30-year bonds.
+ The credit quality of these bonds is of the highest quality.
  There is zero default risk.
+ You can buy these securities at no cost: no commissions
  of any kind. Furthermore, the organization that sells you
  these bonds will maintain your account free of charge to
  you.
+ You can buy these bonds in the privacy of your home,
  via the Internet. You can also set up an automatic
  withdrawal plan through your employer; or you can buy
  these bonds from your local bank.

Sound too good to be true? I have just repeated all the features I described above, because those are the features of I bonds.
They bear repetition because this product is a sleeper: I have seen
almost no mention of it in the financial press. Obviously, brokerage firms do not recommend I bonds even if they could sell them,
because they can't make any money on them. Banks are unlikely
to push I bonds: they compete with CDs, and banks don't make
any money selling you I bonds. But if you compare the features
of I bonds to those of other products designed to provide tax-
deferred income, such as annuities, I bonds are likely to be the
superior product.

I would suggest that if you are looking for a very safe, very predictable investment for some of the assets being put away for retirement, you should investigate I bonds before signing up for expensive and restrictive annuities, particularly if you are going to be investing in fixed-income instruments.

Savings Bonds for Education: The Education Tax Exclusion

Both EE and I series bonds can be purchased to qualify for the education tax exclusion. That means, essentially, that either series of bonds can be used to save for a child's college education, tax free. If the proceeds from savings bonds are used to pay college expenses, no federal taxes are due. Note that only college fees and tuition qualify for the exclusion; board and room, books, and other miscellaneous college expenses do not qualify.

Under normal conditions, either series of savings bonds will in all likelihood be more advantageous than munis. Note, however, that the tax exemption holds only if the bonds are bought in the parent's name (not that of the child whose tuition will be paid). That may not seem logical, but that is the way it is. Also, to be eligible for the tax exemption, the parents' income must meet certain income guidelines. These caps are reset and pegged to the inflation rate. For the year 2000, the full interest exclusion applies to joint incomes under $81,100, with partial exclusions for incomes up to $111,100 ($54,100 and $60,100 for single filers).

Once again, the details are somewhat complex. But the program is attractive enough to be of interest to most families in the middle income brackets.

One final note. The government program for savings bonds is designed to help individual investors save for a variety of purposes. While I have not gone into every possible detail, the government is trying to make this program as simple and user-friendly as possible. There are provisions for all kinds of eventualities; for example, it is possible to replace lost bonds. The program is clearly designed for individual investors. It is surprisingly versatile and worth checking out.

FEDERAL AGENCIES

Most federal agencies that sell debt instruments are classified as *Government-sponsored enterprises* (GSEs). These federal agencies are privately owned. They were created by Congress to reduce borrowing costs for sectors of the economy deemed essential, including farmers, homeowners, and students. Federal agencies sell bonds in order to raise capital, which in turn is loaned to designated borrowers.

Because bonds issued by federal agencies are not direct obligations of the U.S. government, credit quality is deemed to be not as impeccable as that of Treasuries. In spite of this distinction, the credit quality of debt issued by federal agencies is very high. But because of this distinction, bonds issued by federal agencies generally yield more than Treasuries with the same maturities by anywhere from 50 to 150 basis points, depending on current interest rates and supply factors.

GSEs issue two types of instruments: discount notes (similar to T-bills), with maturities under one year, and bonds, with maturities of two years or more. Zeros also exist for agency debt. Only debt sold by the Federal National Mortgage Association (Fannie Mae or FNMA), Federal Land Banks, and Federal Home Loan Banks (FHLB) is exempt from state and local taxes. Other agency paper is not exempt.

This is still a small market compared to the market for U.S. Treasuries. Moreover, it remains primarily an institutional market because minimums required to buy these bonds are high. But if, as anticipated, the U.S. Treasury reduces the amount of debt it will issue, then debt issued by agencies may become a more important source of fixed-income instruments for individual investors. There are some preliminary indications this may happen. A number of agencies have already announced that they will issue debt more frequently and with maturities more similar to Treasury debt. In the future, it is possible that additional accommodations will tailor some of this debt more closely to match the needs of individual investors.

As this book is going to press (in August 2000), Congress may be revisiting the implicit guarantee that Agency debt has traditionally enjoyed. Some members of Congress are concerned that the amounts of debt issued by the various agencies may grow excessively; and that, in the event defaults occur, this will create a situation analogous to the Savings and Loan crisis of the late 1980s, which required massive government bailouts, costing taxpayers well over $100 billion to resolve. To date, the immediate result has been that the spread between the yields of agency debt and those of Treasuries has widened. At this point, it is not possible to predict whether, in the future, agency debt will retain its unquestioned implicit government guarantee, or not.

The two agencies that are likely to be familiar to you are the Government National Mortgage Association (GNMA or, more familiarly, Ginnie Mae) and the Federal National Mortgage Association (FNMA, or Fanny Mae). The bonds issued by these two agencies are described extensively in the chapter discussing mortgage-backed securities. A brief list of some other agencies follows.

Federal Home Loan Banks (FHLBs)

These are the 12 regional banks which back the nation's Savings and Loans (S & Ls). They are actually owned by the private S & Ls. Bonds issued by the FHLBs are known as *consolidated* bonds because they are joint obligations of the 12 Federal Home Loan Banks. That means that in the event one bank experiences financial difficulties, the other 11 banks are under a legal obligation to step in and cover any payments due by the weaker bank. The credit quality of these bonds is very high.

These bonds are issued in maturities of one year or more; are not callable; and are sold in denominations of $10,000, $25,000, and above. The Federal Home Loan Banks also issue short-term securities in the form of discount notes, in minimum amounts of $50,000.

Farm Credit Agencies

These are obligations of the 37 Farm Credit Agencies. Like the FHLB, they are consolidated obligations. The Farm Credit Agencies issue a variety of short instruments that require a minimum investment of $50,000, as well as longer-term paper, in denominations of $1,000 and up.

Student Loan Marketing Association

This agency is colloquially known as Sallie Mae. It provides liquidity for private lenders participating in a number of loan programs for students. Sallie Mae is allowed to purchase and offer investors participation in student loans. Sallie Mae issues unsecured debt obligations in the form of discount notes. It also issues floating-rate, short-term debt, zero coupon bonds, and some longer-term paper.

Debt of any of these agencies can be purchased from banks or from brokerage firms. Brief tables of yields of agency bonds are published daily in the pages of national financial newspapers and on the weekend in *Barron's*. They can also be found on websites maintained by financial publications and on websites specializing in financial data, such as *Bloomberg*. The listings for agency debt follow the same format as those of Treasuries.

Treasuries and Savings Bonds vs. Bank CDs

Insured CDs of banks are a popular alternative to short and intermediate Treasuries. No doubt the bank CDs owe their popularity to the fact that they are insured. Because both are extremely safe, let's go over some of the advantages and disadvantages of each.

Treasuries have the following features. They have no credit risk. They are more liquid than CDs. They can be sold any time with no interest penalty. There is no upper limit on the amount that is "insured." Finally, interest is exempt from state and local taxes. Their major disadvantage compared to CDs is that if you sell a two-to-five-year note before maturity, changes in interest rate levels may result in some loss of principal.

Interest earned on CDs is subject to state and local taxes. Due to the savings and loan crisis that occurred during the late 1980s, there have been a number of proposals in Congress to limit the amount that the government will continue to insure in thrifts or in savings and loans accounts. Although to date all of these proposals have died, they resurface from time to time and one version might finally be adopted.

Note also that many large brokerage firms sell insured CDs. The advantage is that these firms stand ready to buy back your CDs if you need to resell before they mature. This feature makes them more liquid than ordinary bank CDs. But then, of course, the value of the principal in the CD fluctuates with interest rates.

As explained earlier, the various bonds offered through the Savings Bonds program (I, EE, and HH) have undergone many changes and offer increasingly attractive options: market-based interest rates; the opportunity to invest sums as small as $25 or as large as $30,000 per calendar year; numerous tax advantages, including tax exemption from state and local taxes; tax exemption for many although not for all, investors, if interest income is used for paying college tuition; and tax deferral until the bonds are redeemed. Finally, I bonds are indexed to inflation and therefore offer important purchasing power protection to anyone planning to hold these bonds for long time periods.

Will the Long Bond Continue to Be the Bellwether Bond?

In late 1999 and early 2000, the U.S. Treasury made a number of startling announcements. The Treasury Department let it be known that from this time on forward, due to the large surplus generated by the U.S. economy, it would hold auctions of the 30-year bond only once a year. Furthermore, the Treasury would also buy back some bonds issued earlier.

These announcements created a good deal of uncertainty in the credit markets. The Treasury's 30-year bond (the long bond) has been the anchor for the credit markets in the United States, and indeed, the bellwether for credit markets worldwide. But this was not always the case. In the 1960s, bonds issued by utilities and by major corporations were considered the key sectors. This domination ceased because the U.S. government became the largest issuer of bonds in the world. As a result, the market in U.S. Treasuries became the largest and most liquid bond market worldwide.

It is too early to tell what the long-term effects of these announcements are likely to be. The immediate reaction in the credit markets was a rush to buy 30-year bonds on the part of major institutional investors who buy large numbers of long-term bonds to meet future liabilities. Paradoxically, this resulted in a decline in interest rates at a time when the Federal Reserve was widely believed to be trying to raise interest rates in order to slow down the growth rate of the U.S. economy.

Many issues remain unresolved. One of these is whether the United States will curtail its issuance not only of 30-year bonds,

but of other maturities as well. There has also been a lot of speculation about what other issue might replace the 30-year bond as
a bellwether. The assumption during most of 2000 has been that
the ten-year bond would replace the 30-year as the bellwether
issue. That is not certain, however. Many sources of financial news
now list both the ten-year and the 30-year as bellwethers. Other
candidates have also appeared. Some federal agencies, for example, have declared that they will issue bonds more frequently, with
maturities similar to those of Treasuries, in order to appeal to investors who up to this time favored Treasuries.

To date, none of these issues has been resolved. While many
experts are claiming that the ten-year bond is now the bellwether
bond, most sites continue to list the 30-year as the bellwether issue. It is too early to tell what effect, if any, this will have on the
credit markets of the future.

Treasuries on the Web

The website maintained by the Bureau of the Public Debt *public-
debt.treas.gov* is in a class by itself. This website is detailed, updated continually, and easy to use. It is your best source of information about any debt instrument issued by the US government.
You can buy Treasuries online, with no commission, through *Treasury Direct* and sell Treasuries through *Sell Direct* for a modest fee.
The friendly Fed will also maintain an account for you, at no cost,
through Treasury Direct.

For Savings Bonds, the Treasury maintains an interactive
website: *the Savings Bond Wizard*. The Wizard is also accessed
through *publicdebt.treas.gov,* The Wizard enables you to maintain
an inventory of any savings bonds you own from any series, and
to calculate their current value and how much they are earning.
The site will also give you all types of information on any bond
you are tracking, including the yield to date and the final maturity
date of any old bonds you own. It has a spread sheet format and
update functions. In short, it will keep complete track of your
bonds for you. You can, of course, order savings bonds online.

If you do not remember the exact web addresses for this site,
just type the words: "Treasury Bonds" or "Savings Bonds" into
any search engine, and you will also reach the Treasury's website.

Treasuries, incidentally, are sold by all brokers, including on-line brokers. Markups on Treasuries are usually extremely modest, because Treasuries are the most liquid of all debt instruments. But since you can buy Treasuries online through Treasury Direct, why would you ever want to buy through any other broker? For two reasons. One would be to buy Treasury zeros. Those are not sold directly by the Fed. And markups on those may be high. So comparison shopping on the web may pay off for zeros. Also, if you want to buy older, not off-the-run, securities, particularly for longer maturities, in order to lock in the highest yields, there too buying from an online broker would enable you to buy bonds not sold directly at auctions.

All financial websites list yield information for benchmark issues of Treasuries, as well as Treasury yield curves. *Bloomberg*, *investinginbonds.com*, and *GovPx* update treasury yields several times daily, and that is the closest you can come to realtime quotes in the fixed-income market.

SUMMARY

Treasury bills, notes, and bonds are the safest and the most liquid securities that can be bought for any maturity. Historically, Treasury notes with maturities between two and five years have had a better total return than either T-bills or long-term bonds. They are particularly attractive investments for anyone looking for safety of principal and predictable returns. Increasingly, the Savings Bonds Program also offers numerous advantages for investors planning to hold bonds for long time periods.

SUMMARY: QUESTIONS TO ASK WHEN BUYING TREASURIES

How much interest rate risk am I assuming?

Where on the yield curve is the best current trade-off between yield and interest rate risk?

CHAPTER 7

Municipal Bonds

This chapter discusses

- Unique characteristics of municipal bonds
- When it pays to buy municipal bonds (taxable-equivalent yield)
- Credit quality: general obligation vs. revenue bonds
- Municipal bond insurance and other credit enhancements
- Municipal bonds with special features
- Municipal bond pricing
- Buying and selecting municipal bonds

WHAT IS UNIQUE ABOUT MUNICIPAL BONDS?

Municipal bonds, "munis" for short, are issued by city, county, and state governments, as well as by enterprises with a public purpose, such as certain electric utilities, universities, and hospitals. For individual investors, the chief attraction of municipal bonds is that they are federally tax exempt. If you live in the state issuing the bonds, with a few exceptions, they are also exempt from state and local taxes, or, as the ads proclaim, triple tax free.

The Tax Reform Act of 1986, which eliminated many loopholes and tax shelters, left municipal bonds as one of the last genuine tax shelters available to the individual investor. This Act, moreover, made munis much less attractive to former institutional buyers (mainly banks and insurance companies). As a result, the municipal market is the only sector of the bond market where the primary buyers are individual investors. This has led issuers to add features to munis that make them more attractive to individuals. It has resulted, for example, in the phenomenal growth of bond insurance.

Overwhelmingly, munis deserve their popularity among individual investors. Even though there are thousands of issues outstanding, muni securities are sound and relatively uncomplicated instruments. Nonetheless, munis require more caution than Treasuries. Interest risk should be a concern, but it is sometimes ignored. Credit quality is an important consideration. But ratings are not always understood. Also, in spite of the tax exemption, many investors would earn more after taxes on alternative investments. Commission costs, particularly for selling munis, are high. This almost dictates a buy-and-hold strategy.

In addition, it is difficult to obtain information concerning munis. Coverage of munis in the daily financial press is virtually nonexistent. Few stockbrokers have any real interest in this area. Industry sources tell me that this situation may actually have worsened as we cross the millennium. Because of the enormous bull market in equities, many talented and ambitious brokers have exited the bond market to sell equities. As a result, finding a salesperson who really knows this market may be difficult. For most individual investors, however, obtaining accurate pricing information continues to be the major hurdle. It is still virtually impossible to determine the size of the markup, that is, the spread between the "bid" and the "ask" price. Every dealer has a different markup, and so far, virtually no one discloses the markup.

This situation is beginning to change, but slowly. An effort to improve disclosure and to move towards what is called in the industry greater "transparency" has been under way since 1991. At that time the Municipal Securities Rulemaking Board, which functions as an arbiter for the industry, together with underwriters and firms that disseminate information to major broker-dealers, approved the establishment of a centralized data bank or electronic library which would function as a central clearing house

for information. At long last, this initiative has had some results. A limited amount of pricing information is now available
on the Internet on the website of the Bond Market Association:
investinginbonds.com. Another website: *munistatements.com* contains
the official statements of many older issues trading in the secondary market. Both of these websites will be discussed in greater
detail further on in the chapter.

All of this means that buyers of munis must still make a
special effort to understand exactly what they are buying and why.
Munis are not the right product for every investor. Let's see if they
belong in your portfolio.

SHOULD I BUY MUNIS? (OR, TAXABLE-EQUIVALENT YIELD)

No one likes to pay taxes. But not everyone benefits from buying
tax-exempt bonds. If you are in a low tax bracket, you may actually earn more by buying taxable bonds and paying the taxes.
Yet a surprising number of individuals buy tax-exempt bonds
when it makes no economic sense for them. It would appear that
they are suffering from a disease called "taxaphobia."

If you are considering buying munis, your first step should
be to determine whether you will earn more by buying munis or
by buying taxable instruments. That decision requires some arithmetic. The method used most often is to calculate how much you
would have to earn on taxable investments to earn as much as
you net on municipal bonds. This is called the "taxable-equivalent
yield." Exhibit 7–1 shows what some municipal bond yields are
worth in various tax brackets.

If tax brackets or yields change, the taxable-equivalent yield
is easy to calculate The first step is to determine your exact tax
bracket. The formula for computing the taxable-equivalent yield
is:

$$\text{taxable-equivalent yield} = \frac{\text{tax-exempt yield}}{(1 - \text{tax bracket})}$$

For example, suppose you are in the 39% tax bracket and you are
considering purchasing a muni yielding 5% (YTM). To obtain the
tax-equivalent yield, convert percentages to decimals. Your calculation looks like this:

E X H I B I T   7–1

Tax-Exempt and Taxable-Equivalent Yields

TAX BRACKET	15%	28%	31%	36%	39.6%
TAX-EXEMPT YIELDS (%)	TAXABLE YIELD EQUIVALENTS (%)				
2.0%	2.35%	2.78%	2.90%	3.12%	3.31%
2.5	2.94	3.47	3.62	3.91	4.14
3.0	3.53	4.17	4.35	4.69	4.97
3.5	4.12	4.86	5.07	5.47	5.79
4.0	4.71	5.56	5.80	6.25	6.62
4.5	5.29	6.25	6.52	7.03	7.45
5.0	5.88	6.94	7.25	7.81	8.28
5.5	6.47	7.64	7.79	8.59	9.11
6.0	7.06	8.33	8.70	9.37	9.93
6.5	7.65	9.03	9.42	10.16	10.76
7.0	8.24	9.72	10.14	10.94	11.59

Source: *investinginbonds.com* (website of the Bond Market Association). Reprinted with permission.

$$\text{taxable-equivalent yield} = \frac{.05}{1 - .39} = .082 \text{ or } 8.2\%$$

Translation: you would have to earn 8.20% in a taxable security in order to earn an equivalent yield.

If you are in the 15% tax bracket, the same calculation results in a taxable-equivalent yield on the same 5% muni of 5.88%. You may actually earn more by buying a taxable instrument.

Many buyers in states with high taxes, such as New York, California, Massachusetts, and Minnesota, prefer to buy munis free of state taxes. But again, demand for a tax-exempt paper from these states may be so high that you may earn more on out-of-state munis (federally tax exempt, but not exempt from taxes in your own state) than on munis from your own state. The yields in Exhibit 7–1 and in the preceding examples should be further adjusted for state taxes.

To determine whether in-state bonds are more attractive than out-of-state bonds, another procedure is to compute the net-after-tax yield—that is, what you are left with after paying the tax. Suppose, for example, that you are considering two tax-exempt securities: one in-state and one out-of-state. The out-of-state bond yields 6%. The in-state bond yields 5.6%. Which will earn more? To calculate, subtract the state tax from 100% and multiply the out-of-state interest by that amount. This tells you what you would keep after paying the state tax. For the preceding example, if you assume an 8% state tax, the calculation is as follows:

- Subtract 8% from 100%, to get 92%.
- Convert to decimals and multiply the out-of-state yield of 6% by 0.92.
- The net-after-tax yield is 5.52%. In this case, the in-state bond yield is slightly higher.

Finally, before purchasing, consider other factors, such as maturity length, credit quality, or liquidity.

There are some fine points to remember when comparing taxable-equivalent yields. First, remember that Treasury and some federal agency paper are both exempt from state taxes. Particularly in high-tax states, either Treasuries or securities issued by certain agencies may net you more, net-after-taxes, than municipals. This is particularly true if you are buying short maturities because the yield curve of munis tends to be more steeply upward sloping than that of taxable bonds. Also, if you are considering purchasing discount muni bonds, remember that the YTM for those bonds includes a capital gains component, which is federally taxable. Particularly if the discount is substantial, you may want to determine how much the capital gains taxes would decrease the total YTM. Finally, if you are comparing two different bonds, make sure that you are comparing the same quoted yield. Usually it will be the YTM.

As a rule, taxpayers in the highest tax brackets benefit from buying tax-exempt bonds; those in the lowest do not. Whether tax-exempts make economic sense for investors in the middle depends on the relationship between taxable and tax-exempt yields at the time of purchase (these change continually), as well as on current tax laws, and of course on your income. Whenever any of these change, by all means recalculate.

CREDIT QUALITY: GENERAL OBLIGATION VS. REVENUE BONDS

Much of what has been previously published concerning municipal bonds is devoted to elaborate guidelines for analyzing individual municipal credits. Unfortunately, this information may not be particularly useful. Few investors have either the time or the access to information to perform extensive credit analyses. First, you would need a prospectus. For new issues, the prospectus may be unavailable for several days until after the bond sale. For issues trading in the secondary market, the prospectus may not be available at all. Secondly, when your broker "shows" you a bond, you may have only a few hours to decide whether to buy. So what is a poor investor going to do?

In practice, most individual investors rely on the ratings assigned by the rating agencies (see Chapter 3). But there is so much confusion concerning municipal ratings that I would like to clear up some common misconceptions and to describe the essentials that any investor should understand.

Municipal bonds come in two varieties: "general obligation" and "revenue." General obligation bonds (also called GOs) are issued by states, cities, or counties to raise money for schools, sewers, road improvements, and the like. Monies to pay interest to bondholders are raised through taxes and some user fees. Revenue bonds are issued by a variety of enterprises that perform a public function, such as electric utilities, toll roads, airports, hospitals, universities, and other specially created "authorities." Money to pay interest to bondholders is generated by the enterprise of the issuer. Electric utilities depend on the fees paid by users of electricity; hospitals depend on patient revenues; toll roads depend on tolls, and so on.

One misconception concerning municipal bonds is that GOs are much safer than revenues. There are strong and weak credits in each bond sector. The supposed safety of GOs is ascribed to the fact that they are backed by the taxing power of the issuer. Theoretically, that power is "unlimited" because bond indentures state that general obligation bonds are backed "by the unlimited taxing power of the issuer." In the real world, however, the power to tax is limited by political and economic considerations. The classic

question any analyst has to ask is, in the event there is an economic crunch, who will the issuer pay, its teachers, police, and
fire department, or the bondholders? If municipalities could tax
at will, all GOs would be AAA, and as we know, this is not the
case.

Similarly, the supposed lower safety of revenue bonds is
based on the fact that issuers run businesses whose revenues cannot be predicted with certainty. Again, that bears little relationship
to what goes on in the real world. Most electric utilities and toll
roads can, and do, raise rates to pay for increasing costs. Consequently, many revenue bonds, particularly those issued for essential services such as electric power, sewer, or water, are high-
quality credits. So are many toll roads or state authorities.

How much importance should you ascribe to differences in
rating among sound quality credits (A or A+, or higher)? Not as
much as you might expect. It's more important to understand
what is behind the rating. Ratings of GOs are determined by the
overall economic strength of the tax base compared to debt service
requirements. AAA issuers have flourishing tax bases, a strong
and diversified economy not dependent on a single industry, low
levels of overall debt, and/or a strong tradition of prudent fiscal
management. But factors other than the economy are also critical
to GO ratings. One of them is size. Small cities or counties which
come infrequently to market, even those with prudent fiscal management, are generally not rated higher than A. They may nonetheless be strong credits, particularly if you know the communities
and are purchasing intermediate maturities. Some wealthy communities have issued so little debt that they do not even have a
rating!

Ratings of revenue bonds revolve around an analysis of revenues generated by sales, compared to money needed to cover
interest payments (debt service). In practice, the rating is determined by a key ratio known as the "debt service coverage ratio,"
which is defined as the amount of money specifically available for
payment of debt service divided by the amount of debt service to
be paid. This ratio is calculated for the past. How much money
was actually available for debt service last year or for the past five
years? It is also estimated for the future. How much money is
going to be available next year, and the year after, and so on, for

debt service? The past ratio is called "the historical debt service ratio."

An historical debt service ratio of at least two is generally required for an A rating. That ratio indicates that monies reserved for payment of debt service were equal to twice the amount needed for debt service. An historical ratio of five or six times debt service is considered fantastic. An historical ratio below one, indicating there wasn't enough money in the till to cover debt service, would almost guarantee a below investment grade rating. Nonetheless, no matter how sound their management or how strong debt service coverage has been, revenue bonds are almost never rated AAA on their own merit. This does not make them unattractive investments—just the opposite. They yield more than GOs.

In the late 1980s, hospitals were viewed as particularly risky because of the stresses on the medical system. But even in this area there were some very strong credits: for example, teaching hospitals affiliated with outstanding universities, such as Massachusetts General, which is affiliated with Harvard University, or strong chains, such as the Sisters of Charity hospitals in the Midwest.

Also, in practice the boundary lines between revenue and general obligation bonds are sometimes fuzzy. For example, some counties and cities own hospitals and/or electric revenue plants, sometimes both. Therefore, the revenue bonds they issue have both general obligation and revenue backing. These bonds are sometimes called "double-barreled" credits.

Among GOs, the weakest credits are found in two groups: GOs of large cities with deteriorating downtown cores and large social outlays, and older, small cities or districts with shrinking populations, a shrinking tax base, and deteriorating economies. Among revenue bonds, the riskiest bonds have been hospitals with strong dependence on government reimbursement (government programs do not cover hospital expenses in full); bonds issued by developers of nursing homes (many of these are highly speculative); and so-called private purpose bonds (also called industrial development bonds, or IDBs). These are issued by specially constituted authorities on behalf of private businesses.

When you buy a municipal bond, it's important to get a very clear sense of the factors underlying its rating. Who exactly is the issuer? Where does money to pay debt service come from? These factors should be extremely specific. For example, in 1990, both the Port of Authority of New York and New Jersey, and the Denver Airport issued private purpose bonds on behalf of Continental Airlines, which then went into bankruptcy proceedings. It is probable that some buyers of those bonds did not realize that Continental, whose financial troubles were well publicized, was responsible for debt service, and not the Port Authority.

Therefore, you should ask very specific questions:

+ Who pays debt service?
+ How adequate are sources of revenue?
+ For a utility bond, has the power plant been built and is it a going business? (if not, don't buy).
+ For a functioning utility, what is the historical debt service coverage ratio?
+ For a housing bond, where will the development be located, and how is real estate doing in that area? (If nothing has been built, the bonds may be very speculative.)
+ If the bond is a GO, does the locality normally run a balanced budget, or does a deficit threaten continually?
+ Finally, find out the rating history and not just the current rating. Has the rating been stable? Has it gone up and down a lot? Is the credit quality improving or is it deteriorating?

You need not do an extensive analysis to obtain answers to these questions. Even if a prospectus is not available, a knowledgeable broker should be familiar with the outstanding credit features of specific bonds and should be able to answer these questions. If she can't, find another broker!

Note also that the AAA rating of many bonds is based on insurance. Some brokers do not differentiate between bonds rated AAA on their own and those that are rated AAA because of the insurance feature. Bonds rated AAA on their own are stronger. The bond market differentiates between the two, and you should do the same.

Finally, remember that the rating is only one of many factors to consider when buying munis. As always, maturity length and potential total return should be equally important considerations.

MUNICIPAL BOND INSURANCE AND OTHER CREDIT ENHANCEMENTS

Municipal Bond Insurance

Bond insurance is relatively recent: it had its inception in the late 1970s. It owes its existence primarily to the shocks created by the Washington Public Power (WPPSS) default and the near default of New York City bonds. Bond insurance has proved very popular with individual investors and has continued to expand. Currently, as many as 50% of all municipal bonds come to market with bond insurance. Insurance, however, does not remove all of the risks of buying bonds. And it comes at a cost. Let's see why.

Insurance is purchased by an issuer when bonds are brought to market. The insurance guarantees that in the event the issuer experiences financial problems, the insurer will step in and take over payment of both interest and principal. Generally, an entire bond issue is insured, and it is insured for the life of the bond. Occasionally, only part of an issue is covered: perhaps only specific maturities (the longest-term bonds), or perhaps only the reserve fund. (The reserve fund is a sum placed with a trustee which would cover a number of interest payments in the event the issuer experiences financial distress.) Occasionally, bonds trading in the secondary market are insured to upgrade a specific portfolio.

A number of firms insure municipal bonds. The oldest and best-known bond insurance firms are Municipal Bond Insurance Association (MBIA), Financial Guaranty Insurance Company (FGIC), and American Municipal Bond Assurance Co. (AMBAC). A fourth firm, Financial Security Assurance (FSA), entered the market in the early 1990s. All of these firms are rated AAA by the major rating agencies, and the bonds they insure are consequently rated AAA as well. The AAA rating of the major bond insurance firms indicates that in the opinion of the rating agencies, the insurers have sufficient reserves to back up their guarantee even under a simulated severe depression scenario.

As in any other industry, however, changes occur. One major change is that several new firms have appeared on the scene. And unlike the older firms, these firms are not rated AAA. Asset Guaranty (AG) is rated AA, and therefore so are the bonds it insures. Another firm, American Capital Access (ACA), is rated only A. It insures mainly lower quality credits; and those are also rated A, based on the rating of that insurer.

There have been a variety of other changes as well. One bond insurance firm, Bond Insurance Guarantee (BIG), sold its portfolio to MBIA and went out of business. Its bonds are now insured by MBIA. Also, recently AMBAC purchased a subsidiary known as Connie Lee, which at one time insured bonds on its own but is no longer doing so. Initially, all bond insurance firms were monoline: that means that their only business was insuring municipal bonds. In order to increase revenues, some are now beginning to enter additional lines of business. Finally, a number of European firms are considering entering this area. Inevitably, further changes will occur in the area of bond insurance.

Issuers who have a strong credit history (A+ or better) generally come to market without insurance. Issuers who need "enhancements" in order to attract buyers are most likely to insure their bonds. These would include credits that are marginally investment grade, are not well-known, or may be undergoing temporary difficulties. In effect, bond insurance transforms a potential lemon into lemonade. Instead of coming to market with a rating that may be barely investment grade, the bond comes to market with a AAA rating, based, however, on the rating of the insurance firm.

For municipal bond insurers, municipal bond insurance has proved a dream product. These companies screen bonds very carefully. Only issuers deemed unlikely to default are granted insurance. Some minor defaults have occurred, but to date no major bond insurance firm has taken a hit that has been significant enough to threaten its rating.

For individual investors, there are a number of pluses to bond insurance. For starters, the insurance does confer a layer of protection against default. As a result, the bonds are more liquid, which means there is a lower markup to buy or to sell. If a major issuer is downgraded, the insured bonds of that issuer decline less in price than the uninsured bonds of the same issuer. Also, bond insurance functions as a second opinion on credit quality. Someone other than the rating agencies—and who, moreover, has money on the line—has carefully screened a possibly marginal issuer for credit quality.

On the minus side, however, insurance protects only against default risk. It does not protect against fluctuations in the price of a bond due to changes in interest rates. Also, insurance comes at a cost: a somewhat lower yield than the issuer would have to pay based on its own rating.

Nor is there any guarantee that the rating of the bond insurance firms will not be downgraded. As noted earlier, many changes have already occurred among bond insurance firms. More are likely to occur. Insurers may continue to prosper, and they may not. In the event any of the bond insurance firms is downgraded (certainly a possibility), all the bonds guaranteed by that firm would be downgraded as well to reflect the new rating of the insurer. This, in turn, would result in some decline in the price of the insured bonds, due to the downgrade.

There may also be a misconception concerning the relative safety of insured bonds compared to AAA bonds. In the market, insured bonds rated AAA are not considered quite as gilt edged as bonds that are rated AAA on their own merit. The yield of bonds rated AAA based on the rating of an insurer tends to track AA credits and not, as their rating would suggest, AAA credits. To an individual investor, this means that insured bonds yield somewhat more than AAA bonds, and that may be considered a plus. The yield (and therefore the price) of an insured bond is actually based both on the insurance and on the underlying credit of the issuer. For that reason, you should find out how the bonds would be rated if they were not insured. To check the rating of the issuer, find out, if you can, how uninsured issues of the same issuer are rated.

If a broker offers you a AAA credit, be sure to inquire if the bond is rated AAA on its own or if that AAA rating is based on bond insurance. Many brokers do not differentiate between the two, but the distinction is important.

Is bond insurance a good deal for the individual investor? On balance, for most individuals, the answer is yes. The main advantage is that bond insurance adds a layer of protection against totally unforeseeable risks. This is particularly desirable for bonds with maturities longer than ten years; or if you are buying riskier credits such as hospitals; or if you have a relatively undiversified portfolio (any portfolio consisting of a few individual issues).

Letters of Credit

Letters of credit (LOCs) are issued by banks and insurance companies as a form of credit enhancement. They are similar to bond insurance, but they do not confer the same degree of protection.

An LOC does not obligate the bank to actually take over interest payments. Rather, a letter of credit is a line of credit. It obligates the bank issuing the LOC to lend money to the issuer if the issuer does not have enough cash on hand to cover interest payments. But LOCs differ in the degree of "obligation" imposed on the bank. Some are irrevocable. Others obligate the bank to make the loan only under certain stipulated conditions.

Even though they afford more limited protection than insured bonds, bonds with LOC backing are rated either AA or AAA, based primarily on the LOC backing.

LOC backing is no longer a major factor in the municipal market. It has been largely replaced by bond insurance.

"Refunded" Bonds

If you want to be sure that you are buying high quality credits, there are many possibilities other than insured bonds.

Any bonds rated A+ to AAA on their own are sound investments. The strongest credits, however, are those of "refunded" bonds (sometimes called "pre res" for short). These are high coupon bonds, usually selling at a premium. They are backed by U.S. Treasury bonds held in escrow. How can that be? Well, suppose a municipality issued bonds years ago, when interest rates were much higher than current rates, say, 8%. Suppose also that, due to the original call provisions, the municipality cannot just call the bonds. How can that municipality lower its interest costs?

The answer is that the municipality may "refinance" by issuing new bonds at the current lower coupon rate (say, 5 1/2%). The newly issued bonds are known as "refunding" bonds. The municipality issues an amount of bonds sufficient to cover interest payments and to redeem principal of the older bonds (the 8% bonds) at the first call date. The proceeds from the sale of the refunding bonds (the 5 1/2% bonds) are used to purchase U.S. Treasury securities, which are then placed in an escrow account. The coupons of the Treasury bonds are used to pay the coupon payments on the older bonds (the 8% bonds), now called the "re-funded" bonds. At the first call date, the remaining assets in the escrow account are used to redeem the refunded bonds.

The refunded bonds are totally free of default risk since monies to pay the bondholders are held in escrow and invested in Treasuries. Whatever the initial rating of the bonds may have been, it now jumps to AAA. This is not automatic, however. Technically, the issuer has to apply for a new rating—because the rating agencies want their fee. In the event the refunded bonds are not rerated, they will generally trade like AAA bonds. The re-funding bonds (that is, the newly issued 5 1/2% bonds), on the other hand, trade with the rating of the issuer.

Refunded bonds offer several other advantages. Maturities tend to be short; therefore, interest rate risk is low. Also, since most of these bonds trade at a premium, they offer higher cash flow and often, somewhat higher yields than other bonds with similar maturity and credit quality.

A number of states, such as Maine and Virginia, issue bonds for small localities through very well-run and highly rated "bond banks." Other states, such as New York and New Jersey, add a layer of protection to the bonds of local school districts by reserving state aid payments for debt service if the school district is in financial difficulty.

Many other possibilities will no doubt continue to turn up as the markets and economic conditions change. This is one reason for dealing with a knowledgeable specialist who can assist you in uncovering new opportunities.

MUNICIPAL BONDS WITH SPECIAL FEATURES

This is a partial listing of some features that may be of interest.

Taxable Municipal Bonds

This is not a mistake: some municipal bonds are taxable. Taxable bonds are issued by the same entities that issue the more familiar tax-exempt bonds. What determines whether the bonds are taxable is the purpose for which they are issued: taxable munis are issued for so-called private purposes; that is, purposes not deemed essential for the public good. Those might include, for example, bonds issued to finance sports facilities, or certain types of housing bonds.

This is still a small segment of the market, but it is growing. For individual investors, taxable munis may represent a very good opportunity. The yields of taxable munis are comparable to those of investment-grade corporate bonds. The advantage is that taxable munis are far less difficult to analyze than corporates. Many are general obligation bonds, backed by the unlimited taxing power of the issuer. They are free of the major land mines found with corporates, such as event risk or tricky call provisions.

Taxable munis can be found in a range of maturities, from short to long. You can also find zeros. As one example, at the end of 1999 you could have purchased a zero coupon taxable muni, with a 16-year maturity, yielding approximately 7.6% (at a time when 30-year Treasuries were yielding 6.3%). The price would have been somewhere in the neighborhood of $250 for a $1000 par value bond.

Taxable munis can be useful for a variety of purposes. If you are retired and not in a high tax bracket, you may earn more (net after tax) by buying taxable munis than you would by buying tax-exempt bonds. Taxable munis can also be used in tax-deferred accounts for that part of your portfolio you want to allocate to bonds.

Municipal Notes

Municipal issuers issue debt with maturities under three years, with names such as "revenue anticipation notes" (RANs), "tax anticipation notes" (TANs), or "bond anticipation notes" (BANs). As these names suggest, these securities are issued in anticipation of revenues from one of two sources: taxes or bonds. Notes are rated, but their ratings differ from those of long-term bonds. The higher quality ratings are "MIG 1" and "MIG 2" by Moody's and "SP 1+" or "SP" by Standard & Poor's.

Notes are purchased mainly by institutional investors, but they can be purchased in amounts as low as $10,000. And if the yield curve is normal (that is, upward sloping), these securities yield more than tax-exempt money market funds by perhaps 50 to 100 basis points.

Because the yield curve of municipal debt instruments is usually more sharply upward sloping than that of Treasuries, the yields of tax-exempt notes are comparatively low. They would be of interest mainly to individual investors in a high tax bracket, for parking money that will be needed within a period of less than one year. But limit your purchases of notes only to those with impeccable credit quality.

Municipal Zeros

Muni zeros are sold under a variety of names: "municipal multipliers," "principal appreciation bonds," "capital appreciation bonds," or zeros. Whatever their name, they share a number of features. They are issued at a deep discount from par. At maturity, they are redeemed at par. The difference between the issue price and par represents a specified compounded annual yield.

The volatility of municipal zeros is comparable to that of Treasury zeros. Volatility is particularly high for munis with long maturities. But there are some major differences between muni zeros and Treasury zeros. For starters, since muni zeros are federally tax exempt, no tax needs to be paid annually on "phantom" interest. Another major difference is that the credit quality of muni zeros varies with the issuer. For muni zeros, credit quality is critical because no interest is paid until the final maturity date. If the zero defaults after several years, you would not have had the consolation of even a single interest payment. (This is one instance where bond insurance would make a lot of sense.)

In addition, muni zeros are subject to call. Muni zeros are called at stipulated *discounts* from par, and not, as some investors assume, at par.

At one time, muni zeros had the reputation of being expensive to resell. There is now a much more active secondary market for zeros. And markups are comparable to those of other munis. Remember, however, that the costs of selling munis are high and that the volatility of zeros makes them high-risk investments if you plan to resell. Because of this, they are appropriate purchases mainly if you plan to hold them to maturity.

Bonds with Put Provisions

A "put" is the exact opposite of a call. A put feature gives the purchaser the option of tendering (or "putting") a bond back to the issuer at stipulated intervals or dates at par. This is a form of protection for the bondholder since if interest rates rise, she can redeem her bond without incurring any loss of principal, and she can then reinvest the proceeds at a more attractive rate. Because of this feature, put bonds are less volatile than other long-term bonds, and they normally trade at or close to par. But since there is no free lunch, there are a couple of disadvantages. First, the coupon interest is usually lower than that of bonds with a similar maturity: total return may therefore be lower. And second, if interest rates decline, put bonds appreciate in value much less than other long-term bonds.

"Supersinkers"

"Supersinkers" are a variety of housing bonds with specifically designated maturities singled out for early retirement in the event mortgages are prepaid. This means that some of the bonds may be called early. The name "supersinker" derives from the fact that monies to retire the bonds accumulate in a "sinking fund." The retirement date is uncertain because prepayments are unpredictable.

The potential early call feature of supersinkers is considered attractive because, since there is not a specific call date, the yield of the bond—and its price—are determined by the maturity date, not by the uncertain call date. Supersinkers normally mature well before their maturity date. In effect, the purchaser earns a long-term yield on a short-term security.

Be very cautious, however, if a supersinker is selling at a high premium. An early call would result in a loss of principal.

MUNICIPAL BOND PRICING

Call Risk

Munis—mainly those with long-term maturities—are subject to call. You will remember that this means the issuer may choose to redeem a bond before its maturity date.

Call provisions on most munis are straightforward. Typical call provisions for 30-year bonds stipulate an initial call date ten years after issue, at a price slightly above par (typically 101); and several additional consecutive call dates (in 15 years at 102, and so on). Housing revenue bonds, however, may have unusual call features. This can happen, for example, in the event that the money raised by the bonds is not needed for actual mortgages. The difference between those call provisions and ordinary call provisions is that no date is mentioned. The bonds may be called as early as a few months after issue, and this has happened.

Under normal circumstances, issuers are likely to call munis only if interest rates drop substantially. The higher and the more attractive the yield to the investor, the more expensive the interest for the issuer and the more likely it is that a bond will be called. As explained, be particularly careful to investigate call provisions for any bonds selling at a premium. Be doubly careful for housing bonds selling at a premium. Housing bonds are sometimes subject to extraordinary calls. A broker should quote both the YTM and the yield to the first call date (that will usually be lower than the YTM). In the event the bond is called, the yield-to-call becomes the actual return.

"Dollar" Bonds and "Basis" Bonds

Some munis are called "dollar bonds" because the price of these bonds is quoted in dollars. Other bonds are priced "to the basis." Instead of a dollar amount, the YTM is quoted. Therefore, the buyer has to work backwards from the quoted yield to compute the price (the broker will pull out his trusty calculator).

"The Dated Date"

This is the date on which the bond begins accruing (earning) interest.

Markups

The author of a book on municipal bonds characterized pricing in the muni market as "let the buyer beware" or "what the market will bear."[1] For an individual investor, commission costs vary from under one point ($100 per $10,000 of par) for actively traded issues with short maturities and high credit quality to about four points ($400 per $10,000 par value bond) for inactively traded bonds with long maturities.

Small lots (under $25,000 par value) are considered a pain by brokers and are marked up accordingly. This makes them particularly expensive to sell. Brokers, in fact, have an expression for the pricing of these lots: they "punish the coupon." Translation: the commission costs for selling small lots are extremely high. Dealers who buy a small lot from you do so with the understanding that they are doing you a special favor. Paradoxically, the dealer will be anxious to get rid of small lots and will price them attractively for resale. What this means is that you can sometimes find attractive prices if you want to buy a small lot. But then, don't plan to resell!

Pricing of munis remains a quagmire. It is almost impossible to generalize about commissions in the muni retail (i.e., individual investor) market. The chief characteristic of municipal pricing (and, as a result, municipal yields) is that every dealer charges a different price, even for very similar bonds. When I wrote the first edition of this book, in order to research pricing inconsistencies, I pretended to be selling a number of small lots of munis that I had inherited. I called seven different firms to see what prices they would offer. Among the lots was a high-quality, widely traded New Jersey Turnpike bond; one very controversial credit, Philadelphia, whose financial difficulties were highly publicized at the time; and some infrequently traded issues.

I was offered prices all over the lot. The prices were closest on the New Jersey Turnpike bonds. This was not unexpected, since I live in New Jersey and New Jersey Turnpike bonds are actively traded. Nonetheless, even on this lot, offers varied by 150 basis points on a price of 98. Since I was "selling" a $40,000 par value lot, that translates into a price difference of $612.00 between the highest and the lowest offer. The largest difference occurred on an out-of-state housing bond (375 basis points, almost 4% or $1,500

---

1. James J. Cooner, *Investing in Municipal Bonds: Balancing Risks and Rewards* (New York: John Wiley & Sons, 1987), p. 44.

on a $40,000 lot). A number of dealers refused to bid on some of the lesser-known names.

Surprisingly, the situation has changed very little. In fact, a recent article in *The New York Times*[2] indicated that even dealers find pricing information concerning municipal bonds difficult to obtain and need to shop around. Predictably, according to the same article, individuals shopping for the same bonds have to pay higher prices and therefore receive lower yields.

Pricing Information on the Internet

In response to the demand for more transparency in the pricing of municipal bonds, some pricing information is now available on the Internet.

A number of websites currently post pricing information on the Net. The most useful one, *investinginbonds.com* is maintained by The Bond Market Association, and it is free. It publishes daily a list of prices for approximately 1,000 bonds that traded at least four times the *previous* day. You can search this website based on a variety of sorts, including:

+ Location (state)
+ Credit quality
+ Maturity
+ Coupon
+ CUSIP number (this identifies the exact bond)
+ Volume traded
+ Number of trades

Exhibit 7–2 shows a listing, which appeared July 26, 2000. Reading from left to right, the listing specifies:

+ The Bond rating (AAA by both Moody's and Standard & Poor's—denoted as S and M). Note that the AAA rating is based on insurance by the Bond Insurance Firm, FSA.
+ The issuer (New Jersey Health Care Facility). The CUSIP number, identifying the exact bond issue which traded, is listed directly under the name (64579CP87).
+ The size of the coupon (6.5%).

---

2. 27 June 1999, *Finance*, p. 10.

E X H I B I T   7–2

Municipal Bond Trade Data

▶ Ratings ▶ Issue			▶ Maturity	Call	▶ Hi $ Price		
Insur. ▶ CUSIP	▶ St ▶ Coupon	Calls		Prices	▶ Lo $ Price	▶ %YTM	▶ %YTC/P
AAA S	NEW JERSEY HEALTH	NJ	6.500% 07/01/2011		**108.684**	5.435	
AAA M	CARE FACS FING				**104.955**	5.879	
FSA	AUTH REV GEN HOSP						
	CTR AT PA						
	64579CP87						

▶ Volume of $ 60,000 for ▶ 4 trades. ▶ Show Trade Details
▶ Search MuniStatements.com for official statements on this issue.

Source: *investinginbonds.com* (website of the Bond Market Association). Reprinted with permission.

- ♦ The maturity date (07/01/2011).
- ♦ The highest price at which this bond traded: 108.684 (that is, $1,086.84) and the lowest price (104.955, that is, $1,049.55 per bond).
- ♦ The YTM resulting from each price: 5.88% for the lowest price; and 5.43% for the highest price.
- ♦ While they do not appear on this particular listing, call provisions and yield-to-call would also be listed, if applicable.
- ♦ Finally, just below the listing, there is a summary of the total par amount of bonds that were traded, and the number of trades (in this example, $60,000 in four separate trades).

Investinginbonds.com now supplies a second level of information, and that level provides a fascinating insight into the pricing of municipal bonds. When you click on "Trade Details," a second box appears, which supplies additional details concerning the trades. Exhibit 7–3 shows the box which would have appeared if you had "clicked" on trade details for the trades shown in Exhibit 7–2.

This level tells you:

- ♦ The time each trade took place.
- ♦ The par amount of bonds for each trade ($15,000)
- ♦ The price at which each trade took place (lowest: $104.955; highest $108.684).
- ♦ The YTM of each trade (highest: 5.88%; lowest: 5.43%).

E X H I B I T   7–3

Trade Details for Exhibit 7–2.

Trade Time	Par Traded	Price	%YTM	
09:38	$15,000	$107.130	n/a	DD
11:07	$15,000	$105.330	n/a	DD
11:10	$15,000	$104.955	5.880	CS
12:00	$15,000	$108.684	5.435	CB

CB: Customer Buy (dealer sale to customer)
CS: Customer Sale (dealer purchase from customer)
DD: Inter-dealer trade

Source: *investinginbonds.com* (website of the Bond Market Association). Reprinted with permission.

+ Whether the trade was inter-dealer (dealer to dealer),
denoted by the letters DD; a customer buy (CB); or a
customer sell (CS).

When you look at Exhibit 7–3, what jumps out is the major
price difference between the highest and lowest prices. If you do
the arithmetic, you will see that difference amounted to $559.35
on a $15,000 trade, or about 3.7%. Note further that the customer
who sold received only $1,049.55 per bond. The customer who
bought paid a much higher price, $1,086.84 per bond. That would
amount to a spread of nearly 4%. To be fair, since the listings are
anonymous, there is no indication that the same dealer was on
each side of these trades.

The trade details of Exhibit 7–3 are somewhat unusual in that
each trade involved a relatively small lot, in each case, furthermore, an odd lot. (It is a coincidence that all trades were for the
same par amount of bonds.) But you can readily see how wide
the spreads are between customer buys and customer sells, and
between prices dealers pay and those individual investors pay.
Note further that in this example, the bond that traded was insured. Insured bonds are presumed to be reasonably liquid, and
therefore, you would think, should trade in a narrower band.

Most trades listed on *investinginbonds.com* are for far larger lots. Exhibit 7–4 shows the trade details of a more typical listing, which also appeared on July 26, 2000, showing seven separate trades of bonds issued by the New Jersey Turnpike. This is a very actively traded revenue bond. This issue, moreover, was insured by MBIA, and therefore, rated AAA. You will immediately notice that the spreads between the highest and lowest prices at which these various trades took place are much narrower than those in Exhibit 7–3, no doubt due to the much larger size of the lots. All trades listed, including customer buys and sells, are for institutional size lots. But note again: the lowest price ($984.75 per bond) and therefore the highest yield (5.50%), was obtained by the customer who bought $1.4 million bonds. Customers buying $100,000 and $200,000 lots paid a somewhat higher price ($1,000 per bond). That represents an additional 1.6% per bond, and the yield is correspondingly lower: 5.37%. (Note that even in this example two dealer trades were done at the two lowest prices.)

E X H I B I T   7–4

Trade Details for N. J. Turnpike Bonds

Trade Time	Par Traded	Price	%YTM	
13:00	$200,000	$98.450	n/a	DD
13:44	$200,000	$98.375	n/a	DD
14:52	$1,400,000	$98.475	5.503	CB
15:17	$200,000	$100.000	5.375	CB
15:28	$500,000	$98.625	5.491	CS
15:50	$30,000	$98.853	n/a	DD
17:06	$100,000	$100.000	5.375	CB

CB: Customer Buy (dealer sale to customer)
CS: Customer Sale (dealer purchase from customer)
DD: Inter-dealer trade

Source: *investinginbonds.com* (website of the Bond Market Association). Reprinted with permission.

A second source of pricing information is a table published daily by *Bloomberg.com*. Exhibit 7–5 shows a table that appeared on August 22, 2000.

As its title indicates, Exhibit 7–5 shows a small sample of actively traded tax-exempt revenue bonds that traded on the *previous* day. The small print further specifies that prices (and yields) are for round lots $250,000 or larger, which means that these are all institutional size trades. These are clearly benchmark yields, available only to dealers. Reading from left to right, the table includes:

+ Changes in yield compared to the previous day (the first three columns). In this instance, yields for five-to-ten year maturities declined (prices went up); the yield on the two-year went up (prices for that maturity declined); and

E X H I B I T   7–5

National Municipal Bond Yields

NATIONAL MUNI BOND YIELDS						
Triple-A Rated, Tax-Exempt Insured Revenue Bonds.						
	8/21	8/18	Change in	31% eq	8/14	7/24/00	2/21/00
Maturity	Yield	Yield	Yield	Yield	Yield	Yield	Yield
Two year	4.42%	4.40%	0.02%	6.41%	4.42%	4.54%	4.59%
Five year	4.60%	4.62%	-0.02%	6.67%	4.66%	4.77%	5.02%
Seven year	4.72%	4.75%	-0.03%	6.84%	4.78%	4.89%	5.17%
Ten year	4.90%	4.92%	-0.02%	7.10%	4.95%	5.04%	5.38%
Fifteen year	5.32%	5.32%	0.00%	7.71%	5.33%	5.44%	5.80%
Twenty year	5.56%	5.56%	0.00%	8.06%	5.57%	5.66%	6.09%
Thirty year	5.68%	5.68%	0.00%	8.23%	5.69%	5.78%	6.18%

This information is provided by The Bond Market Association and Bloomberg L.P. to be used solely as a benchmark for particular categories of municipal bonds. The yields for maturities beyond ten years represent a callable bond. The yields are a composite of round lot ($250,000 or above) prices based on bonds which have coupons that reflect current market conditions. Taxable equivalent yields would be higher for bondholders subject to a Federal marginal tax rate of more than 31%.

Source: Bloomberg L.P. *Bloomberg.com*

yields for the 15 through 30 year maturities did not change.

♦ The tax-equivalent yield for investors in the 31% bracket (fourth column).
♦ Yields for similar bonds for earlier periods: one week earlier, one month earlier, and six months earlier.

Although this table lists only a small number of bonds, it provides some information not available on the website of the Bond Market Association. It gives you some idea of the current shape of the yield curve in the municipal market because yields are provided for maturities ranging from two years to 30 years. Moreover, the columns showing yields for earlier periods enable you to see how the yield curve is changing in the municipal market; and if so, whether those changes have created buying opportunities in particular sectors of the yield curve.

Why am I calling this information limited? Both information sources have shortcomings. The 1,000 listings of the Bond Market Association may sound like a lot, but they constitute only a minuscule fraction of the over 1.4 million issues that are outstanding. Moreover, the prices (and yields) listed on both that website and the Bloomberg are representative of yields that would be available to institutional buyers. Also, the prices are stale (for trades that occurred on the previous day); they are updated only once a day; and markups are not listed anywhere. At best, this information provides representative rather than specific prices. You are left to estimate how bonds that have similar credit quality and maturity would trade. That is difficult because features of bonds (such as call provisions, or sinking fund provisions) affect the price at which individual bonds trade. Even if you find a bond you want to buy, the price at which you can buy or sell it will be different because it will be a different size lot; you will buy or sell it a day later; and different dealers will price it with different markups. Still, this is a beginning.

Before leaving this tour of websites, let us note another type of information available on the Internet. At the bottom of Exhibit 7–2, there is a link to *Munistatements.com.* If you click on that link, you can read the official statement for the issue in question. You can also try to locate official statements for older issues directly on that website, although not all of them are available. To look up older issues, you need to know the CUSIP number.

The Blue List

One of the oldest sources of information for bonds trading in the secondary market is the "Blue List." If you can get your hands on it, the Blue List remains a good source of information on prices and yields in the municipal market.

The Blue List is published daily by Standard & Poor's, on blue paper, in blue ink (no, I am not pulling your leg). It lists the "floating supply" of bonds that dealers currently own and would like to sell and the price at which the dealers would like to sell these bonds. (The "floating supply" is the entire total of bonds available for sale. It usually varies between $1 billion and $4 billion per list.) The format follows the usual conventions for listing municipal bonds.

This list does not tell you the price at which the bonds actually sell. Also, if you owned one of the bonds on the list and wanted to sell it, you would get a lower price. (Remember that there is a spread between the bid and the ask price. You sell at the lower.) Furthermore, by the time you get your Blue List, it is likely to be several days old. Many bonds will have been sold, and many prices will be stale. Nonetheless, it remains a good source of information because the prices on it are actual prices at which the dealers would like to sell the bonds, at the time the listing appears. Almost any firm that sells a lot of municipal bonds will have a copy of the Blue List and should make it available to you.

The Blue List is now available on the Internet, but only to subscribers, for a fee. It is updated daily.

Finally, in the absence of any other source, you can consult the tables published daily by the *The Wall Street Journal* and *Investor's Business Daily* and on the weekend by *Barron's*. These tables show prices and yields of a small number of very actively traded bonds. But the yields listed are accurate only for wholesale (that is, very large) trades.

Finally, one additional source of pricing information, available for a fee, is a pricing service offered jointly by Standard &

Poor's and the Bond Market Association (1-800-BOND INFO). This service will quote representative prices and yields for specific bonds, but it is not a brokerage service and the quotes are not exact.

BUYING MUNICIPAL BONDS

There are many sources for buying municipal bonds.

The traditional sources have been full service brokerage firms, brokerage firms that specialize in municipal bonds; banks, and discount brokers. All of these are still available. To all those sources, you now have to add online brokers. Increasingly, the lines are being blurred. Both discount brokers and full service brokers will probably sell bonds online, if they don't do so already.

Online brokers

According to recent surveys, perhaps as many as 50 brokers now sell munis online. But, as this is going to press, for all the reasons explained in Chapter 2, it would be a mistake to assume that buying from online brokers guarantees you will be getting a better deal than if you buy from either a full service broker, or from a discount broker. First of all, very few online brokers own any inventory, and if they do, it is extremely limited. Most of the bonds posted on the websites of brokers are listings obtained from *Bond Express*. If you order a bond, the online broker will need to buy it, in order to then sell it to you.

When it comes to price, bear in mind that the price displayed by an online broker includes at least one, and sometimes two markups. Most online brokers also add a small additional fee per bond on top of the markup, which is listed either as a transaction fee or as a commission, and which is in addition to the markup. Virtually none of the online brokers discloses the markup, that is, the spread between the bid and the ask. Finally, the bonds listed on the website may no longer be available, or the price may be different from the listed price.

Similarly, again as noted in Chapter 2, buying and selling online is still not as convenient or as simple as you would expect although over time, that should improve. As emphasized, selling bonds is particularly costly. Your best bet is to deal with a broker who will solicit multiple bids, whether that is an online broker, a full service broker, or a discount broker.

A number of recent surveys indicate that at the current time, the online broker with the largest selection of municipal bonds for immediate purchase is *E*Trade*. E*Trade also has some nifty software that allows you to build a laddered portfolio, lay out its cash flow, and determine its average weighted maturity and duration. (For a discussion of a laddered portfolio, see Chapter 15.) But E*Trade's current status may change. Schwab has announced that it will be developing a larger web presence for municipal bonds in the third quarter of 2000. It will be joining forces with the bond broker *ValuBond.com*. It is not clear how this site will differ from sites currently online. Schwab is not planning, for example, to display the spread between bid and ask prices. I was unable to obtain more specific details from Schwab. Fidelity has also announced that it will expand its municipal bond offerings later this year.

Two online brokers deserve special mention because they specialize in municipal bonds. The first, *eBondTrade.com* is based in California, and specializes in California bonds. It is oriented mainly towards other brokers and investment advisers. The minimum amount for each trade is $25,000. Two innovations are that it is planning to make a market in the bonds that it sells. It also displays the spread between bid and ask prices; and claims that it will charge a flat commission per bond. The second, *MuniDirect.com*, has also announced that it will make a market in the bonds that it sells; will also charge a flat commission; and that it will post bid and ask prices.

Just as we are going to press, *The Bond Buyer* of August 22 has a Page One story about still another new entrant that will specialize in municipal bonds: *eBondUSA.com*. This site, however, intends to add features not found on other websites. First, *eBondUSA.com* intends to provide real-time estimates of the value of the portfolios of investors, based on market conditions and the thinking of traders. The site will also provide customers with prices for the five most recent trades for a given CUSIP or five comparable trades for a given CUSIP. Finally, this entrant also intends to provide a venue for buying new issues. This site is due to be online toward the end of the year 2000.

To sum up, online brokers represent another window into the bond market: a good source of pricing information, and possibly, a source for buying some bonds. But up to now, inventory of most of these brokers is far too limited to be your only source. Moreover, at the moment, buying municipal bonds online is not much more convenient than buying from a broker. Finally, buying online does not guarantee that you are getting a better deal. You still need to shop around to protect yourself on price. On the other hand, as online resources and information expand, and as dealers begin to compete anonymously on the basis of price, spreads will narrow in this market as in others.

But bear in mind that when you shop online, you are on your own. If you are currently dealing with a knowledgeable broker, I would suggest using online resources for information, and continuing to work with your broker.

Buying at Issue

Both *The New York Times* and *The Wall Street Journal* list upcoming sales of municipal bonds every Monday. There are definite advantages to buying at issue. For a few days, the bonds are priced at par (or at a uniform price) by all the dealers in the syndicate. They remain at par until the bonds "break syndicate" and are allowed to trade at what the market will bear. During that time, moreover, prices—and therefore yields—are usually attractive because dealers are anxious to sell the bonds. The buyer also receives the longest possible call provisions.

If you would like to buy bonds at issue, you may need to shop around. Major brokerage firms that participate in bringing bonds to market usually have them. Smaller brokerage firms, or discount brokers, may not have them. Regional firms that specialize in bonds from your geographical area should also have bonds at issue for that area.

SELECTING MUNICIPAL BONDS

Let's mention some factors you might want to consider before buying municipal bonds.

Other Tax Features of Municipal Bonds: The Alternative Minimum Tax (AMT); "de Minimus" Tax

While the exemption of interest income from federal income taxes is the main tax feature of municipal bonds, there are a number of additional wrinkles in the tax law affecting municipals that you should consider before buying municipal bonds.

One is the alternative minimum tax (also known as the AMT). The *Tax Reform Bill of 1986* provides for direct federal taxation of certain categories of municipal bonds. Only bonds specifically designated as "nonesssential" bonds, issued after August 7, 1986, are subject to this tax, and then only in the event that the individual investor's tax bracket makes him subject to the alternative minimum tax.

Because there is the possibility that the bonds may be taxable, however, these bonds yield somewhat more than other municipal bonds. Therefore, for those individuals not subject to the alternative minimum tax (and that's almost everyone not in the highest tax brackets), these bonds will result in a somewhat higher yield.

The AMT is of concern mainly to individuals with large incomes or very large municipal portfolios. If you are in that category, you need to calculate your tax bill in two different ways. The first is the standard method. The second requires a number of adjustments to taxable income and the addition of the amount of tax owed on the bonds subject to the AMT. The two tax bills are then compared. The higher tax is the one you pay. Whatever your tax bracket, you can avoid the AMT by making sure that you do not purchase bonds subject to the AMT.

Another tax wrinkle is the "de minimus tax." Again, this tax is of concern mainly to individuals in the highest federal tax brackets. It is levied on discount bonds which are bought below a specified value and subsequently rise in price or are redeemed at par. That value is determined by multiplying the number of years outstanding until maturity by 0.25. For example, for a bond that matures in ten years, that amount would be $97.50 (that is, a price of $975.00 for each $1,000 par value amount). If you purchase that bond at a price below $975.00, the difference between the purchase price and the selling price is treated as ordinary income for tax purposes, and not as a capital gain. This creates a tax liability when the bond is sold, and obviously the higher the tax bracket, the higher the liability. This tax liability lowers the real yield for the bond. The "de minimus" rule applies to any discount bond, whether it is an original issue discount bond or a bond selling at a discount in the secondary market. Therefore, if you are in a high tax bracket, you might want to check with your accountant before buying muni bonds selling at a deep discount.

Finally, note that even though munis are federally tax exempt, when you sell or redeem your municipal bonds, you may incur either a capital gain or a capital loss, and those create tax issues. Also, if your bonds have declined in value because interest rates have gone up, you may want to sell your bonds in exchange for other municipal bonds in order to generate a tax loss. This is known as a swap. Swaps are discussed in Chapter 15 of this book. If you are in a high tax bracket, or own a large portfolio of municipal bonds, or trade bonds actively, then tax issues become more complex and may require you to consult a tax accountant.

Discounts vs. Premium Bonds

Your broker telephones. She has just gotten some terrific bonds in inventory: one a discount and the other a premium. Both yield 5 1/2% to maturity. Which should you buy?

Well, you reason, I should buy the discount bond because if I buy the premium bond, at maturity, I will lose for each bond the amount of the premium over par.

Wrong, but a common misconception. If you are looking primarily for income—all other factors, such as credit quality and maturity, being equal—you should buy the premium bond. Premium bonds generally yield more than discounts. Here is why.

It is a common error to think that one "loses" the difference in price between par (the price of the bond when it is redeemed at maturity), and the amount of the premium. The yield quoted for the premium bond is based on redeeming the bond at par. The premium is not lost. Even if the yield quoted for the premium and the discount bond are exactly the same, the discount bond yield includes anticipated capital gains. That capital gain is taxable, whereas the entire dividend yield of the premium bond is tax free. Hence, the net yield of the discount bond may actually be lower than the quoted yield-to-maturity, whereas for the premium bond it will be the same.

The yield advantage is amplified by several additional factors. First, the premium bond has higher coupons. So you get a higher cash flow. If you are reinvesting coupons, you have larger amounts to reinvest every year and therefore, more interest-on-interest. More importantly, because many investors avoid premium bonds, they are usually offered with higher yields than comparable maturity discount bonds. Finally, premium bonds are less volatile than discount bonds, which protects principal in the event interest rates rise.

Therefore, if your style of investing is to buy and hold, muni premium bonds have distinct advantages: higher cash flow and lower volatility.

If, on the other hand, you are not investing primarily for income, but rather, to fund a future need such as putting away money for a child's college education, or for your own retirement, then, if you are in a high tax bracket, you might want to consider municipal zero coupon bonds, or, alternately, deep discount municipal bonds with good call protection. But then you need to be aware of the "de minimis" tax.

Overall Strategy

You have decided to invest in munis. If you are seeking maximum income and safety, what should you buy?

Opinions differ on this. Some old hands in the industry would say: "Buy bonds rated AAA (for safety) with 30-year maturities and maximum call protection (for highest income)." My objection is that that strategy buys neither. The 30-year maturity exposes the buyer to maximum interest rate risk. And AAA paper has lower yields when compared to bonds with lower ratings.

The strategy I prefer would be to buy intermediates, that is, bonds with five- to ten-year maturities, and buy A to AA credits. Exhibit 7–6, which shows general obligation yields available the week of December 13, 1999, illustrates why.

Exhibit 7–6 illustrates the trade-offs you would have faced at that date.

+ The yield curve of the municipal market was far steeper than that of the Treasury market (260 basis points compared to about 100 basis points for the Treasury market). The yield curve in the municipal market is

E X H I B I T   7–6

Municipal Market Data General Obligation Bonds

	Aaa (pure)	Aaa (ins)	Aa	A	Baa
2000	3.85	3.93	3.90	4.10	4.30
2004	4.53	4.65	4.63	4.80	5.08
2009	4.95	5.08	5.05	5.23	5.58
2014	5.40	5.54	5.50	5.69	6.00
2019	5.71	5.85	5.81	5.98	6.24
2024	5.80	5.94	5.90	6.06	6.30
2029	5.83	5.97	5.93	6.09	6.33

Source: *The Bond Buyer*, 13 Dec. 1999, p. 27. Reprinted with permission from *The Bond Buyer*.

normally steeper than that of the Treasury market, but the contrast was particularly marked at this date because the Treasury yield curve was relatively flat.

♦ Approximately 85% of the highest yield available in any credit quality in the muni market was available at the ten-year mark, but with lower volatility when compared to longer bonds. Notice also that the yield available at the ten-year mark on A-rated paper (5.23%) is almost 90% of the yield available on AAA bonds with 30-year maturities. It would appear the buyer is not being paid for the risk of going long. The flip side of the coin is that reinvestment risk is higher in the shorter maturities.

♦ Insured bonds yield more than "pure" AAA ratings.

♦ Finally, municipal bonds at that date were very cheap compared to taxable bonds. At the 30-year mark, AAA munis at 5.9% were yielding 95% of 30-year Treasuries on an absolute basis. On a net-after-tax basis, that was worth 8.55% to someone in the 31% tax bracket. This was an astonishing value, given the fact that to find an equivalent yield on a taxable bond, you would have had to buy junk bonds.

Clearly, as interest rates change, trade-offs may very well differ from those illustrated in Exhibit 7–6. Munis are not often as cheap, relative to taxable bonds, as they were at the end of 1999.

Within the muni market, there are times when you are paid little for buying lower quality credits; and others when yield spreads widen, and there is a meaningful pick-up in yield. Unfortunately, tables similar to Exhibit 7–6 do not appear routinely in the financial press or on the Internet. But your broker will have one. And it pays to discuss it with him, in order to check out where rates may currently be particularly attractive.

To sum up: if credit safety is your main concern, the safest bonds are (in order of safety): pre-refunded bonds; bonds rated AAA; and insured bonds. If you stick to maturities of ten years or less, you also reduce volatility. For higher yield, go out a bit further on the yield curve, or stick to A or A+ credits. Those are still very safe investments. Only buy 30-year bonds if yields are particularly attractive. If you buy 30-year bonds, only buy bonds with the highest credit quality.

If your total bond portfolio is small ($50,000 or less), it is difficult to put together a diversified portfolio of municipal bonds. You would be incurring high transaction costs. If you are investing for current income, consider pre-refunded or insured municipal bonds and keep maturities under seven years, in order to minimize interest rate risk. If you are investing for retirement, even for money that is not tax-deferred, muni bonds may not be the best way to go. You might consider the various savings bonds available, particularly I bonds, which defer taxes until the bonds are redeemed. If your income tax bracket is low, some of the safer taxable issues (such as taxable munis or CMOs) may yield more for you on a net-after-tax basis.

If you have a large portfolio of municipal bonds, consult Chapter 15 of this book for strategies for managing large portfolios.

It may seem that I have included an unreasonable amount of detail on sources of pricing information. But anyone familiar with that market will tell you that this is a major stumbling block for individual investors. After all, if you are buying municipal bonds primarily to boost your income, overpaying will diminish that advantage. To protect yourself on price, if you are considering either buying or selling a bond, check any quote against that of bonds with similar characteristics: maturity, call features, and credit quality. And shop around. The best indicator is the YTM (or to the first call date). Your broker can also compare any quote to national (or state) scales for similar bonds.

SUMMARY: QUESTIONS TO ASK BEFORE BUYING MUNICIPAL BONDS

When does the bond mature?

Who is the issuer?

What is the rating?

If AAA, is it insured or AAA on its own?

If the bond is insured: who is the insurer? how is the bond rated without insurance?

Who is the issuer and where does revenue from debt service come from?

For a revenue bond, what is the debt service coverage ratio?

What is the yield-to-maturity?

When is the bond callable? at what price? what is the yield-to-call?

What is the price?

What is the coupon?

ADDITIONAL REFERENCES

For additional information on municipal bonds, a number of excellent books have been written. Unfortunately, these were initially published years ago, and many are out of print. If you can still find it, a very clear and readable book is James Cooner, *Investing in Municipal Bonds* (New York: John Wiley & Sons, 1987).

Another excellent reference, which still seems to be in print, is Robert Lamb and Stephen Rappaport, *Municipal Bonds*, 2nd ed. (New York: McGraw-Hill, 1987).

For information on current yields, consult *investinginbonds.com* and *bloomberg.com*, the Blue List, and online broker listings.

For current market conditions, most firms that sell munis to individual investors publish their own newsletters, and many are

extremely informative. One that is particularly well done is published by the New York firm of Gabriele, Hueglin and Cashman
(1-800-422-7435). It's free to customers and it sells bonds nationwide.

Finally, the bible of the municipal bond market is *The Bond
Buyer*, One State Street Plaza, New York, New York, 10004. Sub-
scription to this daily publication costs about $1,750 per year. *The
Bond Buyer* is now available on line for about $1,500 per year.

APPENDIX: THE NEW YORK CITY DEFAULT

Let's briefly look at the highly publicized default that happened
to New York City in the 1970s. This default has almost receded
into ancient history. Nonetheless, if hard times return to the economy, defaults, or the threat of defaults, may recur. While no two
defaults are exactly alike, analyzing a default illustrates very
clearly how the market for municipal bonds works. In addition,
defaults may create attractive speculative opportunities, as this
one did. Therefore, it is instructive to examine how the default
developed.

In April of 1975, New York City found itself in a cash crunch.
As a result, the City deferred an interest payment on a short-term
note. (Long-term bonds were never involved.) Technically, this delay constituted a default, and it was highly publicized. But the
interest payment was ultimately made, and no investor lost
money unless he sold bonds that had dropped in value because
of the publicity surrounding the default. (Note: to this day, some
New York City officials insist that there was never a real default.)

In September, the state passed the Financial Emergency Act,
putting the city under the authority of the Emergency Financial
Control Board. The crisis was resolved through cooperation between three sectors: the unions, which agreed to use their pension
funds for assistance; the state, which extended cash advances; and
the banking community. Ultimately, the crisis was resolved
through the creation of the Municipal Assistance Corporation
(MAC), which was empowered to issue bonds on behalf of the
city. Note that even though these were issued for the city, MAC
bonds were not obligations of the city of New York. The revenues
to pay debt service were backed, not by the taxing power of the
city, but by the state of New York, and by a special lien on the

city's sales tax (there were distinctions between the first and subsequent liens) and on a stock transfer tax.

In retrospect, New York City's default was not at all that surprising. The city's financial problems had been widely reported in the press. They included revenue shortfalls due to economic decline; inability to contain spending within revenues; and poor fiscal management (for example, funding long-term expenditures through short-term borrowing). Under these circumstances, a downgrade should have been anticipated.

Because of the publicity surrounding the city's financial woes, and despite the fact that MAC bonds were not obligations of the City, the MAC bonds came to market with yields well above then-current market rates: 10% as compared to 8% for securities with comparable maturity and credit. From the beginning, MAC bonds represented a very solid investment. The bonds were secured by very strong revenue sources. Debt service coverage was predicted to be very strong and turned out to be even stronger than anticipated. In 1990, it reached 11 times on first lien bonds, and between four and five times on second lien bonds. MAC bonds were initially rated A, but because of the excellent historic debt service coverage ratio, by 1990 they were rated AA.

What can be learned from this episode? First, that defaults can and do occur and will continue to occur. Can they always be anticipated? In this case, yes. The city's financial troubles were well publicized and the default was preceded by several downgrades.

Finally, this episode demonstrates why it pays, literally, to be very precise about exactly which revenue streams back debt service. In this instance, MAC bonds were tarred by the woes of New York City, even though they were not obligations of the city and rated higher than direct obligations of the city. And that is the main reason why even though MAC bonds represented a very solid investment from the start, their yields were so high.

CHAPTER 8

Mortgage-Backed Securities

This chapter discusses

- The unique nature of GNMA cash flows
- The vocabulary of GNMA returns
- Premium, par, and discount GNMAs
- Sons of GNMA: Fannie Mae & Freddie Mac
- Collateralized Mortgage Obligations (CMOs)
- Stripped mortgage-backed securities
- Asset-backed securities based on assets other than mortgages
- Buying mortgage-backed securities

The market for mortgage-backed securities has changed a good deal since the first edition of this book. At the time, GNMAs (securities backed by the Government National Mortgage Association) constituted the largest and the most liquid segment of that market. Collateralized Mortgage Association securities (CMOs) were still new. The impact of changes in interest rates on the price of mortgage-backed instruments was not fully understood or anticipated. As a result of the sometimes violent interest rate changes that occurred during the early 1990s, and the poor investment returns of many investors in these securities during that period, new structures were developed that better met the needs of both individual and institutional investors. If you want to invest in mortgage-backed securities, you may find that CMOs now meet your needs better than the earlier GNMAs. But since GNMAs remain the prototype for all mortgage-backed securities, and since later structures (including CMOs) are created out of GNMAs, an understanding of GNMA cash flows is basic to an understanding of any of the other instruments. So we will start with GNMAs and discuss newer structures later in the chapter.

WHY GNMAs ARE UNIQUE

GNMAs were the earliest mortgage-backed securities, first issued in 1970. Since that time, GNMAs and instruments structured like GNMAs have become one of the largest segments of the bond market. Currently, a staggering amount, close to two trillion dollars, is estimated to have been issued.

GNMAs were, and continue to remain, mainly an institutional product. The minimum required to purchase a new GNMA is $25,000, although older GNMAs can be purchased for less. Banks, insurance companies, and pension funds, as well as mutual funds, are the primary buyers of GNMAs.

The appeal of GNMAs to individual investors is based on a number of factors: impeccable credit quality (GNMAs have the unconditional backing of the U.S. government); high cash flow (unlike other bonds, interest is usually paid monthly); and higher current yield than Treasury securities. But there is never a free lunch. If GNMAs yield more than Treasuries, then they must have features which make them less desirable than Treasuries. And this, of course, is the case.

In reality, GNMAs are complex. Anyone who tries to tell you GNMAs are simple does not understand the product. While they have no credit risk whatsoever, they are not riskless. Like other bonds, they expose the buyer to interest rate (and price) risk. More importantly, when you buy an individual GNMA, you will not know the exact amount or the timing of its cash flows, or indeed, how long the GNMA will be outstanding. Finally, each GNMA is unique. Two GNMAs with similar coupons and quoted maturities may ultimately perform very differently.

Analysis of a GNMA is totally different from that of any other fixed-income instrument. Analysis focuses on two elements: the probable longevity of the security—that is, how long coupon payments are likely to continue—and its total return. Both are uncertain. Professional investors rely on extensive statistical analysis in their decision process. Individuals usually do not have access to these models.

Analyzing GNMA cash flows requires mastering a whole new set of conceptual tools and vocabulary. But you should not purchase individual GNMAs (or any other mortgage-backed security) unless you are prepared to spend some time mastering the peculiarities of these securities. Within the scope of this chapter, I can only cover some basics.

Note also that GNMAs are taxable both at the federal and at the state level. Since Treasuries are exempt from state taxes, this erases some of the yield advantage that GNMAs have compared to Treasuries, particularly in states with high tax rates.

GNMA Cash Flows

The easiest way to start is to describe how a GNMA security is created. GNMA stands for "Government National Mortgage Association," which is an agency of the U.S. government within the Department of Housing and Urban Development (HUD). That agency does not issue bonds. Rather, its role is that of an insurer and facilitator.

The process of creating GNMA securities (or as they are also known, GNMA pools) begins when a builder or a developer puts up a development. At the point where the builder has obtained financing and sold a number of houses to individual homebuyers (who have obtained individual mortgages), the builder—or more precisely, the mortgage originator—applies to the GNMA for a pool number and GNMA backing. Only mortgages insured by the Veterans Administration (VA) or the Federal Housing Administration (FHA) are accepted. Because these mortgage payments are insured by government agencies, GNMA is able to unconditionally guarantee timely payment of interest and repayment of principal. The mortgages are then bundled together by a servicer into one pool totaling a minimum of $1 million. Pieces of this pool are then sold to investors. You might consider this pool as similar to a mutual fund, except that in this case the fund is made up entirely of mortgage payments. Exhibit 8–1 illustrates how this process works.

When you buy a GNMA (colloquially known as "Ginnie Mae" or "Ginnie" for short), you are buying a percentage amount

E X H I B I T   8–1

Origination of a GNMA Pool

GNMA Pool Organization

Mortgage lender gives commitment to the home buyer.

Mortgage lender obtains guarantee from GNMA.

Buyer settles on house; mortgage is obtained.

Lender pools similar mortgages and delivers to securities dealer but retains responsibility for servicing.

Securities dealer sells mortgage pools, in whole or in part, to investors and advises GNMA of new owners.

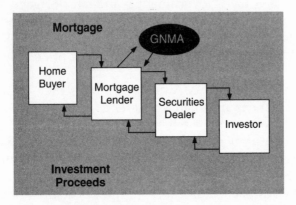

After the pool is originated, the lender collects monthly payments of principal and interest from the home buyer by the 30th of each month and forwards them to GNMA.

GNMA disburses payments to investors by the 15th of the following month whether or not payment has been received from the home buyer.

Source: T. Rowe Price Associates. Reprinted with permission.

of the pool. This pool consists of mortgage payments, which have been repackaged (the Wall Street word is "securitized") in order to create a debt instrument with a fixed coupon. Through the magic of investment banking, individual mortgages have been transformed into debt instruments. But the cash flows of GNMAs differ from those of other bonds. The cash flows of GNMAs are exactly those of the underlying individual mortgages "passed through" from the original homeowners to the purchaser of the Ginnie Mae security. (That is the reason that mortgage-backed securities such as GNMAs are sometimes also called "pass-throughs.")

Let's take a closer look at a typical GNMA pool. Each pool is made up of mortgages bundled together because they share a number of characteristics. All mortgages are fixed rate; they are issued for 20 to 30 years and at the same interest rate, based on prevailing interest levels. The servicer acts as middleman. He receives the mortgage payments made by homeowners and sends them to the purchasers of GNMA securities, charging 1/2 of 1% for his services. As a result, the coupon rate of GNMA securities is 1/2 of 1% lower than the homeowner's interest cost. For example, 8% mortgages would be bundled together into GNMAs with a 7 1/2% coupon. (There are also adjustable rate pass-throughs, but that's another topic.)

When you buy a GNMA, the payments you receive are percentage amounts of those sent by homeowners to their bank. Each homeowner sends a fixed monthly amount to his bank that includes both interest and principal. On a 30-year mortgage, during the first few years a small fraction of the monthly payment pays down principal. That percentage gradually increases through the life of the mortgage based on a preset schedule, called the "amortization schedule." As the amount paying down principal increases, the amount of interest correspondingly declines. Table 8–2 shows the cash flows for a mortgage with a servicing fee. (The assumptions are that the mortgage loan totals $100,000. The term of the loan is 30 years—equal to 360 months. The servicing fee is 0.5%; the mortgage rate is 9.5%.)

This is the first aspect of GNMA monthly cash flows, which differentiates them from those of other fixed-income instruments. Every month you receive some principal and some interest. When the last payment has been made by the last homeowner in a

T A B L E   8–2

Cash Flow for a Mortgage with Servicing Fee

Month	Beginning Mortgage Balance	Monthly Mortgage Payment	Net Interest for Month	Servicing Fee	Principal Repayment	Ending Mortgage Balance
1	$100,000.00	$840.85	$750.00	$41.67	$49.19	$99,950.81
2	99,950.81	840.85	749.63	41.65	49.58	99,901.24
3	99,901.24	840.85	749.26	41.63	49.97	99,851.27
4	99,851.27	840.85	748.88	41.60	50.37	99,800.90
...	...	...	...	...	...	...
...	...	...	...	...	...	...
...	...	...	...	...	...	...
98	92,862.54	840.85	696.47	38.96	105.69	92,756.85
99	92,756.85	840.85	695.68	38.65	106.53	92,650.32
100	92,650.32	840.85	694.88	38.60	107.37	92,542.95
...	...	...	...	...	...	...
...	...	...	...	...	...	...
...	...	...	...	...	...	...
209	74,177.40	840.85	556.33	30.91	253.62	73,923.78
210	73,923.78	840.85	554.43	30.80	255.62	73,668.16
...	...	...	...	...	...	...
...	...	...	...	...	...	...
...	...	...	...	...	...	...
357	3,297.89	840.85	24.73	1.37	814.75	2,483.14
358	2,483.14	840.85	18.62	1.03	821.20	1,661.95
359	1,661.95	840.85	12.46	0.69	827.70	834.25

Source: Frank Fabozzi, ed., *The Handbook of Fixed Income Securities*, 5th ed. (New York: McGraw-Hill, 1997), p. 508.

GNMA pool, the entire principal has been paid back. (There is not a large sum remaining to be redeemed as there is when other bonds mature.)

Bear in mind that the principal payments are not income. The principal payments received each month are your own money being returned to you. If that is not immediately obvious, consider the following analogy. Suppose you lend someone $100 to be repaid in ten equal monthly installments with interest. Each month you would receive $10.00 worth of principal, in addition to the interest payment. At the end of the ten months, your entire principal would have been repaid; no more would be forthcoming.

But the story does not stop here. Remember that your GNMA is made up of small pieces of many mortgages. Few homeowners hold mortgages for 30 years. Whenever a home is sold, its mortgage is prepaid in full. Homes may be sold for many different reasons. Some of these reasons have to do with lifestyle decisions. Homeowners may buy a larger house. They may retire, or divorce. Or they may have to move because of a job change or a birth or a death in the family. But homeowners may also prepay a mortgage for economic reasons. If interest rates decline, many homeowners refinance their mortgage in order to reduce monthly payments. If you own GNMA bonds, this is the key factor to keep in mind: it ties prepayments directly to declines in interest rates.

Whenever a mortgage is prepaid, the prepayments are *passed through* directly to the holders of GNMAs. Prepayments radically complicate GNMA cash flows. Much of the time, payments on a GNMA cease well before the original term of the mortgage loans. Whenever a mortgage is prepaid, a number of things happen. First, you get back some principal. But bear in mind that you receive interest only on the principal amounts that remain outstanding. Therefore, as principal comes back to you, your interest income decreases. Moreover, if many of the mortgages in your GNMA pool are paid down, interest payments on those mortgages cease altogether. As a rule, prepayments speed up the return of principal and shorten the amount of time a GNMA remains outstanding. As a result, even when GNMAs are made up of 30-year mortgages, they are viewed by the market as intermediate, rather than as long-term, securities.

In addition, due to the unpredictable timing of prepayments, no pool behaves exactly like the average. As a result, when you buy a GNMA, you cannot predict either the timing or the speed of prepayments. You also cannot know the final date when all payments cease. This, in turn, means that any yield quotes are, at best, highly inexact estimates.

Let's sum up the differences between GNMA cash flows and those of other bonds. When you buy a bond, you receive interest payments in the form of coupons, usually twice a year. At the bond's maturity, you receive a much larger sum, the principal, which is redeemed in full in what is in effect a large balloon payment. You know at the time of purchase exactly how much you will receive for each coupon payment; the dates of these coupon payments; and the date of repayment of the principal balloon.

Payment schedules for GNMAs, however, differ radically from the above. You receive a check each month that consists of some principal and some interest, based on the amortization schedule. Principal is paid off not in one balloon at the bond's maturity, but carved up into little monthly increments. Whenever mortgages are prepaid, the amount of principal you receive increases; but concurrently, the amount of interest declines. GNMA payments continue until the last mortgage in the pool is paid down. At that point all payments cease. No one, not the servicer, not the builder, and not the GNMA, can predict with certainty either how long it will take before all mortgages are prepaid or the timing and size of prepayments. So while a GNMA has a stated final maturity date, when you buy a GNMA, you cannot know how much you will receive each month or how long it will take before that particular GNMA is paid down.

In the bond market, however, you are compensated for uncertainty: all these uncertainties are one reason that GNMAs yield more than Treasuries. Another reason is that the interest rate on the underlying mortgages is higher than concurrent interest rates paid by Treasury securities.

How Do Interest Rate Changes Affect GNMAs?

GNMAs, like any debt instrument with a fixed coupon, react to changes in interest rate levels. But again, they do so in their own unique way. Once again, prepayments are the complicating element. Elsewhere in the book, I emphasized that when interest rates decline, the value of your bonds goes up, and that when interest rates rise, the value of your bonds declines. That volatility is directly tied to maturity length. But for GNMAs that relationship is modified. Here is why.

Suppose, for example, that interest rates decline substantially. In that event, homeowners are likely to rush to refinance their mortgages. If you own a GNMA, this is bad news. First, prepayments are likely to speed up dramatically. A large percentage of your GNMA pool is likely to be paid down far earlier than you assumed. And secondly, you get lots of principal back, just when rates are lower. Now you have to reinvest at lower rates. The result is: not only won't your GNMA appreciate in price as much as other bonds with similar maturities, but in some cases your GNMA may actually decline in value. Also, the total return you earn on the GNMA is likely to be substantially lower than you initially anticipated for two reasons: you will be reinvesting large amounts of money (the principal being returned to you) at much lower rates than the coupon interest of your original GNMA, and because of this, the price of your original GNMA is likely to have declined. As a result, in rising markets the upside potential of GNMAs is more limited than that of other bonds with similar maturities.

Now suppose interest rates rise. This also is bad news. First, prepayments slow so that the life of your GNMA pool is likely to increase. In this instance, you will have to hold on to your GNMA longer than you anticipated. What is more, at this juncture, the coupon of your GNMA is lower than rates currently available in the market. Therefore, you guessed it: the price of your GNMA is likely to decline more steeply than that of other intermediate bonds.

Both of the preceding scenarios are simplified. Premium, discount, and par GNMAs react differently to interest rate changes. Also, volatility in the face of interest rate fluctuations is cushioned for GNMAs by the fact that the market treats them as intermediate, rather than long-term, instruments. But interest rate fluctuations may create a kind of "heads I lose, tails I lose" situation. In rising markets, GNMAs underperform other bonds. In declining markets, they may decline somewhat less, but not much less than other bonds. So while GNMAs yield more than Treasuries on a current yield basis, when total return is considered, there are time periods when individual GNMAs may not perform as well as Treasuries. Moreover, the total return of an individual GNMA, as we shall see, is far more uncertain than that of Treasuries.

THE VOCABULARY OF GNMA RETURNS

Let's assume you are being "shown" a GNMA pool, that is, an individual GNMA security. Your salesman will no doubt be looking at a *Yield Table*, derived from a Bloomberg (professional) terminal. This is very different from the free *Bloomberg* website available on the Internet. The Bloomberg (professional) database has become ubiquitous in the trade. It contains an extraordinary range of data concerning all types of securities. For GNMA securities, each Bloomberg GNMA Yield Table is based on cash flow scenarios contributed by several leading brokers. In effect, it represents the consensus estimate of the cash flow patterns and returns for that particular GNMA security. If you are shown a quote on paper, it will look like Exhibit 8–3. The quote will look busy and confusing. But it contains a lot of information that is not self-explanatory.

Exhibit 8–3 shows a GNMA with a 7.5% coupon, based on 8% underlying mortgage interest rates. The number at the very top (GN499399) is the pool number of the GNMA. That number is assigned by the GNMA when the developer obtains GNMA backing. The other long number (36210QX49) is the CUSIP number which identifies the specific GNMA. The date (7/15/29) is the final maturity date for the GNMA, that is, the date when the very last mortgage in the pool will be totally paid down.

What follows is an explanation of the terms which you need to understand in order to evaluate the GNMA.

Face Amount, Factor, and Remaining Balance

These terms do not appear on the quote, but the corresponding numbers do. They are in the top box, on the left. The *face amount* is the initial amount of mortgage principal ($17,763,596) still outstanding for this particular security. Expressed as a decimal, the *factor* (0.929599120000) is the percentage of the mortgages in the pool that has not been paid down. (Factors are published by the GNMA for all outstanding GNMA mortgage pools.) Factors change over time. The *balance* ($16,513,023) is the principal amount of the original mortgages that has not been paid down, in dollars. The balance is calculated by multiplying the face amount by the factor. It is, in a sense, the current par value of this particular pool.

Next Pay, Record (rcd) Date, and Accrual

These are bookkeeping terms. *Next pay* (9/15/00, monthly) is the next date you would receive a check. As specified, the check will be paid once a month. *Accrual* indicates the amount of time interest has already accrued. Like accrued interest on municipal bonds, it will be added to the current offering price, when you buy the GNMA. The *record date* (8/31/00) is the date of record for the

EXHIBIT 8–3

Yield Table for a GNMA from a Bloomberg Terminal

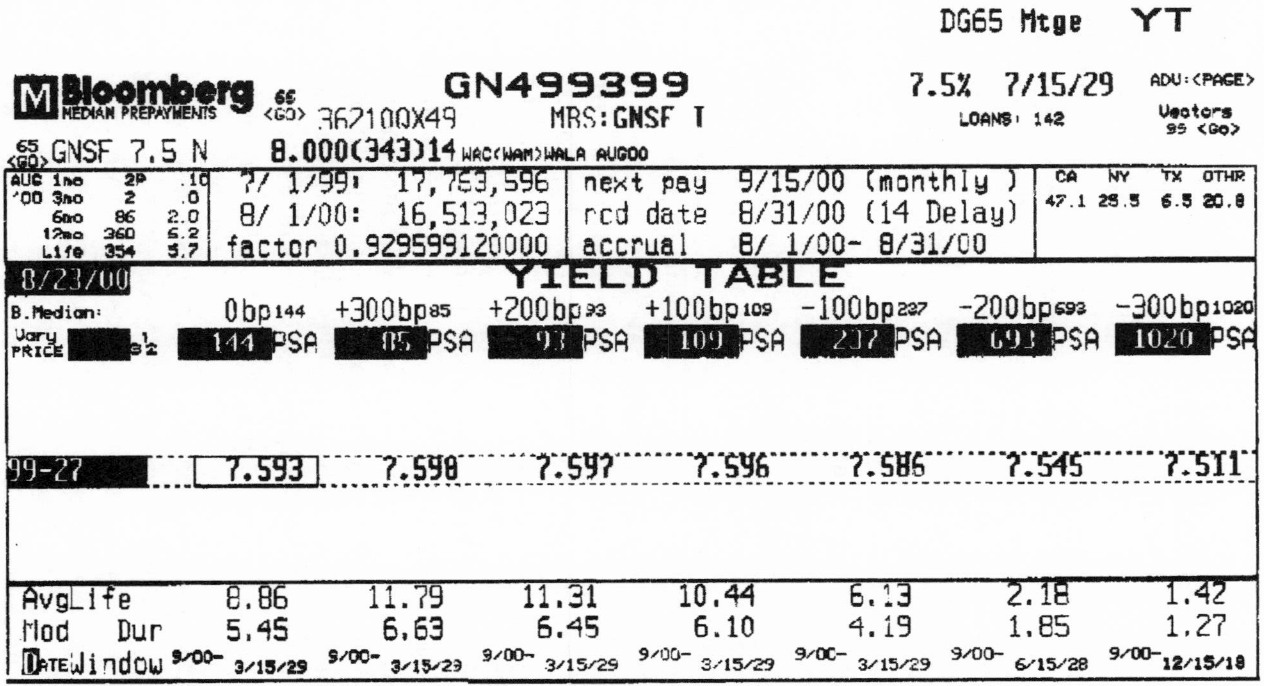

DG65 Mtge YT

Bloomberg MEDIAN PREPAYMENTS 66 <GO> GN499399 7.5% 7/15/29 ADU:<PAGE>

362100X49 MRS:GNSF I LOANS: 142 Vectors 95 <Go>

65 <GO> GNSF 7.5 N 8.000(343)14 WAC(WAM)WALA AUG00

AUG '00 1mo 2P .10; 3mo 2 .0; 6mo 86 2.0; 12mo 360 6.2; Life 354 5.7	7/ 1/99: 17,763,596; 8/ 1/00: 16,513,023; factor 0.929599120000	next pay 9/15/00 (monthly); rcd date 8/31/00 (14 Delay); accrual 8/ 1/00- 8/31/00	CA 47.1, NY 28.5, TX 6.5, OTHR 20.8

8/23/00 YIELD TABLE

B.Median:	0bp 144	+300bp 85	+200bp 93	+100bp 109	-100bp 237	-200bp 693	-300bp 1020
Vary PRICE 1/32	144 PSA	85 PSA	93 PSA	109 PSA	237 PSA	693 PSA	1020 PSA
99-27	7.593	7.598	7.597	7.596	7.586	7.545	7.511
AvgLife	8.86	11.79	11.31	10.44	6.13	2.18	1.42
Mod Dur	5.45	6.63	6.45	6.10	4.19	1.85	1.27
DATE Window	9/00- 3/15/29	9/00- 3/15/29	9/00- 3/15/29	9/00- 3/15/29	9/00- 3/15/29	9/00- 6/15/28	9/00- 12/15/18

Source: Bloomberg Professional. Reprinted with permission.

origination of the pool. The "14 delay" notation simply indicates that the servicer of the GNMA pool sends the check 14 days after receiving mortgage payments.

Current Offering Price

The current offering price (99.27) is stated in multiples of 100, as it is for any other bond. In this instance, as is the case for Treasury bonds, the number after the decimal (.27) should be read as 27/32nds. The price therefore, would be $990, plus 27/32 times $10.00, that is $998.44. Because this is a relatively recent GNMA security, it trades at a small discount from par. (GNMAs, like other bonds, can also trade at a discount, at par, or at a premium.)

Prepayment Assumptions

For GNMAs, yield quotes are meaningless unless they are tied to specific prepayment assumptions. You will notice that several yields are quoted, starting with 7.593 through 7.511. Each yield is listed under a specific prepayment assumption, which is listed as "PSA" plus a number. This requires an explanation. Let's first explain how to interpret *prepayment assumptions* and PSA.

Prepayment assumptions have gone through a number of different formulations. The basic method used has been to compare the prepayment history of each pool to a benchmark. During the early 1990s, the benchmark most often used by brokers selling GNMAs to individual investors was based the data compiled by the the Federal Housing Administration (FHA). Periodically, the FHA published updates of past prepayment patterns, based on the latest nationwide figures. The GNMA maintained statistics for each pool, expressed as a percentage of current published "FHA experience"; that is, the latest FHA data. If prepayments were an exact match of FHA experience, the pool was said to prepay at 100% FHA experience; if at twice the speed, it was said to pay at 200%.

Using FHA experience as a yardstick, however, proved cumbersome because, whenever data were revised, so was FHA experience. In other words, the yardstick (FHA experience) kept on changing. To cope with this shortcoming, two other models came into use. The first to be developed was known as "Constant Prepayment Rate" (CPR). As its name implies, CPR is a constant.

Prepayment patterns, which change continually, are expressed as multiples of CPR. The CPR for any period is the percentage of mortgages outstanding at the beginning of the period which terminate during that period. For example, if a pool of mortgages prepays at a constant rate of 1% per month, then 1% of the outstanding balance (in addition to scheduled principal repayments) will be prepaid each month.

Currently, the industry standard is the Public Securities Association (PSA) model. That model combines features from both of the preceding models. It is based on data published by the FHA. And like CPR, it assumes a rate of prepayment of principal. But that rate is not *one* constant. Rather, it is expressed as a series of prepayment rates for the entire life of the GNMA pool. The PSA benchmark (denoted as 100% PSA) assumes a series of CPRs that begin as 0.2% in the first month and increase by 0.2% each month thereafter. These prepayments level 30 months after mortgage origination to 6%. If a particular GNMA pool is said to prepay at 200% PSA experience, that would mean that for the first 30 months, principal would prepay at 0.4%, leveling off to 12% after 30 months.

An older GNMA pool will have a prepayment history. Older and new pools will both list a number of future prepayment scenarios.

Yield
The *yield,* technically, is called the *cash flow yield.* The yield is comparable to what is known for other bonds as yield-to-maturity. YTM, as you will recall, takes into account all the cash flows earned by a bond: interest; interest-on-interest (assumed to be based on reinvestment at the initial YTM rate); and redemption of the security at par.

You can readily see why quoting such a yield poses problems for a GNMA security. There is simply no way to predict when the mortgages that make up the GNMA will be paid off, or when prepayments will begin. This is where the prepayment assumptions become relevant. In order to quote a yield for a GNMA, estimates have to be made about prepayment possibilities. So instead of quoting just one yield, a typical Bloomberg quote, like the one above, lists a range of prepayment assumptions, based on specific PSA speeds. Those PSA speeds themselves are tied to a range of scenarios about changes in interest rate levels. This is very concentrated information. Starting from left to right, read:

- 0bp. That means, if interest rates stay flat, we assume 144 PSA. The yield would then be: 7.593%.
- Next +300bp. Read: if interest rates go up 300 basis points, PSA speeds slow down to 85. The yield would be 7.598%.
- Let's move to the last number (−300 bp). Read: if interest rates decline by 300 bp, then prepayments speed up rapidly. We then assume a PSA speed of 1020. The yield would then be 7.511%.

None of these yields should be interpreted as a prediction of the actual return. Rather, the different scenarios indicate a possible range of returns, depending on what happens to interest rates, and how those changes affect prepayment speeds. In this particular example, because the price of the GNMA is close to par, there is only a small difference from lowest to highest yield. If the GNMA was trading either at a discount, or at a premium, the range of yields would be much wider. Bear in mind, also, that yield quotes are based on the assumption that prepayments occur at par, and that the GNMA is redeemed at par.

Average Life and Duration

Duration (in this quote) has the meaning that it always does. But note that for this security, it is tied to another term, *average life*. Average life is a technical term which pinpoints the approximate point in a GNMA's life when half of the principal will have been paid back. If you are considering buying individual GNMAs, this number is important. The market prices GNMAs based on these midpoint measurements and totally ignores the final stated maturity date of the mortgages. In effect, this number is the market's estimate of how long the GNMA will remain outstanding.

If you are comparing a GNMA to other securities (Treasuries, for example), you would compare the cash flow yield of the GNMA to the YTM of a Treasury whose final maturity was about the same as the average life of the GNMA. For example, compare the cash flow yield of a GNMA with an estimated average life of two years to the YTM of a two-year Treasury; and one with an estimated average life of 12 years to a 12-year Treasury.

Note that the term "average life" is somewhat confusing. Even though the market treats this number as if it denotes the anticipated longevity of the security, in reality, average life describes the average number of years that each principal dollar will be outstanding. Average life is weighted for time and is related to speed of prepayments. The higher the prepayment speed, the shorter the average life.

In Exhibit 8–3, take a look at the numbers listed as possibilities for average life: they range from 8.86 years to 1.42 years. This is not an unusual range. This series of numbers pinpoints very precisely the risk you incur when you buy this security. It is impossible to predict how long it will remain outstanding. If interest rates go up, prepayments slow down. The GNMA then becomes a much longer security. If interest rates decline, on the other hand, prepayments speed up. The GNMA becomes much shorter.

Window

This is the date when you would start receiving payments and prepayments of principal. For GNMAs, the window is always open. That means you start receiving principal payments immediately. On this security, if you assume interest rates stay flat for the entire life of the GNMA—a most unlikely possibility—(the 0bp assumption), you would receive principal for almost 30 years: from 9/00 to 3/15/29. If, on the other hand, you assume interest rates decline (−300bp assumption), and if, as a result, prepayments occur much more rapidly, most of the principal would have been repaid by 12/15/18. (As we will see later, for CMOs, there is a lockout period so that the window is defined more narrowly.)

The only yield measurement that is computed for GNMAs exactly like that of other bonds is current yield, which, as you will remember is coupon divided by price. In Exhibit 8–3, the yield, 7.5%, is divided by the price, which is close to 100. Therefore, current yield is approximately also 7.5%.

Before proceeding further, a few important caveats are in order.

1. *Your total return will differ from any of the quoted yields.*

GNMAs are sometimes purchased because the quoted yields appear high when compared to other high-quality credits such as Treasuries. So let's review the assumptions underlying the yield.

This will make clear why it is highly unlikely that yield will actually be earned.

The assumptions underlying the yield are:

+ That all interest received will be reinvested rather than spent. Spending monthly payments will lower return.

+ That interest and principal payments will be reinvested at the same rate as the quoted yields. This is highly unlikely for individual investors, particularly if the quoted yield is high. If, for example, the yield is 8%, and monthly checks are swept into a money market account, which yields less, then that too will lower the actual return.

+ Quoted yields are tied to specific prepayment assumptions. In the event prepayments speed up or slow down substantially, the total return will differ considerably from any of the stated yields. Prepaid principal may be returned at a lower—or higher—price than your cost, resulting in capital gains or losses. Also, both principal and interest will then be reinvested at rates differing from the cash flow yield quoted at the time of purchase.

+ Bear in mind that prepayment speeds will affect the price at which you can sell the GNMA if you need to sell before the GNMA is retired. Suppose, for example, that interest rates decline. Prepayments will speed up and that will shorten the life of your GNMA. But this shorter life will not result in the same price changes for all GNMAs. If, for example, you bought a premium GNMA, and prepayments speed up, the principal is returned at par, and therefore, at less than your cost. Also, you now have to reinvest returned principal at a lower interest rate. In that event, if you need to sell, you sell at a loss. On the other hand, if you bought your GNMA at a discount, and prepayments speed up, principal is returned to you faster than initially anticipated, and at a price higher than your cost. This means you can sell at a profit.

2. *Don't confuse cash flow yield and monthly cash flow.*

Yield measures only interest income. Cash flow is the total monthly check you receive, which includes three different items: regularly scheduled principal payments, prepayments of principal; and interest. Some dealers (or mutual funds) lump together both interest and principal and call it monthly income. That results in inflated yields. Remember that the principal is your own money that is being returned to you. It is not income.

3. *Bear in mind that prepayment patterns are not predictable.*

Prepayment patterns have proved remarkably difficult to predict. During the early 1990s, the assumption, based on FHA experience, was that after 12 years only 17% of 30-year mortgages would still be outstanding. This assumption is no longer used.

Intuitively, the pattern of prepayments you might expect would be: low prepayments in the early years of a mortgage, acceleration thereafter; and finally, a leveling off in the later years. But significant changes in interest rates (and therefore in mortgage rates) have played havoc with prepayment assumptions. Large declines in interest rates such as those that occurred in 1993 and in 1998 caused massive prepayments and resulted in chaotic conditions in the GNMA market. Even this factor, however, is not consistent across GNMA pools. Some homeowners may behave in ways that do not seem to make economic sense. They may, for example, not refinance even if interest rates decline, because they may not be able to afford the cost of getting a new mortgage. They may also pay off existing mortgages with very low mortgage rates, just for the satisfaction of knowing they own their home free and clear. They may move for any number of reasons. All of this makes prepayment patterns of any one pool impossible to predict accurately.

One final note. Much of the preceding discussion may appear academic and irrelevant. But the reason for its inclusion is simple. GNMAs are purchased mainly for their higher yield compared to other securities with high credit quality. Therefore, it is important to understand how prepayments will affect your total return. The quote illustrated in Exhibit 8–3 is intended to clarify the uncertainties you face when you buy a GNMA. I have gone into a lot of details because if you are considering buying a GNMA, it is unlikely that you will actually be shown a detailed yield table, such as the one shown in Exhibit 8–3. When I wrote this section,

I approached several brokers, pretending to want to buy a GNMA, and most just quoted *one* yield, and the final maturity, as if that was sufficient. When I asked to see a quote from a Bloomberg on paper, some brokers refused. The reason, no doubt, is that brokers have had to deal with a lot of unhappy clients, who thought they had purchased a totally safe and predictable security, and found out otherwise.

Before turning to other mortgage-backed securities, let us note that all the terms used to describe GNMAs apply equally to all securities which are described in the remaining sections of this chapter. If you are considering purchase of any mortgage-backed security, you should insist at least on a verbal description of the key terms in the Yield Table, and better still, on being shown a quote on paper.

Differences Among Par, Discount, and Premium GNMAs

Because GNMAs have been issued since the mid-1970s, GNMA coupons range from about 6 to 17%. New GNMAs are constantly coming to market. Consequently, you can purchase GNMAs trading at a discount, at a premium, or at par. Each has advantages and disadvantages.

The *par GNMA* is the easiest to understand. GNMAs normally trade at par only when they are issued. They would therefore have no prepayment history and would be priced based on average expectations. Typically, for GNMAs with underlying mortgages of 30 years, average life might be anticipated to be about 12 years. Nonetheless, the Bloomberg will list a variety of prepayment assumptions and cash flow yields. Since none of the mortgages in par pools have yet been prepaid, par GNMAs are likely to be outstanding longer than either discount or premium GNMAs. Note that at the current time, you can also find GNMA pools based on underlying mortgages of 15 years or of seven years. Average life for these would be considerably shorter than for the GNMAs based on 30-year mortgages.

Discount GNMAs have coupons that are lower than current interest rates on mortgages. If interest rates remain stable, prepayments are less likely to speed up, since coupon rates are lower than current rates. Mortgages would be prepaid mainly for considerations other than interest rates. Therefore, cash flow is a little more predictable than for par GNMAs.

On the other hand, discount GNMAs are more interest rate sensitive than either par or premium GNMAs. This translates into steeper price increases or declines as interest rates fluctuate. Again, the reason for this is to be found in prepayment patterns. If interest rates decline, prepayments occur faster than anticipated. This boosts total return because prepaid principal which was purchased at a discount (since this is a discount GNMA) is returned at par. But if interest rates rise, prepayments slow. Average life becomes longer, and the longer maturities cause price declines to accelerate. Discount GNMAs then plummet in price.

Premium GNMAs were issued at a time when interest rates were higher than current rates. They, too, are older pools. In the event that interest rates rise, the high coupon acts as a brake and cushions against declines in price. Therefore, premium GNMAs are a hedge against rising rates.

But the high coupon can be a disadvantage if interest rates decline, particularly if the fall is steep. In that event, prepayments can speed up significantly. You will then have to reinvest both principal and interest at significantly lower rates. In all likelihood, you will hold the GNMA for less time than you initially expected. Ultimate total return will then be far lower than initially anticipated.

Also, steep declines in interest rates constitute a particular risk to anyone who purchases a GNMA at a premium. That is because the principal amounts of the mortgages, purchased at a premium (remember: this is a premium GNMA) are prepaid at par. Speedier prepayments always translate into capital losses for premium GNMAs. If the prepayments occur shortly after purchase, this can result in a very significant loss of principal.

Varieties of GNMAs

While GNMAs on single-family homes were the initial prototype, the market expanded to include a variety of GNMA pools. The cash flows of any of these pools are analyzed in the same manner, but the underlying mortgages differ. These are the main types still in the market.

GNMA I pools. Those are the "plain vanilla" GNMAs, such as the prototype just analyzed. They are composed of 12 (or more) fixed-rate 20- to-30-year mortgages and they total at least $1 million face value, all issued at the same interest rate.

Midgets. Those are composed of underlying mortgages with a 15-year maturity. Average lives would be much shorter than for GNMA I pools. Because of this maturity difference, GNMA midgets trade at a premium to regular GNMAs with the same coupons.

GNMA II pools. These have been issued only since 1983. They differ from GNMA I pools in a number of ways:

+ They are larger than GNMA I pools.
+ They are based on multiple rather than single issuer pools.
+ They have a wider range of interest rates than the original.

The larger size of the pool serves to even out prepayments somewhat. But because of the varieties of coupons and maturities, they are more difficult to analyze than GNMA I pools. They generally yield a bit more for that reason.

GNMA GPMs. GPM stands for "graduated mortgage payments." These are based, not on fixed rate, but on graduated mortgage payments. The cash flows are even more complex than for ordinary GNMAs. Also, the market for these is smaller and less liquid than for ordinary GNMAs.

GNMA mobile homes. These are based on mortgages for mobile homes. They have a shorter history than other GNMAs and have not been as exhaustively analyzed.

CMOs AND OTHER SONS OF GNMA

At the current time, GNMAs no longer dominate the market for mortgage-backed securities. The variations are of three kinds:

1. Who backs the mortgages.
2. Restructured cash flows.
3. Securities based on payment streams other than mortgages.

Let's briefly look at each category.

Who Backs the Mortgages: Federal National Mortgage Association (FNMA) and Federal Home Loan Bank (FHLMC)

In addition to the GNMA, two other agencies back mortgage-backed securities. All three agencies were created by Congress at various times in order to increase the amount of capital available for housing loans. The oldest of these is actually the *Federal National Mortgage Association* (colloquially known as FNMA or "Fannie Mae"), which was created by Congress in 1938 to help solve some of the housing problems brought on by the depression. In 1968, the original FNMA was separated into two different organizations: GNMA and FNMA. GNMA remains within HUD. Its mandate continues to be to facilitate government-assisted housing programs. FNMA was rechartered by Congress as a private institution to establish a secondary market for conventional mortgages, that is, for loans that were not insured by either the VA or FHA. FNMA is a publicly traded corporation whose stock trades on the New York Stock Exchange. The *Federal Home Loan Bank* (colloquially called "Freddie Mac") was initially owned by the 12 Federal Home Loan Banks. But in 1989, it too became a private corporation, much like FNMA.

The main difference between securities issued by the three agencies is that GNMAs are considered to be direct obligations of the government, backed by its full faith and credit; and therefore of the highest credit quality. Fannie Mae and Freddie Mac are Federal agencies which can borrow from the U.S. Treasury. Up to the present time, the ability to borrow from the U.S. government has conferred an *implicit* AAA rating on the debt of both of these agencies. Essentially, the market treated the securities issued by the three agencies as equally credit-worthy. As this book is going to press, some members of Congress, worried about the explosive growth of both Freddie Mac and Fannie Mae, were floating proposals which potentially might remove the implicit AAA rating. The immediate result has been that the spreads between securities issued by both Freddie Mac and Fannie Mae have widened somewhat, compared to GNMAs.

The three agencies also differ in the composition of the pools. GNMA pools consist of VA and FHA mortgages that are assumable. They tend to be concentrated regionally. FNMA and FHLMC (Freddie Mac) pools consist of larger conventional mortgages that are not assumable. The pools also tend to be larger and less regionally concentrated. Those differences might affect assumptions underlying potential prepayment speeds, and quoted cash flow yields would reflect those assumptions.

Initially, GNMA securities constituted the largest sector of the mortgage-backed market and consequently were also the most liquid. That is no longer the case. At the current time, FNMAs are probably the largest segment of the market, and the most liquid.

Private Issuer Backing

There are also so-called "private label" pass-throughs. These pools are issued by banks, investment banks, and thrifts. Typically, they are based on so-called jumbo mortgages, which are very large mortgages. The home buyers taking out these mortgages typically are affluent and sophisticated individuals, and this affects prepayment patterns. While private label pools are not insured by any government agency, they are rated by the major rating agencies (Moody's and Standard & Poor's), and most are rated either AAA or AA based on a variety of credit enhancements such as private insurance.

At the current time, this market is still much smaller than any of the agency markets, and it remains primarily an institutional market. But this too may change.

Restructured Cash Flows: Collateralized Mortgage Obligations (CMOs)

In 1983, after GNMAs came Collateralized Mortgage Obligations (CMOs). Another term that is now used interchangeably with CMOs is "REMIC," which stands for "Real Estate Mortgage Investment Conduit."

This is a segment of the market that has undergone enormous growth and change since the first edition of this book. Collateralized Mortgage Obligations consist of cash flows from mortgage-backed securities that have been diced and sliced and redivided (in Wall Street terms: "restructured") in order to eliminate some of the prepayment and longevity uncertainties of the original pass-throughs. The cash flows of the underlying securities are redirected and reconstituted into a series of bonds with more predictable average lives and prepayments than the original.

CMOs are based on much larger pools than GNMAs, ranging in size from $50 million to $1 billion. Each deal has features unique and specific to that particular CMO. The key difference between older mortgage-backed securities and CMOs is that CMO payment streams are redistributed to a number of different "tranches" ("tranche" is a French word meaning slice or portion). A CMO may have as few as three or as many as 50 different tranches.

The simplest CMOs are what would be called today *sequential pay* or "plain vanilla" CMOs. To illustrate how that works, let us assume that we are putting together a CMO, comprised of several GNMA pools. The CMO will have three tranches. All three tranches receive interest payments. Unscheduled prepayments, however, are sent *sequentially* to each tranche. The first tranche (or slice) receives all unscheduled prepayments made, say, during the first three years. Thereafter, that tranche is retired. In effect, it would be sold initially as a bond with an approximate three-year maturity. Unscheduled prepayments made during the next three years then go to the second tranche. That tranche is then retired, say, in eight years. The third tranche would then receive all remaining prepayments. The whole idea is to make the time the CMO remains outstanding more predictable. Investors seeking shorter-term maturities would buy the earlier tranches. Investors seeking longer-term securities would invest in the later tranches. The buyers of the later tranches would initially receive only interest payments. They would not receive prepayments until earlier tranches had been retired.

Companions, Planned Amortization Tranches (PACs), and Targeted Amortization Class (TACs)

The sequential CMO structure seemed to solve many of the uncertainties associated with GNMA pools. But once more, interest rates failed to cooperate. In 1993, interest rates declined precipitously. As a result, massive prepayments occurred: average lives of CMOs shortened dramatically. In 1994, however, interest rates did an about-turn. The Federal Reserve Bank raised interest rates seven times. Suddenly, prepayments slowed down to a crawl.

This is the exact reverse of prepayment risk, and in fact it has been given a name: *extension risk*. That risk is based on what happened to the anticipated prepayment patterns of CMOs in 1994. Since prepayments dried up, the average lives of CMOs became totally unpredictable. Tranches that were issued with anticipated average lives of two or three years suddenly were treated by the market as if their maturity had been extended to much longer terms. The price of these tranches plummeted.

To further limit this risk, another innovation occurred in the structure of CMOs. Two new types of tranches were created: *Planned Amortization Class* (PACs) and *companions*. The idea behind these two types of tranches is that the role of the companion is to protect the cash flows of the PAC tranches by absorbing either earlier prepayments or later prepayments. This is accomplished by redirecting prepayment cash flows that occur either too early or too late for the desired maturity of the PAC tranche to the companion tranche. Because it absorbs unscheduled or unwanted prepayments, the companion tranche is clearly the more volatile, and riskier, of the two types of tranches. For that reason, it usually sells with a higher yield. Companion tranches with the least predictable prepayment patterns have the highest yields.

The structure of CMOs divided into PACs and companions varies with each deal, as does the number of tranches. The schedule of principal prepayments is based on prepayment rates known as "PAC bands." These bands are targeted at a percentage of PSA speed: for example, 95% of PSA speed for early prepayments and 240% of PSA speed for later prepayments. This would enable the issuer to target cash flows to the PAC in a tighter maturity range. The average life of the PAC, theoretically, is then much more predictable; much less elastic than it would be without the PAC bands.

A similar but somewhat less tightly defined structure involves tranches called *Targeted Amortization Class* (TACs) and companions. You may also encounter the term "busted PAC," which indicates that the companion bands of a PAC have already absorbed all the prepayments that could have been targeted to it. As a result, the PAC is now "busted." That means that it is now trading without support, very much like older GNMA pools: it has become a less predictable, less liquid security, and for that reason it is likely to be quoting a higher cash flow yield.

Note also that as the market has continued to evolve, ever more complex structures have been devised. Some CMOs now come to market with several layers of PACs and several layers of companions.

The "Z" or Accrual Tranche

There is one more type of tranche that you might encounter: the "Z" or "accrual" tranche. The CMO structures described earlier (sequential pay, PAC, TAC, and companion) all redirect prepayments of principal. The Z or accrual tranche redirects payments of both principal and interest.

Think of the Z as resembling zero coupon bonds. A Z tranche receives no payments of any kind—either interest or principal—until specified tranches are retired. (This is called interest and principal lockout.) When the CMO comes to market, the Z tranche has a very small face value. During the years of principal and interest lockout, the Z tranche generates coupon interest at the same coupon rate as other tranches in the CMO, but this coupon interest is not paid out. Interest payments are said to "accrete," which is another way of saying they are added on to the original price of the Z bond, on a monthly basis. Once the classes preceding the Z bond are paid down, the Z bond begins to receive both principal and interest payments, based on the "accreted" value.

When Z tranches first came to the market, they were typically the last tranche of any CMO deal and invariably, therefore, had extremely long average lives. That is no longer the case: Z bonds can now be placed at different stages of the CMO structure. Z tranches have much the same appeal as zero coupon strips: during the accretion phase, there is no reinvestment risk. But because the average life of Z bonds (particularly those which are the last tranche of a CMO deal) is difficult to predict, these can be extremely volatile. For that reason, the yield is high: the higher the uncertainty, the higher the yield.

Let's sum up some of the key points concerning CMOs.

+ CMOs are a structure compatible with any guarantor.
  There have been CMOs backed by GNMA, by FNMA, by
  FHLB, and by private corporations. Some older CMOs
  that have become illiquid have been recycled into newer
  CMOs.

+ With the exception of Z (accrual) tranches, most CMOs
  pay interest monthly. Most CMOs have a principal
  lockout period, during which only interest payments are
  received. The period during which payments of principal
  are received is known as the "payment window." Both
  the payment window and the lockout period may change
  once the CMO is outstanding, depending on what
  happens to interest rates and how those changes in
  interest rates affect prepayments.

+ CMOs based on GNMAs, FNMAs, and Freddie Mac
  securities are deemed to have the same credit quality as
  the underlying cash flows. CMOs composed of private
  label issuers are rated by the rating agencies. Most are
  rated AAA or AA.

+ While companion tranches and Z tranches are designed
  to lessen the uncertainties associated with cash flows of
  CMOs, they limit but do not eliminate prepayment risk.
  Sudden sharp changes in interest rate levels can play
  havoc with planned maturity structures and cash flows.

+ CMO structures are constantly evolving. Major changes
  have occurred during the last decade, and more are
  likely to occur.

Advantages and Disadvantages of the CMO Structure

The CMO structure lessens some of the cash flow uncertainties
inherent in older pass-throughs. This is particularly true for PACs
and for earlier tranches in sequential pay (plain vanilla) deals.
These tranches protect the buyer from both interest rate risk and
prepayment risk. As a result, they yield less than later tranches or
companion tranches.

If you wanted to lock in a higher yield for a longer period
of time, you would buy the later tranches of a sequential pay deal.
By so doing, you would enjoy, in effect, a kind of call protection,

since the later tranches cannot receive any principal repayments until earlier tranches are retired. For higher yield, you could also buy either companion tranches or Z (accrual) tranches.

Finally, let's put the risks of CMOs in even plainer English. Because credit quality of these securities is very high, you know that you will get your money back. You just don't know when you will get it back, particularly for later tranches in sequential pay CMOs, companion tranches, or Z tranches. Moreover, sudden sharp changes in interest rates can throw off planned prepayment patterns even for CMOs with anticipated short average lives. If that happens, the price of these CMOs can plummet. What happens then is similar to what happens with zeros: if you hold your security until the last mortgage is paid down, you will get your entire investment back, plus interest. But if you need to sell anytime in between, you cannot know ahead of time the price at which you will resell. That price may be higher or lower than your initial purchase price.

In spite of the complex nature of CMO deals, CMOs as a group now appear to better meet the needs of individual investors than GNMAs because the structures that have evolved have a higher degree of predictability than older pass-throughs. In addition, they can be bought for as little as $1,000 minimum investment. It bears repeating, however, that while the CMO structure limits prepayment risk, it does not eliminate it.

If you are interested in buying these securities, I would suggest that you try to deal with a broker who has a lot of experience in this area. While the theory behind CMO structures is not difficult to understand, analyzing the cash flows and pricing of specific CMO tranches requires a high degree of information about the market for these securities; enough familiarity with prepayment patterns to be able to formulate reasonable assumptions about both the potential total return and the risks of a particular tranche; and the ability to analyze whether on that basis a specific tranche is appropriate for your investment needs.

Restructured Cash Flows: Stripped Mortgage-Backed Securities

Like any other bond, mortgage-backed securities can be stripped. Several types of strips exist, including interest-only strips (IOs) and principal-only strips (POs). There are also two classes of "floaters": floaters and inverse floaters. These are strips with floating rates. The coupon of a floater moves with interest rates. The coupon of an inverse floater moves in a direction counter to interest rates. These strips are all extremely sensitive to interest rate changes, and they are all highly volatile.

To understand some of the reasons behind the extreme volatility, ask yourself what would happen to any of these strips if interest rates move up or down. Let's use the "interest-only" strip as an example. An IO has no par value. Bear in mind that interest rate payments continue only on mortgages that remain outstanding. Therefore, the IO will receive interest payments only as long as underlying mortgages remain outstanding. Now ask yourself what would happen if interest rates declined and prepayments sped up. The answer is that interest payments to the interest-only strip would diminish and might disappear altogether. Clearly, therefore, a decline in interest rates can result in disastrous price declines for the interest only strips. On the other hand, if interest rates rise, that does not mean that the IO strip will automatically go up in price. Under certain circumstances, its price may actually decline.

Strips based on mortgage-backed securities are as volatile as the more volatile zero coupon bonds, but much less predictable. I mention these securities only to alert you to their existence and to their volatility. Any detailed analysis of these securities is beyond the scope of this book. They are used primarily by managers of institutional portfolios, as a tool for hedging. Using them as stand-alone securities is highly speculative.

Asset-Backed Securities Based on Assets Other Than Mortgages

Almost any type of loan can be repackaged and resold as an asset-backed bond. Many types of loans in addition to mortgages have been so repackaged. There is now a fairly significant market for asset-backed securities based on credit card loans, automobile loans, home equity loans, mobile homes, boat loans, and the like. Typically, the cash flows of these asset-backed securities are somewhat easier to analyze than those of mortgages. For one thing, the loans are not issued for as long as those of mortgages.

As one example, auto loans usually last four years, and pre-payments are less likely to occur than with mortgages. Average lives of auto-backed loans are in the 1.8–2.2-year range, with four to five years payment windows. Automobile loans usually carry a AAA rating, based on expected losses, structure, and credit support. They appeal to investors looking for securities with high credit quality and short maturities. In addition, many of the specific asset classes underlying these asset-backed bonds include a large percentage of subprime loans, that is, loans which may not be repaid. (The impact of defaults is offset by the fact that the loans are collateralized by assets which can be repossessed, and that the asset-backed bonds may be overcollateralized: for example, backed by 125% of the value of the loans. The overcollateralization feature insures that even if loans default, there will be sufficient coverage to pay back bondholders.)

Credit card loans currently make up the largest segment of the asset-backed market. Bonds created out of these loans may be very short: under one year. But the structure of asset-backed loans backed by credit cards is different from that of mortgage-backed securities. A large number of factors affect the credit quality of these loans. Among them are the underwriting standards of the credit card company; the number of credit card holders who fail to pay off their credit card loans; and the structure of the security, which differs considerably from that of other asset-backed or mortgage-backed securities.

At the current time, these newer asset-backed securities remain primarily institutional products: they are tailored to the needs of institutional buyers. Most of them are considered to be high quality credits. But the history of the market is that sooner or later, institutional products are eventually sold to individual investors. As always, before buying, check the spread against securities with similar maturities and credit quality. And check the past volatility of these securities in the market.

BUYING MORTGAGE-BACKED SECURITIES
Tax Considerations

Taxes on any type of mortgage-backed security are a bit of a nightmare. Interest on any mortgage-backed security is subject to federal and state taxes. Return of principal is not. Therefore, make sure you know how much of your cash flow is interest and how much is principal. If you own any pass-throughs, it is essential to maintain good records. Otherwise you will overpay your taxes.

In addition, if you sell your mortgage-backed security before final payments cease, you may incur either a capital gain or a capital loss (depending on the difference between the price you paid and the price at which you are selling). When prepayments occur, they too may subject you to a capital gain or a capital loss.

Because the tax considerations of pass-throughs are complex, if you have a large portfolio of these securities, it is advisable to consult with a tax adviser or accountant.

Some Tips for Buying Mortgage-Backed Securities

Even though technically GNMAs are still considered to have the highest credit quality, for most purposes there is little pricing difference between mortgage-backed securities based on credit quality. The critical factor for both yield and pricing is the level of uncertainty concerning the underlying cash flows. The higher the uncertainty, the higher, potentially, is the yield. The attraction of mortgage-backed instruments is the monthly cash flow, the higher current yield than Treasuries, and the credit safety.

While GNMAs were the original mortgage-backed instruments, CMOs now dominate that market for individual investors because they have been structured to reduce the prepayment and cash flow uncertainties associated with the initial GNMAs. Particularly for shorter tranches and PACs, cash flows of CMOs are now much more predictable. But remember: while prepayment risk has been reduced, it has not been eliminated.

The different CMO structures make them suitable investments for a variety of different purposes. If you are using them in tax-deferred accounts and you want the highest possible yields, then you might want to buy Z tranches, companion tranches, or later tranches. If you are in a relatively low income bracket and are looking for current income and high cash flow, then CMOs might provide you with a higher net-after-tax income than some of the shorter securities available, such as Treasuries or even municipals. (Because the yield curve of municipals is generally more steeply upward sloping than that of Treasuries, municipal bonds with short maturities typically have yields that are quite low and would be of benefit only to individuals in very high tax brackets.) Note, however, that GNMAs are taxable at both the state and federal level. Bear in mind, also, that if monthly income is spent rather than reinvested, then you are spending down principal.

Interest-only strips (IOs) and principal-only strips (POs) are highly speculative instruments. They are appropriate investments primarily for institutional investors and are purchased as tools for hedging a total portfolio.

That said, unless you have a large and well-diversified portfolio, it might be more convenient and efficient to purchase mortgage-backed securities through a mutual fund. The size and diversification of a mutual fund even out monthly cash flows. Furthermore, investing through a mutual fund simplifies reinvesting both interest and principal payments.

Here is a summary of points to remember when buying mortgage-backed securities.

♦ Buy mortgage-backed securities only if they yield more than Treasuries by a significant amount. That level varies with interest rates. In the past, mortgage-backed securities have been a good buy when the spread was at least 150 basis points above Treasuries. Remember to compare mortgage-backed to Treasuries on the basis of the estimated average life and not the stated final maturity.

♦ Ask to see cash flow yield based on a variety of prepayment assumptions. Make sure those assumptions are spelled out in terms of prepayment speeds.

♦ Be sure that you understand how faster or slower prepayments would affect the particular security you are considering. Would the security go up in price or down in price if interest rates rise (or if they fall)? Would faster or slower prepayments mean you would hold the security longer or less time?

♦ If you are investing a small amount of money, it may be more efficient to buy mortgage-backed securities through a well-managed mutual fund.

♦ Once again let me repeat: because any mortgage-backed security is complex, it pays to deal with a broker who can explain in specific detail the pricing and the risks of the specific securities you are considering. Bear in mind that CMOs are extremely large deals and that each is structured in unique ways. If you are considering buying a CMO tranche, you need to find out if it is a companion tranche and how the rest of the deal is structured in order to properly assess the risk of any tranche. Be particularly leery of anyone who is trying to sell you any mortgage-backed securities primarily because the quoted yield is high.

♦ Virtually no online broker currently sells mortgage-backed securities. But even if you can find them, given the complexity of these securities, I would suggest buying only through an experienced broker.

Current pricing and yield information concerning mortgage-backed securities is extraordinarily scanty. The major financial dailies publish very brief listings of a few representative issues. A typical listing would include the information contained in Exhibit 8–4.

Exhibit 8–4 lists prices and yields which you would have seen Monday, April 10. The listing includes prices and yields for a variety of mortgage-backed securities, including Freddie Mac, FNMA, and GNMA, as well as Collateralized Mortgage Obligations (CMOs). Some of the pass-throughs are based on 15-year mortgages and others on 30-year mortgages. For CMOs, the listing indicates the anticipated time the tranche will be outstanding and whether it is a sequential or a PAC tranche. The terms in the listing should all be clear based on this chapter. Yield refers to cash flow yield, calculated to average life. The spread, in all instances, is the spread to Treasuries whose maturity is close to the average life of the CMOs listed. As you would expect, the highest yields are quoted for longer maturities, which have the greatest amount of uncertainty. All cash flow yields are based on PSA prepayments speed assumptions, which are listed.

SUMMARY

In conclusion, mortgage-backed securities offer the buyer certain advantages, such as credit safety, monthly payments, and a high

Newspaper Listing for
Mortgage-Backed Securities

MORTGAGE-BACKED SECURITIES
Indicative, not guaranteed; from Bear Stearns Cos./Street Pricing Service

		Price (May) (pts-32ds)	Price Change (32ds)	Avg Life (years)	SPRD to Avg Life (Bps)	Spread Change	PSA (Prepay Speed)	Yield to Mat.*
30-Year								
FMAC Gold	6.5%	94-12	+02	10	162	+5	120	7.48%
FMAC Gold	7.0%	96-21	unch	9.6	175	+6	135	7.63
FMAC Gold	7.5%	98-22	−01	9.3	190	+7	150	7.80
FNMA	6.5%	94-10	+02	10.1	161	+6	120	7.46
FNMA	7.0%	96-19	+01	9.6	173	+6	135	7.61
FNMA	7.5%	98-19	−02	9.4	188	+7	150	7.78
GNMA	6.5%	95-00	+03	11	148	+6	100	7.32
GNMA	7.0%	97-13	unch	10.2	163	+7	120	7.48
GNMA	7.5%	99-12	−03	9.9	181	+8	135	7.67
15-Year								
FMAC Gold	7.0%	98-12	−02	5.6	128	+5	150	7.43%
FNMA	7.0%	98-12	−02	5.7	124	+5	150	7.38
GNMA	7.0%	98-27	−02	5.7	117	+4	145	7.31

COLLATERALIZED MORTGAGE OBLIGATIONS
Spread of CMO yields above U.S. Treasury securities of comparable maturity. In basis points (100 basis points = 1 percentage point of interest)

Mat	Spread	Chg from Prev Day
Sequentials		
2-year	91	unch
5-year	132	unch
7-year	143	unch
10-year	168	unch
20-year	181	unch
PACS		
2-year	78	unch
5-year	110	unch
7-year	125	unch
10-year	148	unch
20-year	169	unch

*Extrapolated from benchmarks based on projections from Bear Stearns prepayment model, assuming interest rates remain unchanged.

cash flow. GNMAs were the first and remain the prototype for mortgage-backed securities. But they had significant disadvantages. Prepayment patterns proved remarkably difficult to predict. As a result, total return was uncertain; and reinvestment risk very high.

CMOs have reduced many of the cash flow uncertainties associated with earlier GNMAs, but have not eliminated them. The level of uncertainty concerning prepayments varies depending on which tranche of a CMO deal you buy.

This is a sector of the market which has changed a lot since the first edition of this book. New types of pass-throughs are continually being added, and no doubt the market will continue to evolve.

SUMMARY: QUESTIONS TO ASK BEFORE PURCHASING A PASS-THROUGH

What kind of yield is being quoted (current yield, cash flow yield)?

What are the prepayment assumptions?

If prepayments speed up (or slow down), how will that affect this security? Will it mean that the security will be outstanding for a longer (or for a shorter) period of time? How will that affect the value of this security?

For a CMO: how is this deal structured? What type of tranche am I being offered: is it a companion? A PAC? A TAC? A Z (accrual) tranche?

What is the first payment date?

To whom could I sell this security if I need to resell? Do you make a market in this CMO?

ADDITIONAL REFERENCES

If you want to find out more about these securities, the definitive book is Frank Fabozzi, ed., *The Handbook of Mortgage Backed Securities*, 4th ed. (New York: McGraw-Hill, 1995). This book is brought up to date periodically.

CHAPTER 9

Corporate Bonds

This chapter discusses

- The classification of corporate bonds
- Risk factors of corporate bonds
- Corporate bonds with special features
- Junk bonds
- Buying corporate bonds

WHAT IS UNIQUE ABOUT CORPORATE BONDS?

Bonds issued by major corporations are known as corporate bonds, or corporates for short. They are commonly classified into four major groups. The first group, utilities, consists of both electric and telephone companies. These used to be highly regulated and, as a result, were considered among the safest of all corporate bonds. Since deregulation, that is no longer the case, particularly for bonds in the telecommunication sector. The second group, transportations, includes the bonds of airlines and railroads. The third group, industrials, is the largest and most heterogenous of the four groups. It contains bonds of some of the premier corporations in the country, such as General Motors, Exxon, and International Business Machines. It also contains so-called junk bonds.

The fourth group consists of finance companies such as banks and insurance companies.

Corporates are also classified on the basis of the security being pledged by the issuer as collateral for the bonds. The collateral may consist of mortgages (mortgage bonds); financial obligations (collateral trust bonds); or railway rolling stock (equipment trust certificates). Corporates that are not secured by any collateral are known as debentures or notes.

Over the past few years, the appeal of corporates for individual investors has declined significantly. As this chapter will make clear, for individual investors some corporates make sense but in limited situations, such as in tax-sheltered accounts.

If you were to consider yield only, corporate paper would appear attractive. As a group, corporate bonds always yield more than Treasuries. However, for individual investors the higher yield is partly offset by the fact that income from corporate paper is fully taxable at every level: federal, state, and local.

Moreover, corporate paper is far trickier to evaluate than either Treasuries or even munis. Credit quality varies from very high to extremely poor, and credit risk is a genuine concern. There is a lot more uncertainty concerning the future economic fortunes of corporations than there is concerning issuers of munis. Call provisions are more complex for corporates than they are for munis. Also, in the 1980s, corporate bonds developed a unique set of risk factors, described under the rubric: "event risk." Finally, whereas current yield is always higher for corporate paper than for Treasuries, over time, total return, particularly for lower-quality corporates, may be far lower.

This chapter will first discuss the risk factors that are unique to corporate bonds. It will then discuss corporate bonds that would interest individual investors because of specific features.

RISK FACTORS OF CORPORATE BONDS

Event Risk: How the Market Changed in the 1980s

The market for corporate bonds changed radically during the 1980s. This was due mainly to the emergence of the junk bond

market and to the wave of takeovers, restructurings, and leveraged buy-outs that swept corporate America in the 1980s, with
devastating results to some bondholders. The phrase "event risk"
entered the lexicon to designate the uncertainty created for holders
of corporate debt by the takeover phenomenon. This wave of takeovers and restructurings resulted in massive downgradings, sometimes overnight. As a result of these events, the price of many
corporate bonds dropped like a stone, sometimes also overnight.

As the 1980s progressed, and as takeovers involved ever
larger companies, event risk loomed as an increasing menace. This
uncertainty was compounded by the fact that takeovers were impossible to predict.

As a direct result of this turmoil, and in order to sell new
debt, corporations found it necessary to add a variety of induce-
ments—sometimes called "bells and whistles." Some, such as so-
called poison pill provisions, were intended to prevent takeovers
by making takeovers more expensive to the potential acquirer.
Other innovations, such as floating-rate notes and put bonds, were
intended to protect the bondholders against interest rate risk (see
below). Many of these bells and whistles have become permanent
features of the corporate bond market.

During the 1980s, partly as a result of event risk, maturities
in this market became much shorter. That trend has partially reversed, however. Indeed, some corporate bonds have been issued
with very long maturities: during 1997 and 1998, a number of
corporations (Disney, for example) issued 100-year bonds. At the
same time, maturities in the high-yield (or junk) market typically
remain in the five-to-seven-year range.

Credit Risk

The credit quality of corporate issuers varies enormously, from
AAA for some of the premier corporations in the country to as
low as C for highly speculative junk.

Evaluating credit quality for corporates is a more complex
process than for munis. The analyst must look at a variety of factors:

♦ Overall economic trends
♦ Trends within each industry

♦ The relative ranking of the individual corporation within its industry
♦ The quality of its management

There is, in addition, one major difference between corporate bond ratings and those of munis. Ratings are assigned to each individual issue, not to the issuer. Separate bond issues of a single issuer often have different ratings because bonds are ranked in order of priority for payment in the event of default. Senior debt is paid first. Less senior debt—either "subordinated" or "junior"—would be paid after the claims of senior issuers had been satisfied, and so on. Senior debt generally has a higher rating than junior debt.

Rating symbols for corporates are identical to those for municipals. But rating changes among corporates occur more frequently than years ago, partly as a result of event risk and partly due to generally declining credit reassessments. Moody's evaluates the bond indentures of corporate bonds for protection against takeover risk and incorporates those factors in its ratings. Two senior debt issues, for example, may have different ratings, based on event risk protection. Standard & Poor's rates corporate bonds for event risk under a special rating system called "event risk covenant rating." Bonds are rated from E1 to E5, E1 representing the lowest degree of protection, and E5 the highest. It should be stressed that although event risk appears dormant at the present time, it could spring back to life at any time. It should not be ignored. Very short-term corporate debt (that is, commercial paper) has its own set of ratings. Standard & Poor's has the most categories, from A (highest quality) to D (lowest quality, and in default). "A" paper is further subdivided into A1 (strongest of the A group) to A3 (weakest). Moody's has three ratings: P-1 (strongest) to P-3 (weakest).

Default Rates of High-Quality Corporate Bonds

Moody's publishes annual studies of default rates. Past studies have indicated that between 1970 and 1988, no bond rated AAA defaulted while rated AAA. The most recent study (dated 2000) shows that between 1920 and 1999, of the bonds that defaulted, fewer than 9% were rated investment grade one year prior to default. In other words, bonds rated investment grade have a low probability of default: the higher the rating, the lower the probability of default.

Therefore, if you are purchasing corporate bonds, you can protect principal against credit risk by limiting purchases to bonds rated at least A+ and monitoring those ratings periodically.

Call Risk

Like municipals, corporates are subject to call risk. But call features are more complex for corporates than for munis, and there is more risk of capital loss. Here's why.

With some exceptions, call provisions for munis are governed by interest rate considerations. Munis are callable if interest rates decline, at a price stipulated in the indenture.

Corporate bonds, on the other hand, may be called under a variety of circumstances. Like munis, corporate bonds may be called if interest rates drop, at a price and time stipulated in the indenture. But corporate bonds may also be called under a number of contingencies designated as refundings. If a corporation obtains sources of capital cheaper than the interest it pays on its bonds, it may use these proceeds to redeem (that is, to call) its bonds. These sources of cheaper capital include retained earnings, monies raised by selling assets, or proceeds from a stock offering. Finally, some bond indentures require a sinking fund, which means that a certain percentage of bonds have to be retired every year regardless of interest rate levels or refunding contingencies.

Sinking fund redemptions sometimes work to the advantage of the bondholders because some bonds are retired at par when interest rates have gone up and when the price of the bonds would normally decline. The lucky investor can then take his principal and reinvest it at higher interest rates. However, calls or refundings always protect the issuer and not the bondholders. Although bonds are called (or refunded) at par, that generally occurs at a time when interest rates have dropped and when principal has to be reinvested at lower interest rates. Particularly onerous to bondholders are calls that occur when bonds are trading at a premium to the call price. Such calls can result in a substantial loss of capital to anyone who purchased the bonds at the premium price.

Call protection is more "absolute" than refunding protection because call protection includes protection against refundings. Short to intermediate bonds are generally callable in three to seven years. Many long-term bonds have ten years of refunding protection but are callable at any time. Unfortunately, call and refunding provisions are sometimes obscure, and the broker selling the bonds may not be aware of them.

To protect against unwelcome calls, always investigate the call and refunding features of any bond that you are considering for purchase. Another strategy is to purchase only discount bonds. They are less likely to be called than either premium or par bonds. In the event discount bonds are called, the buyer is protected against a loss of principal (compared to premium bonds) by the lower purchase price.

CORPORATE BONDS WITH SPECIAL FEATURES

Put Bonds

A put feature gives the purchaser the opportunity to "tender" (that is, to resell) a bond back to its issuer at par, before the bond matures, at time periods specified in the indenture (typically every six months).

While a call protects the issuer, a put protects the bondholder. If interest rates go up, the bondholder can "put" the bond back to the issuer, that is, resell his bonds to the issuer at par, and reinvest the entire principal at a higher rate. Put features in a bond are designed to protect principal against interest rate risk. The ability to resell the bond to the issuer at par is intended to keep the bond trading at or close to par (assuming no credit deterioration). Effectively, the put feature turns the bond into short maturity paper at periodic intervals.

In practice, while put features have provided some protection against interest rate risk, they have not proved to be a panacea. Whenever major sudden changes occur in the interest rate environment, the put provision may not take place rapidly enough to prevent a price decline. There are also some undesirable features to put bonds. Typically, interest rates on put bonds are lower than on bonds with similar ratings and maturities—as one would expect, given their effectively shorter maturity. Moreover, put bonds trade like shorter paper, and this limits their upside potential in rising markets, when interest rates decline (compared to bonds with similar maturities but without the put features).

Floating-Rate Notes and Bonds

Like puts, floating interest rates on a bond are intended to provide protection against interest rate risk by maintaining bond prices close to par. Floating interest rates are far more prevalent in foreign markets than in the United States. They were introduced to the United States during the early 1970s.

The main feature of floaters is that the coupon rate is reset periodically, usually every six months, based on a stipulated benchmark. The benchmark used to reset the coupon is usually a short-term Treasury (the floater rate might be 3/4 of a point higher). It may also be LIBOR (the London Interbank Offer Rate), which is a key rate for European investors. Sometimes floaters also have a "floor"; that is, a rate below which the coupon will not fall. Some floaters give the bondholder the option of exchanging the floater against a long-term bond, at specified intervals, though at rates which may not be as attractive as those of the long-term bonds.

The rationale for floaters is that as interest rates change, resetting the coupon rate at periodic intervals will tend to maintain the price of the bond at or close to par. In practice, this has tended not to work out quite as well as had been hoped, for a number of reasons. First, during times of extreme interest rate volatility, rates are not reset quickly enough to prevent price fluctuations. Secondly, the coupon rates of floaters are usually well below those of long-term bonds and often not very attractive when compared to shorter maturity bonds.

Floaters are issued chiefly by major banks, such as the Chase Manhattan Bank and Citicorp.

Convertible Bonds

As the name implies, convertible bonds are issued by corporations with the proviso (in the indenture) that they can be exchanged for the common stock of the corporation at a specified price. The buyer has the advantage of a fixed coupon and the potential to share in the possible appreciation of the stock.

If the price of the common stock does not appreciate, as long as there is no default, the downside risk is limited, since the buyer will continue to receive coupon payments and can redeem principal at maturity. In theory, convertibles are somewhat less risky than the common stock. But they have the potential of capital appreciation if the stock does well.

Because of this feature, the price of a convertible bond fluctuates mainly in tandem with the price of the stock, and not in response to interest rate changes. Analysis of convertible bonds is therefore more closely related to equity analysis than to bonds, but with its own unique twists. Convertibles are regarded as a very specialized form of investment. That kind of analysis, however, is not within the scope of this book.

Corporate Bonds with Equity Warrants

This feature gives a purchaser the right to purchase the stock of the issuer at a specified price at some future date. In effect, the purchaser of the bond is being granted options to buy the stock at what is hoped will be an attractive price at some future date. This type of structure is sometimes used by fast-growing companies with limited cash flow to attract buyers to its debt: it enables the issuer to pay a lower interest rate than might be warranted by its low credit quality. *Amazon.com*, for example, was able to issue bonds with equity warrants at very favorable interest rates in 1999, in spite of the fact that it was losing money and the bonds were rated as junk. The purchaser of the debt, on the other hand, is hoping that the price of the stock will rise quickly so that he may realize a profit.

Bonds of U.S. Corporations Issued in Foreign Currencies

In the late 1980s, a number of corporations, including Anheuser Busch, Bankers Trust, Bank of Boston, General Electric, Sallie Mae (Student Loan Association, an agency of the U.S. government), Eastman Kodak, and Procter & Gamble issued bonds in New Zealand or Australian dollars, at interest rates of 14% to 17%, typically maturing in three years or less. Those bonds were available to U.S. investors, in the United States. And they were obligations of corporations that were highly rated at issuance.

These bonds had a number of attractive features. Yields were very high compared to those available for the same corporations in the United States at the same time (the spread was between 500 and 700 basis points). And interest rate risk was low since the securities were relatively short-term, maturing between two and three years.

The greatest risk incurred in buying such obligations is the currency risk. Before purchasing the bonds, the U.S. investor converts U.S. dollars into the foreign currency and reconverts into U.S. dollars at maturity. The coupon is received in the foreign currency. So to the usual sources of income from bonds (interest and interest-on-interest) the investor must add any appreciation or decline in the price of the bond due to currency fluctuations.

If the dollar falls against the foreign currency, the investor actually realizes a gain in addition to the interest coupons because the price of the bond goes up. However, if the dollar rises against the foreign currency, the investor incurs a loss because the price of the bond goes down. For the bonds mentioned above, a 5% to 6% rise in the U.S. dollar against the foreign currency would be sufficient to wipe out the interest advantage. This represents a substantial risk since currency exchange rates are even more volatile than interest rates and less predictable.

At the current time (mid-2000), the dollar is very strong. But if the dollar were to decline against foreign currencies, similar bonds might represent very attractive opportunities. Conditions that would make such bonds attractive would include interest rates substantially higher than those available in the United States on bonds of similar quality and maturity; and issuance in currencies considered particularly strong, in countries with low inflation rates.

Such bonds would also be advantageous to anyone who spends considerable time, or does business, in the country whose currency is being purchased. These bonds would in effect constitute a hedge against currency fluctuations.

The trend of issuing bonds abroad has expanded considerably, mainly in the Eurodollar market (see Chapter 10, on international bonds).

JUNK BONDS

Junk bonds—also known as "high-yield," "noninvestment grade," or speculative debt—have been so controversial and so significant since the 1980s that they deserve a more detailed discussion.

Junk bonds are unique because risk is almost entirely related to credit quality. The term properly designates bonds whose rating is lower than Baa3 by Moody's and lower than BBB by Standard & Poor's. Maturities of junk bonds have been in the five-to-ten-year range, so that interest rate risk is relatively low.

There have been speculative bonds as long as bonds have existed. The term "junk" bonds actually dates back to the 1920s, when it was used by traders to refer to debt instruments that were below investment grade. But that area remained the province of a few specialists. Up to the 1980s, the term "junk" or "speculative" bond was used to describe bonds of companies that suddenly found themselves in financial difficulty. These companies may have been about to go bankrupt or they may have been trying to emerge from bankruptcy. Their bonds were also known as "fallen angels." They were considered attractive speculations for any investor who could figure out which of those companies would ultimately survive and pay off, since they could be purchased at very deep discounts from par—sometimes as little as ten cents on the dollar.

In the mid-1980s, largely due to the activities of Mike Milken, of Drexel, Burnham and Lambert, a new type of junk bond was created: bonds that were issued primarily to finance merger and acquisitions activity. The most controversial of the junk bonds were designed to finance two types of takeovers: leveraged buy-outs and hostile takeovers.

During the mid-1980s, junk bonds flourished. They initially sold at a spread to Treasuries of about 400 basis points. A body of thought developed (among institutional investors and among academics) which maintained that junk bonds would continue to provide very high returns compared to higher-quality bonds. The reasoning was that, even in spite of potentially high default rates, the higher interest income would eventually result in higher total return than for higher-rated bonds. Institutions, including banks (mainly thrifts) and insurance companies, flocked to buy junk bonds. So did individual investors, mainly through the purchase of mutual funds. As a result of all this buying, at one point the spread between junk bonds and Treasuries narrowed to about 200 basis points.

In 1989 and 1990, junk bonds began to plummet in value. Declines were horrendous. When spreads between junk and Treasuries widened to about 700 basis points, some investors saw this as a compelling buying opportunity. Junk bonds (and junk bond funds) rallied briefly, only to decline in value again as the fear of an approaching recession spread. This time the declines in price were even more horrendous.

In November 1990, spreads between junk and Treasuries reached an unbelievable 1,200 basis points, on an aggregate basis. It is not an exaggeration to say that the selling of junk bonds during 1989 and 1990 reached panic proportions. At the height of the panic, junk bonds were being sold for 30 to 40 cents on the dollar, with yields-to-maturity ranging from 20% to 40%.

These extraordinary declines were due to a number of factors. Hanging over the market was a major liquidity crunch, which began with the exit of Drexel Burnham Lambert, Inc., the primary market maker in the junk bond sector, from this market. Suddenly the junk bond market seemed to have only sellers and no buyers. In addition, individual investors were bailing out of junk bond funds and forcing these funds to sell into the already illiquid market. Even worse, government regulators ordered thrifts and banks to get rid of any junk bonds they owned. Finally, default rates on junk bonds reached 5.6% in 1989 and 7% in 1990. There was increasing worry that default rates would go even higher if a recession occurred.

The panic was overdone. In early 1991, a very strong rally ensued. Since the early 1990s, in the aggregate, junk bonds slowly regained their luster—but again not without sinking spells and bouts of panic. The worst decline occurred during the economic crisis of 1998, particularly after Russia defaulted on its debt. At that point, a huge "flight to quality" occurred, which sent the price of Treasuries soaring. Yield spreads widened for all lower-quality bonds: the price of junk bonds plummeted. Again they recovered, but this time only slightly. Even after adding back the interest income, total returns for 1998 and 1999 range from negative to very low. Nonetheless, in spite of the occasional devastating declines, for the decade of the 1990s, average total returns for an *index* of junk bonds have exceeded those of higher quality credits. Returns for individual junk bonds, however, are all over the lot, from outright default to upgrades and significant gains.

Proponents of junk bonds like to point to a number of factors in their favor. First of all, the market for junk bonds has changed a good deal since the mid-1980s. No longer are these bonds used primarily for takeovers. While the term "junk" conjures up images of companies barely able to keep financially afloat, many large, well-known American companies now fall into that group. Approximately 20% of all corporate debt is now rated as junk. Moreover, the junk bond market has become much more diversified. It now includes new "growth" companies such as telecommunications companies (cable and wireless). In fact, the largest group of corporations whose debt is rated as junk are the newer telecommunications corporations, such as MCI WorldCom. Note, in passing, that a number of Internet firms, such as Amazon.com, have issued bonds that are rated as junk.

The junk sector also includes old, mature companies downgraded to the high-yield category. In the late 1990s, that group included well-known companies such as Boise Cascade, ITT, Pennzoil, Time Warner, and Polaroid. Finally, note that some companies reemerge to profitability after being downgraded to junk and operating under bankruptcy. Examples of that process include Continental Airlines and Federated Department stores, which now owns Bloomingdale's and Macy's.

Another argument in favor of junk bonds is that they provide diversification for a large portfolio because returns do not correlate precisely with either the stock market or with other sectors of the bond market such as Treasuries or GNMAs. Correlation is actually somewhat higher with the stock market—about 70%—than with the bond market. Proponents argue that junk bonds in a portfolio help to "smooth out" ups and downs of the total portfolio and that as a result, overall, junk bonds reduce the risk of the total portfolio.

Finally, proponents argue, in spite of higher default rates, the spread between the yield of junk bonds and higher-rated debt is large enough to compensate investors for the risk of investing in junk. Ultimately, the higher interest income, particularly when reinvested and compounded over long holding periods, will result in higher returns than investment-grade debt.

Key to this debate is the actual default rate of junk bonds. Surprisingly, even this aspect of junk bonds elicits some disagreement due to the fact that different methods are used to calculate default rates. One authority on junk bonds, Edward Altman of New York University, calculates the default rate by comparing the value of defaulted bonds to the par value of junk bonds outstanding. Moody's rating service, on the other hand, calculates default rates by comparing the value of defaulted bonds to the principal value (that is, the market price) of junk bonds outstanding. Moody's also includes the debt of emerging markets in its calculations, whereas Altman does not. The two methods for calculating default rates result in different ratios. As a result, for any period you will see different ratios published for default rates of junk bonds.

Finally, however the default rate is calculated, what really matters to investors in junk bonds is less the actual default rate than the actual loss in dollars. Even defaulted bonds do not automatically go to a value of zero. There is some salvage value to almost any defaulted bond.

The current buyers of junk bonds are primarily large institutional investors: insurance companies, pension funds, and mutual funds. Individual investors buy junk bonds mainly through mutual funds. Since the 1980s, spreads between junk and Treasuries have varied between a low of approximately 250 basis points (that is, junk yielding only 250 basis points more than Treasuries) in 1989 and in 1997, to a high (at the end of 1990) of close to 1,200 basis points. Clearly, purchasers of junk are being compensated more generously for the risk of purchasing junk when spreads are wide. When spreads are narrow, you have to wonder whether you are being compensated adequately for the risk.

So, how should you view junk bonds?

First of all, it is important to distinguish between the total returns of an *index* of junk bonds and the total return of individual issues. All parties to this debate agree that individual junk bonds are high-risk and volatile securities. Also, individual junk bonds continue to remain highly illiquid. Finally, total return of the individual junk bonds is highly unpredictable from year to year. The argument that junk bonds (as an asset class) actually lower the total risk of a portfolio must be viewed in the context of modern finance theory, which evaluates the amount of risk any one element of a portfolio contributes to the risk of an entire portfolio. Basically, this view is relevant only to investors who own very large, well-diversified, and probably mainly institutional-size portfolios. It emphatically does not mean that junk bonds are safer than investment-grade securities and belong in every portfolio. Nor does it mean that everyone should own some junk bonds.

Most individual investors should continue to regard junk bonds (or junk bond funds) as speculative. That means that they are suitable investments for investors who can afford a loss, or who can afford to take a long-term view and not sell during periods of negative returns. Moreover, because it would be utter folly to purchase junk bonds without diversifying, it is best for any individual investor who wants to buy junk bonds to do so through a mutual fund. Regardless of how well or poorly managed any mutual fund investing in junk might be, at least a mutual fund will provide diversification and lower risk than individual junk bonds.

BUYING CORPORATES

Corporates are purchased mainly by institutions such as pension funds and insurance companies. Inherently, this works to the disadvantage of the individual investor who purchases smaller lots. Inevitably, he will buy at lower yields and higher spreads than institutional investors.

Listed Bonds

Most corporate bonds are bought and sold like munis, over the counter. But bonds of a few well-known corporate issuers that are actively traded trade on the New York Stock Exchange (NYSE). A very few trade on the American Exchange. These are called "listed bonds." Tables of listed bonds appear daily in the major financial papers. Table 9–1 shows the prices and yields that would have appeared on Wednesday, August 16, 2000.

Reading from left to right, for the third bond listed, the table specifies:

T A B L E   9–1

Table of Listed (Corporate) Bonds

Bonds	Cur. Yld.	Vol.	Close	Net Chg.
CORPORATION BONDS				
Volume, $7,320,000				
AES Cp 4½05	Cv	25	217	+ 21
AMR 9s16	8.8	10	101⅞	+ ⅛
ATT 5⅛01	5.2	35	98¹⁵⁄₁₆	...
ATT 7⅛02	57.1	90	100¼	+ ¼
ATT 6¾04	6.9	15	98½	...
ATT 5⅝04	5.9	26	95	...
ATT 7½06	7.4	127	100¾	¼
ATT 7¾07	7.6	50	102¼	− ¾
ATT 6s09	6.7	100	89½	− ½
ATT 8⅛22	8.1	160	99¾	− ¼
ATT 8⅛24	8.1	45	100¼	+ ¼
ATT 8.35s25	8.2	90	101½	− ⅜
ATT 8⅝31	8.4	145	102⅝	+ ⅝
Aames 10½02	14.2	2	73¾	+ ¼

- The name of the issuer (American Tel & Tel, ATT)
- The coupon (5 1/8)
- The maturity date (01, that is, 2001)
- The current yield (5.2%)
- How many bonds were traded (35)
- The closing price on the preceding day, as a percentage of par (98 15/16)
- The price change compared to the previous trade (in fractions of a point: in this case, no change)

Note two peculiarities of this table. Unlike other bond tables, this table lists the current yield of the bonds, not the YTM. Also, only one price is given rather than the usual bid / ask spread. That should not be taken to mean there is no bid / ask spread.

These listings afford the individual investor a measure of protection because price quotes can be compared against actual trades. This is not possible for corporate bonds that trade over the counter.

The Bloomberg website, *Bloomberg.com,* also gives a list of representative quotes.

Corporate Bonds on the Web

Pricing information on corporate bonds is limited. A number of sites give very general indications of yields in the corporate sector. For example, once a day, *bondsonline.com* publishes tables of spreads between various sectors of the corporate bond market and Treasuries. These indications are so general that they are not very useful.

The best information at the current time is to be found on the website of the Bond Market Association: *investinginbonds.com.* This website publishes a daily report of actual trades that took place on the *previous* day. Exhibit 9–2 shows a listing that appeared on July 26, 2000. The listing is somewhat different from the newspaper tables of "listed" bonds. Reading from left to right, it specifies:

- The CUSIP number of the bond (36158FAC4) and its rating (AA)
- The name of the issuer (General Electric Global Insurance)
- The coupon (7.5%)
- The yield (7.537%). In this instance, the yield listed is the YTM.
- Its maturity date (6/15/2010)
- The spread to a benchmark ten-year bond (150 basis points)
- The price at which the trade took place (99.7343) and the size of the trade ($10 million)

Where call provisions exist, the yield-to-call would also be listed.

This report is similar to those available on the same website for municipal bonds, but it is far more limited. Transactions are listed only for investment-grade corporate bonds and only for extremely large lots, $5 million or higher. Individual investors buying much smaller lots would receive far lower yields. Also, there is no second level (as there is for municipal bonds) which allows you to view trade details. Only one price is listed. Still, limited as

E X H I B I T 9-2

Corporate Trade Data

▶ CUSIP	▶ Issue					Benchmark	▶ Price
▶ Ratings	▶ Sector	▶ Coupon	▶ Maturity	▶ Yield	▶ Spread		▶ Size
36158FAC4	GENERAL	7.500%	06/15/2010	7.537	10Y		99.7343
Aa1 M	ELECTRIC				150		<$10M
AA S	GLOBAL						
	INSURANCE						
	Financial Services						

Source: *investinginbonds.com* (website of the Bond Market Association). Reprinted with permission.

this report may be, this is the best information available on actual trades for nonlisted bonds at the current time.

The availability of corporate bonds through online brokers is also extremely limited. At the current time, *E*Trade* sells some corporate bonds. Schwab sells listed bonds only. Again, this is bound to change. But at the current time, all the usual caveats about buying bonds online apply.

When to Buy Corporates

The advantage of corporate bonds compared to Treasuries is that they yield more, sometimes as much as 100 to 150 basis points more for high-quality (AA or better) corporate bonds. Lower-quality issues, which include rating grades all the way down through junk, yield more than Treasuries by considerably wider spreads, depending both on the rating and the demand for junk at a particular time.

On a total return basis, the yield advantage of corporate bonds is less compelling. According to Ibbotson and Sinquefield, during the 1980s, long-term corporates had average compounded annual returns of 13%, compared to 12.2% for long-term government bonds. For the decade of the 1990s, through 1998, long-term corporates had average annual returns of 10.2%, compared to 10.7% for long-term governments. For those eight years, the total return of corporate bonds actually lagged behind that of governments.[1]

---

1. Roger G. Ibbotson and Rex A. Sinquefield, *Stocks, Bonds, Bills and Inflation: 1998 Yearbook* (Chicago: Ibbotson Associates, 1998).

Bear in mind that the aggregate total return of the corporate bond sector is boosted by the fact that it includes lower-rated corporate bonds, which yield more than higher quality debt. Indeed, some professionals feel that for individual investors, really high-grade corporates do not have a spread to Treasuries that is wide enough to compensate individual investors for some of the uncertainties of corporate bonds, such as event risk, or credit downgrades should the corporation run into economic difficulties. These professionals reason, moreover, that lower-grade corporate bonds are not worth the uncertainty.

As a group, corporate bonds are somewhat less predictable than munis, for all the reasons described above. The yield advantage over Treasuries is further diminished by the fact that Treasuries are exempt from state tax. As a rule, this is worth about 50 to 60 basis points.

For individuals in the higher tax brackets, corporate bonds are most appropriate for purchase in tax-sheltered or tax-deferred accounts (IRAs, Keoghs). Corporate bonds would also be appropriate investments for someone in a lower tax bracket. On a net-after-tax basis, they might yield more than Treasuries.

For those of you who want to buy corporate bonds, here is a list of appropriate precautions:

+ Buy listed bonds (preferably those listed on the New York Stock Exchange).
+ Buy bonds rated A+ or better. This group includes many utilities (electric power utilities) and such corporations as IBM, Exxon, and Amoco.
+ Monitor the ratings.
+ Buy only if the spread to Treasuries of comparable maturity is at least 100 basis points.
+ Stick to maturities of 10 years or less.
+ Investigate call provisions before you buy.

CONCLUSION

Some of the highest yields in the taxable bond sector are to be found in the corporate bond market. But they are trickier to buy than other taxable bonds because they are subject to many uncertainties. Bonds of corporations that are commonly described as "junk" have the highest yields but should not be purchased unless you have a high degree of expertise in analyzing these bonds.

For most individual investors, if you want to buy taxable bonds that yield more than Treasuries, mortgage-backed securities and agency debt would probably present fewer risks and uncertainties than corporate bonds.

SUMMARY: QUESTIONS TO ASK BEFORE BUYING CORPORATE BONDS

What is the credit rating?

What are the call provisions?

Is the bond a listed bond?

On which exchange does the bond trade?

What is the spread to Treasuries of a similar maturity?

ADDITIONAL REFERENCES

The best book on corporate bonds is Richard Wilson and Frank Fabozzi, *Corporate Bonds: Structures and Analysis* (Frank Fabozzi Associates, 1996).

CHAPTER 10

International Bonds

This chapter discusses:

- ◆ Currency risk
- ◆ Categories of international bonds
- ◆ Emerging Markets Debt: Brady bonds
- ◆ The case for investing in international bonds

In the first edition of this book, I included international bonds only briefly, in the chapter on bond funds. For individual investors, bond funds are probably still the most prudent and practical method of investing in international bonds. Nonetheless, the rationale for a brief introduction to the foreign bond market is that there has been a veritable explosion in the availability of foreign bonds. Most of that has occurred precisely since this book was initially published, during the decade of the 1990s. It is likely that this market will continue to grow in importance, given the enormous capital requirements of most regions of the globe, and particularly of underdeveloped countries. Hence, what follows will be a brief introduction to what is admittedly a very complex topic, a review of some of the most basic basics.

In this book, international bonds are defined as any bond whose issuer is not geographically located in the United States, whether that issuer is a corporation or a foreign government.

Many international bonds are denominated in a foreign currency, but many are also denominated in U.S. dollars.

CURRENCY RISK

International bonds are subject to the same risks as bonds issued in the United States: namely, interest rate risk, determined by a change in the level of interest rates, and credit risk, that is, the risk that the issuer will be unable to make payments of coupon interest on time, or redeem principal when the bond matures. But what makes international bonds different and complicated is a unique risk, namely, currency risk.

If you have traveled outside the United States, and if you have had to purchase foreign currency, you have experienced a form of currency risk. You know that at different times a dollar will buy a larger amount, or a smaller amount, of the foreign currency, and that will affect the cost of hotel rooms, restaurant meals, and so forth. If, for example, you had traveled to France in 1982, one dollar would have purchased approximately ten francs. Each franc would have cost approximately ten cents. During most of the 1990s, however, the prevailing rate was approximately one dollar to five francs. That meant that the cost of each franc rose to about 20 cents. Putting it differently, the dollar declined against the franc by approximately 50%. Assuming all other factors had remained equal (we know that was not the case), the cost of a trip to France had doubled (approximately).

The value of the currency of any country is one of the major factors that affects its economy. Unfortunately, shifts in currency values are even more difficult to predict than interest rate changes. In 1998, for example, a number of Asian currencies suddenly collapsed vis-à-vis the dollar, and those declines were followed by virtual collapses in their equity markets. Yet just a few months earlier, those economies were being hailed as participants in the "Asian miracle." It may be less widely realized that changes in the value of the currencies of well-developed countries with well-developed markets also occur, and they can also be major. For example, over the last decade, one dollar has purchased as many as 200 yen and as few as approximately 80.

What causes currency fluctuations? Many factors can be cited, among them: balance of payments imbalances; soaring government deficits; differing inflation rates; economies growing at different rates; differences in the regulatory environment and in government policy toward business; capital flight (for example, Mexican nationals taking Mexican pesos out of Mexico to deposit them in U.S. securities—cited as a major cause of the devaluation of the Mexican peso in 1995); a poorly functioning banking system. I could go on. The main point I want to make is that no expert, no government official, has predicted either major changes in the value of a foreign currency or currency crises with consistent success.

One reason that currency fluctuations are so difficult to predict is that policy towards currency is subject to many crosscurrents. For example, do you think the Japanese would be in favor of a weak yen vis-à-vis the American dollar, or of a strong yen? Exporters of Japanese goods, whether automobiles, televisions, or computers, would probably welcome a decline in the value of the yen because it would mean that their goods became cheaper for American buyers. On the other hand, a decline in the value of the yen means that a whole lot of goods that Japan imports, including oil and food, become a lot more expensive for Japanese consumers. Moreover, whether the Japanese favor a strong yen or a weak yen, they may not be able to control fluctuations in the yen vis-à-vis other currencies. Similarly, some U.S. administrations have favored a policy of trying to maintain a strong dollar in order to keep inflation down; while others have favored a weaker dollar, in order to stimulate exports. Policy has varied from administration to administration. And so has the ability of any administration to influence the value of the dollar.

What Is the Impact of Currency Changes on Total Return of Foreign Bonds?

Over short holding periods (a year or less), fluctuations in the value of currency are often the most significant component of total return, dwarfing both interest income and changes in price resulting from interest rate movements. Bear in mind that you have to convert the price of an international bond into the foreign currency when you initially purchase the bond; and again, you have to convert the price of the bond into U.S. dollars when you sell. This creates risk at both ends of the transaction. It is not unusual for a bond to have a positive return in the local currency, and a negative total return in dollar terms, and vice-versa. This can be illustrated by Exhibit 10–1, which shows the impact of currency fluctuations on total returns to an investor who purchased German bonds with dollars between 1994 and 1999.

The preceding example involves currency fluctuations that are moderate. The impact of a currency crisis, such as those that occurred when Mexico devalued its currency, or after the meltdown that occurred in Asia in late 1998, is of a different order of magnitude. Virtually overnight, some bonds lost as much as 50% or more of their value. At about the same time, the value of Russian bonds plummeted to near zero after the Russian government defaulted.

Some experts believe that over long holding periods (defined as ten years or more), currency fluctuations tend to cancel each other out. But that is by no means certain. It might be noted that there was a prior period during the twentieth century when U.S. investors invested heavily in foreign bonds. That occurred early in the century. By 1920, Moody's was rating the bonds of 50 sovereign borrowers. Many of these investments proved disastrous, due either to hyperinflation (in Germany, for example) or to revolution (in Russia). As a result of these catastrophic losses, as well as capital controls imposed by foreign governments, the international bond market virtually shut down in the United States between 1930 and 1970.

E X H I B I T   10–1

The Impact of Currency Fluctuations on German Bond Returns for U.S. Investors

	Local Market Return	+(−)	Local Currency Appreciaton/Depreciation vs. U.S. Dollar	=	Return to U.S. Investors
1994	−1.8		11.8%		10.0%
1995	16.3		9.6		25.9
1996	7.3		−7.7		−0.4
1997	6.2		−15.2		−9.0
1998	10.9		8.9		19.8
1999	−2.1		−14.3		−16.4

Copyright: T. Rowe Price Associates. Data source: Salomon Smith Barney. Reprinted with permission.

Sophisticated investors, such as pension funds or hedge funds that invest in foreign currencies, use hedging techniques to reduce currency risk. Whether or not hedging is a good idea is a hotly debated topic in finance. What is certain is that, whether or not hedging is advisable, hedges cost money. In an up market, hedges reduce total return. Note also that if you are investing in international bonds through a bond fund, the cost of hedging comes directly out of the NAV of the fund.

If, in spite of all of the above, you decide to invest in international bonds, do you want to see the dollar rise against foreign currencies, or do you want to see it decline against those currencies? The answer is: you want to see the dollar decline against the foreign currency you are buying. To illustrate: suppose you are purchasing Japanese bonds that cost 10,000 yen. Further suppose that one U.S. dollar buys 200 yen. That bond will cost you $50.00 (10,000/200). Now suppose that a few years later, the dollar has declined so that it buys only 100 yen (in other words, the yen has appreciated against the dollar). Assuming all other factors have remained the same, you can now sell your bond for $100.00 (10,000/100). You have doubled your money.

Finally, while currency risk is the main complicating risk in buying international bonds, note that at the current time, purchasing international bonds poses a whole list of additional obstacles. Very few brokers have any inventory or information concerning these bonds. Settlement dates and procedures vary all over the lot. Getting custody of the bonds may be difficult. One factor has changed for the better: the major rating agencies have reentered the international bond market. They are now providing ratings for many large issuers of international bonds, both for bonds issued by governments (called sovereign issues); as well as for corporate issuers of debt. As markets everywhere become increasingly global, it may become easier to buy foreign bonds.

CATEGORIES OF INTERNATIONAL BONDS

The market for international bonds is extraordinarily complex. While currency risk is a major factor for all international bonds, additional risks vary depending on the issuer. Credit quality varies enormously. Many international bonds are issued by governments of countries with strong economies, stable governments,

and relatively stable currencies, or by corporations with international reputations and strong balance sheets. Credit quality for
these bonds would be high. At the other extreme are the bonds
of so-called emerging markets. Emerging markets are defined in
a variety of ways, but the most accepted definitions are based on
a country's gross domestic product or per capita income. Emerging market countries, in a nutshell, are very poor. Bonds issued
by emerging market governments or by corporations located in
emerging markets should be viewed by individual investors as a
subsector of the market for riskier junk bonds: potentially high
return, but extremely volatile and high risk.

The term "globalization" has been used to indicate that markets are becoming increasingly interdependent. The international
bond market is a prime example of globalization. Many major U.S.
corporations issue bonds denominated in foreign currencies: in
euros, for example, or in yen. There are a number of reasons why
U.S. corporations issue bonds abroad. One might be to obtain
more favorable financing, that is, to borrow at lower interest cost.
Another, for multinational corporations with plants abroad, might
be to lay off some currency risk. Similarly, many foreign issuers
issue bonds denominated in U.S. dollars. Again, they do so for a
variety of reasons. One is that the U.S. market is the largest, most
liquid bond market in the world. Another is that issuing bonds in
the United States confers a degree of prestige to foreign issuers.
Foreign issuers may issue bonds denominated in U.S. dollars in
the United States, and others may be issued in foreign markets.

This intermingling of issuers and currencies has resulted in
a confusing terminology. So first, let's define some of the key sectors of the international bond market for a U.S. investor.

International bonds fall into a number of categories.

+ *Domestic* bonds are issued within a foreign country in
  that country's currency. Examples would be bonds issued
  in baht in Thailand, or in pesos in Mexico. These bonds
  are issued, underwritten, and traded under the
  regulations of the country of issue.
+ *Foreign* bonds are issued by a borrower located outside a
  country but intended primarily for domestic investors.
  An example of this would be so-called *Yankee* bonds,
  which are registered with the SEC, denominated in U.S.

dollars, and issued and traded within the United States. Yankee bonds are issued primarily by foreign governments (also called sovereigns) that have high quality credits and by sovereign guaranteed issuers (such as Italy, the province of Ontario, the province of Quebec, or Hydro Quebec).

♦ *Eurobonds* are issued simultaneously in a number of foreign markets in a variety of currencies, including U.S. dollars, German marks, Japanese yen, and Italian lira. Eurobonds are not registered with the SEC even if they are denominated in U.S. dollars. For that reason, U.S. investors are unable to participate in the primary market (that is, they cannot buy at issue), although they can buy these bonds in the secondary market (that is, once they start trading). In practice, however, the euromarket is dominated by foreign, that is, non-U.S. investors. "Euro" has come to mean "offshore." London has become the center of the Euromarket. Issuers in that market include sovereign governments, large corporations, and supranational agencies such as the International Monetary Fund (IMF).

Eurodollar bonds are eurobonds, denominated in U.S. dollars. In other respects they are issued and trade like other eurobonds, that is, primarily offshore. Major issuers in eurodollar bonds include sovereign governments, large corporations, and supranational agencies such as the World Bank and the IMF.

♦ *Global* bonds are a hybrid. They may be issued and traded in the United States or offshore, in the euromarket. Most global bonds are denominated in U.S. dollars.

For a U.S. investor, the most critical distinction is whether international bonds are denominated in U.S. dollars or in a foreign currency. As noted earlier, a wide variety of foreign borrowers, many of them with high credit quality, issue bonds denominated in U.S. dollars. These may include sovereigns, supranational agencies such as the World Bank or the IMF, or large foreign corporations. These bonds may present U.S. investors with an opportunity for earning higher yields than would be available on U.S.

bonds with comparable credit quality and maturity. The critical factor for U.S. investors is that, regardless of the issuer, bonds denominated in U.S. dollars track U.S. interest rates. The one exception to this are Brady bonds, which will be discussed separately (see the section below concerning Brady bonds).

International bonds issued in a foreign currency are called *foreign pay bonds*. At the present time, individual investors in the United States have only sporadic access to these bonds. That usually happens if some brokers see an opportunity and selectively try to sell such bonds to their clientele. At the current time, foreign pay bonds can be purchased mainly through mutual funds.

Credit Ratings for Sovereigns

Bonds of foreign governments are rated by the major credit rating agencies. The credit rating evaluates both the ability of a government to pay and its willingness to pay. It is not a given that a government that is able to pay its debts will always be willing to do it: some defaults are rooted in a political situation where a government will simply decide to renege on its foreign debts.

The first question you might ask is, how frequently do foreign governments default on their bonds? The answer surprised me. Between 1970 and 1996, a survey by Standard & Poor's of the debt of 113 governments numbered 69 defaults on foreign currency debt. The governments that defaulted include Angola, Argentina, Brazil, Ghana, Vietnam, Russia, and Venezuela. Note that Standard & Poor's included as defaults debt "rescheduling" and "restructurings" that eventually gave rise to the Brady market. Many countries, however, are rated AAA, and are unlikely to default. As you would expect, these are mainly countries with well-developed economies and stable governments, including Canada, France, Germany, Japan, the Netherlands, and the United Kingdom.

As is the case with the U.S. market, however, ratings change. For example, in 1996, Malaysia was rated AA+ and Thailand AAA. That was one year before the Asian crisis and the collapse of their currency and their bond market.

For sovereign governments, Standard & Poor's assigns separate ratings to debt denominated in the local currency and to debt denominated in a foreign currency. The rationale behind this is that theoretically, debt denominated in the local currency is backed by the unlimited taxing power of the government. But in reality, however, that taxing power is limited by the political situation. Suppose, for example, that the government of a third world country tried to raise taxes in order to pay debt. It might be argued that such a policy would stifle the economy. Or, suppose the same government is asked to cut spending in order to pay foreign investors. That may also be impossible, for political reasons. Finally, some countries may simply be unable to collect taxes. Russia is a current example. On the other hand, to pay off debt denominated in a foreign currency, a country must have on hand a supply of reserves in the foreign currency. This is usually obtained through trade, mainly through exports. This too raises a host of problems for many countries. Nonetheless, defaults have been much more numerous on debt denominated in foreign currency than on debt denominated in the local currency. In the survey cited above, while 69 countries defaulted on debt denominated in foreign currency, only eight defaulted on debt denominated in local currency.

EMERGING MARKETS DEBT: BRADY BONDS

In 1982, Mexico declared a moratorium on debt payments, and a number of other Latin American countries followed suit. This left several of the largest American banks holding many billions of dollars of loans in default. Over the next several years, a market began to develop for trading the defaulted bonds at a discount. "Brady" bonds are named after the former U.S. Treasury Secretary Nicholas Brady, who played a leading role in solving what had become a major international debt crisis. The Brady plan developed a number of structures that enabled the banks to swap the defaulted loans for bonds issued by the Latin American governments. The basic formula called for a steep write-off of the loan amount and also stretched out repayment of the debt over a period of as much as 30 years. In return for this debt relief, the governments issuing the bonds agreed to implement a program of reforms to their economies. The entire program was developed jointly by the U.S. Treasury, the World Bank, and the International Monetary Fund. In order to attract American investors, the bonds were to be issued in U.S. dollars.

This program was enormously successful. During the late 1980s and the 1990s, a very large and very liquid market developed for trading these bonds. While initially developed to solve the Latin American debt crisis, the Brady program was extended to emerging market governments in every region of the globe: in Eastern Europe, in Africa, and in Asia. The formula remained similar to the original Brady plan: in return for capital and debt forgiveness or debt relief, governments of underdeveloped countries agreed to economic reforms demanded by the IMF and the World Bank. At the present time, the term "Brady bond" has become virtually synonymous with emerging market debt from any source.

The market for Brady bonds is characterized by a number of unique characteristics. First of all, initial yields were extremely high, ranging from 9% to 25%. In a sense, this is the ultimate "junk" bond market for U.S. investors. But volatility in this market is the highest of any bond market. Potential profits are enormous; but so are catastrophic losses. Nonetheless, this is a highly liquid, highly developed market supported by a large number of derivative instruments. Individual bond issues are extremely large: some are larger than certain U.S. Treasury issues. Finally, the Brady market is a constantly evolving, expanding, and changing market.

The initial Brady plan offered banks a variety of options for restructuring their loans. These options, in turn, resulted in several different types of bonds. Option number one was to exchange the amount of the loans for an identical amount of 30-year bonds at below-market interest rates. A second choice was to exchange a discounted amount of the loans (usually at a 35% discount) for a floating rate keyed to a specified lending rate. The third choice was to extend new loans stretching out over four years to cover 25% of the initial loan amount.

In order attract investors, Brady bonds incorporated a number of attractive features. The most important of these is that principal of many Bradies, as well as some interest payments, is collateralized. In most cases, the collateral takes the form of U.S. Treasury zeros, purchased at the time the Brady bonds are issued, in an amount sufficient to cover the principal value of the bonds *when they mature*. This amount is placed in escrow in a Federal Reserve Bank in the United States. In addition, an amount sufficient to cover coupon interest for 12 to 18 months (two or three coupon payments) is also placed in a Federal Reserve Bank escrow account. This is a "rolling interest" guarantee, meaning that as each coupon payment is made, the collateral remains in place to guarantee successive coupon payments. In the event of a default, however, there is no obligation to replenish the collateral. Bear in mind that while both forms of collateral were intended to limit potential losses, this does not eliminate risk. In the event of a default, an investor would have to wait for possibly as long as 25 to 30 years to recover principal, and during that time he may collect little or no interest. Therefore, in every case, an investor must carefully assess the probability of a default.

In order to attract institutional buyers, Brady bonds were issued with a whole array of bells and whistles too numerous to analyze in detail: as par bonds; as discount bonds; with rights or warrants linked to indexes of oil export prices (for major oil exporting countries such as Mexico, Venezuela, or Nigeria); and so on. In all cases, however, the critical variables are the credit quality of the government issuing the bonds; as well as the nature of the collateral.

Valuation (that is pricing) of Brady bonds is complex. The reason for this is that each bond is viewed as having three different components, which are priced separately. The first two, and the easiest to price, consist of the principal fully collateralized by U.S. Treasuries, and the collateralized rolling interest guarantee. These are priced in the same manner as any comparable U.S. Treasury, with similar maturities and coupons. But valuing the bond's remaining cash flows is far more difficult because that is where the major riskiness lies. The remaining cash flows consist of future coupon payments which are not collateralized, as well as potential changes in the price of the bond. To value the risky cash flows, therefore, you have to assess the ability of the issuer to make future interest payments (don't forget that these may have to be paid off at very high interest rates). Even more difficult to value, however, are potential changes in price of the bond (up or down). These can be caused by a number of different factors, including but not limited to, exchange rate or currency fluctuations, interest rate changes in the United States, and interest rate moves in the country of the issuer. Quite a tall order!

Pricing the separate components of a Brady bond is only the beginning of the process. Professionals back out the price of the collateralized components. This price is then subtracted from the price of the Brady bond, and the yield of the risky cash flows is then calculated. That is called the "stripped yield." The stripped yield is viewed as the "market's" view of the risk of the bond.

Since its inception, there have been periods when the entire Brady bond sector has experienced very sharp price moves both up and down. But during other periods total return may vary significantly from country to country and year to year. This creates what professionals call "inefficiencies," which are viewed as potentially profitable investment opportunities.

Initially, Brady bonds were purchased primarily by large institutional investors such as pension funds or hedge funds. Increasingly, they are being purchased by a wide variety of mutual funds: most obviously by mutual funds specializing in emerging market bonds, but also, and less obviously, by "high-yield" (junk) bond funds and by international stock funds, both "value" and "growth." If you own a mutual fund investing in international stocks or bonds, you might want to check what percentage of the fund is invested in Brady bonds: these holdings have the potential to boost returns significantly when the market rises. But if a significant percentage of the fund's holdings is in Brady bonds, this will increase the volatility of the fund.

Returns on Brady bonds have been very high both in 1999 and in the first half of 2000. If this trend continues Brady bonds will no doubt begin to be pitched to individual investors. If that is the case, and you are quoted outsize yields-to-maturity, bear in mind that while YTM and total return are always different for any bond, when it comes to Brady bonds, YTM and total return may bear no relation to each other. Any YTM quote on a Brady bond should be considered a wild guess. To understand why, review the paragraphs above dealing with pricing of Brady bonds.

Note also that the high returns of Brady bonds are due, in part, to a narrowing of spreads. As this book is going to press, spreads have come down from about 1,200 basis points at the height of the debt crisis in 1998, to approximately 550 basis points (compared to Treasuries), even less for certain sectors, such as Mexican bonds. Many domestic (U.S.) junk bonds have higher yields. At these levels, you have to ask yourself: are you being compensated for the high degree of risk inherent in Brady bonds?

Currently, almost all Brady bonds are rated as "junk" by the major rating agencies. In spite of their junk rating, up to 1999, no government had defaulted on Brady debt. In 1999, however, Ecuador defaulted on a Brady bond. Unlike the currency crises that followed defaults in the 1990s, this default attracted little notice.

IS THERE A CASE FOR INVESTING IN INTERNATIONAL BONDS?

Evidence has shown that total returns from international bonds cannot be predicted with any real degree of certainty, given the unpredictable nature of exchange rates. Since no one disputes this fact, is it possible to make a case for investing in international bonds?

The case for investing in foreign bonds is based on a number of arguments. Let's briefly examine them.

One argument is diversification. This is based on the fact that it has been shown that total returns of international bonds do not correlate exactly with the total return of U.S. bonds. According to modern finance theory, holding assets whose returns are not closely correlated lowers the volatility of the total portfolio even if each of the assets is volatile. While this argument has some merit, applying it to a bond portfolio is appropriate mainly for very large, extremely diversified portfolios of bonds, such as those of insurance companies, pension funds, and the like. For individual investors with a few bonds or even a few bond funds, the diversification argument is irrelevant and particularly so if the objective for investing in bonds is safe, predictable income.

Another argument is that a portfolio which includes international bonds may earn higher total returns. There is no question that during some time periods, portfolios of international bonds would have earned higher total returns in dollars for U.S. investors than portfolios holding only U.S. bonds. These time periods can always be selected with hindsight. But, as Yogi Berra is reputed to have said, making predictions is very difficult, especially for the future. In the case of international bonds, selecting the appropriate bonds for higher total returns means you have to be right about timing (when to buy the international bonds). You also have to be right about which currency or which international market to choose. The strongest case for potentially higher returns can be made for investing in the Brady market, that is, in the bonds of "emerging markets." But as we saw, this is a very high-risk, extremely volatile market. Some analysts believe, in fact, that adding such bonds to a portfolio would increase the volatility of the total portfolio rather than lower it.

The final argument for investing in international bonds, which seems to be the most relevant to individual investors, is that, in effect, this represents a way for individual investors to hedge against a falling dollar, should the dollar go into a serious decline. Again, predicting the value of the dollar against other currencies is not for amateurs. Over the past decade, the dollar has remained extremely strong, in spite of the fact that the United States has had a large deficit in its balance of payments. For many foreign investors, in fact, the dollar has replaced gold as a reserve currency. How long this will continue is anybody's guess. Before the inception of the euro, for example, it was widely predicted that the euro might challenge the U.S. dollar as the world's strongest currency. (The euro is the new currency which supersedes and is likely to displace the currency of a number of European countries, including France and Germany.) However, to date, since its inception, the euro has actually declined significantly against the dollar. But if the U.S. equity and bond markets were to experience a sustained downturn, financial assets denominated in U.S. dollars might no longer be as attractive to foreign investors as they have been during the past decade. A strong case could then be made for investing in international bonds.

How can any of this information be of use to you? This would be determined mainly by your financial objectives. If you are investing in bonds mainly in order to have a safe and predictable income stream, then the arguments for investing in foreign bonds are not very convincing. If your portfolio is large, or if you feel you have enough information to be able to speculate in an informed manner, then including foreign bonds for a percentage of your portfolio may make more sense. In either case, at the moment, the easiest method for investing in international bonds is through bond funds, but for no more than 10% or 20% of your bond portfolio.

OBTAINING INFORMATION ON INTERNATIONAL BONDS

At the moment, I am tempted to say: don't even try. While the financial press in the United States barely covers the credit markets of the United States, it almost totally ignores foreign bonds.

There is some regular coverage of foreign interest rates in *Barron's* and in *The Financial Times* of London, and also on some websites, which are listed at the end of the chapter.

CONCLUSION AND SUMMARY

The international bond market has grown tremendously in the last decade. It is likely to continue to grow in importance because of the enormous capital needs of the underdeveloped world, and of developed economies which seek to catch up with the United States. International bonds are subject to the same risks as U.S. bonds, namely, interest rate risk and credit risk. But another far more major risk is currency risk. For U.S. investors, it is still extremely difficult to purchase international bonds on an individual basis. U.S. investors can purchase these bonds mainly through funds. Total return of international bonds is highly unpredictable, and the case for investing in these bonds is not convincing for most investors.

ADDITIONAL REFERENCES

There are no recently issued books that cover the international bond markets. Any book published more than five years ago would be obsolete.

The best print information concerning international bonds (or international markets) are: the *Economist* magazine and *The Financial Times* of London.

Your best source of current information on international bonds is the Internet. Bloomberg (*Bloomberg.com*) publishes daily price and yield information for representative issues of international bonds, including Canadian, French, German, Italian, Japanese, and U.K. government bonds, in maturities ranging from 30 months to 30 years, depending on the maturity structure of the bonds of a particular country.

There is extensive coverage of Brady bonds on *bradynet.com*. *Brady net* has also added a premium service (fee based). The websites of the major rating agencies (*moody's.com, standardandpoors.com,* and *fitch.ibca*) all carry ratings and stories on foreign bonds and foreign markets. Quite a lot of information is available for free.

Also, if you are interested in a specific market, for example, the bonds of Thailand, typing the phrase "Thai bonds" into your favorite search engine can yield a surprising amount of information. By typing in this phrase, for example, I turned up several interesting articles, including one from *The Bangkok Post* on the spread of Thai bonds to ten-year Treasuries; as well as several interesting articles on *geoinvestor.com*.

PART THREE

Investing Through Funds

Since I wrote the first edition of this book, in no area of the bond market have there been as many changes as those that have occurred with bond funds.

Bond funds represent a relatively recent development in the mutual fund universe. Few bond funds had their inception prior to the 1980s. Subsequently, bond funds underwent explosive growth. New bond funds were being created almost daily. Hard as it may be to believe at the current time, during the 1980s and through the early 1990s, more money went into bond funds and money market funds than into stock funds. Only in 1993 did the amount of money flowing into equity funds begin to surpass the amount of money flowing into bond funds. Note that this has not stopped bond funds from proliferating. Whereas in December of 1987 the Lipper survey listed 888 bond funds (excluding money market funds), in December of 1999, the numbers had reached a staggering 4,581 (again excluding money market funds), divided between 2,411 taxable bond funds, and 2,170 tax-exempt bond funds. Fund categories and assets had also multiplied.

In spite of this explosion of bond funds, since the middle of the 1990s, the percentage of money going into bond funds has been declining compared to the amount flowing to equity funds. In large part this is due to the spectacular bull market in stocks which has marked the 1980s and 1990s. Returns from investments in bonds (or in bond funds), which have actually been high for most of that period (by historical standards), look puny compared to the more dramatic stock market returns. But another reason for the decline in popularity of bond funds may be that, to be blunt, a large number of bond funds have been disappointing investments: promising low risk and high returns and delivering, instead, outright losses or low returns.

The fault may lie partly with poorly worded or misleading information concerning the risks of investing in bond funds. Advertising of many bond funds focuses on two themes: high yield and safety of principal. Ads indicate only in fine print that assets invested in bond funds can go down as well as up. Many investors do not realize that they can lose money even in funds investing in securities guaranteed by the U.S. government. Sadly, many investors come to this realization only after the value of their fund has gone down. Moreover, all bond funds are not equally low risk. Returns for some categories of bond funds are almost as variable and as difficult to predict as those of equities.

The purpose of this part of the book is to enable you to evaluate both potential total return and potential risks of bond funds in a more informed manner. These chapters will tell you which funds can indeed provide safe predictable income; which are volatile (go up and down in price) and why; and which might provide higher total return, and at what risk.

Most of this section is devoted to open-end funds—ordinary mutual funds—which are by far the largest segment of the industry. Chapter 11 discusses the essential aspects of investing in bond funds. Chapter 12 classifies bond funds and also discusses their risk factors and historical returns. Both chapters together should enable you to anticipate total return and risks under a variety of market scenarios. Chapter 13 briefly discusses two additional types of bond funds: closed-end bond funds and unit investment trusts.

Mutual Funds:
An Overview

This chapter discusses

- ◆ Characteristics of bond funds
- ◆ Differences between bond funds and individual instruments
- ◆ Measures of bond fund returns
- ◆ The costs of investing in bond funds
- ◆ Why the NAV of your bond fund will go up and down
- ◆ Some guidelines for selecting, buying, and monitoring bond funds
- ◆ Taxes and bond funds

WHAT IS A FIXED-INCOME FUND?

Mutual funds are technically known as open-end funds, as opposed to unit investment trusts (UITs) and closed-end bond funds. Each fund is comprised of a portfolio of securities that is managed by an investment adviser—technically known as the management company—usually as one of a number of funds managed by the same management company. These management companies are better known to individual investors as mutual fund "families" or groups.

The mutual fund's price per share, also called net asset value (NAV), varies daily. The main characteristics of a mutual fund are that an investor can buy or sell shares in that fund on any business day at the closing price per share (NAV) on that day; and that the portfolio changes continually both because investors buy and sell shares and also because the manager buys and sells securities.

Bond funds differ from each other in many significant ways. The most obvious difference is that they invest in different sectors of the bond market: there are municipal bond funds, funds investing in junk bonds, funds investing in international bonds, and so on. Also, only money market funds have a constant share price. The price per share of all other bond funds can be expected to go up and down, and with it the value of your assets in the fund will go up and down.

Funds differ both in degree of riskiness and potential total return. Generally, the higher the risk, the higher the potential total return, but also the higher the unpredictability of return. This chapter and the next will discuss the various factors that affect both riskiness and total return.

What Are Some of the Major Differences between Individual Bonds and Bond Funds?

While you can invest in any sector of the bond market either through a bond fund or by buying individual bonds, the two are radically different investments.

The main difference is that an individual bond has a definite maturity date and a fund does not. If you hold a bond to maturity, on that date it will be redeemed at par, regardless of the level of interest rates prevailing on the bond's maturity date. Assuming a default has not occurred, you get back 100% of your principal. You have also earned a predictable income for the period that you have held the bond, consisting of the coupon interest and, if coupons were reinvested, of interest-on-interest.

This is not the case with a bond fund. Bond funds are comprised of a great many issues. While a number of individual issues may remain in the portfolio until they mature, there is no single date at which the entire portfolio of the fund will mature. (There is one exception to this rule: a small group of funds that are structured to mature on a specific date, called "target funds.") In fact, most bond funds maintain a "constant" maturity. For example, the maturity of a long-term bond fund will always remain long term, somewhere between 15 and 25 years. The maturity of a short-term bond fund, on the other hand, will always be short, that is, somewhere between one and three years. Consequently, unlike an individual bond, the NAV of a fund does not automatically return to par on a specified date. Rather, the NAV of the fund will move up and down in response to a variety of factors, including changes in interest rates, credit quality, and, for international bonds, currency values.

As a result, the price at which you will be able to sell shares of a bond fund cannot be known ahead of time. It will be determined by conditions prevailing in that sector of the bond market when you sell your fund. This price may be higher than your initial cost in the fund, or lower, depending on what has happened to the value of the underlying portfolio. The fact that you can sell fund shares any day you wish does not guarantee that you can sell at the price you paid.

To illustrate this basic difference, let us assume that you are considering buying either an intermediate municipal bond fund or a five-year New York State bond. If you buy the New York State bond, you can be reasonably certain that—barring the unlikely occurrence of default—in five years your bond will be redeemed at par and you will have earned the coupons and any interest-on-interest on reinvested coupons. If you buy the bond fund, however, you cannot predict what the price per share will be in five years. The value of the shares will depend, among other factors, on interest rates prevailing in the municipal sector of bond market at that time. Another way of looking at this difference is that, if you own an individual bond, each year, its market value (its price) moves one year closer to par. But because it has a constant maturity, the NAV of a bond fund follows interest rates. For that reason, its future value is not predictable.

Because the price of a bond fund does not return to par at a specified maturity date, it cannot quote a yield-to-maturity. As a result, any comparison between the potential return of an individual bond and a bond fund is imprecise. You are comparing apples and oranges.

MEASURES OF BOND FUND RETURNS

How much you earn in a bond fund is measured by three different numbers: yield, NAV, and total return. Yield is a measure of the distributions (that is, the interest income) that the fund posts to your account, divided by your invested principal. Total return sums up what you have really earned from all of the cash flows of a bond fund. Bond fund advertising focuses on yield. But total return is actually the more meaningful number. So let's first clarify what these two numbers really tell you.

Yield

When you invest in a fund, you receive "distributions" (that is, interest income), which are posted each month. You may choose to receive these in cash or to reinvest them to buy additional shares. The distributions constitute the income portion of your fund, and that is the number measured by yield. When you see a quote for the yield of a fund, chances are that quote is what is technically called the distribution yield, that is, the dollar amount of dividends distributed for the previous month. Most bond funds quote a 30-day yield (based on the average share price for the last 30 days). The distribution yield is comparable to the current yield you would be quoted for an individual bond, that is, dividend income divided by price.

As we saw in the discussion of individual bonds, however, the key number quoted to buyers of individual bonds is the YTM. Since there is no date at which the entire portfolio of a bond fund matures and returns to par, a bond fund does not have a maturity date, and consequently a bond fund cannot quote a YTM. Instead, there is a different quote, known as the SEC standardized yield.

The standardized SEC yield is a snapshot of the actual returns of the fund for the past 30 days. By far the greatest portion of that yield consists of the interest income accrued by the fund for the past 30 days. In addition, however, like the YTM quoted for individual bonds, the 30-day SEC yield includes small increases in the price of bonds in the portfolio as they rise towards par (this would be the case for discount bonds) or (for premium bonds) small declines as the price of these bonds falls towards par. The SEC yield also reflects the fund's expenses during the 30-day period, which are subtracted from the gross income received.

The main purpose of the 30-day SEC yield is to enable a purchaser to compare the yields of mutual funds accurately to those of similar funds. The use of the standardized formula ensures that the yields are calculated in exactly the same way. Prior to the imposition of the SEC standardized rule in 1988, it was not uncommon for funds to manipulate and inflate yield quotes. Now, if you are comparing two GNMA funds, or two muni bond funds, and you ask for the SEC yield for the same 30-day period, you know the quotes are exactly comparable for the past 30 days.

But because the SEC yield measures return only for the past 30 days, that number is not directly comparable to the YTM quoted for individual securities. The SEC yield can be used as a rough guide for comparing a fund to individual bonds since no other number comes close; but you should understand that the two numbers are really not equivalent. That is because (as already noted) the YTM of an individual bond is based on the assumption that the bond will be redeemed at par. And there is no date at which the entire portfolio of a fund "matures" and returns to par. Moreover, you cannot know at what price you will redeem a bond fund. That distinction is particularly important for bond funds whose NAV can be expected to be volatile, such as long-term bond funds, funds investing in junk bonds, or in bonds of emerging markets.

The SEC yield differs by a small amount, usually not more than 20 basis points, from the fund's actual cash payout. But if the discrepancy is larger, that is a red flag. It indicates that the fund may be stuffed with premium bonds that have high coupons. When those are redeemed at par at maturity, that represents a capital loss and a decline in NAV.

Note in passing that bond funds occasionally distribute capital gains. These distributions occur when bonds are sold from the portfolio at a profit. By law, these capital gains must be passed on to shareholders. Capital gains distributions represent taxable income and are taxed like any capital gains. This makes them particularly unwelcome when they occur in municipal bond funds. Capital gains are excluded from yield calculations by SEC regulations.

NAV

The price per share of a bond fund, also known as its net asset value (NAV), varies daily, like that of any mutual fund. The NAV is the closing net asset value for the day. To determine the NAV, the value of all the assets in the fund (less any minor liabilities) is tabulated at the end of each trading day. The total net assets

(TNA) are then divided by the total number of shares outstanding, and the resulting number is the net asset value per share for that day. Any change in NAV translates directly into a corresponding change in the value of the assets in the fund. If you own 1,000 shares of a fund whose NAV is $10.00 (for a total value of $10,000), and the value of those shares declines to $9.95 the next day, then your assets in the fund are now worth $50.00 less than the previous day, or $9,950. If the NAV goes up by 5 cents, then your assets in that fund are now worth $10,050.

While this point may seem elementary, I stress it at the outset because there is a widespread misconception that somehow if you are investing in a fund of high-quality bonds such as Treasuries or other government-guaranteed securities, then your invested principal cannot decline in value. That is not the case. A bond fund is not a CD. With the exception of money market funds whose NAV remains a constant $1.00 per share, the NAV of all bond funds should be expected to go up and down, and with it the value of your assets in the fund will go up and down.

The NAV of most of the larger mutual funds is printed daily in the financial pages of major newspapers. You can monitor the value of your funds as often as you care to. Exhibit 11–1 shows the format of mutual fund listings. The listing includes both bond funds and stock funds and includes only relatively large funds.

Note that the listing includes a good deal of information in addition to price. Whenever two prices are quoted for a fund, that tells you that the fund is sold on a commission basis. The spread between the "bid" and the "ask" is the amount of the commission charged by the fund. If the fund is sold without commission, only one price is quoted and the letters "NL" (for No Load) appear after the fund name. An "r" after the fund's name indicates a redemption fee is charged. Funds with a 12b-1 plan are marked with a "p." A "t" indicates both redemption and 12b-1 plan fees. (All of these terms will be explained below.)

Total Return

The yield quoted by bond funds—whether the dividend yield or the 30-day SEC yield—is a measure of the fund's dividend distributions. It is valid only for the immediate past. It cannot be used as a projection of future returns. Its biggest shortcoming, however,

E X H I B I T   11-1

Format of Mutual Fund Listings

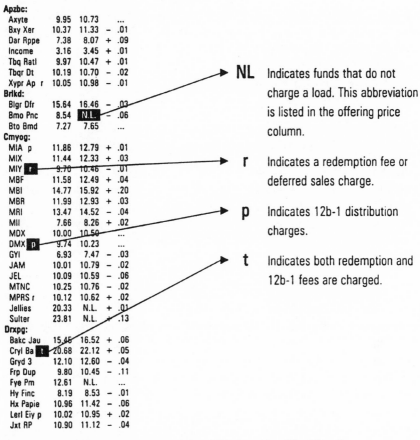

Apzbc:

Axyte	9.95	10.73	...
Bxy Xer	10.37	11.33	– .01
Dar Rppe	7.38	8.07	+ .09
Income	3.16	3.45	+ .01
Tbq Ratl	9.97	10.47	+ .01
Tbqr Dt	10.19	10.70	– .02
Xypr Ap r	10.05	10.98	– .01

Brlkd:

Blgr Dfr	15.64	16.46	– .03
Bmo Pnc	8.54	N.L.	– .06
Bto Bmd	7.27	7.65	...

Cmyog:

MIA p	11.86	12.79	+ .01
MIX	11.44	12.33	+ .03
MIY r	9.70	10.46	– .01
MBF	11.58	12.49	+ .04
MBI	14.77	15.92	+ .20
MBR	11.99	12.93	+ .03
MRI	13.47	14.52	– .04
MII	7.66	8.26	+ .02
MDX	10.00	10.50	...
DMX p	9.74	10.23	...
GYI	6.93	7.47	– .03
JAM	10.01	10.79	– .02
JEL	10.09	10.59	– .06
MTNC	10.25	10.76	– .02
MPRS r	10.12	10.62	+ .02
Jellies	20.33	N.L.	+ .01
Sulter	23.81	N.L.	+ .13

Drxpg:

Bakc Jau	15.46	16.52	+ .06
Cryl Ba t	20.68	22.12	+ .05
Gryd 3	12.10	12.60	– .04
Frp Dup	9.80	10.45	– .11
Fye Pm	12.61	N.L.	...
Hy Finc	8.19	8.53	– .01
Hx Papie	10.96	11.42	– .06
Lerl Eiy p	10.02	10.95	+ .02
Jxt RP	10.90	11.12	– .04

NL Indicates funds that do not charge a load. This abbreviation is listed in the offering price column.

r Indicates a redemption fee or deferred sales charge.

p Indicates 12b-1 distribution charges.

t Indicates both redemption and 12b-1 fees are charged.

Source: Investment Company Institute pamphlet, "FAQ about Mutual Fund Fees."

is that it does not include any decline (or increase) in the value of principal caused by declines (or increases) in the fund's NAV. Over long holding periods, the only measurement that accurately measures a fund's actual return to you is total return.

Total return consists of:

- Dividends + capital gains distributions, if any
- Interest-on-interest from reinvesting dividends
- Plus or minus any changes in NAV

Changes in NAV have a major impact on total return. Suppose, for instance, that you are tallying total return for the past year. Assume that your fund's dividend yield was 5%. Further suppose that the NAV of your fund declines by 10%. This will translate directly into a 10% decline in the value of your principal. (For the sake of simplicity, at this point I am ignoring reinvested dividends or interest-on-interest.)

Total return for the year will be:

Dividend distribution	+5%
Decline in value of principal	−10%
Total return	−5%

If you had invested $10,000 at the beginning of the year in this fund, at the end of the year your investment (including dividend distributions) would now be worth approximately $9,500. On the other hand, suppose that the fund's NAV goes up by 10%. Then the total return calculation would look like this:

Dividend distribution	+5%
Principal gain	+10%
Total return	+15%

If you had invested $10,000 at the beginning of the year, your investment would now be worth $11,500. If you do not sell the shares, either the gain or the loss in the value of the shares, is said to be "unrealized." But you, as a shareholder, can sell the shares in the fund and realize the gain.

Note that for both of the above examples, whether the NAV has gone up by 10% or down by 10%, the bond fund would continue to advertise virtually the same dividend yield: approximately 5%. The yield quote would change only slightly as the NAV changes. But there would obviously be a major difference in the value of your investment at the end of the year.

The major financial newspapers as well as many financial magazines periodically list total return for longer periods, ranging anywhere from one to 20 years. Whenever total returns of bond funds are listed for any period over one year, the convention is to assume that dividend distributions, as well as capital gains distributions, are reinvested. As a result, total return numbers include interest-on-interest. But if you spend the interest income to meet daily expenses, then you will earn only simple interest and not the total return numbers published for these longer periods. Note that the two preceding examples for total return over a one-year period do not include interest-on-interest on reinvested dividends. Over long holding periods, however, reinvesting dividends and earning interest-on-interest make a significant difference on total return because of what, earlier in the book, I called the "magic of compounding."

Total return for periods of over one year may be listed in several different ways. *Cumulative* total return is simply an addition: the cumulative return adds up total return from all cash flows of the fund over a period of years. For example, for a ten-year period, total return would add up all the returns earned during the entire ten years. *Annual* returns may be listed in either of two different ways. Annual returns may be listed separately for every year, as they are, for example, in a prospectus which will show you returns for every calendar year for ten years. But more often, tables that summarize total returns over a period of years list total returns which are *compounded* (that is, interest-on-interest is assumed to be reinvested) and then *averaged on an annual basis.*

One additional note concerning total return: tables of total returns overstate returns in a number of ways. Commissions or loads are not subtracted from the total returns of load funds. Neither are taxes. There is some movement in the direction of adjusting total returns for both of those factors. But, in all fairness, those returns would vary significantly from investor to investor, depending on the exact date the fund was purchased and on tax brackets. Just be aware of how your own tax situation or the timing of your purchases would affect the total returns listed.

Finally, if you are comparing total return numbers for different funds, make sure you are comparing total returns computed in the same way and over the same period of time. Sometimes, even a difference of a few days can make a significant difference in the total return of a fund.

THE COSTS OF INVESTING IN BOND FUNDS

There are two types of fund expenses. The first, called "shareholder fees," are what used to be called "commissions" or "loads." They may be deducted from your investment when you buy a fund or when you sell your fund. The second, known as the "fund operating expenses," are deducted daily from fund assets before the NAV is figured.

The issue of fund expenses is discussed exhaustively by John Bogle, the founder of the Vanguard Mutual Fund Group and one of the truly distinguished men in the mutual fund industry, in his books *Bogle on Mutual Funds*[1] and *Common Sense on Mutual Funds*.[2] Both of these books place fund expenses front and center. The case is overwhelming that investors should make expenses one of the primary criteria in selecting bond funds. Here is why.

What Is a Load?

There was a time when the answer to this question could be stated in a few words: a load is a sales commission. A no-load fund charges no commission. A load fund does. The answer, however, is no longer as simple: commissions, or loads, now come in a wide variety of guises, some of which are not immediately recognizable as loads.

The simplest loads are still the commissions paid at the time of purchase. They consist of a percentage of the money invested and are deducted from the amount you invest at the time of purchase. Standard commissions vary between 4% and 5%. Some so-called "low-load" funds charge less, between 1 1/2% and 3 1/2%. A very few funds charge as much as 7% to 8%, and this is almost unconscionable.

But now the matter becomes more complicated. Some funds charge graduated amounts. For instance, the commission might be 4% if you invest less than $100,000. It may decline to 3 1/4% for up to $250,000 and to 2 1/2% if you invest more than $250,000. Some load funds, incidentally, deduct commissions not just from the initial sum you invest, but also from every amount invested subsequently including reinvested distributions.

Another form of commission is charged when you sell shares. These loads go under a variety of names, including "exit fee," "back load," "deferred sales charge," "redemption fee," "contingent deferred sales charge," and the like. These fees are usually

---

1. (New York: Dell, 1994).
2. (New York: John Wiley & Sons, 1999).

higher for shorter holding periods. They decline if you hold a fund for longer periods of time. For example, you might pay a stiff 6% exit fee if you hold the fund for only one year. The back load might drop to 5% after two years, to 4% after three years, and so on until it disappears if you hold for five to seven years.

In addition, many funds have added a variety of charges that fall somewhere between a commission and annual expenses. They are more insidious because you, the shareholder, may not be aware of either their existence or of their true cost. Some funds now charge shareholders an annual fee for the cost of advertising and selling new shares. These fees, known as 12b-1 fees, are imposed in addition to the usual annual fund expenses and are deducted directly from assets invested in the fund. For no-load funds, 12b-1 fees are capped at 25 basis points (1/4 of 1%). For load funds, 12b-1 fees are capped at 75 basis points (3/4 of 1%).

To complicate matters further, some fund groups are listed with an alphabet soup of fees and commissions. These fund groups offer different classes of shares: Class A, Class B, Class C. These groups allow you to choose the poison you prefer. Class A shares generally charge a front-end commission (or load). Class B shares may charge a 12b-1 fee and a deferred sales charge. Class C shares may not charge either a front or a back load, but then will charge a higher 12b-1 fee. *These distinctions vary from fund group to fund group.* But they are continuing to multiply.

To end this litany of fees and loads, let's note a particularly objectionable form of commission known as a "contractual plan." Under this type of plan, the investor contracts to invest a fixed sum (say $50 or $100) per month for a specified number of years, perhaps ten or 15 years. Commissions are about 8% for the entire life of the contract. These commissions, however, are paid up front. Over 50% of the total invested during the first year consists of commissions. Contractual plans were prevalent in the 1960s.

As far as I know, only one mutual fund group (First Investors) was still using contractual plans to sell funds in the early 1990s. It has now discontinued this practice. Unfortunately, shareholders who purchased funds under an earlier contractual plan may still be under obligation to continue buying shares under the plan. A number of states have passed laws that enable those investors to exit without incurring large penalties. First Investors now sells A shares with a 6 1/4% up front load and B shares with a back load ranging from 4% for funds held for two years or less to zero for funds held for seven years. Needless to say, those are very hefty loads, and I would not suggest you buy bond funds with costs that are this high.

What Is the Effect of Loads on Total Return?

Suppose you are investing in a fund yielding 6%. Let's assume you pay a load (or commission) equal to 5%. There are two ways in which this reduces total return. The first is that the 5% load eats up practically the entire interest for year one. The second is that 5% is deducted from the monies that you invest. Only 95% of principal is actually invested. Therefore, less of your money earns interest for as long as you own the fund.

The ultimate effect of commissions on total return depends partly on how long the fund is held. If you hold a fund for one year or less, a 4% to 5% load eats up the entire year's worth of dividends. So would a back load of 4% to 6%. But if you plan to hold a fund for five years or more, an initial commission may be cheaper in the long run than an equivalent percentage as an exit fee. The latter will represent a percentage of a larger amount each year you own the fund if the fund does well.

Surprisingly, if you plan to hold a fund for over five years, the most expensive form of commission may be the 12b-1 fee. Consider, as an example, that you have invested in a fund that levies an annual 12b-1 fee 3/4 of 1%. If you hold the fund for ten years and multiply the annual fee by ten times, this results in a commission cost equivalent to 7.5%. Actually, that number understates the true cost of such a plan because, as your assets in the fund increase annually, each year you are charged a percentage of ever larger amounts.

Annual Fund Operating Expenses:
The Expense Ratio

Broadly defined, fund expenses are all the recurring expenses which are charged against assets in a mutual fund. They would include transaction costs for buying and selling bonds, salaries for management, overhead expenses, mailing costs for reports to shareholders—in short, all the costs associated with running the bond fund. These expenses are deducted directly from the monies invested in the bond fund. If you divide total annual expenses by the total amount of assets in the fund, the resulting number is what is known as the "expense ratio." For example, if a fund has $1 billion in assets and the total cost of managing the fund is $10 million, the expense ratio will be 1% ($10 million divided by $1 billion, or 100 basis points). If the total cost is $5 million, the expense ratio will be 1/2 of 1% (50 basis points). The expense ratio is commonly stated in basis points. Obviously, if all other factors are equal, the lower the expense ratio, the higher the total return of the fund.

Fund expenses vary all over the lot. The low cost leader is Vanguard, with annual expenses of around 20 basis points (1/5 of 1%) for its bond funds. A number of fund groups maintain subgroups which cap annual expenses at approximately 50 basis points (1/2 of 1%): T. Rowe Price for its Summit Funds and Fidelity for its Spartan Funds. The high end of the range is approximately 2% in annual expenses (not including 12b-1 fees). When you see total returns listed for a bond fund, operating expenses have already been deducted.

Why Fund Expenses Matter!

It is one of life's clichés that you usually get what you pay for. Therefore, you might assume that bond funds that charge commissions or have higher annual expense fees somehow do a better job for their shareholders than the lowest-cost bond funds. Investors must believe that is the case because there is approximately three times as much money in load funds as in no-load funds.[3] And yet the overwhelming evidence is that low-cost funds actually do a far better job for their shareholders than funds that charge higher fees.

You might also expect that load fund groups (mutual fund groups that charge commissions) would compensate their shareholders with lower annual expenses. But, as Bogle has shown, precisely the opposite is true. As a group, the no-load funds are low-expense leaders. Many load funds charge higher annual expenses.

----

3. Bogle, *Common Sense on Mutual Funds*, p. 179.

Therefore, investors in load funds (of whatever stripe) may be doubly penalized: a percentage of their assets is lost to commissions, and on an annual basis higher management expenses come directly out of total return.

A few years ago, when long-term Treasuries yielded 8% or 9% and investment-grade corporates somewhere around 10%, investors could afford to be more cavalier about commissions and expenses. But now, with long Treasuries at approximately 6%, the difference between annual management expenses of 20 basis points and 1.5% is eye-popping. Some simple arithmetic can show you why seemingly small differences (for example, 1% a year) matter a lot. Assuming a fund invests in bonds with a 6% yield, on a $10,000 initial investment, total return for the low-cost leader will be $580 (6% − 0.20%). On the high-cost fund, total return would be $450 (assuming that the high-cost fund buys securities with similar risk characteristics). That is a $130 difference, *or approximately 22% of total return for year one.* Admittedly, a 1.5% expense ratio is extremely high. But if you consider all possible expenses, including loads, 12b-1 fees, exit fees, etc., 1.5% total expenses a year would not be an unrealistic amount for load funds with high expense fees.

Even more astonishing is the difference higher expenses make in total return over longer holding periods. That is due to the wonder of compounding. This is illustrated in Exhibit 11–2, which shows how much difference an extra 100 basis points (1%) in expenses costs over long time periods.

If you have invested in bond funds for a while and if you have researched returns, you may object that quite often load funds or funds with high expense ratios turn up as the best-performing funds for certain time periods. And that is true. But that leads to the other side of the story: namely, how high expenses affect the riskiness of a fund. Ask yourself: if you were the manager of a fund with high management expenses or high sales loads, how could you compete with lower-cost funds?

The answer is obvious. Debt instruments with similar characteristics (credit rating, maturity length, duration) have virtually identical returns. But in the world of bonds, one can always reach for higher returns by taking on more risk. It follows that, in order to compete with his lower-cost cousins, the manager of a higher-cost fund must take on higher risk. To use a sports analogy, high-expense funds begin the race with a large handicap. Much of the

E X H I B I T   11-2

How Costs Consume Bond Fund Returns Over Time

| End of Period (Years) | Initial Investment of $10,000 | | | |
| | Capital Value | | Capital Lost | |
	6% Return	5% Return*	Amount	Percent*
1	$ 10,600	$10,500	$ 100	17%
10	17,900	16,300	1,600	20
20	32,100	26,500	5,600	25
30	57,400	43,200	14,200	30
40	102,900	70,400	32,500	35

*Lost capital as percentage of market appreciation.

Source: Bogle, *Common Sense on Mutual Funds*, p.181. Reprinted with permission.

time, this translates into inconsistent returns. Outstanding returns for one year are often followed by much less stellar returns in subsequent years.

To be sure, costs are only one of a number of factors that make up total return. John Bogle estimates that on average, fund expenses account for 35% of total return. But the evidence presented by John Bogle is overwhelming that over long periods of time, lower-cost funds investing in higher-grade securities consistently rank above higher-cost competitors in total return.

You might ask: are there no star managers in the bond world? Is there not a Warren Buffett or Peter Lynch who consistently beats the bond market? To date, the answer is no. That does not mean that bond funds are not managed capably and honestly. But given the fact that bonds with similar risk characteristics have almost identical returns, it is very difficult for a manager to obtain higher returns without taking on more risk. I know of no star manager who has consistently outperformed the bond market, year after year, managing a higher-cost fund. And if one were to come along, *how would you identify that manager ahead of time?*

The obvious conclusion is that, as a first cut, investors should consider as potential candidates for their investments only those bond funds that have low management costs, no commissions of any kind, and no 12b-1 fees. Remember also: it makes little sense to invest in a high-cost fund if a less risky lower-cost fund is available which posts similar returns.

WHY THE NAV OF YOUR FUND WILL GO UP AND DOWN

This section will discuss some of the major risks associated with investing in bond funds. Since bond funds are debt instruments, they are subject to the same risks as individual bonds. But bond funds are also subject to a number of unique risks. Let's examine them now.

Interest Rate Risk

For most bond funds, the most important risk factor is interest rate exposure. A bond fund responds to changes in interest rates like an individual bond. If interest rates rise, the NAV of a bond fund declines. If interest rates decline, NAV goes up.

How much NAV goes up or down is tied directly to maturity length. Most bond funds invest in a specific segment of the yield curve: short (three years or less); intermediate (three to ten years); or long term (15 to 25 years). As the average maturity of a bond fund increases, so does volatility. Volatility of NAV is negligible for short-term bond funds but very high for long-term bond funds. (Note that for bond funds, maturity is weighted by the size of each issue in the portfolio. For that reason, the term "average weighted maturity" is used to describe the maturity length of a bond fund portfolio.)

This aspect of bond fund investing is the one that has been most puzzling to novice investors. The widespread misconception exists that money invested in high quality credits (AAA municipal bonds, GNMAs, or Treasuries, for example) is totally safe. At the risk of being tiresome, I repeat: that guarantee extends only to credit quality. For bond funds investing in high quality credits, credit risk is virtually nonexistent. But interest rate risk is alive and well. In fact, if you are buying bond funds, you should be more aware of interest rate risk than if you are buying individual bonds.

If you buy a bond fund, you need to be aware that for your fund, interest risk does not diminish with time. Every year, the price of an individual bond moves closer to par as the bond gets closer to its maturity date. But there is no date at which all the bonds in a bond fund reach maturity. Therefore, unlike that of an individual bond, the price per share of a bond fund (that is, its NAV) does not move closer to par. Indeed, because a bond fund maintains a constant maturity, its level of interest rate risk also remains constant as long as you own the fund. If you hold an individual bond, you need not concern yourself with day-to-day fluctuations in the price of the bond, as long as you intend to hold it to maturity. But you will be very much aware of the day-to-day changes in NAV of your bond fund. You will see them in your newspaper and in your monthly statements. And you will not know at exactly what price you can sell your shares, even tomorrow.

Duration and Total Return

Can you estimate potential volatility before you buy a bond fund? Surprisingly, that is actually quite easy to do. What you need to know before you buy a bond fund is its duration. Duration is listed by only a few of the publications that dispense information about bond funds. It is usually included by Morningstar. But you can always find out the duration of any bond fund: simply telephone the toll-free number of the fund group, and ask.

Duration, as we saw in the section on individual bonds, is a very accurate measurement of the sensitivity of a bond to interest rate changes. The same holds true for bond funds. A fund's duration can be used as a rough guide to determine how much the NAV of a fund is likely to move up or down in response to a change in interest rates of 100 basis points (1%).

As an example, let's suppose you own a fund investing in long-term Treasuries (the Treasury's long bond). Let's assume the fund has a duration of eight years and is yielding 6%. If the yield on the Treasury's long bond were to go up to 7% (a move of 100 basis points), then you can expect that the NAV of the fund would decline by 8%, that is, by the duration of the fund.

Moves of this magnitude are not unusual. Larger moves have occurred. As a recent example, between September of 1998 and

January of 1999, the yield on the Treasury's long bond went from a low of approximately 4.8% to a high of approximately 6.7%, a move of almost 200 basis points. Total return of bond funds investing in long-term Treasuries were devastated: the NAV of these funds declined by as much as 20%. (The exact number varied from fund to fund based on the exact makeup of each fund.) Ironically, this move reversed a move that had occurred the preceding year, when the yield on the Treasury's long bond declined to under 5% from above 6%, resulting in a gain in NAV of about 12%.

While the preceding example focused on a change in yield of the Treasury's 30-year bond, since all bonds key off U.S. Treasuries, during 1999, declines occurred in virtually all sectors of the bond market and consequently in all types of bond funds: corporates, GNMAs, municipals, and even, to some extent, international bond funds. The extent of the decline varied from fund to fund and from sector to sector.

Average weighted maturity of bond funds and duration are closely related. But two funds with identical average weighted maturities may have different durations, based on whether the fund invests in premium or in discount bonds, zeros, derivatives, and so on. In general, bond funds with short average weighted maturities (two to three years) have an approximate duration of two years. The duration of intermediate bonds funds with average maturities of 8 to 12 years ranges between four and five years. The duration of long-term bond funds, whose average weighted maturity may vary from 15 to 25 years, varies from approximately six to eight years. Note that for so-called target funds, which invest in zero coupon bonds, duration and average weighted maturity are equal. Therefore, the NAV of a bond fund with a duration of 25 years may move up or down by as much as 25% in response to every 1% change in yield.

As we saw in Chapter 4, these guides are approximate and will vary depending on whether interest rates are moving up or moving down. Nonetheless, for bond funds whose major risk factor is interest rate risk, duration numbers provide better information concerning the potential volatility of the fund's NAV (and therefore its potential riskiness) than any other kind of information you can find. Duration is particularly useful because it is a forward-looking number, as opposed to total return, which tells you what happened in the past. Duration enables you to predict how exposed you are to interest rate moves.

But remember that fluctuations in the NAV of a fund are only part of its total return. Over time, the interest income of a bond fund cushions its downside risk. Suppose, for example, that in the example cited above, the 1% rise in yield (from 5% to 6%, in a fund with a duration of eight years) occurs over a one-year period. Your total return for that year would be a negative 3% (+5% interest income and −8% decline in NAV). If interest rates were to decline by 1%, then the total return for the same fund would rise to 13% (+5% interest income and +8% rise in NAV). Interest income mitigates declines in NAV in down markets and adds to total return when NAV goes up.

Over short holding periods (two years or less), significant changes in interest rates, and resulting changes in NAV, dominate total returns. But for very long holding periods (ten years or more), interest rate moves are likely to offset each other. For long periods of time, the income portion of a bond fund consisting of interest income, and interest-on-interest, are more likely to dominate total return.

NAV "Erosion"

This aspect of investing in bond funds has received very little attention. It was brought to my attention by a number of excellent articles in *Morningstar* and by the "Principal Only Fixed Income Reports" published by Lipper.

What I mean by NAV erosion are declines in NAV that are not recoverable and that, in fact, represent a permanent loss of principal. There is a big difference between what I am calling NAV erosion and a change in NAV due primarily to interest rate changes. If you buy a long-term bond fund when interest rates are at 5%, you know that if interest rates rise to 6%, the NAV of your fund will decline. But if interest rates return to 5%, you have the right to expect that at that time the NAV of your fund will again be approximately what it was initially when you bought the fund. (That is what would happen to an individual bond.) In other words, you would expect to recoup principal in full. In the meantime, you would have earned the interest income and interest-on-interest.

Many bond funds, however, do not meet this test. If you compare their NAV at intervals of several years when interest rates were roughly at similar levels, you may be in for a major shock.

The NAV of many funds is well below what it was in earlier years when interest rates were at similar levels.

Why would this occur? The shocking answer is that, in some instances, this erosion is the result of deliberate accounting policies on the part of fund management, which emphasize yield at the eventual cost of loss of principal. Funds that are guilty of this abuse often trumpet high yields in their advertisements. In order to quote a higher yield, the portfolio is often stuffed with premium bonds. When these bonds are called, or sold, at par or below, each redemption results in a loss of principal and therefore, a loss of NAV. In effect, these managers sacrifice principal in order to advertise a higher yield. Sadly, many taxable bond funds, including government bond funds and GNMA funds, have been among the most flagrant abusers.

NAV erosion may also be the direct result of strategies designed to boost yield or total return. In the process of managing a bond fund, the manager typically makes a variety of bets: on the direction of interest rates, for example; on potential upgrades or downgrades of bond credit ratings; on potential turnarounds for defaulted bonds; on derivatives and so on. Some of these bets are low risk; others high risk. If the strategy backfires, then a manager may use possibly riskier strategies in order to recoup lost principal. A high expense ratio is also an indirect contributor to NAV erosion since it forces the manager to take on comparably more risk than lower cost funds. Also, since it eats up return constantly, it eventually results in far lower total return for investors.

At various times, Morningstar has also run numbers and come up with lists of bond funds that "grow" NAV. This would reflect "successful" bets, that is, correctly anticipating a variety of changes in the bond market. And no doubt many managers make decisions which pay off. Unfortunately, too many of one year's brilliant strategies become next year's disasters. The history of the bond market shows that it is unlikely that any manager will consistently outperform a sector of the bond market.

How can you guard against NAV erosion? Before you buy a fund, look up its history. Some red flags would be: the SEC yield being much lower than the distribution yield; a high expense ratio; and a high portfolio turnover. Also, be leery of bond funds that promise to achieve high returns by using "sophisticated" models or "state-of-the-art" strategies, particularly if these funds are very new and have no track record. The term "sophisticated" is a euphemism for quantitative strategies using derivatives or complex mathematical models. As noted in the section dealing with derivatives (see below), the history of bond funds is littered with anecdotes of "sophisticated" strategies that have blown up and resulted in major losses. Funds with conservative management and low expense ratios tend to do a better job of preserving NAV over long holding periods.

Derivatives Risk

1994 was the year derivatives got a lot of press. No, derivatives were not invented in 1994. But prior to that year, use of derivatives in bond funds received little notice. That does not mean derivatives were not in use. In fact, some of the best-performing bond funds had used derivatives to soup up returns. Few investors noticed or complained.

In 1994, however, market conditions changed. Many bond funds suffered steep declines. Some of the steepest declines were attributed to the use of derivatives. At that point, the financial press took notice. Use of derivatives suddenly became a major topic in the financial press.

First of all, what are derivatives? A derivative is defined as any financial instrument which derives its value from another instrument. It cannot be priced independently. The term, however, is a catch-all that covers a very broad spectrum of financial instruments, some fairly well known (such as options and futures) and others so obscure and arcane that only professionals engaging in the most complex strategies understand them. Derivatives cannot be priced independently. New derivatives are constantly being created, and unfortunately, even if I understood them all, there are far too many derivatives for me to discuss them in detail.

You should, however, be aware that derivatives are an important tool for managing bond fund portfolios. They have two very different uses: they can be used to boost yield, and therefore total return, or to hedge against losses. It is in the nature of derivatives to magnify both losses and gains. When derivatives work as intended, the gains can be significant. Derivatives, however, often behave in totally unanticipated ways. In that case, losses can be major.

As an example, some of the significant gains of municipal bond funds in 1992 and 1993 were due to the use of derivatives known as "inverse floaters." (Inverse floaters are floating-rate bonds designed to rise in price as interest rates fall.) As interest rates declined in 1992 and 1993, inverse floaters performed as hoped, resulting in nice gains for some municipal bond funds.

One problem with derivatives, however, is that even the most experienced managers cannot anticipate the conditions which might cause their strategy to backfire. When interest rates turned up in 1994, the price of inverse floaters plummeted. The municipal bond funds that had souped up returns in 1992 and 1993 with inverse floaters became the biggest losers of 1994.

Another example involved a well-known fund which went by the reassuring title of "Institutional Government Income Fund." (This is a real fund, but I am leaving out the name of the fund group.) The fund was marketed as a conservatively managed, safe fund which invested primarily in bonds guaranteed by the U.S. government. Between February and April of 1994, the share price of that fund declined by a catastrophic 25%. (In other words, within a space of three months a $10,000 investment shrank to $7,500.)

This fund had made use of derivatives the cornerstone of its investment strategy: at least half of the fund's assets were invested in derivatives based on mortgage-backed securities. That particular strategy had been responsible for the outstanding returns of the fund prior to 1994. Up to that time, fund management had received high praise in the financial press for their brilliant strategy. Indeed, the fund had received a five-star rating from Morningstar. (That rating is not only the highest rating conferred by Morningstar but is also adjusted for risk.) As a result, money poured into the fund. Fund assets grew to over a billion.

It is unlikely that many investors in that fund were aware that the fund's strategy could backfire in the event of a rise in interest rates. The fund name and prospectus gave no clue that the manager might be pursuing a high-risk strategy. Most investors in the fund probably viewed the fund holdings as very safe, high-quality instruments. But as interest rates rose, suddenly some of the securities held by the fund became virtually worthless almost overnight. Similar losses occurred in other funds pursuing similar strategies. Many of those funds had also been marketed as low-risk funds.

How concerned should you be about derivatives? The question is difficult to answer. At the present time, derivatives have receded from public consciousness, but that does not mean they have disappeared from bond funds. Indeed, even though derivatives are used widely, it may be difficult, if not impossible, to find out if your fund uses derivatives, and if so, how. The prospectus of a fund usually does not address the issue. Neither does Morningstar.

As always, the best defense is to investigate a fund before you buy. One red flag might be returns that seem very high compared to similar funds for the same period. Try to find out how these returns were earned. Also, be suspicious of any fund that promises to use "sophisticated" or "state of the art" economic models. Those phrases, or others like them, imply the use of the newest, fresh-off-the-computer, untried derivatives. Be an aware consumer. Be skeptical of promises that sound too good to be true. If you don't like or fully understand the answer, find another fund.

"Sell-Off" Risk

What would happen if too many investors wanted to sell their shares on the same day? This would be the equivalent of a run on the banks. Articles speculating on this possibility have appeared occasionally in the past. But as I write this, in early 2000, I do not recall seeing anything of the kind recently. Does this mean that the risk of sell-offs has disappeared permanently from bond markets? The facts do not support this assumption.

Bond funds, like other mutual funds, permit investors to redeem their shares any time they wish. This has worked well because most of the time the money to meet those redemptions is available. New money comes into funds on a daily basis. And managers keep some cash on hand for the purpose of making redemptions. Most of the time the daily redemption of shares does not materially affect the fund.

But what happens if there are more sellers than buyers? Then the manager has no choice except to sell some of the securities held by the fund. In weak markets, even normally liquid securities become illiquid, that is, hard to sell. Managers are forced to sell their best, their most liquid, holdings first. If the decline continues, eventually, managers are forced to sell holdings no one wants, at fire sale prices.

Steep sell-offs are not just a theoretical possibility. On a number of occasions, particular sectors of the bond market have experienced massive sell-offs resulting in steep losses. In 1989 and 1990, junk bonds went into a tailspin. During that time, the NAV of some junk bond funds declined by as much as 50% (that is, $5,000 per $10,000 investment) within a six-month period. Similar though briefer and less steep waves of selling hit municipal, corporate, and Treasury bonds prior to the 1987 stock crash and GNMA funds in 1981 and 1982. 1994 was characterized by intense selling and steep losses in every sector of the bond market. The NAV of riskier bond funds plummeted, sometimes by 10% to 15% in a matter of weeks. Total NAV losses for some bond funds exceeded 30%. In 1998, the bottom fell out of bonds of emerging markets, and NAVs of bond funds in that sector declined by 50% or more. Finally, 1999 was a dismal year for investors in all types of bond funds: the worst year for the bond market since 1994. Steep declines occurred in almost every sector of the bond market.

This is not written to alarm anyone. But if you are investing in a bond fund, you should be aware that the risk of price declines is real, and particularly acute in volatile bond funds. Your choice of bond funds should be partly governed by an awareness of what these risks would mean to you in the event of a steep decline or a multiyear bear market in bonds, such as the one that occurred between 1979 and the end of 1981.

A number of mutual fund groups have taken steps to protect their shareholders in the event of panic selling. Some mutual fund groups, for example, have established lines of credit with banks which would enable them to have enough cash on hand to meet shareholder redemptions even under panic selling conditions. But some possibilities might be more disturbing to investors. For example, somewhere in the fine print of their prospectus, many mutual funds reserve the right to hold back checks for redeemed shares for a period of seven days if redemptions are very high. Another possibility is that shareholders would be paid for redeemed shares not in cash but "in kind," that is, with actual bonds from the portfolio (presumably because management could not find a buyer for the bonds). I am not aware at this time that either of these eventualities has ever actually occurred.

Of course, once again, the other side of the picture is that many sell-offs present speculative opportunities once the waves of selling have run their course. But of course, there is no way to know when a decline has run its course except in retrospect, and there is no guarantee that all declines will eventually reverse.

Credit Risk

With the exception of funds investing primarily in bonds that are below investment grade (such as bond funds investing in junk bonds, or debt of emerging markets), credit risk is a less significant factor for holders of bond funds than it is for holders of individual bonds. Bond funds are, by their nature, diversified. The larger the fund, usually, the more diversified it is. Most large funds hold dozens of different issues. Particularly if those securities are investment grade or higher, diversification becomes an important safety factor. Few issues comprise more than a small percentage of total assets (usually less than 2%). In addition, many funds are monitored for credit quality by in-house credit analysts. Deteriorating credits may be sold before the problem becomes significant.

This is one clear advantage bond funds have compared to individual bonds: you can boost yield without incurring significant risk of default by investing in bond funds that buy investment grade credits or better. And you do not have to limit yourself to buying only bonds with the highest credit quality (as you might wish to do with individual bonds). But note that in comparing one bond fund to another, it would not make sense to purchase a fund with a high expense ratio and riskier bonds if a lower expense fund with a less risky portfolio provides an equal or higher yield.

What Happens to Your Money if a Management Company Goes Belly Up? Is There Any Fund Insurance?

No, there is not any kind of insurance. Nonetheless, even if the management company of your mutual fund goes belly up (a very unlikely occurrence), your investments will probably still be safe.

In order to explain why, it is helpful to look at the structure of a typical mutual fund family. While there are differences among complexes, the typical structure consists of a management company (the mutual fund group) that manages a group of funds. The individual mutual funds and the management company are separate entities. The management company functions as an investment adviser. It manages the assets of individual funds. But it does not actually hold the assets of these funds. Also, each fund is actually set up as an individual corporation or business trust. The assets of the individual funds are kept entirely segregated from those of the management company. The securities in those funds are held in trust by a custodian such as a bank—again, not by the management company. A transfer agent usually maintains and administers the individual accounts.

If the management company (the mutual fund group) were to find itself in financial difficulty, the assets of the individual funds would continue to be held by the custodian and would remain segregated from those of the management company. All of this is very strictly regulated by the SEC. It is, therefore, unlikely that the financial misfortunes of a management company would adversely affect assets held in mutual funds.

Remember also that the greatest asset of mutual funds is the confidence of the investing public. Management companies typically exercise very tight controls to prevent malfeasance or fraud on the part of employees. In addition, most management companies carry insurance in the form of a fidelity bond to protect assets under management against possible fraud or malfeasance on the part of employees.

SELECTING, BUYING, AND MONITORING BOND FUNDS

Should I Buy a Fund or Individual Bonds?

This question is hotly debated, but it does not have only one correct answer. A case can be made for investing in individual bonds or for investing in bond funds. Some individuals feel more comfortable buying individual bonds. Others prefer mutual funds. Each has advantages and disadvantages. Direct comparison between funds and individual securities is, at best, imprecise.

For example, will you earn a higher return by investing in individual bonds or in a bond fund investing in securities with similar maturities?

Most brokers would tell you that you will earn more by buying individual bonds. The broker will point out that a fund's management expenses come directly out of your return. This is true, but incomplete. If you are buying one or a few bonds, credit safety becomes paramount. You do not want to own the one bond that defaults. So you buy high quality credits, even though by doing that, you are sacrificing yield. If, on the other hand, you are buying a bond fund, you can safely invest in a fund with somewhat lower quality credits without impairing credit safety, because the fund is broadly diversified.

Whether you buy a fund or individual instruments, your actual total return will be determined by many variables:

- The size of the markup, for an individual bond; or for a fund, the expense ratio and commissions
- The maturity length of the securities
- Their credit quality
- Reinvestment rates
- Whether you buy and hold or trade
- The length of the holding period
- The price at which you redeem

On a total return basis, for investors who buy and hold over long periods of time (more than five years) and who reinvest dividends, certain features of funds boost their return when compared to individual securities. Any large fund can buy securities more cheaply than any individual. Also, a mutual fund distributes dividends monthly. This is an advantage both if you rely on dividend checks for income and if you reinvest. More frequent compounding also boosts return. So does reinvesting at higher than money market rates. The higher reinvestment rate and monthly compounding of higher-yielding bond funds boost total return over long holding periods. Over very long holding periods (ten years or longer), bear in mind that interest income and interest-on-interest comprise the greatest part of total return. On the other hand, if you buy a fund with a large expense ratio or high commission costs, then this reduces total return.

Funds offer a number of advantages compared to individual securities. They enable an investor to buy a diversified portfolio cheaply and efficiently. They are convenient. They simplify collecting and reinvesting dividends as well as record-keeping. They offer liquidity. If you want to resell, you always have a ready buyer.

On the other hand, let's address the issue of preservation of capital. If you are unwilling to lose any part of principal and want to be certain to at least earn the coupon, then you should buy individual bonds. The intermediate range (two to seven years) generally provides a reasonable buy point: it provides perhaps 80% to 90% of the return of long-term bonds, with far less volatility. The main advantage of buying the individual securities—rather than a fund investing in those securities—is that, as noted above, you are guaranteed return of your entire principal at maturity. And in addition, if you hold to maturity, you will have earned the coupons. Finally, your return will not be reduced by fund expenses.

If you want the highest degree of safety, whether you are investing $10,000 or one million dollars, put that money in a laddered portfolio of short Treasuries. This is as safe as anything can be in this world.

As a rule, if you are investing less than $50,000 (total) in bonds, and if you are buying securities other than Treasuries or high quality short maturity munis, then you might feel more comfortable buying mutual funds rather than individual securities. If your portfolio is larger, and you are able to buy individual securities at a good price (without excessive commissions), then individual securities may be a better option, particularly if you prefer to buy and hold rather than to trade.

Even if you feel comfortable buying some individual securities, you may want to include funds in your portfolio in order to diversify core holdings. Also, if you would like to buy securities that are complex and require a lot of expertise, then it makes sense to invest in those through funds. As a rule, the greater the expertise required to navigate within certain sectors of the bond market, the better off you would be choosing a fund, as opposed to individual securities. If you want to invest in junk bonds, or in any international bonds (whether high quality or emerging market debt), then do so through a mutual fund. Due to the unique nature of pass-through cash flows and some of the complex features of corporate bonds, it may also be simpler to invest in those through funds.

These, however, are guidelines. All choices involve trade-offs. Funds and individual securities are different enough so that your choice can be governed by what feels most comfortable for you.

Finally, one important reminder. Don't expect conservatively managed bond funds to outperform significantly their sector of the bond market. They generally don't. This, however, is not meant as a criticism of funds. Nor does it lessen their usefulness to individual investors. It means only that individuals should realize that performance of bond funds will in all likelihood track that of the sector of the bond market in which they invest.

How Concerned Should You Be About Potential Changes in NAV?

You should always be concerned about changes in NAV if they are due to what I called earlier "erosion of NAV" because that is simply tantamount to destruction of principal. The question I am raising in this section refers to changes in NAV due primarily to changes in interest rates.

The answer depends on a number of factors. The first one is when you intend to use the money. You should never buy a long-term fund (or any fund whose NAV is going to be volatile) for short holding periods. If you are going to need the money in two years or less, major changes in NAV will clearly affect total return far more than dividend yield.

On the other hand, over long holding periods (ten years or longer), income produced by reinvesting interest income and reinvesting dividends, compounded, should dominate total return, assuming, of course, that dividends are reinvested and not spent. The reason for this can be explained through the concept of duration. Theoretically, there is a point corresponding to the duration of your bond fund at which changes in NAV become irrelevant to total return. If you own a fund with a duration of eight years, that point will be reached after eight years. If, during those eight years, interest rates go up, you will be buying shares at a lower price, but you will be receiving higher interest income. If interest rates decline, then the NAV of your fund will go up. In fact, it has been shown that if interest rates rise, this will result in higher total return (even if NAV declines) because you are reinvesting at higher rates.[4]

The problem with this viewpoint is that total return for any long period is not predicable because any large and sudden increase in rates, particularly if it occurs towards the end of the holding period, can depress the average returns of many years. This happened in 1999, for example.

Finally, consider your comfort level with volatility. Don't buy any long-term fund if you are not comfortable with a certain amount of volatility and uncertainity.

Sources of Information Concerning Bond Funds

The problem nowadays is not finding information. Rather, it is information overload. The financial press, magazines, newspapers and newsletters, finance channels on television, and the Internet all issue barrages of information about mutual funds. Most of the information concerns equity funds, with occasional attention paid to bond funds, usually after a particular sector has had a good run. Unfortunately, much of this information is hype and not very useful. Some excellent sources of information do exist, however, and these will be discussed below.

Why Not Just Buy the Fund that Had the Highest Return Last Year?

A great deal of the information published concerning mutual funds consists of rankings of top-performing funds. Most financial publications periodically issue lists of top-performing funds, some as often as every month or every three months. So a legitimate question would be: why not just buy the bond funds that had the highest total returns last year?

The main reason would be that, for bond funds past performance simply does not predict future performance. Generally, bond funds track the sector of the market in which they are invested. If

---

4. John Bogle, *Bogle on Mutual Funds* (New York: Dell, 1994), pp. 36–37.

a particular group of funds does well one year and conditions change, so will returns for these funds. If, for example, interest rates go up in a particular year, then bond funds with short maturities will be standouts that year. If interest rates decline, long-term funds, or funds investing in zeros, will be the winners. Next year's conditions will dictate winners and losers next year.

Another caveat is that the top-performing funds in any group are likely to be the riskiest funds in that group. In order to have a higher total return than funds investing in comparable securities, a fund manager has to take on more risk. According to one of the leading experts on bond funds, Michael Lipper,[5] if a fund manager wants to be at the top of his respective peer group, he has to be willing to take the chance that next year he will be at the bottom. Very few funds turn up as top-performing funds year after year. Moreover, you are unlikely to be able to predict from a list of past winners which are likely to be next year's winners.

Finally, the objectives and investment policies of the top-performing funds may not be appropriate for your investment needs. If the top-performing funds are volatile, and you need stable, predictable income, then those funds are not for you.

There is a use for surveys of top-performing funds. You can use them to locate funds that you might want to investigate further. But don't just look for the top-ranked fund. Rather, look first for funds that are no-load, have low expense ratios and no 12b-1 plans. Secondly, focus on funds that have operated for at least five years (more is better) and preferably through both strong and weak markets. You want to look for funds that have held up relatively well during bear episodes and that have done okay during bull markets. Basically, you are looking for consistent performance and relatively conservative management. Over the long run, those are the funds most likely to preserve both capital and income.

Surveys of top-performing funds, however, rarely go into enough detail to enable you to evaluate whether the fund is an appropriate investment for your needs. To dig further, there are a number of avenues.

---

5. Quoted in *The Handbook of Fixed Income Securities*, ed. Frank J. Fabozzi and Irving M. Pollack (Homewood, Ill.: Dow Jones-Irwin, 1987), p. 492.

Morningstar

I am mentioning Morningstar first because chances are that you have seen references to it in advertisements for funds or on the Web.

Morningstar started out as a newsletter about mutual funds. Currently, it is available in two forms: a printed newsletter, which comes out on a monthly basis and on the Internet. Both are now available in many public libraries.

The printed version publishes detailed, one-page analyses of major mutual funds, including bond funds, on an annual cycle. Major funds are reviewed once a year. These one-page summaries contain a lot of information: fund objectives, expense ratios, average weighted maturity, duration, an analysis of the manager's past track record, and annual total returns for ten years or since inception for more recent funds. A style box, which looks like a tic-tac-toe box, summarizes the sensitivity of the fund to interest rates and its credit quality.

The Internet version comes in two flavors: a free website and a more in-depth "premium" version, intended for professionals, which costs about $10.00 a month. The free website (*morningstar.com*) has a variety of features including articles and background analyses. It also has an easy-to-use database which enables you to generate a list of funds in a given sector (municipal, international, taxable), ranked according to criteria you select (best performing for one year or for five years, for example). Once you have generated a list, you can "click" on individual funds within that list and zero in for more detailed information about these specific funds. This will generate a one-page summary. These summaries are not as detailed as the printed version. The "premium" subscriber version is the most complete and is updated monthly. Finally even if you are not a subscriber, using the Internet, you can also order in-depth reviews of any fund that interests you, for a modest fee (currently $2.00 per report).

The feature of Morningstar's analysis which has received the most attention is its star ratings: Morningstar awards from one to five stars to selected funds. The star rankings are intended to single out the best performers within a specific investment "objective." Only funds that have been in existence at least three years are considered for any stars. Further, according to Morningstar, the rankings depend on a mathematical formula, not on subjective judgment. The rankings include an adjustment for risk, also developed by Morningstar and proprietary to it.

These star rankings have become ubiquitous. Any fund that is rated four or five stars trumpets this fact in advertisements. Surveys indicate that many individuals buy only funds that have earned four or five stars from Morningstar.

You should be aware of the limitations of star rankings concerning bond funds. While the star rankings may point you to well-run funds within specific objectives, that is all they do. The list of four- and five-star funds will not necessarily identify the specific funds with the highest future total returns, or the least volatile funds, or the ones with the lowest expense ratios. Like other bond funds, four- and five-star funds track the sector of the market in which they invest. The list of five-star bond funds, for example, includes many long-term municipal bond funds and some high-yield (i.e., junk) funds. These funds go down in down markets and up in up markets, as do other bond funds in the same sectors. Note also that some bond fund categories include no funds at all with four or five stars—international, for example. The "high-yield" sector includes a number of five-star funds, but that does not make them a safe investment for everyone.

Morningstar, however, does supply some very useful information. But instead of looking at the stars, focus on the expense ratio, the duration of the fund, its credit quality (those two are summarized by the style box), and the table of annual returns for the past few years.

Note some additional caveats. Morningstar presents detailed analyses only of major funds in large mutual fund families. You will not find information on many smaller funds. Also, some of the funds that are analyzed (for example, trusts and "prime rate" funds) are really closed-end funds rather than true mutual funds, but they are identified as such only in very small print. Moreover, the Morningstar database is not as complete as Lipper's. But while many major financial newspapers and magazines use Lipper data to compile their mutual fund listings, the Lipper analyses themselves are not as accessible to the general public as Morningstar's.

Many financial websites have links to Morningstar, mainly to generate lists. It is much more useful to go directly to the Morningstar website.

The Dow Jones newspapers (*Barron's, The Wall Street Journal*) use the Lipper database to compile their fund rankings and returns. Many other publications, including *The New York Times* and many financial websites, use the Morningstar database. This can be somewhat confusing because Morningstar and Lipper classify funds based on different criteria. Also, the Lipper database includes many funds not rated by Morningstar. As a result, you will sometimes see different funds turn up as the top-ranked or top-performing fund in a given objective. Also, at one time Morningstar did not separate funds by maturity. It now does that on its website. But newspapers using Morningstar data do not necessarily make use of that distinction.

Finally, note that many financial publications, both in print and on the Internet, publish weekly tables of fund returns compiled by Lipper and grouped according to their objectives. For bond funds, the objectives are those defined in the next chapter.

Getting Information Directly from Mutual Fund Groups

Mutual fund groups provide a lot of useful information. It is available for free, directly from the mutual funds themselves. Investigating a fund need not be a lengthy process; and it may save you a lot of grief.

Years ago, material was supplied by mutual fund groups mainly through a document, written in stilted language, called a "prospectus." The language and format of the old prospectus were dictated by legal requirements. While the prospectus supplied lots of good information, it was often difficult to read and confusing.

The good news is that the prospectus has undergone a significant transformation. In 1996, the SEC approved changes to make the prospectus easier to read and more useful to prospective shareholders. In lieu of the old prospectus, many fund groups now publish a very short document (two to four pages long), formally known as a "profile," which contains a lot of the key information you would want to know before buying a specific fund.

The next three Exhibits (11–3 through 11–5) are examples of some key sections excerpted from a fund profile.

The section excerpted in Exhibit 11–3 shows the name of the fund: "*Vanguard High-Yield Tax-Exempt Fund*," and defines its objective: "*to provide a very high level of tax-exempt current income.*"

E X H I B I T   11–3

Excerpt from a Fund Profile for a Tax-Exempt Bond
Fund

Fund Profile—
Vanguard High-Yield Tax-Exempt Fund

The following profile summarizes key features of Vanguard High-Yield Tax-Exempt Fund.

INVESTMENT OBJECTIVE
The Fund seeks to provide a very high level of tax-exempt current income.

INVESTMENT STRATEGIES
The Fund invests at least 80% of its assets in longer-term, investment-grade municipal
bonds, which are securities with ratings of Baa or higher, and up to 20% in bonds that are
rated less than Baa or are unrated. For more information on credit quality, see "Additional
Risk Information" under **More on the Funds**.

Now you immediately want to know: how do they plan to provide
a high level of tax-exempt income? The answer to that question
is provided under the heading "Investment Strategies." The fund
will invest in longer-term municipal bonds, 80% of which will be
investment grade or higher. In other words, the fund will provide
a high yield because it will invest in bonds that have a long maturity. Any reader of this book will immediately realize that the
primary risks of the fund will be that its NAV will fluctuate, due
to interest rate changes. (The reason for this will be explained
more fully in the next chapter.)

   While the statement is reasonably specific, you would want
more precision. Since the primary risk factor in the fund is its
maturity length, you would want to know the average weighted
maturity of the portfolio, or better yet, its duration. Just phone the
toll-free line of the fund. Since both numbers vary from time to
time, that is the best source of information because it is the most
up to date.

   Exhibit 11–4 addresses the issue of risk and ties it to past
performance.

   The section in Exhibit 11–4 shows past performance in several different ways. The bar graph displays total annual return for
each of the past ten years. The highest annual total return was
18.13% (in 1995); the lowest, −5.06% in 1994. Total return was

E X H I B I T   11–4

Excerpt from a Fund Profile for a Tax-Exempt Bond Fund

PERFORMANCE/RISK INFORMATION

The following bar chart and table provide an indication of the risk of investing in the Fund. The bar chart shows the Fund's performance in each calendar year over a ten-year period. The table shows how the Fund's average annual returns for one, five, and ten calendar years compare with those of a broad-based bond market index. Keep in mind that the Fund's past performance does not indicate how it will perform in the future.

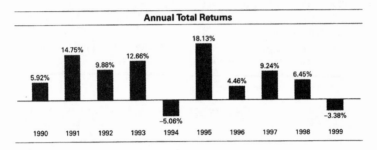

Annual Total Returns

During the period shown in the bar chart, the highest return for a calendar quarter was 7.83% (quarter ended March 31,1995) and the lowest return for a quarter was –5.11% (quarter ended March 31, 1994).

Average Annual Total Returns for Years Ended December 31, 1999			
	1 Year	5 Years	10 Years
Vanguard High-Yield Tax-Exempt Fund	–3.38%	6.75%	7.07%
Lehman Municipal Bond Index	–2.06	6.91	6.89

positive during eight of the past ten years; negative for two out of the past ten years. The narrative directly under the bar chart supplies additional information about variability of total return: the highest total return for one quarter (7.83% for one quarter in 1995) and the lowest (−5.11% for one quarter in March 31, 1995). All of these numbers taken together give you a very good idea of the amount of volatility that you can expect if you invest in this fund. Once again, I repeat that since this fund invests in long-term, high-quality bonds, the variability of returns over the past ten years has been due primarily to changes in the level of interest

E X H I B I T   11–5

Excerpt from a Fund Profile for a Tax-Exempt Bond Fund

FEES AND EXPENSES

The following table describes the fees and expenses you would pay if you buy and hold shares of the Fund. The expenses shown under *Annual Fund Operating Expenses* are based upon those incurred in the fiscal year ended October 31, 1999.

SHAREHOLDER FEES *(fees paid directly from your investment)*

Sales Charge (Load) Imposed on Purchases:	None
Sales Charge (Load) Imposed on Reinvested Dividends:	None
Redemption Fee:	None
Exchange Fee:	None

ANNUAL FUND OPERATING EXPENSES *(expenses deducted from the Fund's assets)*

Management Expenses:	0.16%
12b-1 Distribution Fee:	None
Other Expenses:	0.02%
Total Annual Fund Operating Expenses:	**0.18%**

The following example is intended to help you compare the cost of investing in the Fund with the cost of investing in other mutual funds. It illustrates the hypothetical expenses that you would incur over various periods if you invest $10,000 in the Fund. This example assumes that the Fund provides a return of 5% a year, and that operating expenses remain the same. The results apply whether or not you redeem your investment at the end of each period.

1 Year	3 Years	5 Years	10 Years
$18	$58	$101	$230

rates. Annual total returns for the next ten years can be expected to be equally variable from year to year.

Note that *average* annual total return is also provided for the one-year, five-year, and ten-year periods. Total return for 1999 was negative. (As you will see in the next chapter, that was not unusual for 1999.) But in spite of that, *average* annual total return has been positive for the five-year and ten-year periods. (Even though it is not stated in the prospectus, average annual total return is calculated based on the convention that dividends have been reinvested.) Note also that average annual performance is compared to an unmanaged benchmark index, the Lehman Municipal Bond Index. This particular fund gets high marks on that score because its performance for the ten-year mark exceeds that of the index and comes close for the five-year mark. Since performance numbers for an unmanaged index do not include any expenses, matching the performance of an index is difficult.

Exhibit 11–5 addresses fees and expenses. Both of the expenses described in this chapter are spelled out. These are shareholder expenses (in other words, commissions or loads), which you pay directly either when you buy or when you sell the fund; and annual operating expenses, which are deducted directly from fund assets every year, and which come directly out of total return. Since the fund under discussion is a no-load fund, there are no loads or commissions of any kind, no 12-1b expenses, and no expenses for exchanging assets from one fund to another within the same fund family. Annual fund operating expenses for this fund are exceptionally low: 18 basis points. Note also that a separate section spells out annual fund expenses, in dollar amounts, for periods ranging from one to ten years.

All of this information is clear and easy to understand. Even if you are investing in this fund primarily for income, a few minutes spent looking at the profile enable you to see how total return varies from year to year; and to compare this fund to other funds quoting similar yields and total return.

This fund profile is only one of a number of bond funds profiled within one prospectus. Vanguard, like a number of other large mutual fund groups, groups profiles of a number of funds investing in the same sector within one single brochure. This particular brochure includes all of Vanguard's municipal bond funds. This makes it very easy to compare the various municipal bond funds to each other, for total returns, volatility, etc.

In addition to the profiles of individual funds, you would need to check:

+ The procedures for buying and for redeeming shares
+ The procedures for receiving or reinvesting dividends
+ Available services (check-writing privileges; buying or redeeming shares by phone or over the Internet; switching privileges, again by phone or over the Internet)
+ Whether the fund can be used for tax-deferred plans such as IRAs or Keoghs

Mutual funds are required to publish a number of additional documents, which can be requested separately. One, called the Statement of Additional Information (SAI), is technical and can be somewhat difficult to read. But it includes a lot of useful information, such as a list of all the individual securities in the fund as well as audited financial statements. Once you buy a fund, the management company will routinely send you annual and semi-annual reports which discuss the performance of the fund and relate it to current conditions in whatever sector of the market the fund is invested.

In addition to the prospectus, SAI, and annual reports, mutual fund groups also publish less formally structured documents, typically named "facts on funds" or a similar phrase, which summarize information from all of the brochures just mentioned. A typical "facts on funds" brochure would list:

+ General information about the fund: amount of assets, ticker symbol, etc.
+ Fund objectives and strategy
+ Name of the manager and length of tenure
+ Information on total return for the preceding ten years
+ The fund's largest holdings
+ Fund expenses
+ Commentary on past performance and future outlook of the managers

Many mutual fund families also produce an enormous amount of information concerning a wide range of topics, such as guides to IRA accounts and planning kits for asset allocation or saving for retirement, with detailed questionnaires. Some of these planning kits (which are available for free from the mutual fund groups) are good enough to be used by financial planners, who, incidentally, may obtain them for free from the mutual fund groups and then charge you for their use.

Much of the information supplied by funds is now available both in printed form and on the Internet. Most mutual fund groups now have a website, and many of these are extremely well done. Finally, mutual fund groups all have toll-free numbers, and you can discuss any questions you may have with real persons, some of whom may be genuinely helpful.

Buying No-Load Funds

By that, I mean 100% no-load funds, with no 12b-1 fees. You can still buy funds the old-fashioned way: directly from the fund groups. Here is a list (in alphabetical order) of some of the larger fund groups that have a variety of no-load bond funds, along with their toll-free telephone numbers.

- American Century Investors (800) 345 2021
- Dreyfus (800) 373 9387
- Fidelity (800) 544 8888
- Liberty Stein Roe (800) 338 2550
- Price, T. Rowe (800) 638 5660
- Scudder (800) 225 2470
- Vanguard (800) 662 7447

The expense ratios of the Vanguard funds are consistently the lowest in the industry. Several fund groups (for example, T. Rowe Price and Fidelity) have introduced sub-groups of funds with low expense ratios. While the funds listed do not charge 12b-1 expenses, and do not, as a rule, have either exit or redemption fees, they occasionally impose nuisance fees on specific funds (junk bond funds, for example) to discourage trading. Before buying a fund, it is prudent to double check. Because they do not earn commissions, most brokers do not sell no-load funds.

The procedure for buying no-load funds directly from the management companies is simple. All mutual fund groups have a toll-free number staffed by personnel whose job it is to answer questions from current and potential shareholders. If you are interested in one or more funds, telephone and ask for information. You will be sent a prospectus and usually additional information concerning the funds. If, after reading this information, you still have questions, then telephone the fund's marketing people and ask those questions.

The entire procedure has become even easier since the advent of the Internet. By now, most mutual fund groups have a website. You can read and download any needed information and forms directly from the Web. In order to actually invest in a fund, however, you still are required to fill out some forms and usually to mail or fax them in. The funds need your original signature and need to ask if you have read the prospectus. (That can be the profile described earlier.)

In addition, a number of fund "supermarkets" now make it possible for you to buy no-load funds in one spot. A number of discount brokers now sell no-load funds: Schwab was the first, and remains the best known. But bear in mind that discount brokers charge a small fee for this service. In addition, several large no-load fund groups (including Vanguard, T. Rowe Price, and Fidelity) have established discount brokerages, and they too sell no-load funds other than those of their own group, again, usually, for a modest fee. This enables you to put all your accounts under one umbrella. But there are some drawbacks to these fund "supermarkets." First, although the fees for buying or selling no-load funds may appear tiny, they add up. In addition, frequent sales generate taxes, which should be added to your transaction costs. Also these supermarkets may not send you all the statements a management company normally sends, and those are needed for your tax records.

TAXES AND MUTUAL FUNDS

Suppose you invested $10,000 in the "many happy returns" bond fund three years ago. You sell the shares today for $20,000. What are the tax consequences?

Simple, you say: the difference between my purchase price and my sale price is $10,000. That represents a capital gain, and it will be taxed at the current long-term capital gains rate. Simple, but wrong. And yet, it appears, a very common error.

To calculate your tax liability, you have to determine what is called in financialese the "cost basis" of your shares. This includes not only the money you initially invested, but also dividend income that is reinvested, as well as capital gains distributions. All mutual funds send periodic reports to shareholders which list all taxable capital gains distributions. These are also reported by the mutual fund groups to the IRS. You, the shareholder, must report these annually on your tax forms, whether the fund has gone up in value or down in value. Taxes are paid annually on all taxable distributions.

Let us assume that during the three years that you owned the fund you received dividends totaling $1,000 annually, as well as capital gains distributions of $500 two years in a row. Dividends and capital gains together add up to $4,000. To determine the "cost basis" of your shares, when you sell all the shares in your fund, the total amount of the distributions (that is, dividends plus capital gains) has to be added to the $10,000 that you initially invested. The cost basis rises to $14,000 (instead of $10,000). This lowers your tax liability since you have already paid taxes on the $4,000 of interest income and capital gains. To determine your tax liability at the time of sale, subtract the cost basis ($14,000) from the sale price ($20,000). You owe taxes on capital gains of $6,000—not $10,000.

The procedure I have described briefly is known as the "average cost basis." It is the method used most commonly to determine your tax liability for the sale of shares in a mutual fund. Some mutual fund groups now calculate this cost basis and report it to you (but not to the IRS) when they send you summaries of annual transactions. You are not obligated to use this method to determine your tax liability. It is possible to use other methods to determine taxes due (for example, designating certain shares for sale). And if your portfolio is large, you should consult a tax adviser to determine which method is most beneficial.

If you are selling only part of your shares—not all the shares in the fund—this procedure has to be modified somewhat in order to determine the cost basis of the shares you are selling. The important point to remember is that all distributions, including dividends paid out by municipal bond funds that are not taxable, should be added to your cost basis. This raises the cost basis and lowers taxes due.

When you switch money out of one mutual fund into another, even within the same family of funds, this is considered a sale for tax purposes and will create a tax liability, which may be either a capital gain or a capital loss.

Finally, there are tax consequences to owning funds, even if you just hold them and sell nothing. Each fund generally sends out exact tax information on dividend and capital gains distributions at the end of each year. Dividends are federally taxed as ordinary income (unless the fund is a municipal bond fund). Capital gains distributions are federally taxable, at the rate on capital gains.

It is a good idea to inquire about the schedule for capital gains distributions before you buy a fund. If you buy a fund just prior to a capital gains distribution, you are taxed immediately, even if you have owned the fund for one day or if the fund immediately declines in value.

Paper losses or paper gains create no tax liabilities, but you may want to sell a fund in which you have a paper loss, either to redeploy assets or to offset a capital gain. Similarly, you may want to protect a capital gain by selling shares.

It is essential to maintain good records if you own mutual funds. A simple method is to keep all your records for one fund in one folder and keep those together as long as you own the fund. Even if you do not do all the computations yourself, an accountant will need this information to compute your tax liability accurately.

SUMMARY: QUESTIONS TO ASK BEFORE BUYING A BOND FUND

What securities does the fund hold? What are its objectives and investment policies?

What is the average maturity of the fund?

What is the credit rating of most of the securities in the fund?

What has been the total return for the last year? For the last three years? For the last five years?

How much has the NAV varied from year to year? Am I comfortable with that amount of volatility?

What has been the fund's dividend yield? What has been its 30-day SEC yield?

Is there a commission? an exit fee? a 12b-1 plan?

What are annual expenses?

How long has that fund existed? Has it existed long enough to have a meaningful track record?

How does its track record compare to those of similar funds?

What services are available to shareholders?

CHAPTER 12

Varieties of Bond Funds

This chapter discusses the risk factors and past performance of the following types of bond funds:

- Money market funds: taxable and tax-exempt
- "Plain vanilla" tax-exempt bond funds
- "Plain vanilla" taxable bond funds
- "Specialty funds": GNMA, zero coupon bond funds
- "Funds with equity characteristics": junk bond funds, multi-sector funds. Also, funds investing in foreign bonds: international, global, and emerging markets
- Miscellaneous: bond index funds; loan participation funds

Selecting a fixed-income fund can appear thoroughly bewildering. As of December 1999, excluding money market funds, the Lipper survey of fixed-income funds (the most complete survey of those funds) listed 2,411 taxable bond funds and 2,170 tax-exempt bond funds. How is an investor to choose?

This chapter is a start. It classifies bond funds based on risk factors and potential volatility. This discussion also includes total returns for every type of bond fund, for a variety of time periods ranging from the most recent one-year period (calendar year 1999) to 20 years, for the few categories of bond funds that have been around for that long.

Let's first look at a group of bond funds that are among the oldest in the industry, but that you may not even consider to be bond funds: money market funds.

MONEY MARKET FUNDS

Money market funds occupy a unique place among fixed-income funds. They are the only funds whose NAV does not go up and down; it remains a constant $1.00 per share. The principle behind money funds is very simple. Money funds invest in a variety of debt instruments with very short maturities, usually three months or less. As these securities mature, they are replaced with other equally short instruments. The value of the principal does not change, but the interest income varies as interest rates change. Since their inception, money market funds have ranked among the safest of all investments.

Money market funds were among the first fixed-income funds, and they remain extremely popular. They have become ubiquitous. In December of 1999, an astonishing 70% of all the money in taxable bond funds, and 40% of all the money in tax-exempt bond funds, was in money market funds.

As a group, money funds have been an extraordinarily successful product. They have been profitable both for shareholders and for the companies offering them. In spite of the enormous sums slogging around this market, it has proved remarkably free of scandals, scams, and losses. It is probably almost a forgotten fact that before money market funds existed, individual investors seeking risk-free investments were limited to passbook savings accounts at miserly regulated rates. The major innovation of money market funds was that they made available to the individual investor the high money market yields previously available only to institutional investors.

By law, the maturity of money funds cannot exceed 90 days. Many money funds keep their maturity at 50 days or less. Because of their short maturity, money funds respond very quickly to changes in interest rates. If interest rates rise, so does yield. If interest rates decline, so does yield. This quick response is an advantage if rates are going up; a disadvantage if they are going down.

Money funds are offered in two different guises: taxable and tax-exempt. Both groups can be further subdivided. Taxable money market funds include the following categories:

♦ *General funds.* This is the largest group of money market funds. They invest in a variety of short debt instruments, including short-term Treasury bills, insured CDs, commercial paper issued by corporations, federal agency debt, "repos" (which are overnight loans), foreign obligations, and a constantly growing list of short-term debt instruments.

♦ *Treasury-only money market funds.* This subgroup buys only Treasuries. The yield of Treasury-only money funds is lower than that of money funds investing in a variety of instruments, perhaps by as much as 50 basis points. The exact amount varies with interest rate levels. On the other hand, interest income is exempt from state taxes. This exemption may bring the net-after-tax yield close to that of the more diversified money funds, particularly in states with very high state taxes. The added advantage, for risk-averse investors, is the impeccable credit quality of the securities in the fund.

Tax-exempt money market funds also come in two different groups:

♦ *General tax-exempt money market funds.* This group invests in short-term debt instruments exempt from federal taxes without regard to geographic origin.

♦ *Single-state tax-exempt money market funds.* These funds invest in debt instruments of one state only. They are tax-exempt to residents of that state, as well as federally tax-exempt. Their popularity may be judged by the fact that approximately 45% of all the money in tax-exempt money funds is in single-state tax-exempt funds.

Money market funds are offered through a variety of sources:

1. *Brokerage firms* usually offer money market funds as part of so-called *cash management accounts.* These were initially intended for affluent individuals and they

required minimum initial deposits of $20,000. But many firms now require much lower initial deposits. These cash management accounts offer an extraordinary range and variety of services. They come with a choice of a credit or a debit card (when you use a debit card, charges are automatically deducted from your current balance.) Cash management accounts also usually offer unlimited check writing privileges, as well as a choice between taxable and tax-exempt money market funds. Finally, cash management accounts can be used to consolidate different financial assets (including individual stocks or bonds, or mutual funds) in one umbrella account. Income from any source you designate is then automatically swept into the money market account; and any monies deposited start earning interest on the day of deposit. If you have a Treasury Direct account, interest income and redeemed principal can be directed automatically to the cash management account. The cash in cash management accounts is insured by SIPC for amounts between $100,000 and $500,000. Yields on money market funds in cash management accounts are competitive. Annual maintenance fees vary between $120 and zero. Increasingly, also, these accounts may be accessed via the Internet.

2. *Mutual fund groups* offer at least one taxable money market fund. The larger mutual fund groups offer both taxable and tax-exempt money funds and often a choice among several taxable and several tax-exempt money market funds. Some fund groups now offer their own version of cash management accounts.

Money market funds offered by mutual funds generally require low minimum investments ($1,000 or even less for an IRA). Many mutual funds initially set up money market funds in the hope that money placed in these accounts would eventually migrate to either equity or bond funds within the same group. These accounts offer convenience and a broad range of services. Money can be moved from the equity or the bond funds of the mutual fund groups with a telephone call, and increasingly, these accounts can also be accessed through the Internet. These money market accounts usually have check writing privileges (generally limited) and occasionally charge a fee for each check. Mutual fund money market funds are not insured and are governed by the same rules that govern mutual funds.

3. *Banks* offer money market accounts that are insured by the federal government (up to $100,000). The yields of bank money market accounts are significantly lower than those of either brokerage firms or mutual funds (by as much as 200 to 250 basis points), and in a time of low interest rates, this is a significant disadvantage. But if the insurance helps you to sleep better at night, by all means take your money out of the bank's passbook account and put it in its insured money market fund. You will still boost your yield (compared to a passbook account) and have a totally safe investment. Initial deposits required are low. Note, however, that Treasury-only money market funds offered by brokerage firms invest in direct obligations of the Treasury and are therefore just as safe as bank money funds; but they usually offer higher yields. Note also that in addition, there is no limit on the amount that is "insured." Few banks currently offer tax-exempt money market accounts.

Money Market Fund Yields and Returns

The yield quoted for money market funds is a standardized SEC yield, based on interest income for the preceding seven days and annualized. That number may be simple or compounded. During the 1980s, yields of money funds were extremely high: they actually briefly reached 20% in 1981. Since 1992, yields have varied between a low of 3% in 1993 and a high of 6% in 1996.

To determine whether a taxable or a tax-exempt fund makes more sense for you, you need to do some simple arithmetic. You have to calculate the net-after-tax yield; the calculation is the same as for municipal bonds (see Chapter 7). Although no one likes to pay taxes, except for individuals in the highest tax brackets, the net-after-tax yield of taxable funds is often higher than that of tax-exempt money market funds. That is because the yield curve of municipal bonds tends to be steeper than that of taxable paper and therefore the yields of tax-exempt money funds are extremely low. The same arithmetic needs to be done to determine if single-state tax-exempt money funds are best for you. Whether they make sense for you depends on both your federal tax bracket and your state's tax rate.

The yields of taxable money funds offered by mutual funds and by brokerage firms tend to cluster within a fairly narrow range: within approximately 50 basis points of each other. Unless you have a very substantial sum invested in money funds, the choice of money fund can be determined by convenience. On a $10,000 investment, a 50-basis-point difference amounts to approximately $50.00 per year. (As noted earlier, however, yields of bank money funds are significantly lower.)

Nonetheless, some money funds underperform the averages by more significant amounts. The key, as you would expect, is the expense ratio. Again, the low-cost leader is Vanguard, with an expense ratio for money funds ranging from less than 15 basis points to 30 basis points, depending on the fund. Among other fund groups, expenses can reach 100 basis points, although the average is lower. (Again, bear in mind that high annual expenses force a money fund to adopt somewhat riskier strategies in order to compete with lower-cost cousins.)

Note also that in order to attract your dollars, some money funds adopt a somewhat curious practice: they waive expenses for a period of time which can last for six months or more. This has the immediate effect of boosting the stated yield of the fund. In 1999, for example, the money market fund with the highest yield was actually running the fund at a loss to the parent company in order to be able to advertise that it had the highest yield of any money market fund. Over the years, a number of different fund groups have adopted similar practices. These groups may or may not reveal that the fee waiver is temporary. By all means, if you don't mind the bother of moving money around, there is no harm whatever in enjoying the higher yield as long as it lasts. Just be aware that it is unlikely to last.

How Safe Are Money Funds?

The SEC imposes tight regulations on money funds. Money funds are required to be broadly diversified, and restrictions are placed on the type of securities that funds may buy. Also, as noted earlier, the weighted maturity of a money market fund may not exceed 90 days. Note, however, that a money fund may invest in longer-dated instruments provided that the average weighted maturity of the fund does not exceed 90 days. The tight regulations and short maturities have resulted in an enviable record of safety.

That record, however, is not totally unblemished. On a number of occasions—in 1990, 1994, and 1999—a number of money market funds were found to hold short-term debt of corporations that defaulted. The 1999 episodes involved oddly structured and speculative instruments issued by an obscure insurance company.[1]

The confidence of the investing public in money funds is built on the widely shared belief that NAV will not "break the buck" (that is, that the share price will not drop below $1.00). An erosion of confidence would be extremely costly to money market funds. In 1990 and 1994, in order to maintain the confidence of the investing public, the parent companies of the money funds in question chose to absorb the loss by actually buying the defaulted paper. In 1999, the money funds in question again went to great lengths to prevent an actual default from occurring, setting up lines of credit with banks and securing insurance in order to guarantee access to cash as required to meet the needs of shareholders. To date, no individual investor in any money fund has lost a dime. (Note one exception, however. One money fund actually did "break the buck." In 1994, an institutional money fund which had used derivatives had to be liquidated at an NAV of 94 cents, a loss of 6%. But because this was an institutional money fund, presumably no individual investor lost any money.)

Still, the question arises: why did these potential losses occur at all? In the preceding examples, the managers of the funds in question took on a significant degree of risk in order to boost the yield of the funds by only marginal amounts. Some, no doubt,

---

1. See Sandra Ward, "Fund of Information," *Barron's*, 23 August 1999, p. F3, and 30 August 1999, p. F4.

were attempting to compensate for very high expense ratios. So, while the risk of an actual loss is minor for most money market funds, it is not nonexistent. As is usually the case in the world of bonds, yield is the best indicator of risk. Typically, the highest-yielding money funds are likely to be those that have some degree of risk.

What Percentage of Your Portfolio Should You Keep in Money Market Funds?

Because of their relatively high yields, safety, and convenience, money market funds have become a permanent alternative to bank passbook and checking accounts, as well as a place to keep liquid cash or contingency reserves. Over long stretches of time, however, returns of money funds have been significantly lower than those of stocks or of longer-term bonds and bond funds. Moreover, while safety of principal is high, money funds carry a very high income risk, as well as significant reinvestment risk. Two questions then arise: should you maintain a permanent percentage of a your portfolio in money funds? and if so, how much?

The attractiveness of market fund yields compared to other investments varies with interest rates and with the shape of the yield curve. If the yield curve is flat or inverted, yields may compare favorably with those of longer-term instruments, but usually only briefly. There are also occasional periods when money market funds outperform all other investments. This last happened in 1994, when long-term interest rates rose steeply. Both long-term bond funds and equity funds plummeted. For most of the year, money funds, on average, outperformed both stock and bond funds. Not infrequently, moreover, if interest rates are rising, money funds have higher total returns than most other bond funds. For the 1999 calendar year, for example, money funds all had positive total returns whereas most longer-term bond funds posted negative total returns (total return of long-term bond funds of all varieties was down as much as 10 to 12%).

This is not intended as a suggestion that investors try to "time" the market by going entirely into cash (i.e., into money funds) whenever they feel worried about the bond market or the stock market. There is no evidence that anyone has ever consistently succeeded in timing the market. What this suggests, however, is that most investors need to hold a certain percentage of their assets in extremely safe assets such as money market funds or very short-maturity fixed-income securities in order to be able to ride out episodes when the stock market or the bond market, or both, may be going through a sinking spell. Some financial advisers feel that for retirees, this should equal whatever amount is needed to meet expenses for at least one year. Longer-term investors may choose to keep only a small percentage of their assets in money funds, anywhere between 5 and 20%, depending on your comfort level with risk.

Over longer time periods, however, real returns from money funds are not likely to outpace inflation. The returns of taxable money market funds generally track those of three-month T-bills. In the 1990s, yields have ranged from a low of 3% in 1993 and a high of 6% in 1996. Yields of tax-exempt money funds have ranged between a low of 2% and a high of almost 4%. For that reason, the permanent percentage of assets in money funds should never exceed 20% of total assets. As a general rule, the longer term your investment horizon is, the less should be permanently in money funds.

To sum up, for parking money over short periods of time, if safety is one of your main concerns, the best trade off between yield and risk is to be found in money funds issued by brokerage firms or in cash management accounts that invest only in Treasuries, or in high-quality commercial paper and insured CDs.

If you want to keep a significant amount of money in very safe instruments for longer time periods, there are some alternatives to money funds which can boost yield without sacrificing safety. One would be to invest in a combination of Treasury bills and short-term notes (two years or less), through Treasury Direct (see Chapter 6). Another would be to invest in three-month, six-month, or one-year CDs. Their yield is usually significantly higher than that of bank money market funds. (Many brokerage firms that offer cash management accounts shop the country for insured CDs with the highest yields.) Still another alternative would be to invest in so-called jumbo CDs. Those require minimum investments of approximately $100,000. Most brokerage firms also shop the country for the highest jumbo CD yields, and they can sell them to you. (Yields of jumbo CDs are listed in the newspaper along with those of money market funds.) But note that while CDs are insured, and while yields may be higher than those of money funds, there may be penalties if you want to sell early.

Finally, let's look at how money market funds have performed over the years. Table 12–1 shows the average annual total returns of two categories of taxable money market funds: general and Treasury-only. These are of interest for two reasons: first, to compare yields of these two types of money funds to each other. Secondly, these yields will serve as benchmarks when we look at the total return of longer-term, riskier bond funds. As we will see, while many longer-term funds have had higher total returns than money funds, some of the more volatile and riskier funds have actually failed to perform as well.

Keeping Informed About Money Funds

All major financial newspapers list sample money market fund yields, and some also list the funds with the highest yields on a national basis. In addition, *The Wall Street Journal* publishes a table of major money market funds on Thursday. This table lists the most recent seven-day yield, the amount of assets in the funds, and their average weighted maturity, in days. Generally, money market funds increase maturity length if they think interest rates are about to decline, and decrease it if they think interest rates are about to rise. *The New York Times* and *Barron's* also publish tables of money market yields on the week end.

On the web, *mutualfunds.about.com* has comprehensive information on money funds, including rankings, yields, and weekly stories on money market funds.

T A B L E   12–1

Average Annual Returns of Taxable Money Market Funds, Through December 31, 1999

	1 yr	5 yr	10 yrs	15 yrs	20 yrs
General money market funds	4.49	4.95	4.80	5.59	7.24
U.S. Treasury money market funds	4.23	4.75	4.63	5.36	6.87

Source: Derived from *Lipper Taxable Fixed Income Performance Analysis*, Dec. 31, 1999. Copyright 1999 by REUTERS, SA. Reprinted with permission.

FUNDS WHOSE PRICE GOES UP AND DOWN

For any sector of the fixed-income market, you can buy either a fund or an individual security. There are funds that invest in municipal bonds, funds that invest in Treasuries, funds that invest in corporates, funds that invest in GNMAs, funds that invest in international and emerging market bonds, and so on.

As stated earlier, with the exception of money market funds, the price of all bond funds can be expected to go up and down, some by a little, many by a lot. This chapter will discuss in detail why this happens, which bond funds are less volatile and why, and which bond funds are most volatile and why. The purpose of this analysis is to give you some idea of the potential returns and volatility of the various categories of bond funds.

A number of factors complicate this analysis. To begin with, there is no general agreement about the riskiness of certain categories of bond funds such as junk bond funds. The Securities and Exchange Commission, the major rating agencies, and the Investment Company Institute have all tried to come up with a system of ratings that would give individual investors some indication of the types of risks they incur when they buy bond funds. To date, no agreement has been reached by all parties.

A second complicating factor is that there is also not one single, generally agreed-upon classification for bond funds. The two main purveyors of data on bond funds, Morningstar and Lipper, come up with different categories. Another word for categories is "objectives." I have adopted the Lipper database and classification because it is more complete.

Moreover, one of the more mysterious aspects of investing in bond funds is that determining exactly how to classify any bond fund is not always obvious. That is because the names of many bond funds obfuscate, rather than make clear, exactly in what corner of the bond world the bond fund invests.

For starters, the name of a fund may be so general that it offers no clue concerning the type of securities in a bond fund, their maturity, their credit quality, and therefore, the main risk factors of the fund. The name, after all, is a marketing device, designed to attract investors. Any number of confusing possibilities exist. So-called "government" or "government-only" funds are a prime example. These funds may be invested primarily in

Treasuries or primarily in GNMAs. They may also include agency securities, or zeros. Or they may include a combination of all of the above. In all cases, the name implies the highest credit quality and very little risk. But of course, we know that interest rate risk affects government securities to the same extent as any other securities of the same maturity length. I shall point out additional instances of confusing fund names where appropriate.

Also, many bond funds invest in more than one sector of the bond market. Occasionally, the name of the fund indicates as much. That would be the case, for example, for funds labeled "multi-sector" or "total return" bond funds. But even when the name of a fund mentions a specific corner of the bond market, that does not mean that the fund owns only that type of bond. Whatever their name, many bond funds include a range of maturities and a variety of credits, from high to low. Many bond funds also include a sprinkling of holdings designed to confer some type of total return advantage. These may include high-yield debt, derivatives, or even stocks. This may boost total return in good times but exacerbate declines in weak markets, and these holdings may not be listed in the general information about the fund. The Lipper categories generally specify that, to be put into a specific category, at least 65% of all the bonds in a fund should clearly belong to that category. For example, for a fund to be classified as a corporate bond fund, at least 65% of the bonds in that fund should be corporate bonds, and not some other type of bond. But that means that, for most bond funds, 35% of all the bonds in the fund belong to a different category.

In order to come up with some indication of how predictable risk factors and total return might be for different bond funds, I have subdivided Lipper's classification into three basic groups: "plain vanilla bond funds," "specialty funds," and "funds with equity characteristics."

"Plain vanilla bond funds" are the most straightforward to describe and understand. For these funds, interest rate exposure— and therefore maturity length—is the primary determinant of both a fund's volatility and its total return.

"Specialty funds" are those funds whose total return and riskiness are determined by factors unique to that type of fund. This group includes, for example, bond funds investing in mortgage-backed securities and bond funds investing in zeros.

I am calling the last group "funds with equity characteristics" not because they own stocks but because, as for stock funds, their risk factors are more complex. Total returns for these funds are less predictable and vary the most from year to year and from fund to fund within a single category. Bond funds placed in this group include junk bond funds, international bond funds, emerging market debt bond funds, and multi-sector bond funds.

There is, of course, the inevitable "miscellaneous" category.

Lipper divides bond funds into two main groups: taxable and tax-exempt. The tax-exempt group includes all bond funds investing in debt instruments which are federally tax-exempt. Taxable funds, by definition, invest in debt instruments that are taxable.

All tax-exempt funds can be characterized as plain vanilla. The taxable sector, however, is much more diverse. It includes plain vanilla bond funds; as well as specialty funds, funds with equity characteristics, and miscellaneous funds.

PLAIN VANILLA FUNDS

For this group of funds, both total return (dividends plus any change in the share price) and volatility of share price (that is, how much share price goes up or down) are related directly to the average maturity length of the fund's portfolio. This is due to two factors. Assuming a normal "upward-sloping" yield curve, dividend yield is higher for longer maturities, lower for shorter maturities. Therefore, funds with longer average maturities normally yield more than funds with shorter maturities.

But higher yield always comes at a cost. The cost here is that the share price of funds with longer average maturities (or duration) goes up and down more steeply in response to interest rate changes than that of funds with shorter maturities. As noted in the preceding chapter, a bond fund responds to changes in interest rates very much like an individual security. Furthermore, the potential change in NAV can be predicted if you know the duration of the fund. For example, if interest rates rise from 6% to 7%, the NAV of a long-term bond fund with a duration of eight years would decline in value by approximately 8%. The same increase in interest rates would cause the NAV of an intermediate fund with a duration of five years to decline by 5%, and it would cause the NAV of a short-term fund with a duration of two years to decline by 2%.

For this reason, over short-term holding periods (under one year), the total return of long-term funds is unpredictable. It may be higher than the dividend yield if interest rates decline (because the NAV of the fund will go up); about the same as the dividend yield if rates remain stable; but lower than the dividend yield if interest rates rise (the NAV of the fund will decline).

Over long holding periods (higher than ten years), long-term funds should have higher total returns than shorter-term funds. That is due to the fact that over a long stretch of time, the income portion of the funds (dividend income plus interest-on-interest) dominate total return. But that needs to be qualified. If interest rates are stable or decline, long-term bond funds will continue to post higher total returns than shorter-term funds. But because of the high interest rate risk, during a period such as the 1970s, when interest rates climbed inexorably for most of the decade, long-term funds would be poor investments. Also, as we shall see, over the short term, an abysmal year such as 1999 can significantly reduce what had been very solid returns for the entire preceding decade.

MUNICIPAL BOND FUNDS

The most popular plain vanilla funds, and by far the most profitable for individual investors, have been municipal bond funds. They were among the first bond funds. Some had their inception in the 1970s. Their peak popularity occurred in the second half of the 1980s and the first half of the 1990s, when returns were exceptionally high. Nonetheless, in spite of the diminishing popularity of municipal bond funds, excluding money market funds, approximately one half of all the assets in bond funds remain in the municipal sector. The major attraction of these funds is that interest income is federally tax-exempt (but subject to state taxes if you do not reside in the state issuing the bonds). The municipal corner of the bond market is much less diverse, much more homogeneous than the taxable sector. It is also the only sector of the bond market that is dominated by individual investors.

Before discussing these funds in greater detail, let's look at Table 12–2, which summarizes average annual total returns from

T A B L E 12–2

Average Annual Total Returns of Municipal Bonds Funds, Through December 31, 1999. All Distributions–Dividends and Capital Gains–Are Assumed to Be Reinvested.

	1 yr	5 yrs	10 yrs	15 yrs	20 yrs
Tax-exempt money market funds	2.68	3.03	3.17	3.70	4.22
Short (1–3 years)	1.69	4.32	4.69	5.19	5.55
Short-intermediate (1–5 years)	0.31	4.43	5.17	5.91	–
Intermediate (5–10 years)	–1.65	5.55	5.91	7.25	7.24
Long-Term: (10 years or more)					
General	–4.63	5.76	6.18	7.96	7.87
Insured	–4.69	5.68	5.96	7.87	7.30
High yield	–4.16	6.06	6.14	7.81	–
Single-state:					
Money market	2.65	2.99	3.10	3.67	–
California (Long-Term)	–5.16	6.08	6.08	7.55	6.86
New York State (Long-Term)	–4.89	5.68	6.09	7.49	–

Source: Derived from *Lipper Tax-Exempt Fixed Income Fund Performance Analysis* Dec. 31, 1999. Copyright 1999 by REUTERS SA. Reprinted with permission.

June 30, 1979, through December 31, 1999. Total return is the average annualized compounded total return, based on reinvestment
of all dividends and capital gains distributions, if any, plus
changes in share price. Average annual returns of tax-exempt
money funds are listed first for purposes of comparison.

First, let's briefly take a closer look at the various categories,
beginning with Lipper's definitions.

♦ The largest subgroup is the category of *general municipal
  bond funds*. General municipal bond funds are the most
  broadly diversified municipal bond funds: by type of
  bond (general obligation, revenue); geographically (they
  include bonds from many states issuing tax-exempt
  bonds); and by credit quality (although Lipper stipulates
  that at least 65% of bonds in the general municipal bond
  category must be investment grade).

♦ *Insured municipal bond funds* invest at least 65% of their
  portfolio in insured bonds.

♦ *High-yield municipal bond funds* invest at least 50% of their
  portfolio in lower-rated municipal bonds. This stipulation
  differentiates high-yield municipal bond funds from the
  general funds. In other words, the credit quality of
  Lipper's high-yield fund category is largely below
  investment grade.

♦ *Short, short-intermediate, and intermediate* municipal bond
  funds all have weighted average maturities shorter than
  the long-term funds. The average weighted maturity of
  short municipal bond funds is three years or less, that of
  short-intermediate funds is three to five years, and that of
  intermediate funds is five to ten years. In other respects,
  these funds are broadly diversified: geographically, by
  type of bond, in credit quality, etc.

♦ *Single-state municipal bond funds* invest primarily in bonds
  of one state. They are exempt from federal taxes and also
  from state and local taxes to residents of the state in
  which they are issued. Lipper lists single-state funds for
  27 states. Most of these are long-term funds. (The
  average returns of the two largest states are listed in
  Table 12–2. Average returns for the group as a whole are

not listed, however, because the group includes all three
maturity ranges: short, intermediate, and long.)

Lipper's definitions of these categories (or objectives) are
fairly narrow. The Lipper organization decides, based on their
own criteria, which category a fund belongs to. (This is important
to fund managers because Lipper's rankings within a group in
part determine their salaries!) Even so, these definitions, with their
quantified criteria, point up how difficult it can be to characterize
a fund based only on its name. In practice, mutual fund families
label their funds much more loosely than does Lipper. A prime
example are the labels "high-yield" and "high income," which are
used with different meanings in different mutual fund groups.
Some fund families label their longest term funds "high yield" or
"high income" to indicate that they will have high yields because
they invest in long-term bonds. However, credit quality for these
high-yield funds may be very high. Other fund families designate
funds as "high yield" or "high income" because they invest in
lower-quality, and hence higher-yielding, bonds. (Note also that
even within Lipper's classification there is a room for some over-
lapping.)

To interpret Table 12–2 properly, you need to realize that
more than 90% of the bond funds listed are long term. That includes the general, insured, high-yield and single-state categories.
The only municipal bond funds that are not long term are those
that are specifically identified as having shorter maturities: short,
short–intermediate, and intermediate. The combined assets of
these shorter maturity funds comprise only about 10% of the total
in municipal bond funds.

If you bear this in mind, a number of facts stand out:

♦ For the past two decades it has paid to buy long-term
  bond funds and just hold. As a group, the longer-term
  funds have higher total returns than shorter-term funds
  for most time periods.

♦ Differences other than maturity length have played a
  much lower role in total return, as demonstrated by the
  fact that average total returns of long-term funds have
  not varied significantly from group to group. Average
  total returns are in the same range for all funds with

long average weighted maturities, whether the funds are insured, high-yield (in Lipper's objectives, below investment grade), or general. This has been a much debated topic because for some brief periods the high-yield sector has had higher total returns, and during other time periods, the insured sector has had higher total returns. Bear in mind, however, that Table 12–2 shows average returns for entire groups. Returns of individual funds will be somewhat higher or lower than the averages for all categories.

♦ For 1999, total returns of the longer-term funds were negative even after adding back interest income. This reflects the significant decline in NAV caused by the rise in rates that started in late 1998 and continued throughout 1999. Total returns for 1999 are higher for all categories of shorter-term funds: the shorter the maturity, the higher the total return. For 1999, the best returns were turned in by tax-exempt money market funds.

Over the total 20-year period, the generally higher returns of longer-term funds were due to two factors: the very high interest rates which prevailed during most of the 1980s and 1990s, and the general trend of declining interest rates through much of that period. The general trend of declining rates added a chunk of capital gains to the dividend income earned by the funds. Total returns were highest during the early 1980s, which experienced both the highest interest rates, as well as the steepest declines in rates from 1982 onwards.

What this table does not show, however, is the variability of returns for long-term funds over short holding periods. Swings in NAV can be sudden, steep, and nasty. The sharp spikes upwards in interest rates which occurred in 1987, 1994, and 1999 caused very sharp declines, as much as 10 and 20% of NAV ($1,000 to $2,000 per $10,000 investment) within the space of less than a year. Total returns of long-term funds were negative in 1987, 1994, and 1999. In fact, the abysmal returns of 1999 depressed *average* annual total returns for the prior two decades. The effect of this is particularly marked for funds held for five years or less. Average annual returns are significantly lower than they would have been a year earlier for the preceding five years.

Finally, although Table 12–2 shows that the average total returns of long-term funds are generally higher than those of intermediate funds, on an individual basis some of the better managed intermediate funds have actually had higher total returns than many longer-term funds, in spite of their lower interest income. This is due to a combination of lower volatility and low expense ratios. For the decade of the 1990s, the negative total returns of 1994 and 1999 at the long end brought the total returns of the longer-term funds and those of the intermediate and shorter funds much closer together.

Let us now take a look at individual categories of municipal bond funds.

General Long-Term Tax-Exempt Bond Funds

The general, long tax-exempt bond funds are the veterans of the industry: a few had their inception in the early 1970s. As noted earlier, these are the most broadly diversified municipal bond funds. Average weighted maturity is typically in the 16-to-25-year range, and duration somewhere between six and eight years. That long duration has been the main contributor to both the volatility of these funds and their total return.

The pattern of returns of this group follows the general pattern discussed above for long-term bond funds. Due to their long average weighted maturity and duration, short-term swings in NAV are highly unpredictable and can be violent. On the other hand, credit risk is not significant, both because the funds are highly diversified and because there is usually ongoing monitoring of credit quality. Over the ten- and 20-year periods illustrated in the chart, total return of the best managed of these funds has been the highest of any of the municipal bond funds.

For many years, general municipal bond funds were extremely popular. This was due, no doubt, in part to the very high total returns generated by the funds through the decade of the 1980s and the early 1990s. On a tax equivalent basis, in fact, total returns of these funds exceeded those of almost all categories of bond funds. This popularity led to a number of more specialized variations.

Tax-Exempt High-Yield Funds

The first to emerge were the tax-exempt high-yield funds. (The term "high-yield" is used here, as in Table 12–2, to designate funds investing in lower quality credits.) In spite of the similarity in name, there is simply no credit analog in the municipal market to the high-yield (or "junk") bonds issued by corporations. Tax-exempt high-yield funds hold issues in the riskier sectors of the tax-exempt market (for instance, hospitals, nursing homes, electric power, private-purpose bonds, and the like, as well as some of the riskier GOs). Credit quality for these funds clusters around investment grade or just below, but that is a far cry from corporate junk bond funds. The default rate of municipal bonds even in this lower-credit-quality range has been far lower than that of corporate junk bonds.

Since their inception in 1985, for much of the time, high-yield municipal bond funds posted higher total returns than muni funds holding higher-quality paper. This advantage has been less clear-cut in recent years. One advantage of high-yield muni funds, however, seems to have been maintained, which is that, for reasons that are not entirely clear, volatility of these funds (when interest rates have spiked upwards) has actually been somewhat lower than for funds holding higher-quality paper (you would expect the exact opposite). If a severe recession were to occur, however, the lower credit quality of these funds (compared to general or insured municipal bond funds) might become a more significant risk factor. For that reason, in spite of their overall excellent performance, it may be prudent to regard these funds as somewhat riskier than other municipal bond funds.

One new wrinkle in this sector occurred in February 2000. An investment management firm, Saybrook Capital, is proposing to start a municipal bond fund which would invest only in defaulted bonds. This would actually be a single-state bond fund, investing in defaulted State of California municipal bonds. (Note that the fund would bear an inviting name: it is to be called the "Saybrook Tax-Exempt Opportunity Fund.") But its portfolio, consisting only of defaulted bonds, places it in the riskiest sector of the high-yield category. While so far, this is the only such fund, another fund family, American Century, has rewritten the prospectus of its high-yield municipal bond fund to allow it to purchase defaulted municipal bonds. Both fund groups specify that they will research the defaulted bonds carefully to try to identify bonds likely to be upgraded. At this point, it is difficult to say how profitable or how risky this strategy is likely to be. There is virtually no secondary market for defaulted municipal bonds, and as a result, these bonds are highly illiquid.

Municipal–Insured (Long-Term) Bond Funds

This is the most recent group of general municipal bond funds to emerge, and it remains the smallest. Insured municipal bond funds invest most of their portfolios in insured municipal bonds. Most of these funds are long term, although a few have somewhat shorter average weighted maturities: around 12 years, with correspondingly shorter durations. The name of the fund may not reflect the shorter maturity.

The appeal of these funds is clearly to the most risk-averse investors. Buying a bond fund investing in insured bonds is a little bit like wearing a belt and suspenders. The insurance feature adds little in the way of credit safety compared to a broadly diversified general fund investing in high quality credits, where credit risk is very low.

On the other hand, insured bonds yield somewhat less than uninsured bonds. Therefore, one would expect insured bond funds to have lower total returns than either general or high-yield funds. And Table 12–2 demonstrates that on the whole, that has been the case. There have been some exceptions, however. During 1989, for example, total returns of insured bond funds were as high as those of high-yield funds. No one at the time was quite sure why. On the other hand, if a recession were to occur, and there was a flight to quality, insured bond funds might do slightly better than other general bond funds.

Intermediate (and Shorter) Municipal Bond Funds

This is still a small group of funds, but it deserves to be more popular. Funds in this group are broadly diversified. For the intermediate sector, maturity has clustered between seven and ten years and duration around five. The rationale behind this group of funds is that they capture a high percentage of the total return of longer funds, but with lower volatility. And indeed, because the yield curve of municipal bonds tends to be quite steep, the total return of the best-managed intermediate municipal funds has matched or even surpassed the performance of some long-term funds, and with lower volatility. As Table 12–2 demonstrates, due to the sharp losses experienced by long-term municipal bond funds in 1999, the total return of the entire intermediate group edged much closer to that of the long-term funds. If interest rates continue to be highly unstable, this group merits consideration as an alternative to longer-term funds.

If you are interested in a municipal intermediate fund, compare it to other bond funds with approximately the same duration. There is a significant difference between the best- and the worst-performing funds in this sector, so look at a number of alternatives before you leap.

Ultra-Short Municipal Bond Funds

A number of well-managed mutual fund groups offer municipal bond funds that limit weighted average maturity to three years or less. A very few even limit maturity length to one or two years. The duration of these ultra-short bond funds varies between one and two years. (These funds are offered, for example, by T. Rowe Price and by Vanguard.) At this point, this remains a tiny group, although several of the individual funds have been around for as long as 20 years.

The rationale behind these funds is that this maturity sector will capture a higher yield than is available in money market funds, and that the very short maturities will produce negligible volatility. Bear in mind, also, that due to the very short maturities of the bonds in the portfolio, the entire portfolio of bonds matures within less than three years. As a result, risk to principal is also exceedingly low. But one drawback is that reinvestment risk is significantly higher than for longer-term funds.

Since their inception, these funds have achieved their objectives with mixed success. Volatility has been dramatically lower than for longer-term or intermediate funds. Current yield numbers vary between 50 and 130 basis points higher than those of tax-exempt money funds, depending on the shape of the municipal yield curve. In 1999, however, as shown in Table 12–2, the total return of the shortest funds was positive. The very shortest funds had the highest total return. And because of the stable NAV, total returns for the five-year mark were almost as high as for the intermediate group.

These funds make sense for you if you are trying to lift yield and total return above that of money market funds, while incurring minimal risk to principal. Funds whose maturity is under three years are particularly attractive when interest rates are highly unstable, and the future of interest rates is particularly cloudy.

Note that occasionally, if the yield curve inverts, the yield of very short funds may go below that of money market funds. This was the case in 1988.

Alternatives to these funds would depend on your objectives. For maximum liquidity, consider a money market fund. For higher income, you might wish to go out a little further on the yield curve to the intermediate group. If you have more than $10,000 to invest and can hold the security for two to five years, consider either short-term tax-exempt paper or Treasuries. (See the sections on Treasury Direct and on pre-refunded tax-exempt bonds.)

Municipal—Single-State Bond Funds

Another wrinkle in tax-exempt bond funds has been single-state bond funds. Most of the funds in this category are long term, which means that total return and volatility track those of other long-term municipal bond funds. The appeal (and advertising) of these funds is based heavily on the double tax-exemption (federal and state to residents of the state) or sometimes even triple tax-exemption (federal, state, and city). The yield is usually slightly lower than that of general municipal funds. But the net-after-tax yield will vary with both the federal and state tax rates.

These funds have become extremely popular: there is now almost as much money in this group as in the more broadly diversified municipal bond funds. As a result, they have become much more specialized. For the larger states with high tax rates, such as New York, Florida, and California, there are now funds with intermediate or short maturities, high-yield funds, and insured bond funds. No doubt more will be started. There is even a New York City bond fund.

The main disadvantage of any single-state fund (aside from its possibly lower overall total return) is that these funds are not diversified. If the region experiences an economic downturn, the credit quality of many of the bonds in the fund can deteriorate simultaneously and this may result in a decline in the fund's NAV.

"Oddball" Category: Taxable Municipal Bond Funds

No, this is not an error. Some municipal entities issue taxable bonds.

The appeal of this type of bond (and hence bond fund) is that the credit quality of municipal bonds is generally reasonably good: default rates are low. But since there are not many of these bonds, they have to be issued at fairly attractive yields—that is, compared to Treasuries and corporates.

Only a few small bond funds invest primarily in taxable municipal bonds. Some taxable bond funds include a sprinkling of municipal taxable issues. Lipper classifies taxable municipal bond funds as corporate bond funds, and that is entirely appropriate since these funds are taxable. The funds are long term. The credit quality is generally lower than that of governments. The yield is comparable to that of corporate bond funds with similar maturity and credit quality.

Only a few small bond funds belong to this subgroup. They are load funds, with 12b-1 fees and an undistinguished record. I am pointing out that the category exists to alert you not to be misled by the label "municipal" into thinking these are tax-exempt funds with very high yields.

Summary and Conclusion: Municipal Bond Funds

Municipal bond funds had their greatest popularity in the late 1980s and early 1990s. This coincides with their highest returns. During this period, on a net-after-tax basis, municipal bond funds provided individual investors with higher total returns than virtually any other bond funds. In addition, as a group, these funds did a good job of preventing erosion of principal due to what I earlier called NAV erosion. In all likelihood, the better-managed municipal bond funds should continue to do just that.

You should not expect, however, that a municipal bond fund will somehow perform a lot better than its sector of the market. In general, municipal bond funds track their sector of the bond market. If interest rates rise significantly, the NAV of even the best-managed municipal bond funds has declined, and sometimes significantly. While managers of long-term bond funds shorten or lengthen maturities to some extent in order to insulate the fund against market declines, these changes are at the margin. Major changes in maturity would dramatically alter the yield of the fund. And the yield is one of the major factors that attracts investors.

Table 12–2 lists average total returns for the group. Clearly, all municipal bond funds are not created equal. The best-managed funds have higher total returns than the averages; the worst are a lot lower. Differences in total return are due to the factors analyzed in the preceding chapter: expense ratios, credit quality, NAV erosion, management practices, including the use of derivatives, and reaching for yield. In order to give you some idea of these differences, I am including Table 12–3, which lists total returns for the best- and worst-performing funds in these groups for five-year, ten-year, and 20-year periods ending December 31, 1999. I am using *cumulative* rather than *average* annual returns, simply to show more graphically how seemingly small differences in annual returns, compounded over time, begin to amount to real money. Once again, cumulative returns of tax-exempt money funds are included for purposes of comparison.

The popularity of municipal bond funds declined significantly throughout the latter part of the 1990s. One factor, no doubt, was the spectacular bull market in equities. It is also possible that individual investors decided to take their money out of bond funds and invest it instead in individual bonds. During the last quarter of 1999 and the beginning of 2000, there were very large outflows from municipal bond funds. This is somewhat ironic since at that time yields of municipal bond funds were exceptionally high on a relative basis.

Perhaps as a result of this trend, some financial advisers are suggesting that municipal bond funds have outlived their usefulness. I do not necessarily agree with that point of view. In fact, as I am writing this, in February of 2000, the spread between municipal bonds and taxable bonds of all types is extremely narrow by historical standards. Indeed, the yield of many longer term or intermediate municipal bonds is close to that of Treasury bonds. This means that on a net-after-tax basis, municipal bonds would benefit most investors, even those in the lowest tax brackets. This

T A B L E 12–3

Cumulative Total Return of the Best-Performing and Worst-Performing Municipal Bond Funds, Through December 31, 1999. All Distributions—Dividends and Capital Gains—Are Assumed to Be Reinvested.

	Leading Funds			Trailing Funds		
	1 yr	5 yrs	10 yrs	1 yr	5 yrs	10 yrs
Tax-exempt money market	3.33	19.44	45.38	2.33	13.62	31.68
Short	3.01	27.49	64.05	0.76	20.98	54.46
Intermediate	0.86	44.25	90.44	−4.20	22.49	66.30
General	−0.91	40.84	99.18	−8.97	23.06	64.42
Insured	−1.85	45.75	93.58	−7.89	26.86	67.77
High-yield	1.47	45.14	104.65	−12.27	27.74	34.91

Source: Derived from *Lipper Tax-exempt Fixed Income Fund Performance Analysis* Dec. 31, 1999. Copyright 1999 by REUTERS SA. Reprinted with permission.

makes municipal bonds (and municipal bond funds) an attractive buy.

But, as stressed throughout, because of their potentially high volatility, long-term municipal bond funds should always be viewed as potentially volatile and therefore risky. Investors seeking the highest possible income should be cautious about holding most of their bond portfolio in long-term bonds or bond funds. Also, long-term municipal bond funds should not be purchased for holding periods of less than two years, unless you are frankly speculating that interest rates will decline over the short term. You cannot know what the fund's NAV would be if you need to redeem within such a short time frame. For shorter holding periods, a tax-exempt money market fund or a very short municipal bond fund would be more appropriate.

TAXABLE BOND FUNDS

Taxable bond funds are a much more diverse group than tax-exempt funds. To get some idea of the potential number of combinations, consider first all the different taxable bonds available to U.S. investors: corporates, governments (the United States and many foreign governments), federal agencies, and mortgage-backed and asset-backed securities. Consider further that every sector of the taxable bond market comes in short, intermediate, or long maturities. Consider that credit quality for taxable bonds ranges from impeccable to junk. Consider also the number of bonds with unique characteristics: zero coupon bonds or CMOs, for example. Finally, consider that many taxable bond funds invest in more than one sector of the bond market, and to boot, many use a variety of derivatives either to hedge or to leverage total return.

To give some sense of the predictability of returns and risk factors of taxable bond funds, I came up with the three main groupings described in the introduction to this chapter: "plain vanilla" funds, which are funds whose risk factors and total return are primarily determined by interest rate risk; "specialty funds," which invest in bonds with unique risk factors; and the most speculative group, "funds with equity characteristics." Each will be discussed in turn.

Before turning to this analysis, let's again address the issue of fund names. Some fund names give you very precise information about the portfolio of the fund. A label such as "Long-term Treasury" or "Short-term corporate" identifies the primary holdings of the fund; their credit quality; and a probable maturity range. But many taxable bond funds are not so clearly named. Indeed, many names seem intended to mislead rather than to inform. A "government" bond fund, for example, may invest in U.S. Treasury bonds, federal agency bonds, GNMA bonds, or zero coupon bonds, in any combination. Many "government" bond funds (including funds with names like "government-only") in fact, invest mainly in GNMA bonds. Some fund names, such as "corporate," "income," and "high income," are even more vague. These funds may hold corporate bonds, Treasuries, government agency paper, GNMAs, and so on, again in any combination. The name of these funds does not give you a clue about the actual securities in the fund. More importantly, the name tells you nothing about the average weighted maturity of the fund or the credit quality of its portfolio. In fact, some "income" funds invest in stocks as well as bonds.

Secondly, taxable bond funds are much more diverse in their make-up than municipal bond funds. As a result, within any fund category you are likely to find a wider range of total returns than for municipal bond funds. At the extreme, some bond funds allow the manager to invest in any sector of the bond market, anywhere on the planet, in any combination deemed attractive and possibly, to use derivatives. The potential volatility of this type of bond fund is far more difficult to predict. Basically, if you want to invest in this type of fund, you need to analyze the history of specific funds. That would include the track record of the fund's manager, the total return history of the fund, and its current investments. You would be relying primarily on the skill and judgment of the manager.

"Plain Vanilla" Taxable Bond Funds

"Plain vanilla" taxable bond funds invest in a broad variety of investment-grade taxable bonds, including corporates, GNMAs and CMOs, Treasuries, federal agencies and so on. The main risk factor for these funds is our old friend: interest rate risk, determined by average weighted maturity and duration. Many of these funds invest in a broadly diversified group of bonds.

Table 12–4 illustrates the total return of plain vanilla taxable bond funds through December 31, 1999, for time periods of up to 20 years. Total returns are compounded, with dividends and capital gains assumed to be reinvested. Yields of taxable money market funds are listed first for purposes of comparison.

Once again, the categories and definitions are those of the Lipper organization. The taxable bond funds are divided first by average weighted maturity, which ranges from:

+ Ultra-short: 91 to 365 days
+ Short: one to three years
+ Short-intermediate: one to five years
+ Intermediate: five to ten years
+ Long: ten years or more

Each maturity sector is subdivided further based on credit quality. All funds discussed in this section are at least investment-grade. Terms such as "government" and "corporate" should be interpreted primarily as indicators of credit quality and not as a description of the portfolio. Funds investing primarily in Treasuries have the highest credit quality. The lowest rating is corporate, BBB rated, which is the lowest investment-grade rating. Ranked from highest to the lowest, the quality groupings are: Treasury, government, investment-grade, corporate debt, A rated, and corporate debt, BBB rated. With the exception of Treasuries-only bond funds, all other categories (government, investment-grade, corporate) invest in a broadly diversified portfolio of bonds. Again, the Lipper organization decides, based on its own criteria, where to assign a fund.

Over long holding periods, total returns follow a pattern similar to what was seen for tax-exempt funds. The funds with the longest maturities posted the highest total returns over long holding periods. The highest returns occurred during the 1980s, due to the very high interest rates prevailing in that decade, as well as to the decline in interest rates, which started in 1982 and which added a chunk of capital gains to total return. Due to the spike in interest rates which occurred in 1999, Table 12–4 once again shows

T A B L E 12-4

Average Annual Total Returns of "Plain Vanilla" Taxable Bond Funds, Through December 31, 1999. All Distributions–Dividends and Capital Gains–Are Assumed to Be Reinvested.

	1 yr	5 yrs	10 yrs	15 yrs	20 yrs
Money market funds (taxable)	4.49	4.95	4.80	5.59	7.24
Ultra-short (91–365 days)	4.58	5.62	5.59	6.20	–
Short (1–3 yrs)					
U.S. Treasury	1.66	5.95	6.16	7.59	8.52
U.S. government	2.50	5.57	5.66	6.68	7.16
Investment grade	2.80	5.95	6.36	7.50	–
Short-intermediate (1–5 yr)					
U.S. Treasury	–	–	–	–	–
U.S. government	0.64	6.00	6.47	7.71	–
Investment grade	0.89	6.23	6.55	7.76	9.59
Intermediate (5–10 yrs)					
U.S. Treasury	–2.27	6.57	6.66	7.72	–
U.S. government	–1.68	6.35	6.44	1.84	7.82
Investment grade	–1.31	6.79	7.09	8.05	9.15
Long-term (10 years or more)					
U.S. Treasury	–6.17	7.35	7.39	9.30	–
U.S. government	–3.02	6.50	6.63	7.74	9.49
Corporate A rated	–2.61	6.90	7.30	8.77	9.56
Corporate BBB rated	–1.68	7.67	7.98	9.29	9.70

Source: Derived from *Lipper Taxable Fixed Income Performance Analysis*, Dec. 31, 1999. Copyright 1999 by REUTERS SA. Reprinted with permission.

that for that abysmal year, the shortest funds posted the best returns.

You might expect total return to be highest for funds holding
corporates, rather than governments or Treasuries: typically, funds
holding lower-quality bonds yield more than those holding higher
quality credits. Following this line of reasoning, bond funds holding government bonds should have higher total returns than those
holding Treasuries; funds holding A rated corporates should have
higher total returns than those holding governments; and the
highest returns should be found in the corporate BBB rated. But
this has varied from year to year. One reason is that if an economic
downturn is anticipated, the credit ratings of many corporations
are downgraded. As a result, the NAV of corporate bond funds
may decline. Also, when the economic outlook is poor, or cloudy,
a so-called flight to quality occurs. Investors abandon lower quality credits and flock to the security of Treasuries or of higher-
quality bonds. As a result Table 12–4 shows a somewhat erratic
pattern of returns for quality groupings, with Treasuries sometimes posting higher total returns than lower-quality bonds and
lower-quality bonds posting higher total returns some other times.

Table 12–4 shows annualized returns that have been averaged. For that reason, volatility and variability of returns show up
in this table only in 1999, a year during which most bond funds,
particularly those with long maturities, posted negative total returns. The interest rate spikes that occurred in 1987 and 1994 were
equally damaging, but the declines disappear into the averages.

The same caveats apply to long-term taxable bond funds as
to long-term tax-exempt bond funds. Because of their high potential volatility, long-term taxable funds should be purchased for
long holding periods only if you are prepared to live with considerable volatility. Again, unless you are frankly speculating that a
decline in interest rates is likely to occur, long-term taxable bond
funds should not be purchased for holding periods of one year or
less.

Unless you are in a very low tax bracket, taxable bond funds
are appropriate investments primarily for tax-sheltered accounts.
For money not in tax-sheltered accounts, bear in mind that funds
holding Treasuries-only are exempted from state taxes. Whether
such a fund would yield more for you than other bond funds

(whether taxable or tax-exempt) would vary with your tax bracket and the taxes of the state in which you live.

SPECIALTY FUNDS

As noted earlier, this grouping is made up of funds which invest in bonds that have some unique characteristics.

GNMA (and Other Mortgage) Funds

GNMA fund advertising focuses on two very appealing themes: their high dividend yield (GNMAs yield more than Treasuries) and the unconditional government backing, which eliminates credit risk. It is therefore a shock to some buyers of GNMA funds to discover that the high credit quality does not eliminate market risk.

Table 12–5 lists average annualized total returns for funds investing in different types of mortgage-backed securities, through December of 1999, for periods up to 20 years. Total returns are compounded, with dividends and capital gains assumed to be reinvested. Again, total returns of taxable money market funds are listed first for purposes of comparison.

T A B L E   12–5

Average Annual Total Returns of GNMA (and Other Mortgage-Backed Securities) Bond Funds, Through December 31, 1999. All Distributions—Dividends and Capital Gains—Are Assumed to Be Reinvested.

	1 yr	5 yrs	10 yrs	15 yrs	20 yrs
Taxable money market funds	4.49	4.95	4.80	5.59	7.24
GNMA	0.11	7.02	7.01	8.19	8.71
U.S. Mortgage	0.65	6.98	6.95	8.06	8.48
ARMs	4.38	5.79	5.60	–	–

Source: Derived from *Lipper Taxable Fixed Income Performance Analysis*, Dec. 31, 1999. Copyright 1999 by REUTERS SA. Reprinted with permission.

Again, the categories are those of Lipper. Lipper specifies that GNMA funds invest at least 65% of fund assets in GNMA securities. Mortgage funds invest at least 65% of fund assets in a variety of mortgage-backed securities other than GNMAs. Adjustable-rate mortgage funds invest at least 65% of fund assets in adjustable-rate mortgage securities. Note again that many funds investing primarily in GNMAs or other mortgage-backed securities are called "government" or "government income" or "government-only" funds.

Bond funds investing in GNMAs remain the largest of these three categories. During the 1980s, GNMA bond funds attracted enormous sums. Indeed, one GNMA fund, with over $14 billion in assets, was both the largest bond fund and one of the largest of all mutual funds at the time.

Since then, GNMA funds have lost a good deal of their initial appeal. GNMA funds disappointed shareholders in a variety of ways. In order to quote the highest possible yields, some funds pursued policies which led directly to erosion of NAV. For example, in order to be able to advertise high yields, managers of some GNMA bond funds stuffed their portfolio with premium bonds. When those bonds were sold at a lower price, or redeemed at par, NAV declined.

In addition, investors may not have understood the unique risk factor of GNMA funds: prepayment risk. When interest rates decline, homeowners refinance their mortgage at lower rates. What this means to holders of any GNMA security is that their higher-yielding bonds are called away and the proceeds have to be reinvested at lower rates. Whereas declining interest rates benefit other long-term bond funds, declining interest rates may actually cause the NAV of GNMA funds to decline. To add insult to injury, the yield of the fund declines as well.

Total return for GNMA funds is difficult to predict. When interest rates are stable, these funds do well because of the high dividend yield. In volatile markets, however, total return has been disappointing. If interest rates rise, the NAV of GNMA funds declines along with that of other bond funds. But if interest rates decline sharply, GNMA bond funds may show poor total returns because of massive prepayments. GNMA bond funds have experienced a number of years with substantial declines in NAV and poor total returns.

For most of the 1980s and 1990s (through 1998) average annual total return of GNMA funds was actually somewhat below
that of intermediate taxable bond funds and well below that of
long-term corporate bond funds. At the end of 1999, however,
total returns of GNMA funds look somewhat better compared to
other taxable bond funds. Because 1999 was a flat year for many
GNMA funds (compared to a down year for most longer-term
taxable bond funds), average annual total return of GNMA funds
is now slightly ahead of intermediate bond funds. But it remains
lower than long-term taxable funds.

Individual investors usually invest in GNMAs because of
their high cash flow. GNMA funds have a number of advantages
compared to individual GNMAs. They require a lower initial investment ($1,000 as compared to $25,000). The size of a fund also
results in more predictable cash flows (again compared to individual GNMAs). As a result, funds are viewed by some as a better
way for individuals to invest in this security. Also, investors in
GNMA funds are able to reinvest interest and mortgage prepayments automatically, and at a higher rate than money market
yields, which should boost total return over time. Finally, GNMA
funds can buy GNMA instruments far more economically than can
individuals.

Because GNMA advertising focuses so heavily on yield, some
of the more poorly managed funds used to inflate the advertised
yield. SEC regulations have made this more difficult. Nonetheless,
be aware that total return for GNMA funds (from the best to the
worst) varies significantly from fund to fund. The best-performing
GNMA funds manage for total return, which means that they may
not have the highest advertised yield. Before purchasing a GNMA
fund, be sure to check the fund's history and total return compared to other GNMA funds.

While funds investing in mortgage-backed securities other
than GNMAs are listed by Lipper as a separate category, it does
not appear that these funds have either a significant advantage or
disadvantage compared to GNMA funds. This is also a far smaller
group of funds.

If you already own a GNMA fund and are happy with it, by
all means continue holding it, especially if you have already paid
a commission. But if you are investing new money, attractive alternatives may now be available. You can now invest in individual

CMOs with relatively small sums ($1,000 minimum). And you can tailor your choice of a CMO to your own preferences, based on yield or average life. If stability of principal is a primary concern, consider five-year Treasuries. If you are looking for higher total return, consider intermediate or long-term bond funds. Also, for IRA or Keogh accounts, consider mutual funds investing in zeros, or individual zeros, if rates are attractive.

If you are considering investing in GNMAs through a fund, be sure to read the chapter on mortgage-backed securities in order to understand the nature of these very complex instruments.

Adjustable-Rate Mortgage Funds (ARMs)

In 1988, a new type of GNMA fund arrived on the scene. It invests in adjustable-rate mortgages (ARMS), which are floating-rate bonds. The theory behind all floating-rate bonds is that the yield will fluctuate, in this instance as mortgage rates change, but principal value will remain stable. The duration of ARMS funds is extremely short. Consequently, yield should be lower than conventional GNMA securities but higher than money market funds. Risk to principal should be minimal.

In the first edition of this book, I noted that these funds had too brief a history for me to make any kind of meaningful generalization. Now that they have been around for approximately ten years, it would appear that for most of the time they have been a disappointing product. During the early 1990s, ARMs experienced significant prepayments. In spite of the theory behind the funds, principal value, and therefore NAV, declined. Since then, total return has occasionally been somewhat higher than for money market funds, and occasionally lower. In 1999, total return was about equivalent to that of money market funds.

In short, investing in ARMs would seem to be a risk not worth taking: you take on some risk to principal, and at best the gain in total return is marginal.

Zero Coupon Bond Funds

These are Treasury bond funds, on steroids.

These funds invest in zero coupon bonds (strips). Unlike other long-term bond funds, however, zero coupon bond buy securities that all mature at approximately the same date. They have a definite maturity date. For this reason, most are called "target" funds (the target is the maturity date). Average maturities for Target funds vary from short to approximately 25 years. The price behavior of bond funds investing in zeros is analogous to that of an individual zero coupon bond with the same maturity length and duration.

Since these funds invest primarily in Treasuries, their credit quality is impeccable. The risk factor for these funds is interest rate risk, highly magnified. As explained in Chapter 6, zero coupon bonds with long maturities can be more than twice as volatile as ordinary coupon securities with similar maturities. As a result, bond funds investing in zero coupon bonds (particularly those investing in long-term or intermediate maturities) are among the most volatile of all bond funds. In rising markets, zero coupon bond funds with intermediate or long maturities are invariably among the best-performing bond funds. In weak markets, they are a disaster.

There is, however, one excellent use for zero coupon bond funds. The maturity can be selected to coincide with known future expenses: for instance, a child's admission to college; annual tuition payments; cash for retirement years; a trip; and so forth. If the funds are held to the maturity date, there is no credit risk, no interest rate risk, and no reinvestment risk. The actual total return is known and guaranteed. But if zero coupon bond funds have to be sold before their maturity date, their volatility turns these funds into very high-risk investments.

The main advantage of investing in zeros through funds is that transaction costs may be lower than for individual securities. Individual zeros, when sold in small amounts, have high mark-ups. Because volatility is so high, funds holding mainly intermediate or longer-dated zeros should be bought as short-term holdings only if you are frankly speculating on short-term interest moves.

Note also that the tax treatment of zero bond funds is identical to that of individual zeros: taxes have to be paid annually even though no interest is received until the bond matures. This makes them suitable more for tax-deferred or tax-sheltered accounts than for taxable assets.

To be meaningful, total returns for this very volatile group have to be tallied for individual maturities, and for specific time periods. That is the reason I have not included a table of average returns for this group of funds. For 1999, as you would expect, total returns for all target maturity funds was negative. But in spite of the poor 1999 total returns, average annual total return (as tallied by Lipper) for the ten-year mark ending December 31, 1999 was 9.77%; and for the five-year mark 10.89%: the highest total returns for any investment-grade group. Bear in mind, however, that those returns are high due to three factors: the very high initial coupon rates—as high as 9% for the funds with the longest maturities (20 to 25 years); compounding at the initial coupon rate; and, for maturities longer than five years, some capital appreciation due to declining interest rates.

If you buy a zero coupon bond fund at the current time, total return is likely to be much lower than the returns of the past two decades because interest rate levels and also reinvestment rates (built into the structure of a zero) are currently much lower. If you hold a zero bond fund until its target maturity date, the total return is known and guaranteed. If you sell before the target date, however, if rates decline, total return will be higher than the quote at the time of purchase. But if rates go up, total return will be lower than the initial quote.

MORE SPECULATIVE FUNDS: "FUNDS WITH EQUITY CHARACTERISTICS"

These are the bond funds which have the greatest variability of returns, the ones whose total returns are the most variable and hardest to predict. Risk factors are more complex and less easy to define than for either of the preceding group of funds. This grouping includes bond funds that have had some of the highest total returns at various time periods and also some of the largest losses. Total returns for bond funds in this grouping vary significantly from year to year, and from fund to fund within any one fund category.

There is also a good deal of disagreement concerning the riskiness of some of these funds, particularly for longer holding periods. If you like a lot of "action" and want to speculate, then read on.

Table 12–6 lists the average annual total return for two types of funds in this category: high-yield (junk) and multi-sector funds.

T A B L E   12–6

Average Annual Total Returns of High-Yield (Junk) and
Multi-Sector Bond Funds Through December 31, 1999.
All Distributions—Dividends and Capital Gains—Are
Assumed to Be Reinvested.

	1 yr	5 yrs	10 yrs	15 yrs	20 yrs
Taxable money market funds	4.49	4.95	4.80	5.59	7.24
High-yield (junk)	4.53	8.84	10.03	9.86	10.56
Multi-sector	2.57	7.90	8.65	9.08	9.82

Source: Derived from *Lipper Taxable Fixed Income Performance Analysis*, Dec. 31, 1999. Copyright 1999 by REUTERS
SA. Reprinted with permission.

This table summarizes average annual total returns from December 1979 through December 31, 1999. Total return is the average compounded total return, based on reinvestment of all dividends and capital gains distributions, if any, plus changes in share price. Once again, total returns of money market funds are listed first for purposes of comparison.

"Junk" Bond Funds

As of December 31, 1999, this bond fund sector held over $100 billion in assets. This was the largest single category among taxable bond funds, holding approximately 40% of all the assets in the taxable sector! As you can see in Table 12–6, for every period between five and 20 years preceding December 31, 1999, average annual total return of junk bond funds was among the highest of any group investing in domestic (U.S.) taxable bonds. Note also that average annual total return for the entire group was positive in 1999, approximately equal to that of money funds. For 1999, this constituted a very good performance since so many bond funds investing in high-quality debt instruments posted negative total returns.

So-called junk bond funds invest in corporate bonds rated below investment grade. That rating indicates a strong possibility of default. This is the only type of bond fund where the primary source of risk is credit quality. To compensate investors for the probability that defaults will occur, yields quoted for junk bond funds are always the highest of any domestic bond funds: they sell at a spread to Treasuries (that is, above the yield of Treasuries) which has ranged from a low of perhaps 250 basis points to an unbelievably high 1,200 basis points (in 1990).

These funds are a perfect illustration of the fact that high yield does not necessarily translate into high total return. In 1989 and 1990, in spite of diversified holdings, NAV of junk bond funds plummeted as buyers disappeared and the market for junk bonds essentially shut down. Many junk bond funds lost an initial 30% of NAV in about six months in 1989 and another 15% to 25% the following year. As of December 1990, total return was negative for the preceding two years, in spite of a current yield averaging an astronomically high 13% to 15% for 1990. This means that at the end of two years, even after adding back the high interest income, an investment was worth less than two years earlier. At the end of 1990, for the previous five-year period, cumulative total return was lower than for virtually riskless money market funds.

As NAVs declined, investors in junk bond funds began bailing out. As outflows increased, bond fund managers were forced to sell into the decline, causing the decline to steepen. In order to cope with the continuing outflow of assets, junk bond funds instituted a variety of measures. Some cut dividends. Others changed the name of their fund from "high yield" to "high income." Still others merged the junk bond funds with other funds in the same fund family or changed the investment policies of the funds.

As a direct result, in 1991, far fewer genuine junk bond funds were left. Some of the mutual fund groups that continued to provide the real article adopted the policy of routinely advising anyone asking for information on junk bond funds that these bond funds were considered speculative, and furthermore, that the high dividend yield was the result of a dramatic drop in price and was unlikely to be maintained. Some mutual fund families are still maintaining this policy. In addition, a number of no-load fund families have imposed either exit fees or entry fees on the funds in order to limit the appeal of junk bond funds to traders and to "hot money."

Of course, because the market is perverse, 1991 was also the precise point that a rally in junk bond funds occurred. As a result of the very high yields then quoted, and the rally, total returns for these funds was in the range of 20 to 40% for that year. Partly as a result, and because of subsequent high total returns, junk bonds and junk bond funds have regained their luster. In spite of the horrendous declines that occurred periodically in this sector, as Table 12–6 shows, the *average* annual total returns of the group are higher for every period between 20 years and one year than those that invest in higher-rated instruments, and the volatility *appears* somewhat lower. But those returns must be interpreted with caution.

For one thing, these total returns do not include the junk funds that went out of business after the debacles of 1989 and 1990. This bumps up the average returns of the remaining funds in the group. Also, a different ending date would have shown a totally different picture. In 1997 and 1998, for example, after the economic crises that occurred in Asia and the default on Russian bonds, Treasury bonds soared and junk bonds plummeted. That year, returns for junk bond funds were significantly lower than those of Treasuries or more highly rated debt. Moreover, bear in mind that you would have earned those high *average* annual returns only if you held on through bad years as well as good years. Had you bought when junk bond funds were hot and sold when they declined, this would have resulted in investment disaster. Trying to time this sector is extremely difficult. Almost invariably, advisers suggest investing in junk bond funds *after* they have gone up in price and when the spread to higher-quality bonds is narrow. That is usually a poor time to buy.

Chapter 9 includes a brief history of junk bonds, and there is no need to repeat it here. What is clear is that if you invest in junk bond funds, periods of very high returns alternate with periods of miserable returns—and both parts of the cycle may last a long time. Over very long holding periods, exceeding ten years, total returns of junk bond funds may exceed those of higher-rated instruments, but that is not certain.

Proponents of these funds argue that holding junk bonds or junk bond funds will lower the total risk of a portfolio because their returns do not move in tandem with other interest rates. Theoretically, for example, during a boom cycle, interest rates may rise and NAV of long-term funds decline. But during an economic boom, default rates of corporations should be low and total returns of junk bonds high. That argument, however, holds for very large, well-diversified portfolios, such as those of an insurance company or a pension fund. The fact that highly rated bonds and junk bonds do not move in lockstep helps these large institutions to meet their annual liabilities. Most individual investors do not have the same needs. And periods of decline such as those that occurred in 1989, 1990, and 1997 are extremely painful.

Because of the imperative need to diversify and the genuine expertise required to analyze individual junk bonds, mutual funds represent the most practical way for the average individual to invest in junk bonds. If this area attracts you, you should be aware that whereas even a poorly managed junk bond fund will at least be somewhat diversified, a number of the worst-performing junk bond funds have had truly abysmal total returns, well below the average for the group. The worst-performing junk bond funds suffered losses of close to 50% in 1990 after losing 25% in 1988. (This means that an investment worth $10,000 at the beginning of 1988 would have shrunk to approximately $2,500 at the end of 1990, even after adding back the dividends.)

A good rule to follow is that the more aggressive the fund, the higher the volatility. Note that since 1996 and 1997, many junk bond funds have included bonds of emerging markets in their portfolios. Some junk bond funds are managed more conservatively, investing only in the higher reaches of junk and excluding debt of emerging markets. The volatility of those funds is somewhat lower than the average for the group; and their total return is more consistent. Junk bond funds are poor investments during or going into a recession, when defaults can be expected to rise. They are also poor investments if spreads to Treasuries have narrowed significantly: you are not compensated for the high credit risk.

Because overall average annual total return of the group has been high for the decade of the 1990s, some financial advisers now routinely advise all individual investors to include junk bond funds in their bond portfolios. Many experts disagree with this assessment. My opinion is that junk bond funds should be regarded as speculative, that is, for money where you can afford to sustain losses and that you do not need for a long period of time so that you can ride out periods of negative returns. You should invest in such a fund only if you have a very large and otherwise well-diversified portfolio (well in excess of $200,000 in bonds or in bond funds), and certainly with no more than 20% of your bond portfolio in this sector. Also, be sure to investigate the history of any fund which interests you because total returns vary significantly from fund to fund. Finally, be sure to read the section dealing with junk bonds in Chapter 9.

Multi-Sector Funds

These are relative newcomers: few "multi-sector" funds have existed for much more than five years. Most have existed for three years or less. The most popular term in the fund name is "strategic," although "multi-sector" also makes a number of appearances. I shall quote Lipper's definition for this group: "Fund seeks current income by allocating assets among different fixed-income securities sectors (no 65% in one sector except for defensive purposes), including U.S. and foreign governments, with a significant portion rated below U.S. investment grade."

In other words, multi-sector funds manage for the highest possible total return, selecting bonds from any group they deem likely to appreciate the most and to have potentially the highest total return over the short term. Managers of these funds are free to select any bond from any sector, and any maturity length from any nationality. Many of these funds invest in securities that are deemed to be well below investment grade (read: rated as junk), not only in the United States but also in emerging markets. A few rely heavily on mathematical, quantitative models. Leveraging techniques (buying or selling futures contracts, writing options) may also be permitted. The hope, of course, is that the freedom given to the managers to invest in high-risk, but potentially high-return securities will enable them to post returns that will be well above average.

I have listed average annualized total returns for the group with some misgivings because once again the averages are somewhat misleading. For starters, even though average returns are listed for up to 20 years, very few funds have existed for more than five years. Also note that because the managers of these funds are totally free to select any currency, and any bond they think will provide high total returns, total returns vary significantly from fund to fund. One fund which bet heavily on rising U.S. interest rates by selling short had a total return of 18% for the first six months of 1999, a spectacular performance for that time period. Other funds which bet heavily on bonds of emerging markets tanked in 1998 but recovered somewhat in 1999. But there is simply no way to predict how any fund in this sector will perform without analyzing the record of its manager. And even that is likely to vary from year to year.

Over longer holding periods, average annualized total returns for the group as a whole are about equal to some much lower-risk fund groups (intermediate index funds, for example, or GNMA funds.) For the one-year period ending December 1999, most "strategic" funds had negative or barely positive total returns. Again, the range of returns was wide: for the entire calendar year of 1999, the best-performing fund had a total return of 12%; the worst, minus 4%. You are not being paid very well for the high level of risk in this group.

It is possible, of course, that some managers will be successful for more than one year. But unfortunately, how likely is it that you can predict who that manager is going to be? and for how long? I would suggest investing in this type of fund with the greatest caution, and with only a small amount of money, until they compile a more meaningful track record.

Bond Funds Investing in Foreign Bonds

Since the first edition of this book, this sector has increased in importance and is likely to continue to increase in importance.

I cannot resist quoting two paragraphs from the first edition of this book:

> If I had to pick the most beleaguered bond fund manager, the manager of an international bond fund would be a strong candidate. This manager may purchase bonds issued in any country, in any maturity. Consider his dilemma. Bonds issued by foreign corporations or foreign governments are subject to the same risks as U.S. securities: credit risk and interest rate risk; and these vary enormously from country to country.
>
> But international bond funds are subject to additional risks. The most important of these is currency risk since bonds are purchased in American dollars. Currencies fluctuate even more unpredictably and dramatically

than interest rates. There is also what is known technically as sovereign risk; that is, the risk deriving from the political and the economic system of foreign countries, some with highly unstable governments, and even less stable economies.

The currency crises of 1997–1998 made these paragraphs look positively prescient!

Total returns of all bond funds investing in foreign bonds have been determined largely by changes in currencies. Bear in mind that these funds represent a bet against the dollar: they prosper when the dollar declines against foreign currencies. A very few funds investing in bonds of foreign countries were introduced in 1985. For the first three years, as the dollar declined steeply, these funds soared. The greatest part of total return was capital gains, resulting from the decline in the value of the dollar. Subsequently, returns went on a wild rollercoaster ride. In 1988 and 1989, as the dollar rose, the funds sank: total return was dismal. In 1990, the dollar dropped; once again, international funds were stars. But in 1991, the dollar rallied: once again, return for these funds was dismal.

This remains a small group of funds: at the end of 1999, bond funds investing in international bonds had a total of less than $22 billion in assets. Few funds in this group had been around for as long as ten years. But because investing in individual foreign bonds remains difficult and requires genuine expertise, individual investors will find that bond funds represent the most practical way to invest in international bonds. Since international bond funds vary a good deal in their make-up, let's briefly discuss the types of international bond funds currently available.

Table 12–7 illustrates the total return of taxable bond funds investing in foreign bonds through December 31, 1999, for time periods of up to 15 years. Total returns are compounded, with dividends and capital gains assumed to be reinvested. Once again, total returns of taxable money market funds are listed first for purposes of comparison.

Global and International Bond Funds

The two largest categories of international funds are the "Global" and the "International" categories. Let's consider these two categories first. These are Lipper's definitions:

T A B L E   12–7

Average Annual Total Returns of Taxable Bond Funds
Investing in Foreign Bonds, Through December 31,
1999. All Distributions—Dividends and Capital Gains—
Are Assumed to Be Reinvested.

	1 yr	5 yrs	10 yrs	15 yrs	20 yrs
Taxable money market funds	4.49	4.95	4.80	5.59	7.24
Global	−2.44	6.33	6.57	10.24	–
International	−4.60	6.45	6.51	–	–
Emerging markets*	24.49	12.76	–	–	–
Short world multi-market	0.99	5.01	4.48	–	–

*2 year: average −1.09
 3 year: average   3.34
Source: Derived from *Lipper Taxable Fixed Income Performance Analysis*, Dec. 31, 1999. Copyright 1999 by Reuters
SA. Reprinted with permission.

 ◆ Global bond funds invest in bonds of at least three
   countries, one of which may be the United States. The
   bonds may be denominated in U.S. dollars or in foreign
   currencies.
 ◆ International bond funds invest primarily in bonds of
   foreign issuers, excluding the United States except in
   periods of market weakness.

As these definitions suggest, the main distinction between
"global" funds and "international" funds is that global funds normally include U.S. debt instruments, whereas international funds
may do so only during periods of market weakness. Theoretically,
overall currency risk may be lower for global funds since they
include some U.S. securities. Both global and international bond
funds may own bonds issued by corporations or by sovereign
governments.
   International bond funds differ widely in their investment
policies. Some invest in bonds of many countries. Others are more
regional in nature, specializing in bonds of developed countries
(Europe, for example). Some funds invest in investment grade

bonds of countries with well-developed economies and solid currencies. Some permit the use of leverage and derivatives. Others do not.

Although a table of group returns was included, once again, for this category, the averages are somewhat misleading. Total returns vary enormously from the best-performing to the worst-performing funds. For the five-year period through June 30, 1999, for example, *cumulative* total returns for the best-performing fund in the global category was close to 70%; for the worst-performing fund, approximately 20%. For the international category, the story is the same: cumulative total return for the five-year period through June 30, 1999, was approximately 75% for the best-performing fund; approximately 11% for the worst-performing fund.

The most striking fact, however, that Table 12–7 illustrates is that for the group as a whole, total returns have been disappointing. Total returns were negative for 1999. For the five-year mark, total returns for the group are only marginally above money market rates. And unfortunately, choosing the fund that has had the best total return over any preceding time period in no way insures that fund will perform equally well into the future.

"Emerging Markets" Bond Funds

Lipper's definition of "Emerging Markets Bond Funds" is that they invest at least 65% of their assets in debt instruments of "emerging" markets. These are primarily Brady bonds denominatd in U.S. dollars. (Brady bonds are analyzed in some detail in Chapter 10, on international bonds.) Emerging market debt is typically rated below investment grade. It is considered highly speculative. This group of bond funds, like junk bond funds, is another perfect illustration of the fact that high yield does not automatically lead to high total return.

This is still a tiny group of funds, with total assets, at the end of 1999, of less than four billion dollars. The group, moreover, has a short history, with only a few funds dating as far back as five years. But this category of funds is likely to increase in size for two reasons. The first is that emerging countries, as a group, need to raise enormous amounts of capital to meet their needs for infrastructure. The second is that in 1999, total returns were spectacular, the highest of any category of bond funds.

Initial returns for the few funds that existed prior to 1997 were very high, because yields of the original Brady bonds were set at very high levels: around 20%. Then came the debt crises of 1997 and 1998. Emerging market bond funds experienced dramatic declines: 50% or more in a few months. Declines of some of the issues in the portfolios of these funds were among the worst experienced in any bond funds in any market. The value of Russian bonds, for example, declined to practically zero after the Russian government defaulted on its debt.

But of course, out of spectacular declines often comes opportunity. Bonds of emerging markets were the standouts of 1999: almost all of the best-performing bond funds of 1999 either invested primarily in the bonds of emerging markets or included a sprinkling of bonds of emerging markets in their portfolio. (This was true, for example, of junk bond funds and of so-called "multisector" funds.)

Average total return for 1999 for this group was extremely high: almost 25%. But differences in total return between funds in this category are extraordinarily wide. For the 1999 calendar year, total returns ranged from 40% for the best-performing emerging market debt fund to negative 9% for the worst.

Volatility for this group of funds is the highest of any category of bond funds. The very high total returns of 1999 derive from the fact that the price of emerging market debt at the end of 1998 was severely depressed, resulting in outsize yields. In 1999, as the economic crisis receded, the bonds recovered some of the value lost in the debacle of the preceding year. The combination of very high interest income as well as capital gains resulted in very high total returns. Anyone lucky enough, or clever enough, to buy at the bottom enjoyed hefty gains in 1999. In spite of these hefty 1999 returns, however, anyone who purchased an emerging market bond fund three years earlier was probably still under water at the beginning of 2000, or may barely have matched the total return of a money market fund for that period. As noted in Table 12–7, according to Lipper data, as of December 31, 1999, average annual total return for the two-year mark was minus 1.09%; and for the three-year mark approximately 3%.

Note one point in favor of emerging market bond funds. For the five years preceding June 1999, the bond funds of emerging markets, as a group, posted higher total returns than stock funds of emerging markets, perhaps because of their outsize dividend yields. This suggests that if you want to invest in emerging markets, it may be safer and sometimes more profitable to do so through a bond fund, rather than through a stock fund. But this relationship does not always hold.

Any investment in emerging market funds should be viewed as speculative and suitable only for very large, well-diversified portfolios. This is not for money you cannot afford to lose. At the current time, however, buying individual securities in this market would be extraordinarily difficult for individual investors. If this area attracts you, investigate a bond fund, but very carefully.

Short World Multi-Market Funds

"Short world multi-market" income funds invest primarily in debt of foreign issuers. As their name indicates, these funds have short weighted average maturities, typically under two years.

This group currently is very small: only a little over $1 billion of assets for the entire group. This represents a significant amount of shrinkage, however. At their inception, in 1990, short world multi-market funds attracted a lot of money. You can guess why. When introduced, these funds were marketed as a higher-yielding alternative to money market funds. The case for these funds sounded convincing. They were able to promise a higher return than money market funds because foreign interest rates were higher than in the United States. They would be low risk because maturities were short. Moreover, currency risk was to be eliminated through cross-hedging.

Initially, the funds delivered: total return was very high, thanks to a combination of higher interest rates abroad and a sinking dollar in the United States. These conditions did not last, however, and as losses piled up, assets exited the funds.

Average total returns listed in Table 12–7 are somewhat misleading in that, once again, returns vary significantly from fund to fund. For the group as a whole, for 1999, average total returns are barely positive. Average annualized total returns were between 3% and 4% for the two-year, three-year, and four-year periods preceding December 1999. They match money market total returns for the five-year period only because that coincided with one of their good years.

It is not impossible that total return for this group may improve at some future date. But if you want to be in a low risk fund (which, after all, is how these funds were sold), why would you invest in a group whose total returns are as unpredictable as this one's?

Summary and Conclusion: International Bond Funds

To sum up, the potential total return of any fund investing in bonds of foreign countries is unpredictable. Risk is high and derives from the inherent unpredictability of currency fluctuations. But, particularly if the dollar declines at some future date, or as the capital needs of other countries are funded, this group is likely to grow enormously.

Once again, it bears mentioning that financial advisers make the argument that investing in international bond funds may lower the total risk of a bond portfolio because these bonds do not move in lockstep with U.S. bonds. And if you look back, it is true that international bonds have had some of their best years (for U.S. dollar-based investors) when the dollar declined and when other dollar-denominated assets were doing poorly. But bear in mind that many international bond funds have only a very short history. To be successful, managers have to pick the right foreign currencies. As a result, total returns vary enormously from international fund to international fund.

Most individual investors should consider the diversification argument skeptically: as valid mainly for very large institutional portfolios such as those of pension funds or insurance companies. International bond funds would be appropriate mainly for individual investors with very large, well-diversified portfolios (at least $300,000 in bonds) for any of three objectives: as a speculation, to diversify the portfolio, or as a hedge against the dollar.

MISCELLANEOUS FUNDS

Loan Participation Funds

This is a hybrid type of fund that is not, properly speaking, an open-end mutual fund. It is similar in some ways to closed-end funds, although it is a hybrid category belonging in neither group. The unique characteristic of loan participation funds is that money invested in these funds can only be redeemed one day each quarter.

These funds go under a variety of names, including "prime rate" funds, "floating rate" funds, "income trust," or some combination of terms that includes these phrases. These funds invest in bank loans, and specifically in loans characterized as "subprime," meaning loans that have high yields primarily because they carry a high degree of credit risk. These loans are fairly short term, usually under two years. Interest rates on the funds are reset periodically, based on a spread to a benchmark rate, usually LIBOR. The theory is that interest rates will vary, but invested principal will not decline significantly in value, because maturities are short.

As a result, these funds are now being marketed as higher-yielding alternatives to money funds. And in fact, several recent articles, both in financial magazines and on the Internet, characterize these funds as "stars" or as a unique corner of the credit market reserved for savvy investors. These funds are sold by brokers (like other closed-end funds). At the current time, five of these funds are exchange traded. Some of these funds carry a 1% deferred sales charge, meaning that you pay it when you sell the fund. Growth of these funds has been rapid. In just one year, the funds now hold well over $35 billion in assets.

As has been stated many times in this book, higher rates always go hand in hand with some higher degree of risk. These funds are no exception. Once again, the clue to this is the total return of the funds. While the quoted yields are high (somewhere between 7 1/2% and 8%), average annual total return for 1999 (according to data supplied to me by the Lipper organization) is much lower: approximately 5.87% for the group, which indicates that most of these funds have declined in value.

Most of these funds were issued with a $10.00 share price. So if a broker is pitching one of these funds to you at a price lower than $10.00, that indicates that some of the loans in the portfolio have experienced difficulties, which are reflected in the lower share price. The worst-performing of these funds went to an approximate 15% discount in 1999, which means that the price per share declined by 15%, a significant loss for a fund marketed as very safe.

As we go to press, the Fidelity group has announced that it is starting a loan participation fund that will permit daily redemption of monies. Other groups may follow. Stay tuned.

If you would like to look up these funds, they are grouped in *Barron's* and *The Wall Street Journal,* with closed-end funds listings. (See the next chapter for more on closed-end funds.)

Bond Index Funds

Bond index funds are not listed as a separate fund category by either Lipper or Morningstar. Individual bond index funds are included, however, among several different categories, based on their average weighted maturity and on the sector of the bond market in which they are invested. These funds are a recent innovation. Vanguard, which pioneered stock index funds, also pioneered bond index funds. The concept has spread, however, and several other groups now offer that option.

While indexing may seem arcane when applied to bond funds, it is simply an extension of the concept of indexing which has become familiar for equity funds. Like equity index funds, bond index funds are managed passively to mirror a specific benchmark index. All index funds have two advantages: a low expense ratio and low turnover of assets. Again, as is the case for equity funds, few managers of actively managed bond funds have managed to consistently outperform specific benchmark indices. The anticipation is that, over long holding periods, bond index funds will have higher total returns than most actively managed bond funds, simply by virtue of the fact that they will match the total return of the benchmark, and that expenses for managing the fund will be low.

In a sense, bond index funds are the ultimate plain vanilla funds. Their risk factors are straightforward: they can be summarized as the average weighted maturity of the fund (or its duration) and its credit quality. At the beginning of 2000, the largest bond index fund is the Vanguard Total Bond Market Index Fund, which is managed to match the total return of the Lehman Total Bond Market Index. This fund has an average weighted maturity of 8.8 years and a duration of five years, which places it in the intermediate sector. Other index funds are managed to match the returns of short, intermediate, and long-term Lehman government or corporate bond indices.

Total return for bond index funds has been high compared to average total returns for similar maturity sectors compiled by Lipper. As an example, through December of 1999, the cumulative total return of the Total Bond Market Index Fund (which, you will remember, is an intermediate fund) was approximately 44% for the preceding five years and 107% for the preceding ten years. That is higher than the average cumulative total return of the Lipper taxable intermediate bond fund grouping, which was 39% for the preceding five years and 99% for the preceding ten years. Even more impressive, the total return of the Total Bond Market Index Fund was higher than the average cumulative total return for the long corporate A rated sector, which was 40% for the preceding five years and 103% for the preceding ten years. Finally, the cumulative total return of the index fund was also higher than the cumulative average of the GNMA funds, which was 40% for the preceding five years and 97% for the preceding ten years. Note that the higher cumulative total return of the Total Market Index Fund was achieved with less risk than for the long-term or GNMA sectors.

To date, Vanguard continues to have the lowest expense ratios of any mutual fund group: 20 basis points or less. So the returns of its bond index funds should be competitive. But if other groups want to be competitive with Vanguard, their expense ratios may also come down.

Index funds are an attractive option if you want to invest in a bond fund. The level of risk is easy to predict: simply find out the duration of the fund and position yourself based on your investment horizon: that is, how long you think you will own the fund. Choose a duration close to that number. Choosing a duration close to the amount of time you want to own the fund lowers interest rate risk (see the section on duration). Credit risk should be minimal; and so should NAV erosion.

To date, bond index funds still constitute a tiny group of funds. Moreover, they have been pretty much confined to the taxable bond fund sector. But it is quite likely that at some future date, indexing will spread to other sectors of the bond market.

Evaluating Future Possibilities

As the market evolves, new varieties of bond funds will continue to appear. Some possibilities would be: bond funds investing in inflation-linked bonds; new types of bond index funds; or more specialized international funds. The criteria used in the preceding sections should enable you to evaluate both potential risk and potential total return of new funds. The questions to ask yourself are the following:

+ What is the average maturity of the fund's portfolio? If it is short (under two years), interest risk is low. If it is intermediate (four to ten years), interest rate risk is higher. Long-term funds will have the highest interest rate risk.
+ Is there credit risk? Credit risk will be significant if credit quality of most of the bonds in the fund is below investment grade.
+ Is there a currency risk?
+ How high is dividend yield expected to be, and what is that based on? Remember that very high yield translates into high risk. Investigate the risk factors before you buy.
+ Finally, how much freedom does the manager have in determining what to buy? If he has total freedom, then what kind of track record has he established?
+ As a result of all these factors, how volatile is NAV expected to be?

Some Do's and Don't's for Buying Bond Funds

Before you buy any bond fund, you should have a clear understanding of its objectives and policies. If the language of the objective appears to be full of jargon, or unclear, ask the fund's information people for clarification. If, for example, the objective states that "the fund will buy speculative securities that are well below investment grade," it is important that you understand that this fund will invest in junk bonds. If the objective states that the fund will purchase "high and upper medium quality securities," ask for specific rating information. Be sure that you understand the risk factors described in the objective. The risk factors should be taken seriously, even if recent fund performance has been excellent. Remember, however, that policies are usually defined in broad enough terms to allow fund managers enough latitude to deal with changing market conditions.

If you are investing in bond funds primarily for reliable, steady income, you will want to locate funds that have existed long enough to have gone through both bull markets and bear markets in bonds. Once again, the mantra is to buy a no-load fund with a low expense ratio, no 12b-1 fees, and a track record of conservative management. Look for funds that have not gone down too much during bear markets but have also done reasonably well during bull markets. If that fund ranks in the top quartile (25%) of its category (whether tabulated by Lipper or by Morningstar), you have found a fund that is likely to have a consistent performance over time.

Remember that in choosing any fund, there will be trade-offs. Longer maturities usually result in a higher yield but more volatility. Shorter maturities result in lower volatility but also less income.

The average maturity of a bond fund determines how much share price goes both up and down in response to interest rate changes and the dividend yield. Normally, longer-term funds have higher dividends than shorter-term funds, but price per share goes up and down more. The price per share of shorter-term funds is more stable (goes up and down less), but dividend yield is lower.

Let's summarize some general principles that should guide the purchase of bond funds:

♦ Don't buy any fund whose share price fluctuates if you are going to need the money in less than a year; you cannot know at what price you will be able to redeem.

♦ If you are investing primarily for "income" and safety of principal is important to you, don't buy the longest-term funds or those with the highest stated yields (those will be the riskiest funds). Instead, stick to funds that have intermediate (or shorter) maturities (whether taxable or tax-exempt) and invest in high-quality bonds.

♦ Where possible, for new money, buy no-load funds, with low expense ratios and no 12b-1 plans.

♦ Before buying a fund, make sure you know exactly what securities are in it; check the current maturity length, or better still, the current duration.

♦ Don't invest more than 20% of your bond portfolio in any bond fund that is long term, international or junk. Invest in these funds only if you have a large, well-diversified bond or bond fund portfolio (minimum: $200,000). It's not necessary to own one of each.

♦ The more complex the security, the more expertise it requires, then the more appropriate it becomes to buy a fund rather than individual securities. Funds are the most efficient way for individual investors to own international bonds, GNMAs, junk bonds, and corporates.

♦ Taxable bond funds are appropriate for tax-deferred (or tax-sheltered) monies that you want to place in fixed-income securities. For those purposes, consider high-quality corporate, GNMA, or zero bond funds. For money that is not in tax-deferred or tax-advantaged accounts, do the arithmetic to determine whether taxable or tax-exempt bond funds will result in the highest net-after-tax yield.

CONCLUSION AND SUMMARY

The preceding discussion indicates that over the past 20 years, certain types of bond funds (long-term funds, intermediate funds, municipal funds, junk funds) have had high total returns. During that period, for most years, also, total return has been almost directly related to maturity length. The longest-term funds had higher total returns than intermediate funds; and those in turn had higher total returns than money market funds.

One would naturally want to know: will longer-term funds continue to have higher total returns than shorter funds? The answer to that question is a qualified yes. Over long holding periods, longer-term funds should continue to have higher total return than shorter-term funds, if for no other reason than that dividend yield is higher. Because of compounding, and because dividends will be reinvested at higher rates, longer-term funds should have higher total returns than shorter-term funds. Over long holding

B O X   1–1

THE DO-IT-YOURSELF BOND FUND

If you are investing in bonds primarily because you do not want to risk any loss of principal and you want to insure a steady source of income, then the safest way to go is the do-it-yourself route. You can use either Treasuries or munis. For Treasuries, buy any combination of maturities between one and five years that suits your needs. Since Treasuries run no risk of default, you do not need to diversify in order to eliminate credit risk: a one-bond portfolio of U.S. Treasuries runs no risk of default. Buy your Treasuries through Treasury Direct. Uncle Sam will maintain the account for you at zero annual expense and will not charge any commission. You can also build a totally safe portfolio using municipal bonds. Stick to short maturities (between one and seven years). Buy any combination of AAA bonds, pre-refunded bonds (i.e., premium munis backed by escrowed Treasuries, and therefore even "safer" than AAA), or insured muni bonds or build a ladder. (For a "ladder," see Chapter 15.)

periods, the income portion of bond funds, that is interest income plus interest-on-interest, should dominate total return.

But this scenario is contingent on what happens to interest rates. If rates remain in a relatively narrow range or decline from current levels, the longest-term funds will continue to have higher total returns than shorter-maturity funds and money funds by a substantial margin. But if rates rise, or if there is great volatility for several years in a row, then total return of long-term bond funds will be highly unpredictable for short holding periods, and may not exceed the total return of shorter or intermediate bond funds. As 1999 has shown, over any short holding period (one or two years), an interest rate spike can significantly depress total returns which were high for the previous decade.

Moreover, for newer categories of bond funds, predictions of future returns are extremely tentative. For example, the exceptional returns enjoyed by emerging market funds in 1999 may very well be tied to a combination of factors unique to that period, and these factors may not repeat. Therefore, in this case it would be prudent to take very literally the standard disclaimer that one finds in any prospectus, namely, that past performance should be not taken as a prediction of future results.

Finally, the golden decade for bond funds was the 1980s. Total returns were exceptional, because the decline in interest rates that occurred in the second half of the 1980s added a chunk of capital gains to the high interest income generated during that decade. As we enter the year 2000, the level of interest rates is a lot lower than it was either in the 1980s, or even, at the beginning of the 1990s. Consequently, total returns generated by all types of bond funds will be a lot more modest than those of the 1980s.

Of course, rates could rise from current levels. But if that prospect makes you smile, remember this: a substantial rise in yields from current levels (say 200 to 300 basis points) would translate into a very substantial loss of principal for the longest-term funds (as much as 25% to 30%).

CHAPTER 13

Closed-End Bond Funds and Unit Investment Trusts (UITs)

While mutual funds constitute the most familiar part of the fund universe, there are two alternate forms of funds, and indeed, these actually antedate mutual funds. The first are closed-end funds; and the second, which reappears periodically under a variety of names, are unit investment trusts (UITs). Both of these include bond funds, as well as equity funds. Each will be discussed, briefly.

CLOSED-END BOND FUNDS

Closed-end funds constitute a somewhat arcane and specialized corner of the market for funds. At the beginning of the year 2000, there were approximately 530 closed-end funds, holding assets worth approximately $160 billion, a relatively small sum compared to the almost seven trillion dollars in open-end mutual funds. Approximately 72% of closed-end funds invest in bonds. By far the largest number invest in municipals.

This is an asset class whose popularity seems to come and go. During the 1980s, closed-end funds experienced several years of great popularity. During the 1990s, their popularity declined. In 1999, a bad year for all types of bond funds, many closed-end bond funds experienced significant declines. But some declines were particularly steep. The municipal sector virtually collapsed.

To understand why this collapse occurred, you have to understand how the structure of closed-end funds tends to magnify both gains and losses.

If you want to invest in closed-end funds, you need to first become familiar with the product, in order to know when the investment is attractive and when it is not. The questions and answers which follow describe some of the major characteristics of closed-end fixed-income funds.

How Do Closed-End Funds Differ from Mutual Funds?

Like mutual funds, closed-end funds are comprised of a diversified portfolio of a specific kind of financial asset (municipal bonds, government bonds, etc.). The portfolio is managed continuously. You can buy closed-end funds that invest in different sectors of the bond market: munis, international bonds, convertible bonds, corporate bonds, and so on, in a range of maturities.

The distinguishing characteristic of closed-end funds, however, is that the funds are sold on the major stock exchanges and trade like any ordinary stock. There are other differences between closed-end funds and mutual funds. You will recall that mutual funds are technically known as "open-end investment trusts." That means that they continually issue new shares. When investors buy shares in a mutual fund, the manager buys more securities and the fund expands. The NAV of shares of the mutual fund is determined entirely by the value of its assets.

A closed-end fund, on the other hand, issues a fixed number of shares at its inception. Since the portfolio is managed continuously, the portfolio may change. But the number of shares of the fund remains fixed. After issue, a closed-end fund trades on one of the stock exchanges. Its price is determined very much like that of any stock: namely, by the demand for that particular stock. That is an important difference between closed-end bond funds and open-end mutual funds. Moreover, and this is another major difference, the price per share of a closed-end fund usually differs from the value of the assets in the fund. If the price per share of a closed-end fund is higher than the value of the assets in the fund, the closed-end fund is said to be trading at a premium. If the price per share is lower than the value of the assets in the fund, the fund is said to be priced at a discount.

Since closed-end funds trade like stocks, on the major stock exchanges you can buy or sell closed-end funds, or track the price per share of a closed-end fund, in the same manner that you buy, sell, or track any stock. The commission structure is the same as it is for any stock. But when you look up a table that lists returns for closed-end funds, you will see the term "NAV." That term may be confusing because for closed-end funds, NAV refers not to the price per share but to the market value of the assets in the fund. You can also consider the NAV to be equivalent to the liquidation value of the assets in the fund.

In other respects, however, closed-end bond funds behave very much like open-end funds. Closed-end bond funds have a continually managed portfolio, typically consisting of 30 to 60 issues. As is the case for bond mutual funds, there is also no date at which the entire portfolio matures. Therefore, there is no date at which the price of a closed-end fund returns to par automatically, like that of an individual bond. Finally, again, as for mutual funds, the price of a closed-end bond fund fluctuates with interest rates, and those fluctuations are governed in part by the average maturity of the closed-end bond fund.

But the price fluctuations of closed-end bond funds are more complex than those of open-end mutual funds because the price of a closed-end bond fund is also partly determined by the demand for its shares. If demand is high, the share price rises, regardless of what is happening to the underlying value of the assets in the fund. In fact, at times the price of a closed-end fund and the value of the assets in the fund move in opposite directions. That is, the share price of the fund may be going up while the value of the assets in the fund is actually declining. Or the opposite may take place.

Note also that some closed-end funds are "leveraged." Since closed-end funds cannot issue more shares, they raise additional capital by selling preferred stock, commercial paper, or rights offerings. That money is then invested in additional securities. If the managers are betting correctly, this will boost interest income and therefore, potentially, total return. But if the bet is wrong, the leverage will exacerbate any decline.

Why Should Closed-End Funds Not Be Bought at the Time of Issue?

There are several different reasons. The first one is that, when a closed-end fund is issued, its initial offering price includes a hidden cost, typically between 7% and 8%. This is the so-called underwriting spread, which goes to the underwriter. This spread means that about $700 to $800 is taken out of an initial investment of $10,000. That is only the first injury to your pocketbook. Typically, once a closed-end fund starts trading, its price goes to a discount. That is to say, the price per share of the fund declines, and with it the value of your principal declines. Note that often, such a decline occurs even though the NAV—that is, the value of the assets in the fund—may not have changed at all. Why closed-end funds move to a discount after they start trading is somewhat unclear. But the existence of this phenomenon has been extensively documented. Unfortunately, brokers are most likely to tout these funds when they first come to market because this is the time that they earn the highest commission.

A second reason is that, when you buy a closed-end bond fund at the time of issue, the portfolio has usually not been constituted; the funds are sold to raise money to put together a portfolio. The manager has no money with which to buy bonds until the shares of the fund are sold. It follows, therefore, that at the time of issue, you do not know what securities will be in the portfolio. All the critical factors that determine total return for a bond fund—namely, maturity, call provisions, yield, and credit quality—are not known. Therefore, you are purchasing an unknown portfolio and yield. Finally, it may take the fund three to six months to become fully invested, and in the interim your money is likely to be parked in Treasury bills.

There is still another reason why purchasing closed-end funds at issue is not a good idea. These funds tend to become popular *after* interest rates have declined and *after* their price has gone up. The typical pattern is that, after existing closed-end funds have run up in value in a particular sector, the financial press takes notice. At that point, there is a rush to issue a lot of new closed-end funds in that sector. Brokers are eager to sell them because they earn high commissions. Buyers, eager to get in on a good thing, buy. Then the funds move to a discount.

It follows from all of the above that buying closed-end bond funds at issue seldom makes economic sense. Buying after a run-up in price has already occurred in a particular sector is a recipe for investment unhappiness and occasionally, for investment disaster.

When Should I Buy a Closed-End Fund?

Many investors purchase closed-end funds primarily as trading vehicles, that is, in order to capture a capital gain. The opportunity for profit derives from the changing size of the discount, as well as from fluctuations in the share price. When the discount narrows, or when the price of the fund moves closer to the value of the assets in the fund (that is, to the NAV), the investor realizes a profit. The ideal trade would involve buying at a wide discount to the value of the assets in the fund (the NAV) and selling when the fund moves to a premium. To realize a profit, however, the fund need only to move to a narrower discount.

This piece of advice, however, is deceptively simple. Discounts can widen rather than narrow, resulting in severe losses. This is what happened to municipal closed-end bond funds at the end of 1999. Professionals who trade closed-end bond funds develop strategies for trading those funds. For example, one leading expert, Thomas Herzfeld, suggests that before you buy any closed-end fund, you track its price for some period of time in order to determine the size of the average discount of the fund. He suggests buying only when the discount is 3% wider than the *normal* discount for that fund.

Closed-end funds occasionally become "open ended." When that happens, the price of the fund rises to equal the net asset value of the bonds in the portfolio. If the fund was purchased at a discount, that would provide a windfall profit. If, however, it was purchased at a premium (or at issue), that would result in a loss of principal. There is no certain way to predict which funds will become open ended, but it happens occasionally.

When Are Closed-End Bond Funds Attractive Vehicles for Income?

If you can buy a closed-end bond fund in the secondary market at a discount to the net value of the assets in the fund, you are, in effect, purchasing the underlying bonds for less than you would have to pay for similar bonds on the open market. If, for example, the fund is trading at a discount of 10% to the value of the underlying assets, you are, in effect, buying each dollar's worth of assets for 90 cents. That raises the net dividend yield that you will earn. Suppose, for example, that the fund you purchase at a 10% discount has a current yield of 6% based on the net asset value of the bonds in the portfolio. Your net yield, compared to the discounted price you paid, will be 6.7%. You will, moreover, be purchasing a continually managed, diversified portfolio, at an attractive commission cost since the transaction costs of buying closed-end funds trading in the secondary market are low. (Remember: the commission you pay is a stock commission.)

Also, even if you purchase a closed-end bond fund primarily for income, if it is purchased at a deep discount, total return may be boosted by capital gains resulting from a narrowing of the discount. This is likely to happen if interest rates fall. But remember that this is a two-edged sword. If interest rates rise, your investment may suffer a double whammy as the price falls for two reasons: because of rising rates, and because investors are selling.

Yield and Closed-End Bond Funds

The yield that is quoted is net investment income per share, divided by share price. That is, of course, a current yield. It is not comparable to the yield-to-maturity quoted for individual bonds; and it is not comparable to the SEC yield quoted for bond funds. It is, therefore, difficult to compare potential return of any closed-end fund to that of individual bonds or of bond funds.

Total return for a closed-end fund consists of interest income and changes in the price per share, that is, the price at which you buy and the price at which you sell a closed-end fund. There is no automatic reinvestment of dividends. If you reinvest interest income through some other vehicle, then that also becomes part of your total return.

How Can I Get Information on Closed-End Funds?

Information on closed-end funds is not reported as widely (or as conveniently) as that of other mutual funds.

If you own a closed-end fund, you can, of course, track its price the way you would track any stock. You can look up the price on any website or in your daily newspaper.

To obtain information prior to buying a closed-end fund, your best source of information is the group that originates and manages the funds. Some of the well-known groups that manage closed-end funds include Nuveen (which is particularly well known for its municipal bond funds), Van Kampen, and Merrill Lynch. You can contact the groups through a toll-free number or look up their websites. Before buying a closed-end bond fund, you would want to know:

+ The fund's average weighted maturity (and duration). As always, funds with shorter maturities (or durations) would be less volatile.
+ The credit quality of the bonds in the fund.
+ The average bond price, or the size of the average coupon. That serves as an indicator of whether the bonds in the portfolio are likely to be called. If the fund has a lot of premium bonds, that would indicate to you that bonds in the portfolio are more likely to be called than if the fund has a lot of discount bonds.
+ If the fund is leveraged or not.
+ The exchange on which the fund trades. The largest funds trade on the NYSE, which would mean greater liquidity.
+ How often the dividend is paid: some funds pay dividends quarterly, others monthly.

If a closed-end fund has been trading in the secondary market, a prospectus will usually not be available. But you can request a recent report, such as an annual or semiannual report, directly from the fund group that manages any closed-end fund that interests you. Also, be aware that closed-end funds do not routinely publish total return numbers. If you do find total return information, you need to find out whether those are derived from the price per share or the NAV.

Exhibit 13–1 shows the format of a typical newspaper listing for closed-end funds. Reading from left to right, the table lists

E X H I B I T   13–1

Format for Closed-End Bond Fund Listings

FUND NAME (SYMBOL)	STOCK EXCH	NAV	MARKET PRICE	PREM/ DISC	12 MO MARKET 7/31/00
VK Tr Inv Grd (VGM)-a	N	16.17	14.13	− 12.6	7.1
VK Value Muni (VKV)-a	N	14.37	12.50	− 13.0	6.5
Single State Muni Bond					
BlckRk CA Ins 08 (BFC)-a	N	16.49	15.00	− 9.0	5.2
BlckRk CA Inv (RAA)-a	A	14.60	13.75	− 5.8	6.2
BlckRk FL Ins 08 (BRF)-a	N	15.62	14.00	− 10.4	6.0
BlckRK FL Inv (RFA)-a	A	14.63	13.13	− 10.3	5.9
BlckRk NJ Inv (RNJ)-a	A	13.90	12.69	− 8.7	5.6
BlckRk NY Ins 08 (BLN)-a	N	15.87	14.50	− 8.6	5.8
BlckRk NY Inv (RNY)-a	A	14.51	14.00	− 3.5	6.2

+ The name of the fund
+ The NAV of one fund share: remember, that is the value of the assets in the fund
+ The price per share of the fund
+ The difference between the price of the fund and its NAV. A minus sign (−) indicates the fund is selling at a discount; a plus sign (+) that it is selling at a premium
+ The yield: remember, that is a current yield

This information is too sketchy to be useful. If a fund is trading at a discount, it might be an attractive buy. But you would need to investigate further. You would want to know how volatile the fund may be; whether it normally trades at a discount, and if so, the size of the average discount. The recommendation is to buy only if the discount is wider than the *average* discount. You would also have to find out more about the make-up of the portfolio. Be particularly cautious if the fund is trading at a premium.

To buy a fund, contact your broker. You can also buy closed-end funds from online brokers, since they are bought and sold like any other stock. The price you would pay would be the listed price, which, like that of any stock, is likely to fluctuate daily, plus the broker's commission.

SUMMARY: QUESTIONS TO ASK BEFORE BUYING A CLOSED-END FUND

Am I buying at issue? If so, what is the underwriting spread?

What is the NAV of the shares?

Is the fund selling at a premium or at a discount?

What is the average discount for this type of fund?

What kinds of bonds are in the portfolio? What is their average maturity and credit quality?

On what exchange does this fund trade?

ADDITIONAL REFERENCES

The best book on the topic remains Thomas J. Herzfeld, and Cecilia L. Gondor, *Herzfeld's Guide to Closed-End Funds* (New York: McGraw-Hill, 1993).

Coverage of closed-end funds in the printed press is sketchy. The most complete listings of closed-end funds are in *Barron's* and in the Sunday *New York Times*. *The Wall Street Journal* also publishes a table of closed-end funds on Mondays. That listing also includes loan participation funds.

A number of websites have useful information on closed-end funds. They are:

- *site-by-site.com*. This site has weekly commentary and reviews of closed-end funds and lots of links. Some of those enable you to request annual reports.
- *mutualfunds.about.com*. This site includes rankings of performance by objectives and lots of data, including return on NAV and on price for periods ranging from one to several years, recent price, whether the fund is trading at a premium or at a discount. The data is supplied by Lipper.
- *icefi.com*. This is the website of the closed-end fund association, but it is primarily a subscription service.

For detailed information on individual funds, your best source is the fund groups which manage the funds. Like open-end mutual funds, these groups have toll-free numbers, which are listed in the quarterly reviews of mutual funds published by *Barron's*. These groups also have websites, such as *nuveen.com, vankampen.com*, etc. The websites have detailed information on the individual funds, including the make-up of the portfolio, whether the funds are leveraged, whether they are selling at a discount or at a premium, market returns, and the like.

UNIT INVESTMENT TRUSTS

Unit investment trusts (UITs) represent a third type of bond fund. They are sold through brokers, either by brokerage firms or by banks, and on a commission basis, usually around 5%.

When you buy a UIT, you are purchasing a diversified portfolio of securities. But that portfolio is quite different from either a mutual fund or a closed-end fund. The key characteristic of a UIT is that, once constituted, its portfolio remains unmanaged. With few exceptions, no bonds are added or sold out of the portfolio. Because the portfolio remains unmanaged, its price should rise towards par as the UIT approaches maturity.

The portfolio of a UIT is typically much less diversified than that of a mutual fund, consisting of perhaps as few as ten issues. While the portfolio is assigned a maturity date, that date is simply the date when the longest term bond in the portfolio matures. Each of the bonds in the portfolio may actually mature at a different date, over a span of time that may last as long as ten years. Each individual issue in the UIT is also subject to call risk. As each bond matures, or is called the principal is returned to shareholders. Varying percentages of the entire portfolio must then be reinvested as the bonds mature or are called.

There are UITs for most sectors of the bond market: corporates, governments, and municipals—in a variety of maturities, from intermediate to long. Merrill Lynch, Van Kampen and Merritt, Bear Stearns, and Nuveen are major sponsors. Some municipal portfolios are insured (the entire portfolio is insured, not each individual issue). There are also single-state municipal portfolios. Sponsors of UITs generally maintain a secondary market. But selling a UIT before it matures is somewhat more cumbersome than selling a mutual fund. Particularly during market downturns, UITs can be illiquid (that is, difficult, and expensive, to sell).

Note also that while a UIT quotes two yields, a current yield and a yield-to-maturity, the YTM must be calculated with a formula that takes into account the different maturities of the bonds in the UIT. Therefore, the YTM is not comparable to the YTM quoted for individual bonds.

Brokers point to a number of features of UITs as advantages. Income is paid monthly, and since the portfolio does not change, the monthly amount is fixed. Moreover, since UITs are not actively managed, there is no annual management fee. This should theoretically result in a higher yield than for mutual funds with comparable credit ratings and maturities.

These arguments do not appear compelling. The yield advantage may be illusory or based on low credit quality. And the coupon is fixed only until the first bond matures out of the portfolio or is called. Thereafter, as various bonds mature (or are called), the monthly coupon changes. Moreover, the shareholder will have to reinvest returned principal and coupons at an unknown rate.

In addition, the portfolio is not managed. There is no protection of any kind against deteriorating credits. You are purchasing a portfolio of issues, which will not change, and not a manager.

Finally, because each UIT is unique, each portfolio must be scrutinized with some care. Since UITs are advertised on the basis of yield, some UITs play games in order to quote higher current yields. They may, for example, buy high coupon bonds which might be subject to call. Or they may buy bonds with questionable credit ratings. Municipal UITs were widely criticized after the Washington Public Power (WPPSS) default for stuffing their portfolios with bonds of the project, which ultimately defaulted. This resulted in substantial losses that were passed on directly to shareholders.

The only advantage UITs offer compared to mutual funds is that since the portfolio has a final maturity date, its price rises towards par as the various isuses in the fund near maturity. This might make UITs attractive to an investor who does not have sufficient funds to buy a diversified portfolio of individual securities but who wants to know that principal is likely to be returned in full when the fund matures.

In sum, UITs offer somewhat more diversification than individual bonds but few advantages compared to mutual funds. Because of the high initial commission, they should be considered for purchase only as long-term holdings.

SUMMARY: QUESTIONS TO ASK BEFORE BUYING A UIT

What securities does the UIT hold?

What is the maturity of the portfolio?

What is the credit quality of the portfolio?

If the portfolio is quoting a relatively high yield, are many of the bonds premium bonds? How likely is it that the bonds will be called?

What is the size of the commission?

To whom could I resell the UIT if I need to sell before the UIT matures?

Do you, the seller, stand ready to buy back the UIT? At what price?

PART FOUR

Portfolio Management

Asset allocation, that is, deciding how to divide financial assets between stocks and bonds, has become a hot topic of discussion. The extraordinary bull market in stocks of the past two decades seems to have swept away the basic principles that financial professionals had used as guideposts for generations. As a result, there are now enormous differences of opinion concerning asset allocation. At one extreme, some "experts" are now claiming that we are genuinely in a new era and that old valuation yardsticks do not apply to the "new" economy—or to the stocks that are the backbone of that new economy. These same "experts" suggest, furthermore, that the unprecedented stock market gains of the past two decades can continue for the foreseeable future and that therefore, asset allocation should consist of putting as much money as possible into stocks, with perhaps a small amount in cash to cover immediate cash needs and emergencies. At the other extreme, other "experts" are saying that stocks are extremely overvalued and that the U.S. stock market is going to undergo a nasty and possibly prolonged decline. You will notice that bonds are absent from this discussion. Indeed, bonds have become almost a forgotten asset class, except for the occasional remark that since everyone knows that in the long run bonds always have lower returns than stocks, why would anyone invest in them?

I am not going to claim that I can resolve this debate. But it may be useful to you, the reader, to review the guidelines suggested in the first edition. The main issue to be addressed is this: were the guidelines outlined in that edition valid? And if they were, are they still valid? Or, to put it differently, should you follow the "new era" pundits and put 100% of your money in stocks? Can you still make a case for bonds?

These issues will be discussed in Chapter 14. Chapter 15 will describe a number of techniques used by professional managers of bond portfolios that can be adapted by individual investors to the management of their own bond portfolios.

Asset Allocation

This chapter discusses formulating a game plan for investing. It discusses

- A model portfolio of stocks and bonds for the defensive investor
- Managing a portfolio in the retirement years

A GAME PLAN FOR INVESTING

For most investors, the foundation of any plan for investing should start with a genuine understanding of compounding. Compounding was discussed in Chapter 4. But this is so important that I am bringing up the topic once again.

Actually, anyone able to balance a checkbook can formulate and carry out an investment strategy. Anyone can accumulate assets, indeed, substantial assets. For most people, financial security is the result, not of making it big on one or more stocks, but rather, of patience, a reasonable game plan, a willingness to save some money—and time, which gives compounding a chance to work. The outsize stock market gains of the 1990s may have skewed perceptions and given you the idea that if you pick the right stocks, you can become rich, quick. No doubt some people can. Most of us won't. But those of us who did not ride the Internet

E X H I B I T   14–1

The Magic of Compounding: What Happens to an
Investment of $100 per Month Earning an 8%
Return, Compounded Monthly*

Year	Cumulative Investment	Total Value
1	$1,200	$1,245
5	6,000	7,355
10	12,000	18,335
20	24,000	59,195
30	36,000	150,252
40	48,000	353,168
50	60,000	805,362

* All dividends reinvested at 8%

boom can still accumulate significant assets for retirement, simply
by putting aside a modest sum periodically, for example, once a
month, and watching it compound. This appears thoroughly
unexciting, until you take a good look at the numbers.

Exhibit 14–1 demonstrates how much can be accumulated by
putting aside $100 a month and allowing it to compound at a rate
of return of 8% for a period of 50 years. While 50 years may appear to be a long time, it is not unreasonable for someone who
begins to set aside money at age 25, with the intention of retiring
at age 65, and hopefully, is still looking forward to a long retirement. I am using an 8% rate of return because, while that may
seem low compared to recent outsize gains in the stock market, it
has the merit of being more in line with historical rates of return
that are achievable by most investors. This table shows that such
a return, even if it appears modest, if it is consistent, over time,
will eventually grow into a significant nest egg. If you can do
better, good for you!

A MODEL PORTFOLIO FOR THE DEFENSIVE INVESTOR

Let's look at the model portfolio I suggested in the first edition of this book, written in the late 1980s. I shall quote from the first edition:

Here is the model portfolio. It should be divided as follows:

- 60 percent two-to-five-year Treasuries (I shall call this the core bond portfolio)
- 40 percent a stock mutual fund: preferably, an index fund.

This looks very boring and ultra simple. But actually, it meets every criterium for sound portfolio management. Let's consider each portion in turn.

Let's first look at the stock portion of the portfolio. I have suggested an index fund; that is, a fund that exactly duplicates a benchmark index. The most frequently used index is the Standard & Poor's 500. By its very nature, an index fund will never beat the market but it will mirror market performance almost exactly. Returns from an index fund will normally be slightly lower than the index. The difference is due to the fact that the index fund has some management expenses. An index does not.

An index fund offers a number of advantages, when compared to other types of stock funds. First of all, while you might assume that if a fund does only as well as the market, its performance will be average, think again. Historically, 70 percent of mutual funds fail to do as well as the Standard & Poor's 500. Or, to put it differently, over time, an index fund beats 70 percent of all stock mutual fund managers. Second, an index fund usually has lower expense ratios than actively managed funds. You keep more of what the fund earns. Third, index funds make fewer capital gains distributions than most stock funds. As a result, over time, a larger portion of your stock investments compounds without annual taxation. Finally, an index fund eliminates the worry that if you select the wrong mutual fund, the market may do well while your fund does not. There is no need to pick the hot manager of the year, or the decade. (The oldest, largest, and most efficiently managed index fund—i.e. with the lowest expense ratio is the Vanguard 500 index fund.)

Now let's look at the bond portion of the portfolio.

There is no need to repeat in detail what was stated in the chapter on Treasuries. But a brief review of the advantages of this core portfolio may be helpful:

♦ This maturity sector yields more than short instruments. It captures about 85 percent to 95 percent of the return available on long-term bonds, but with far less volatility (and therefore far less risk to principal) than long-term Treasuries. Indeed, as the studies quoted elsewhere have shown, over two different time periods, the first lasting about 60 years, and the second lasting about 30 years, two-to-five-year Treasuries have had higher total returns than either long-term bonds or T-bills.

♦ Such a portfolio has zero credit risk. No diversification among different kinds of securities is required since the principal of any Treasury is 100 percent safe, whether you own $10,000 or one million.

♦ For most individuals, the total return of Treasuries will probably be close to seemingly higher yielding fixed-income instruments for two reasons. First, individuals can buy Treasury securities more cheaply (that is, with lower commission costs) than any other debt instrument. In fact, if you buy through Treasury Direct, and hold to maturity, commission costs are zero. Second, a portfolio of Treasury securities is not taxable at the state and local level.

That's it. One can't imagine a portfolio that is simpler to buy and to manage. On the bond side, you eliminate credit risk entirely and a good deal of interest rate risk. On the stock side, you can stop worrying about which stocks or stock fund to buy; and when to buy. Annual expenses for managing such a portfolio are under one quarter of one percent for the stocks; zero for the bonds if you buy through Treasury Direct.

Will this approach to investing earn the highest returns possible? No, that is unlikely. But remember that this portfolio is intended for an investor who does not wish to pursue complicated strategies. Moreover, over time this portfolio should do quite well. It will beat chasing hot tips or pursuing strategies that you may not understand. At the other extreme, it will also beat keeping your money entirely in CD's.

Studies have shown that over time, the most important factor in determining total return is not which specific assets you buy (that is, not whether you buy IBM stock as opposed to General Motors), but which categories of assets you own (that is, whether you own stocks as well as bonds) . . .

Variations on the Basic Portfolio

This portfolio is not intended as a rigid recipe. Rather, it embodies a number of principles:

+ allocation among both stocks and bonds;
+ uncomplicated securities and strategies;
+ low transaction costs;
+ diversification;
+ a growth component and a stable, income producing component.

All of these combined should produce long-term growth. Moreover, such an allocation can be adapted to almost any size portfolio. Diversification is not needed for Treasuries; and the index fund is inherently diversified.

The basic portfolio can easily be altered to meet a variety of needs. Suppose you are in your thirties and you are beginning to put some money aside for retirement which seems to be forever away. You consider yourself a risk taker and want to emphasize growth, rather than preservation of capital. Fine, then switch the proportions around. Invest 40 percent of your portfolio in 2–5 year Treasuries and 60 percent in the stock index fund.

These suggestions may look somewhat timid in the light of the raging bull market in equities of the 1990s. But viewed through the lens of the 1980s, it was good advice. You may be too young to recall the stock market of the 1970s and 1980s. The Dow industrial average first reached 1,000 in 1968. Between 1968 and 1982, a period lasting about 14 years, the Dow, essentially, did not go above 1,000, although it often traded below that level. Anyone who was invested in stocks during 1973 and 1974 will remember the vicious bear market of that two-year period: the Dow declined by over 40%. Many stock funds declined by 50% or more. Some of the more aggressive growth funds (the so-called "go go" funds) declined by 90%. In August 1982, a time when stocks were despised, the stock market began its current bull run. That bull run was stopped by the crash of 1987. Initially, the Dow declined by about 35%. It took well over a year for the stock market to return to its pre-crash highs and during that period, many "experts" were issuing dire warnings of worse declines to come. The crash of 1987 now looks like a blip on most charts of stock returns. But in the late 1980s, that crash was still fresh in people's minds. And it was frightening. Stocks did not look like a sure thing at all.

If you look at the bond side of the portfolio, the 1980s were as turbulent as the equity side. Let's refer back to the history of interest rates illustrated in Chapter 3. You will remember that in 1979, interest rates started climbing steeply. They briefly touched 15% on the long bond in 1981. They subsequently declined, to approximately 8% on the long bond at the end of the 1980s. That eight-year period represents a bull market in bonds that was totally unprecedented. For the 1980s, annual returns on long-term Treasury bonds averaged approximately 12%. But during that decade, on a year-to-year basis, total return of long-term bonds was as volatile, and as hard to predict, as total returns in the stock market.

In addition to the investment backdrop of the times, the portfolio guidelines of the first edition were based on a number of concerns.

First, in spite of the enormous volatility that had prevailed in the stock market during the 1970s and 1980s, data about historical returns of financial assets was very clear that over long holding periods, stocks had higher total returns than any other financial asset, including bonds. Therefore, one of my main concerns was to encourage investors to place assets in stocks, as well as in bonds.

Another important concern, however, was based, not on historical returns of financial assets, but on personality traits. In this, I was following a distinction first made by Benjamin Graham in his classic book *The Intelligent Investor*, between a "defensive" and an "enterprising" investor. The distinction between these two types of investors is one of involvement and expertise. The enterprising investor views investing as equivalent to a business; and seeks to become as proficient as any professional. The defensive investor, on the other hand, is content to forego the highest possible rate of return in exchange for safety and freedom from concern. The enterprising investor is a very active investor; the defensive investor is more passive. Graham further made the point that being an enterprising investor does not guarantee a higher degree of success. Graham (who was a legendary investor) knew very well that it is extremely difficult to beat the market. Most of us, I think, would consider ourselves defensive investors. My portfolio suggestions were formulated for a defensive investor.

Finally, these suggestions were based on several constraints. First, I wanted to put together a portfolio comprised of both stocks and bonds that was uncomplicated enough to meet the needs of a defensive investor. The stock portion would provide the more volatile growth component. The bond portion would provide a steady income stream and a degree of safety. Therefore, for the bond component, I needed to select bonds that would provide the best combination of safety of capital and predictable returns.

Now let's return to the present. The total returns of stocks (averaging approximately 18% for the S&P 500 Index for both the 1980s and 1990s) have been unprecedented. Every previous record has been broken. The total returns of stocks during the 1990s were so high that they bumped up the average annual return of stocks for the entire century to approximately 12%, compared to 10%, at the start of the bull market, in 1982. It is worth noting that for the century, about 40% of the total return of stocks is derived from reinvesting dividends to buy additional shares. For most of the twentieth century, the dividend yield of stocks averaged approximately 5%. A dividend yield of 3% or less was regarded as a sign that stocks were unusually expensive. Currently, the dividend yield of large stocks is at a historical low of about 1%. Therefore, if stocks are to continue to have high returns, these must come from appreciation in the price of stocks, not from reinvesting dividends.

But as a result of the long bull market in stocks, investor psychology has changed dramatically, compared to the late 1980s. The mantra has become: "Buy the dips!" With the wisdom of hindsight, many commentators now view the crash of 1987 as one of the last and great buying opportunities. The issue in the mind of many investors is not how much of their portfolio to allocate to bonds, and how much to stocks, but rather, which sector of the stock market to invest in: large caps, small caps, growth, Internet, and so on. Many financial advisers now recommend a 100% equities portfolio, with perhaps a small amount in cash to meet current cash needs and emergencies. Stock dividends are viewed as unimportant. Bonds are viewed with disdain.

I don't agree; and few historians of the stock market would agree. There are a number of reasons for this.

First, if you look back over the investment returns of the twentieth century, it becomes clear that no two decades have been alike. Don't count on repeats! Periods of stellar returns alternate with periods of poor returns. Earlier in the century, several periods with stellar stock market returns namely the late 1920s, the 1950s, and the 1960s were hailed as new eras, only to be followed by long stretches of poor returns. Optimism is highest after peak stock market returns. Many historians of the stock market point to a phenomenon known as "regression to the mean." Simply put, that is the observation that economic cycles exist; that stock returns track these cycles; and that, as a result, over time, stock market gains will eventually return to historical averages. Based on this viewpoint, the returns of the 1980s and 1990s were exceptional and not sustainable. It would therefore be unrealistic to expect stock returns for the next 20 or 30 years to match the returns of the past two decades.

For these reasons, surprising as it may seem given the current optimism concerning stock returns, I would continue to suggest an asset allocation that includes bonds, as well as stocks. The exact proportions of that allocation can be varied to suit your age, and your tolerance for risk. Clearly, if you are young, or affluent, you can afford to put a higher proportion of your assets in equities.

Furthermore, unless you want to devote most of your spare time to managing your equity portfolio, I would still suggest index funds as the vehicle of choice for investing in equities; and for the reasons explained in the quote.

I could not have known in 1990 that indexing would become as popular as it did: for most of the 1990s, the S&P 500 stock fund of Vanguard had higher total returns than 80%, and during some years, 90% of professional money managers. If few professional money managers are able to outperform an unmanaged index fund year after year, what is the likelihood that the rest of us will do so on a consistent basis *over a lifetime of investing?* For that reason, I continue to believe that unless you are extremely skilled (and lucky!), for most investors, index funds remain the simplest and most efficient vehicle for investing in stocks. Moreover, today you can choose from a much broader selection of index funds than were available at the end of the 1980s, mirroring a whole range of benchmarks, such as the Wilshire (which includes the entire stock market) and indices for foreign stocks.

The Case for Bonds

The case for bonds can be stated briefly. First of all, bonds provide a steady income stream. This is particularly important now that the dividend yield on both the Standard & Poor's Index and the Dow are hovering at the 1% mark, the lowest in stock market history. Bonds, and the cash streams they generate, enable you to get through periods of subpar returns in the stock market. If you have an all-stock portfolio, and if you need cash during a period of poor stock market returns, you have no other recourse than to sell stocks at a loss. This can seriously erode the value of such a portfolio.

Secondly, the returns of bonds and stocks are not correlated. There have been long stretches in the United States (the thirties, for example, or 1968–1982) when stocks had poor returns, and bonds performed as well or better. Think of a portfolio of um-brellas and straw hats. Each has a season, but they are different seasons. Typically, a booming economy will be accompanied by a booming stock market but, possibly, rising bond yields and a weak bond market. In a weak economy, however, the stock market may sag, but declining interest rates may lead to a strong market in bonds. This was the case in the United States in the thirties. The Japanese stock and bond markets provide another more recent example. The Japanese stock market peaked in 1989, with the Nik-kei at 38,000. It subsequently declined by about 60%. In the year 2000, the Nikkei remains about 50% lower than its peak. But in the intervening decade, returns on Japanese bonds have been ex-tremely high. This historical evidence demonstrates that even though total returns in both the stock and the bond markets are unpredictable, investing in bonds as well as in stocks lowers the volatility and the total risk of a portfolio of financial assets.

So let's return to our initial question: does the bull market in stocks of the past two decades prove that an allocation of financial assets among both stocks and bonds is too timid a strategy? That is clearly for you to decide. But I would argue that for most in-vestors, particularly for investors past the age of 50, the traditional 60/40 allocation still makes a lot of sense. The issue is simply this: how much are you willing to bet on the belief that all of past financial history no longer applies? More importantly, if the new era pundits are wrong, how would the volatility of stock market returns affect your standard of living?

Managing a Portfolio in the Retirement Years

While the suggestions of the preceding section may appear too cautious, a report I recently came across suggests that it may not be conservative enough for retirees. Managing a portfolio during the retirement years poses special challenges. If you are retired, and relying for income primarily on a portfolio of financial assets, two questions become critical: How do you allocate your assets between stocks and bonds? and How much can you safely afford to withdraw on an annual basis so that you do not run out of money before you die?

Most of the literature on this topic comes up with recommendations similar to those made earlier in this chapter: continue to invest between 40% and 60% of your assets in stocks because of their historically higher return than bonds. Put the rest in bonds and cash. To meet expenses, don't spend more than 4% to 5% of your assets annually. But a recent article in a newsletter published by T. Rowe Price Associates highlighted a critical variable, namely, *the difference between actual returns and average returns*.[1] True, between 1926 and 1999, annual returns from stocks averaged 12%. But as also pointed out earlier, there have been several stretches (again 1968–1982) when returns from stocks were very low, as well as some years of large losses. The T. Rowe Price article examined the impact such events might have on the portfolio of retirees.

The starting point of this report was a hypothetical couple of retirees with a $250,000 nest egg, allocated 60% in stocks, 30% in bonds, and 10% in cash—considered a very conservative allocation nowadays. This couple is retiring in *1968*. They are planning to withdraw 8.5% the first year. Thereafter, they are planning to increase their annual withdrawals by 3% a year, to maintain purchasing power in spite of inflation, through 1998.

With hindsight, we now know that this portfolio would have produced an average annual return of 11.7% during that 30-year period. (Portfolio performance was based on actual historical returns of the Standard & Poor's 500 stock index, intermediate government bonds, and 30-day Treasury bills, between 1968 and 1998 as reported by Ibbotson Associates.) The 11.7% average annual return suggest that withdrawing 8.5% initially, with 3% annual increases, was a realistic plan.

---

1. "Determining a Realistic Spending Rate in Retirement," T. *Rowe Price Report*, Issue No. 65, Fall 1999, pp. 1–3.

Surprisingly, this turns out not to be the case. For starters, actual returns of this hypothetical portfolio (60% stocks, 30% bonds, 10% cash) averaged only 6.9% for the first 13 years. More importantly, the vicious bear market in stocks of 1973–1974 would have had a devastating impact on the portfolio. (Bear in mind that during those two years, stocks declined by over 50%.) Between 1982 and 1998, average returns subsequently skyrocketed to an annual average of 15.3%. But if our retirees had withdrawn 8.5% a year beginning in 1968, by 1981 their portfolio would have been entirely wiped out by the combination of the poor stock market conditions and the annual withdrawals.

How could our retirees have avoided this disaster? Clearly, our retirees had no control over stock market returns or bond market returns. A more conservative annual withdrawal policy—that is, withdrawing 6% annually—is one component of the answer. But that in itself would have been insufficient to prevent their assets from being depleted by the vicious bear market in stocks of 1973–1974.

A surprising answer is that a more conservative asset allocation (25% stocks, 40% bonds, 35% cash) would have made a dramatic difference. *Average* annual returns would have been much lower over the 30-year period. But assets would have lasted much longer because in its worst year, the steepest decline of the entire portfolio would have amounted to only 2%. The startling conclusion was that a more conservative asset allocation would have supported initial withdrawals of 6%, increased by 3% annually, through 1998.

This report was based on extensive simulations of a wide range of economic scenarios and returns. The conclusion was that *retirees should focus first on their income needs* and only secondarily come up with an asset allocation strategy that has a good chance of supporting that income. The important point to bear in mind is that a more aggressive portfolio strategy, with a high proportion of stocks, does not guarantee that the portfolio will continue to grow throughout the retirement years: a tough stock market environment in the early years can be devastating. Paradoxically, a more conservative approach, allocating a larger proportion to bonds and cash, enables the retiree to make larger annual withdrawals, relatively speaking, because there is more confidence that the portfolio will not be wiped out by a couple of bad stock market years.

If you are retired, and if you depend for your daily income requirements on a portfolio of financial assets, bear in mind that money will be needed regardless of what is happening in the stock and bond markets. Although elswhere I have stressed a total return approach to investing in bonds, in retirement, cash flow becomes paramount: even if the price of a bond declines because current interest rates are climbing, the semiannual interest income will continue to be generated. But that is not true of the stock portfolio. At the end of 1999, the dividend yield of the Standard & Poor's 500 index was approximately 1%. Therefore, to generate income from a portfolio of stocks, you would need to sell shares. That would be fine if the stock market were to continue to rise annually by more than 18% a year, as it did during the 1980s and 1990s. But if the stock market ceases to generate outsize returns, given the current dividend yield, even a few years *of an essentially flat stock market* would severely deplete the stock portion of the portfolio.

Obviously, ultra-cautious strategies are not for everyone. More affluent individuals can afford to be more aggressive. The T. Rowe Price report, however, raises genuine concerns, even though its point of view is unfashionable. Nowadays, anyone with a calculator or a spreadsheet can come up with rosy scenarios based on stock prices increasing at a minimum 12% a year, no more bear markets ever again, and inflation never rearing its ugly head. But if cash flow from financial assets is needed to pay the rent and put groceries on the table (never mind for vacations and medical care), then a less rosy view of the future might be prudent and warranted. Unfortunately, life's bills do not always coincide with stock market peaks.

Let me make one more point concerning saving for retirement. Brokerage firms and mutual fund groups have spawned a virtual growth industry to help you determine how much you need to save in order to maintain a desired level of purchasing power in your retirement years. You answer a questionnaire or click onto a website and plug in numbers: current income, current savings, desired level of purchasing power in your retirement years. You get back a list of numbers which tell you how much you should be saving every year to achieve your desired goals.

These projections, in turn, are based on assumptions built into a model concerning total return on financial assets, as well as future levels of inflation. So bear in mind that, particularly if you are still in your 30s and 40s, the calculations of saving and spending may cover a 50-year span. Therefore, as was pointed out in the section on future value in Chapter 4, make sure that the assumptions underlying the calculations are spelled out very clearly and appear realistic. Furthermore, bear in mind that over a 50-year period, even a difference as small as 1/2 of 1% can make a very significant difference in the final numbers.

For most individuals, the main difficulty in setting up a portfolio such as the one I suggest is psychological. You will have a thousand objections. You may not believe, in spite of overwhelming evidence to the contrary, that an unmanaged stock portfolio (that is, an index fund) will achieve better results than 70% to 80% of active managers, including fund managers. (If you still need convincing, next time you look at a survey of mutual fund returns, check the percentage of managers that have done better than the index fund.) The Internet, moreover, with its proliferation of financial websites, and the emphasis on active management (you too can make 100% next month if you pick the right growth stock) is making this situation even worse. Investing in an index fund doesn't give you many bragging rights. And owning bonds for the long run may appear stodgy, particularly at a time when interest rates appear low, compared to even a few years ago, but particularly compared to the recent outsize returns of the stock market. But then, look again at Table 14–1, on compounding 8% a year for 50 years, and then go out and have fun.

Finally, I can't resist passing along a couple of dumb (but tried and true) rules. For many old hands, the first rule for making money is not to lose money. The second rule is not to forget the first.

You have probably heard of both of these rules. But what do they really tell you? The answer to that question might be called the arithmetic of loss.

Suppose, for example, you lose 50% of your investment. How much do you have to earn to make up for that loss? No, the answer is not 50%. It is 100%. If you are not convinced, calculate that in dollars. Suppose you have a $10,000 investment, and it declines by 50%. It is then worth only $5,000. A 50% gain gets you back only to $7,500. Your money has to double for your investment to be worth $10,000 again. And at that point, you have merely returned to the starting point. You have not earned anything additional.

ADDITIONAL REFERENCES

Two classic books that deal with the stock market and portfolio allocation are:

> Benjamin Graham, *The Intelligent Investor*. This book has had numerous editions. Try to get one dating from before 1950, because more recent editions have been updated by persons other than Ben Graham.

> Burton Malkiel, *A Random Walk Down Wall Street*. Again, this has had many editions. The latest one, in paperback, was issued in June 2000.

You might also want to take a look at *Valuing Wall Street* by Andrew Smithers and Stephen Wright (McGraw-Hill, 2000). This book is an in-depth discussion of asset allocation, highlighting the risks of investing in stocks and the case for bonds, particularly for investors nearing retirement age or for retirees.

CHAPTER 15

Management of Bond Portfolios

This chapter discusses

+ Different portfolio structures: the bullet portfolio, laddering, the barbell portfolio
+ How to spot undervalued bonds using yield spreads
+ Swaps
+ Managing a bond portfolio for total return
+ The main differences among par, premium, and discount bonds

Any investment in bonds starts with a number of questions: What is the ultimate use of the money? What is my time frame? Can I afford to lose any part of my investment? For investments in bonds or in bond funds: Should the money be in taxable or in a tax-exempt securities? To answer these questions, you also need to decide what the ultimate use of the money you are investing is going to be: Is it income? capital preservation? growth?

HOW SHOULD YOU STRUCTURE YOUR PORTFOLIO?

Throughout the book, I have recommended that you stick to intermediate maturities for the greater part of your bond portfolio.

For investors who are buying bonds primarily as a source of steady income or to lower the volatility of their portfolio, the intermediate sector, in the long run, has historically, been the best choice. But depending on your objectives, there are a variety of strategies you can use to maximize returns.

This chapter will introduce a number of concepts that are used by professionals in the management of large bond portfolios and that can be adapted by individual investors in the management of their own bond portfolios to meet specific objectives.

"Maturity Matching," or the "Bullet Portfolio"

If you are saving for a specific purpose and the money will be needed in less than a year, and if your resources are limited, then your options are equally limited. You have to confine your choices to instruments that guarantee that principal will not fluctuate in value. That limits you to money market funds, CDs, or short-term instruments such as T-bills.

You might wonder why it is not advisable to buy longer-term bonds with higher yields and enjoy these yields until you need the money. There are two reasons. First, you cannot be certain that you will recover the entire principal when you need it because you do not know where interest rates will be when you want to sell. Also, as explained in Chapter 2, commission costs are particularly high when you sell small lots. Brokers say that small investors get killed by commissions when they sell.

However, if the intended use goes out somewhat further in time, say between two and ten years, then you have a different alternative, which professionals call "maturity matching." (This is also called a "bullet" portfolio.) You would buy a security which will mature at the time principal is needed. Typical intended uses include saving for retirement, for a down payment on a home; and for a child's college education. Buying securities that will mature at the time the money is needed enables you to go out further along the yield curve and therefore to buy securities that are higher yielding than the shortest cash equivalents (assuming a normal upward-sloping yield curve). At the same time, the bullet structure eliminates the risk that principal will have declined in value due to rising interest rates at the time that principal is needed.

A bullet portfolio does not dictate which instruments you should choose. If, for example, the money is needed in five years, you might buy a five-year Treasury note, a five-year pre-refunded muni, a five-year bank CD, or a five-year Treasury zero. If rates seem particularly attractive (that is, high), then the zero is an attractive option since there is no reinvestment risk.

Another alternative for longer term investors would be to use what is known as a "weighted maturity" structure. This type of structure would be appropriate for a large portfolio of bonds. And it can be varied to suit your needs. The basic idea behind such a structure is that a variety of maturities are selected. But generally, you would choose a combination of maturities whose duration is close to the expected target date when you would use the money. This would protect the bond portfolio against a major erosion of the value of principal. And weighting the maturities would enable you to take advantage of attractive buy points in the yield curve. The selection can be tailored to your preferences and needs, in any desired combination. One possibility, for example, would be to overweight the maturity sector that corresponds to the time the money is needed. Or an investor requiring the highest possible level of income might want to overweight both long-term bonds and pre-refunded shorter bonds.

Laddering

Several more formal portfolio structures have been developed which are variations of "maturity weighting."

A very conservative approach to portfolio structure is called "laddering." Laddering involves dividing your money among several different bonds with increasingly longer maturities. You might buy, for example, a one-year bond, a three-year bond, and a five-year bond. You would put approximately equal amounts of money in each bond. As each bond matures, you would replace it with a bond equal to the longest maturity in your portfolio, in this case the five-year bond.

This is how your portfolio would evolve:

♦ Initial portfolio: beginning of year one. You buy a one-year bond, a three-year bond, and a five-year bond.
Average weighted maturity of the portfolio: three years.

♦ Year two: the one-year bond matures. You replace it with a five-year bond. But your older bonds are now one year closer to maturity. You now have a two-year bond, a four-year bond, and a five-year bond. Average weighted maturity of the portfolio: three years.

♦ End of year three: your three-year bond matures. You replace it with a five-year bond. You now have a two-year bond, three-year bond, and a five-year bond. Average weighted maturity of the portfolio: three years.

A laddered portfolio is not limited to the maturities described above. You can build a ladder to correspond to somewhat longer durations and include longer maturities. But the ladder structure has a number of advantages. Replacing maturing bonds regardless of the level of interest rates is similar to "dollar cost averaging" in the stock market. At the same time, laddering protects you against a variety of risks. Keeping the average weighted maturity of your portfolio somewhat short protects the principal value of your portfolio against downside risk. So does redeeming your bonds as they mature since you are redeeming at par. Finally, if rates have gone up, you can invest maturing bonds at higher rates and boost your income.

Laddering is also flexible enough to enable you to choose a structure appropriate to your needs. If, for example, you are investing for capital appreciation or for income, you would typically choose a ladder with a somewhat longer maturity structure. You might then buy a combination of two-year, three-year, five-year, seven-year, and ten-year maturities. The average maturity of such a portfolio is about half that of the longest maturities. If, on the other hand, you are extremely risk-averse and you are mainly concerned with protecting your principal against erosion, you would structure your ladder to have a shorter average weighted maturity such as the one described earlier.

The online broker *E*Trade* now includes software on its website that automatically enables you to structure a ladder of bonds according to your specifications. The software calculates the average weighted maturity and duration of the portfolio; and lays out its cash flows. If this feature is successful, it will probably be the precursor of similar software on the websites of other online brokers.

The Barbell Portfolio

This is another variation of "maturity weighting" which is more aggressive than laddering.

A barbell portfolio derives its name from the fact that approximately half of the portfolio is in short-term bonds (under two years) and the other half in long-term securities (20 to 30 years). This portfolio does not include any intermediate maturities. But the combination of long and short maturities produces a portfolio that has an intermediate average weighted maturity. Income from this type of portfolio would generally be lower than you would receive if you just bought intermediate maturities.

Institutional investors go to a barbell structure primarily if they think interest rates are about to decline at the long end. If that happens, the longer term bonds appreciate in value. If they have guessed correctly, this gives them the opportunity to boost total return by selling the longer term bonds and "realizing" the capital gains. If they are wrong, at least they would have hedged their bets because the shorter maturities act as a cushion.

Of course, it is always extremely difficult to forecast interest rates. For individual investors, the barbell structure makes the most sense if you want to concentrate your bond portfolio at the long end (for higher yield). Including a large chunk of securities at the short end hedges your bets. But you should be aware that this strategy can backfire. Suppose, for example, that short-term rates drop and long-term rates rise. This happens whenever the yield curve becomes steeply upward sloping, with long-term rates rising and short-term rates declining. At such times, a barbell portfolio suffers a double whammy. The principal value of the long-term securities declines. Simultaneously, yields in the short-term sector also decline.

TAKING ADVANTAGE OF CHANGES IN THE LEVELS OF INTEREST RATES

The portfolio structures discussed up to this point match the maturities of a total bond portfolio to specific financial objectives. But, as we know, interest rate levels go up and down; and with those changes, the value of a bond portfolio goes up and down. Institutional investors have developed strategies to try to take advantage of changes in the level of interest rates in order to boost total return. If you follow the credit markets closely, you too can use similar strategies. Let's briefly describe them.

Finding Undervalued Bonds Using Yield Spreads

Different sectors of the bond market are not always in sync. At any given period, some sectors of the bond market may be undervalued compared to other sectors of the bond market. Sectors become cheap for a variety of reasons. A large increase in supply of one sector of the bond market (a large supply of corporate or of municipal bonds, for example) leads to a rise in yields in that sector. Also, periodically, some sectors of the bond market fall into disfavor. Again, that leads to a rise in yields in those sectors. Two examples that come to mind are the collapses that occurred in the junk bond market in 1989 and 1990, and the panic that occurred in the bonds of emerging markets in 1998. The reverse is also true. If demand increases in a particular sector, yields fall in that sector. An example of that would be the so-called flight to quality buying of Treasuries that occurs when the stock market declines precipitously.

A tool you can use for finding undervalued bonds is yield spreads: that is, the difference between yields in a given sector and Treasuries with comparable maturities. If the spread widens (that is, if the spread becomes larger), then a bond may be undervalued. Finding undervalued bonds has two advantages. You can earn higher interest income. Also, if you are right, as spreads move back towards normal, your undervalued bond goes up in value. Professionals use extraordinarily detailed data to track yield spreads. While much of this data is not available to the public, there is some readily available information that you can use.

Basic yield spread information can be found daily in the financial pages of major newspapers as well as on financial websites. To find this type of information, you would look either for tables that list key rates; or for graphs that contrast yield curves in different sectors of the bond market. Exhibit 15–1 zeroes in on two of the key rates that you would have seen on February 19, 2000.

First, let's define these rates.

• The 30-year T-bond is, of course, the YTM of the
   bellwether (that is, the most recently issued) long bond.

E X H I B I T   15–1

30-yr. T-bond	6.15
Municipal bonds	6.20

♦ The rate listed under municipal bonds is the average yield of a benchmark index of long-term municipal bonds compiled by *the Bond Buyer.*

These rates would have been listed along with several other rates such as rates on T-Bills and Notes; and perhaps corporate bonds. I zeroed in on the rates in Exhibit 15–1 because they show an extraordinary situation: the yield listed for a long-term benchmark index of muni bonds (6.20%) is actually *higher* than the yield listed for the Treasury's long bond (6.15%).

You can compare the two yields simply by subtracting the muni yield from the Treasury yield. Normally, the yield on the Treasury bond is, of course higher than that of the muni bond. On February 19, 2000, however, the yield of the Treasury's long bond was actually lower (by five basis points) than the yield quoted for the muni bond index. Professionals usually gauge the spread by using ratios. To determine the ratio between Treasury yields and muni yields, divide the muni yield (here, 6.20%) by the long bond yield (here, 6.15%). On February 19, 2000, the resulting ratio is above 100%.

This is an amazing situation because historically, munis have yielded somewhere between 80% and 90% of Treasuries under "normal" (by historical standards) conditions. If the 30-year long bond is 6.20%, then you would expect the muni index, yielding 85% of Treasuries, to stand at 5.27%, approximately 88 basis points lower than the Treasury's long bond.

The ratio between munis and Treasuries changes as a result of a variety of factors, including proposed changes in the tax laws, as well as current supply and demand factors. In the past, any ratio above 85% was taken as an indication that for most individuals in higher tax brackets, munis were reasonably attractive compared to Treasuries. A ratio of 90% was usually regarded as a buying opportunity because any investor in a tax bracket above 15% would earn more on the muni on a net-after-tax basis. A ratio of 100% is dramatic. To an investor in a 28% tax bracket, for example, the muni yield of 6.20% is equivalent to a taxable yield of approximately 8.61%; to an investor in the 39% bracket, to a taxable yield of 10.20%. Either of these two yields is dramatically higher than what was available on the same day in any of the taxable sectors of the bond market, except for junk or emerging market debt. (To be totally accurate, it should be noted that for approximately one year prior to this date, munis had been yielding close to 95% of Treasuries.) In other words, munis had been looking like screaming buys, or very cheap, for over one year. This is a classic example of what happens to an asset that has become unpopular.

There is one other instance when muni yields were higher than Treasuries. In 1986, a proposed change in the tax laws led to a momentary panic in the muni market. As a result, for a few months yields of munis were actually 15% *higher* than those of Treasuries. The panic in the muni market turned munis into bargains. The basic arithmetic is simple. If yields of munis are 15% higher than those of Treasuries and subsequently return to a more normal level (for example, munis yielding 85% of Treasuries), that means yields of long-term munis will decline by approximately 30%. Therefore, prices will rise by a similar amount (30%)—a dramatic possibility for capital gains in what is normally a rather sleepy sector of the bond market. In fact, in 1986, some managers of institutional accounts bought munis (rather than corporates) for two reasons: first, because their yield was higher than Treasuries; and second, because they anticipated that if ratios returned to a more normal level, the muni bonds would appreciate in value. This in fact is what occurred. This type of buying is known as "crossover" buying.

In 1999, one reason for the unusually high yields in the muni market can be found, not in the bond market, but rather, in the equity market. Individual investors were selling municipal bonds (there were large net outflows from municipal bond funds) and buying stocks. This trend continued well into 2000. But another factor may also have contributed to this unusual ratio. Because the Fed had announced buybacks of the long bond, the perception became widespread that a shortage of these bonds would develop. This, in turn, caused a rise in demand for the long bond, and as a result, lower yields. If that situation continues, it would be more appropriate to compare the yield of the benchmark index of long-term munis to the yield of 20-year Treasury bonds. That yield would be about 25 to 30 basis points higher than those of the 30-year bond. As an example, as this book is going to press, on August 17 of 2000, my newspaper lists the following yields:

- 30-yr. T-bonds   5.74
- 20 yr. T-bonds   6.05
- Municipal bonds   5.76

At these levels, municipal bonds yield about 100% of 30-year Treasuries and 95% of 20-year Treasuries, which means that, based on either ratio, they are still cheap. The relatively high yields in that sector (compared, for example, to other taxable or even to junk bonds—on a net-after-tax basis) provide an opportunity for higher income, and possibly, for some capital appreciation. At worst, these relatively high yields should provide a cushion if yields were to rise in the Treasury market.

Another good example of changing yield spreads has occurred repeatedly in the junk bond market. In that sector, spreads have become almost a contrary indicator. Before junk bonds became a household word in the 1970s and early 1980s, yield spreads between Treasuries and junk were about 400 basis points. As their popularity increased, yield spreads narrowed to about 200 basis points. The narrowing spread was a signal to alert buyers that the yield of junk bonds was no longer high enough to compensate for their high default risk. Thereafter, the junk bond market crashed. At the beginning of 1991, the spread had widened to an unprecedented 700 to 1,200 basis points (depending on which index you consulted). At that point, the very wide spread pointed to a probable buying opportunity. And indeed, a huge rally ensued. In 1998, spreads narrowed as junk bonds once again became wildly popular. Once again, junk bonds subsequently tanked.

Professional money managers rely on yield spreads to determine which sectors of the bond market might be undervalued at any particular time. Since their transaction costs are very low, they often seek to profit from imbalances between sectors that would be uneconomic for individual investors. But the kinds of imbalances described above are wide enough so that alert individual investors can take advantage of them.

Even if you do not use spreads as guides for exploiting undervalued sectors of the bond market, an awareness of spreads gives you a good idea of how attractive—or how risky—any sector of the bond market may be at any given time. The key is to track the spread to Treasuries: a widening spread indicates prices are getting cheaper; a narrowing spread, that prices are rising.

Changes in the Shape of the Yield Curve

As explained in Chapter 5, the yield curve is the most basic tool for determining buy points for any particular security. For much of the last two decades, attractive attractive buy points for Treasuries have been in the two-to-five-year maturity range; and for munis, in the five-to-ten-year range. These short to intermediate sectors have captured about 90% of the yield available on long-term instruments, but with far lower volatility.

Even during that time period, however, significant anomalies occurred. If you get into the habit of comparing yields, anomalies become readily apparent. Between 1988 and 1989, for example, the Treasury yield curve became steeply inverted. Yields on two-to-five-year Treasuries climbed to above 9% for a brief period of time. The muni yield curve failed to invert as steeply. If, during that period, you had wanted to invest at the short end, and if you had checked the yield curve both of Treasuries and of munis, with the exception of investors in the highest tax brackets, the net-after-tax yield of Treasuries would have been far higher than that of munis. This made two-to-five-year Treasuries doubly attractive: you could buy the safest instruments and realize a higher yield—an unusually attractive opportunity.

Historical Data

Allow me again to quote from the first edition of this book:

> If you have some basic information concerning historic rates of return, just reading the daily financial press will tell you on a relative basis which sectors appear to provide good value. For example, 30-year Treasuries have seldom yielded above 9% for very long periods (with the notable exception of 1979 to 1982, when they reached up to 15%). A yield above 9% (again for Treasuries) is seldom available for maturities of two years or above.

At the current time, yields of 9% are available only on very low quality credits, if at all. I would probably have to change the preceding statement to: if you see yields on Treasuries rising to 8%, no matter what the pundits are currently saying, buy! Note that relatively high yields on Treasury zeros are doubly attractive because those yields include reinvestment rates, and they are guaranteed if you hold to maturity. To put that in perspective, remember that the historic rate of return on stocks was about 10% until the current bull market in stocks.

Swaps

When you swap a bond, you trade a bond for a different bond, rather than for cash proceeds. During the 1970s, swaps used to be an annual ritual for many holders of long-term bonds. These swaps were usually done for the purpose of generating a tax loss. They represented a means of recouping partially the erosion of principal that resulted from annually rising interest rates, or, as some Wall Street wags used to put it, a means of making lemonade out of lemons.

During the 1980s, most holders of long-term bonds had capital gains, rather than capital losses, and for that reason the annual rite of tax selling of bonds diminished significantly. Note also that significantly lower income tax brackets (39% for the top bracket as compared to 70% in the 1970s) reduced the value of tax losses, even when they did exist. But dismal returns in the bond market during 1994 and 1999 revived the popularity of swaps for tax losses. Note also that there are other reasons for swapping than generating tax losses. Bonds may be swapped:

- To upgrade credit quality (a good time for that is when yield spreads between credit ratings narrow)
- To increase dividend income (either by extending maturities or by lowering credit quality)
- To take advantage of anticipated changes in interest rate levels (going shorter or longer along the yield curve)

Any of these swaps might be viewed at different times as improvements of the basic bond portfolio and as a means of increasing total return.

Whatever the purpose of the swap, however, there are good swaps and bad swaps. The chief difficulty in evaluating swaps is that transaction costs are not obvious. When you swap individual bonds, prices are usually quoted net so that the actual commission cost is hidden. On a large trade, for long-term bonds, you should assume that commission costs will equal perhaps 2% to 3% of the value of principal, that is, $2,000 to $3,000 per $100,000.

There may also may be costs to a swap in addition to the commission. To evaluate a swap, you need to compare the total par value of the bonds that are being swapped; the annual coupon interest income; the credit quality of the issues involved; and the maturity of the bonds. Suppose, for example, that you own a $25,000 par value municipal bond, rated A+, with a 20-year maturity and a 7% coupon. You receive annual dividend income of $1,750. Further suppose that you are offered a swap for this bond. Costs of the swap would include any of the following:

+ You are offered a bond with a lower credit rating (say, B+).
+ Coupon income declines by $100 a year.
+ The par value of the potential swap is lower than the par value of the bond you own (say, $22,000 compared to $25,000).
+ You are offered a swap which lengthens maturity to 22 years.

Any of these represents a cost. To evaluate whether or not to do the swap, you need to compare all of the cash flows of the two bonds; their maturity; and their credit quality.[1]

Another wrinkle to consider when doing a swap are some of the tax considerations. Swaps for generating tax losses are disallowed if they run afoul of the "wash sale" rule. The basic rule is that you cannot buy back the same security that you sell for a tax loss for at least 30 days. But this is a barebones formulation of the wash sale rule. To be certain, consult a tax accountant because wash sale rules can be complex.

---

1. Note: for an in-depth discussion of swaps, see Sidney Homer and Martin Leibowitz, *Inside the Yield Book* (Englewood Cliffs, N.J.: Prentice-Hall, 1972), pp. 78–96.

Finally, note that swaps need not be limited to individual bonds: you can also swap bond funds to generate tax losses. The costs of swapping bond funds are easier to determine, particularly if you are using no-load bond funds. You can swap two funds that are similar (for example, sell an intermediate fund, swap into a long-term bond fund, or vice-versa) without significantly altering your position. But because the two funds are not the same, you have not run afoul of the wash sale rule. If you want to swap bond funds, however, you need to be aware of some additional wrinkles. Because bond funds generate monthly interest income, that can extend the wash sale rule to 60 (not 30) days. Note also that mutual fund groups may restrict the number of annual trades they allow. It may be worth it to you, however, to swap between fund groups if that generates significant tax savings.

MANAGING A BOND PORTFOLIO FOR TOTAL RETURN

As was explained in the sections on bond yields and total return, managing for total return involves taking into account all aspects of a bond's total return: namely, transaction costs, capital gains (or losses); and reinvestment rates. This implies a strategy that minimizes transaction costs, maximizes reinvestment rates, and preserves capital.

The following is a summary of some guidelines that will maximize total return:

- To minimize transaction costs, comparison shop. Buy Treasuries at auction. Buy munis at issue when you can.
- Buy maturities and securities with low spreads: that means intermediate maturities, and high quality credits.
- Buy and hold rather than trade. Commission costs are particularly high when you sell.
- As a corollary, if you are investing new money in bond funds, stick to no-loads, with low expense ratios, and no 12b-1 plans.
- If you are investing in securities other than Treasuries, always check the yield against Treasuries of comparable

maturities, and only purchase if the spread to Treasuries is high enough to warrant the additional risk.

♦ Some securities are bought most economically and efficiently through funds: for example, mortgage-backed bonds, junk bonds, and international bonds.

♦ If you are buying individual bonds, the longer you extend maturities, the higher the credit quality you should require.

♦ If you are investing large sums, don't buy smaller lots. It is preferable to buy lots that are at least $25,000. Buying too many small lots raises transaction costs, both when you buy and particularly if you resell.

♦ If you are investing for capital appreciation, over long holding periods reinvestment rates are particularly important. This is because, as mentioned before, over long holding periods, compounding, through interest-on-interest, constitutes the largest part of total return. Boosting reinvestment rates results in higher compounded interest income. To reinvest at higher rates, consider sweeping reinvested interest income into higher-yielding bond funds (for example, intermediate or long-term bond funds) rather than into money market funds. Also consider sweeping interest income from bonds or from bond funds into equity index funds. (This is a strategy that has been adopted by some pension funds. It represents a form of dollar cost averaging into stocks, and can boost returns from a bond portfolio.)

♦ If you are risk-averse, for most of your bond portfolio, two-to-five-year Treasuries and five-to-ten-year munis will provide the best combination of risk and return.

Discounts vs. Premium Bonds

In a number of sections, the disadvantages and advantages of discounts versus premiums were mentioned. Again, since this comes up so often, a summary may be helpful:

For instruments with long-term maturities, bonds selling at a premium usually have higher yields than either par or discount bonds. The higher coupon also provides both a high cash flow,

E X H I B I T   15–2

What Should I Invest In?

Cash equivalents	*Short-Term Uses* (1 to 5 years)
Money Market funds (Taxable)	T-Notes
Money Market funds (Tax-exempt)	T-Zeros
T-Bills	Pre-refunded Munis
CDs	Munis up to 5 years
	CMOs (PACs and TACs)
Long-Term Uses (*more than 5 years*)	
(for taxable income)	*Long-Term Uses* (*more than 5 years*)
T-bonds	(Tax-deferred accounts)
Intermediate or Long Munis	Taxable Zeros (or zero bond funds)
	CMOs—companion or Z tranches
High Cash Flow (current income)	GNMA Bond funds
Premium Munis	Long-Term Bonds: Federal Agencies or
CMOs (PACs and TACs)	High-Quality Corporates
Closed-End Bond Funds (bought at a	Long-Term or High-Yield Taxable Bond
discount)	Funds
To Set Up a Retirement Annuity	*For Call Protection* (*or to lock in yields*)
I (Savings) Bonds	Deep discounts
Zeros—maturing in successive years	Zeros
To make interest rate bets	*For Protection against Inflation*
Zeros	Inflation-Indexed Treasuries
	I (Savings) Bonds
For Capital Appreciation (*Speculative*)	
Junk Bonds (and bond funds)	*To Fund a Child's College Education*
Emerging Markets Bonds (and bond	I and EE (Savings) Bonds
funds)	Muni Zeros
	To Hedge against a Falling Dollar
	International Bonds (or bond funds)

and a cushion in the event interest rates rise. The chief disadvantage of premium bonds is that in the event interest rates drop, they are more likely to be called. Before buying any bond selling at a high premium, be particularly careful in checking call provisions since an early and unexpected call could result in a significant loss of principal. In addition, if interest rates decline substantially, premium bonds generally do not appreciate as much as par or discount bonds.

If you are buying long-term bonds, discounts are more interest rate sensitive. In the event that interest rates decline, they will appreciate more in value than either par or premium bonds. Bonds selling at a deep discount also provide a form of call protection because they are less likely to be called if the coupon is very low. Also, you are more certain to earn the quoted YTM on those bonds than on premiums since a greater portion of the total return is locked in as a capital gain. This, however, is an advantage primarily if rates are relatively high.

In general, investors looking for some capital appreciation and maximum growth would favor discounts, whereas those looking for high cash flow and price stability would favor premiums.

What Bonds Should I Buy?

Elsewhere in the book, specific uses were suggested for fixed-income instruments as they were analyzed. Exhibit 15–2 pulls together and summarizes investment choices and alternatives for specific purposes.

Conclusion

I began work on this book in 1999 and we are going to press sometime in September of 2000.

The first edition of this book ended with two separate conclusions. The first was written when this book was initially published. The second was added when a paperback edition appeared. These conclusions provide a useful time capsule on the state of the bond market during each of those periods.

The first conclusion was dated October 1991. At that time, yields on long-term bonds had come down from the peak levels reached in 1982, to about 8% on the long bond. Taxable money market funds were yielding about 5.5%. Investors who had purchased bonds with long maturities were probably very happy. Those who had invested in shorter term paper, or who needed to reinvest new money, probably considered interest rates available at the time to be low, compared to those available just a few years earlier. Nonetheless, my advice was to stick to short or intermediate bonds, based on studies that had shown that over long holding periods, Treasuries with two-to-five-year maturities, and munis in the five-to-ten-year range provided the best combination of risk and return. In retrospect, it would appear that I was somewhat too spooked by the extreme volatility of long-term bonds during the 1980s. If you still own long-term bonds issued at that time (if they have not been called away), you are probably still smiling.

The second conclusion was written in November of 1994. I noted that the preceding three years had witnessed dramatic ups and downs in interest rates. The long bond had reached a low of 5.73% in September of 1993. Even more striking was the fact that at the same time, T-bill yields had fallen to below 3%. But those declines had come to a sudden halt in October of 1993, when the Fed started raising rates. Before 1994 ended, the Fed raised rates seven different times. And at the end of 1994, all sectors of the bond market had experienced dramatic price declines. Anyone who owned GNMAs or long-term bond funds in 1994 will remember that year with pain. My advice at that time looks a little better. I continued to suggest that, for new money, you should invest in short to intermediate securities. But I also suggested that if you held long-term bonds or bond funds, you should not panic because, after all, total return is a combination of interest income plus changes in the value of principal. In the short term, the dramatic declines in the bond market of 1994 resulted in dismal returns for that year. But, reinvesting to take advantage of the higher rates and compounding would smooth out the bumps over time. The bond market did recover, and the performance of both bonds and bond funds improved over the next several years.

I started updating this book in 1999. It is an odd coincidence that 1994 and 1999 were the two worst years to own bonds of the entire decade of the 1990s. The difference, of course, between 1994 and 1999 is that 1999 (and the beginning of 2000) marked the fifth year of the greatest bull market in equities of the century, making any decline in the value of bonds, the traditional safe harbor of investors, particularly painful. Moreover, the past two and a half years have been extremely volatile for bonds. Between the end of 1998 and the beginning of 2000, interest rates on the long bond went up by approximately 200 basis points, only to promptly go down 100 basis points during the first quarter of 2000.

The year 2000 has been full of other surprises for the bond market. The big story has been the perception that the supply of 30-year Treasury bonds is shrinking. This has led to a significant decline in yields for the long bond, from 6.75% at the beginning of the year, to approximately 5.75% as this book is going to press. As a result, many now view the ten-year bond as the bellwether bond, and this may now be the most widely traded Treasury bond. The decline in yields was most unexpected because it occurred in spite of the fact that the Federal Reserve Bank was raising interest rates, six times at last count. In comparison, when the Fed raised interest rates in 1993–1994, interest rates went up across the entire yield curve, and all sectors of the bond market suffered steep price declines.

The recent decline in yields of Treasuries was accompanied by declines in interest rates in other sectors. But a number of sectors have lagged. Municipal bond yields have declined; but intermediate and long municipal yields remain at between 95% and 100% of Treasuries. That means that on a relative basis, they are still undervalued. Bonds of emerging markets continue to be standouts. The spread of emerging market debt to Treasuries has narrowed from 1,200 basis points at the height of the 1998 debt crisis to approximately 550 basis points, even less for certain countries such as Mexico. You have to ask yourself, at those levels, are you being compensated for the risk? On the other hand, spreads of junk bonds to Treasuries are widening. Some junk bonds are now yielding 13%. Some analysts view this as a sign that an economic slowdown may be on the horizon. The inversion in the yield curve may also be pointing in the same direction. But other analysts view these high yields on junk bonds as a buying opportunity, particularly because junk bonds have performed poorly for the past two years.

While all sectors of the bond market have not participated in the rally by an equal amount, so far, the year 2000 has been a good one for holders of bonds. After the dismal returns of 1999, holders of bonds must be feeling better. As you would expect, the best performers have been zero coupon bonds (and funds) and closed-end bond funds. Some of these are up well over 20% year-to-date. But the great majority of bonds (and bond funds) are having a good year. Longer term funds investing in Treasuries are up perhaps 12%; shorter funds, and funds in other sectors, are up a lesser amount, between 4% and 7%. Even more surprising, for the first time anyone can remember, so far this year, total returns of bonds and bond funds are higher than those of most equity funds, a startling turn when you consider that in the last two years, financial advisers overwhelmingly were telling investors to ignore bonds.

At this juncture, the crystal ball of pundits is unusually cloudy. While no less an authority on the credit markets than Henry Kaufman is predicting that yields on the long bond will decline to perhaps 4% over the next few years, others feel that the economy will continue to grow and that this, in turn, will require the Fed to keep on raising interest rates until the economy slows. They are predicting a rise in rates before further declines can occur.

One common thread runs through all three conclusions: each preceding period saw significant volatility in the bond market. For the last two decades, interest rate levels have been changing more within a few months than they did within a period of several years before 1979. If someone were to ask me what the bond market will do, my answer would be to paraphrase a famous statement about the stock market: it will fluctuate. Because of the inherent unpredictability of interest rates, if you are investing in bonds primarily for safe and predictable income, I continue to believe that the best course is to stay away from both the longest and the shortest instruments, and to stick to relatively straightforward, high-quality securities.

Whatever happens, my hope is that the information contained in this book will help you to put together a portfolio of bonds that meets both your financial objectives, and your tolerance for risk.

So, once again, many happy returns.

Annette Thau
Teaneck, N.J.

INDEX

ABOUT THE AUTHOR

ANNETTE THAU received a B.A. from Douglass College and a Ph.D. from Columbia University. She was elected to Phi Beta Kappa and was the recipient of numerous academic honors and fellowships, including a Woodrow Wilson Fellowship; University Fellowships from Columbia University; and a National Endowment for the Humanities Fellowship for Younger Humanists.

Annette Thau has had several different careers. After teaching both at the high school and college level, she worked as a municipal bond analyst at the Chase Manhattan Bank. She has also been appointed as a visiting scholar at the Graduate School of Business of Columbia University.

Annette Thau's first book was a study of the poetry of Max Jacob, a French poet who was a friend of Picasso and the poet Apollinaire. *The Bond Book* was written in order to fill a need for a book that would explain bonds and the bond market in clear language that could be understood by any individual investor. Sales of the book suggest that it met that need. This second edition was written in order to bring *The Bond Book* up to date.